BY THE SAME AUTHOR

On Shakespeare:

THE WHEEL OF FIRE
(Tragedies)

THE IMPERIAL THEME
(Tragedies and Roman Plays)

THE CROWN OF LIFE
(Final Plays)

THE SHAKESPEARIAN TEMPEST
(Symbolism)

THE SOVEREIGN FLOWER
(Royalism and General Index)

THE MUTUAL FLAME
(Sonnets)

SHAKESPEARIAN PRODUCTION

On other writers:

THE BURNING ORACLE: see p. 104, note
(Spenser, Milton, Swift, Byron)

THE STARLIT DOME
(Wordsworth, Coleridge, Shelley, Keats)

CHARIOT OF WRATH: see p. 22, note
(Milton)

LAUREATE OF PEACE
(Reissued as *The Poetry of Pope: Laureate of Peace*)

LORD BYRON: CHRISTIAN VIRTUES

LORD BYRON'S MARRIAGE

BYRON AND SHAKESPEARE

IBSEN

THE SATURNIAN QUEST
(John Cowper Powys)

THE CHRISTIAN RENAISSANCE

CHRIST AND NIETZSCHE

THE GOLDEN LABYRINTH
(British Drama)

General:

ATLANTIC CROSSING

THE DYNASTY OF STOWE

Drama:

THE LAST OF THE INCAS

Poetry:

GOLD-DUST; *with other poetry*

SHAKESPEARE
and
RELIGION

essays of forty years

by

G. WILSON KNIGHT

A CLARION BOOK
PUBLISHED BY SIMON AND SCHUSTER

for

BONAMY DOBRÉE

with gratitude

PREFACE

THE collection of these essays was not until recently among my plans. I was content to know that they would be in the Bibliography of my writings being compiled by Dr. John E. Van Domelen and to appear in the Bulletin of the New York Public Library [see p. viii]. The decision to publish was made for two reasons. One was the fairly wide demand for publication of my six 'Lift up your Hearts' talks on Shakespeare and Religion in 1964 (p. 227). The other was the conviction, arising from Mr. R. M. Frye's *Shakespeare and Christian Doctrine* and the reviews of it (p. 293), that large sections of the literary public had failed to realize what my forty years of Shakespearian labour has been about.

My brother used often to advise me that anything new had to be repeated, and yet again repeated and repeated, if it were to be driven home; and it seemed that this collection, itself repetitive and composed mainly of pieces in an explanatory style, might succeed where earlier volumes had failed. My complaints against Mr. Frye's misrepresentations may accordingly be countered by the recognition that he is in part responsible for my present book. If readers have been in fact seeing my Shakespearian interpretations as he does, it is as well that someone should have stated it openly: 'There is some soul of goodness...' Nor would I deny that the contours of my work have been in my own mind newly clarified during the composition of my first chapter. The confusion was, to some extent, forgivable. Whenever I have seen Christian elements as part of the Shakespearian synthesis many of my readers have apparently assumed that I must be reading Shakespeare as part of Christianity. What I have been doing is *larger* than they supposed (pp. 103, 311–12, 318).

The book reviews of my Appendix are intended to indicate the relation of my Shakespearian approach to the approaches of my contemporaries; and I would ask that they should be read as pieces coloured by the excitements of my own discoveries rather than as final pronouncements. Were I to reread each book today I might write differently, especially on Middleton Murry, whose *Shakespeare* —which had noted Shakespeare's forecast of Charles I (p. 101 below)—scarcely receives justice in my review. I am aware, too, of the danger of supposing that my own acknowledgments to Bradley, Masefield and Murry as early influences—to which I should perhaps add certain plastic and spatial analogies in Una Ellis-Fermor's *Christopher Marlowe* (1927)—may convey the impression that there were no others, of earlier date; and I would point to my note on p. 306 drawing attention to Dowden's fine statement when writing on *Macbeth* regarding the respect of great writers to what we call 'the supernatural'. Dowden I read as a boy. R. G. Moulton, also referred to in my note, I did not read until much later, but he too deserves re-assessment.[1]

My essays are printed in the order of their composition which is with one exception (IX) the order, or for the cluster of 1964 the approximate order, of publication or broadcasting. Date and place of publication are given for each, but some titles have been changed. Originals now abbreviated or changed were as follows: for IV, 'The Theme of Romantic Friendship in Shakespeare'; for V, 'On the Mystic Symbolism of Shakespeare'; for VI, 'The Vision of Eros in Jesus and Shakespeare'; for VII, 'A Note on *Henry VIII*'; for XVIII, 'Shakespeare's Religion' (as printed in *Radio Times*, though conceived and submitted under my present title); for XX, 'New Light on Shakespeare's Sonnets'; for XXIII, 'Shakespeare and Theology'. Chapters VIII, IX and XVII, being extracts from books, bear new titles devised for my present purpose.

In reprinting old work I have sometimes smoothed the text in regard to punctuation, syntax and obscurities, and deleted the worst horrors of unneeded words, especially link-words at the start of a sentence such as 'And', 'But' and 'Indeed'. References have been

1. I would here draw attention to Lascelles Abercrombie's 1930 British Academy Lecture 'A Plea for the Liberty of Interpreting' which formulated arguments in exact correspondence with those being simultaneously advanced by myself. The lecture is included in the collection, *Aspects of Shakespeare*, O.U.P., 1933 (preface by J. W. Mackail).

tidied and where missing inserted, insertions in proof sometimes forcing the omission of an unneeded phrase nearby. I have done nothing to improve the *general* style, in places distasteful to me now, and have in no instance twisted an old idea in the light of subsequent thought. Where their nature renders it advisable, new footnotes are dated.

After many years of anxiety I have given up attempts to be consistent in the capitalization of 'Comedies', 'Histories', 'Tragedies' and 'Final Plays'. In some contexts capitals look right, in others too assertive. For 'Spiritualism' I generally reserve the capital for the modern movement; 'spiritualism' as a world-wide and age-old experience or pursuit seems better without it. For the possessive case of names ending in 's' I nowadays go by the 'spoken sound. One does not at all naturally say 'E. K. Chamberses *Elizabethan Stage*', but one can, and perhaps does, say 'Powyses *Glastonbury Romance*'. Many names, such as 'Keats', seem indeterminate. Classical names cannot bear the extra syllable.

My act, scene and line numerals apply to the Oxford Shakespeare, but I have preserved freedom in punctuation and capitals. For page references to my present volume I use the letter 'p.'; for all other page references, the numeral alone. I have been unable to trace G. K. Chesterton's lines quoted on p. 108. They were, presumably, published in a periodical.

To all who have invited and often in effect, since such short pieces do not come easily to me, forced me to compose these essays, I express my gratitude; for I am now glad to have them. I am indebted to Dr. Sylvia England and Miss Olivia Mordue for help with the checking of references; to Mr. John D. Christie for reading my proofs and pointing out a number of technical slips; to Dr. Patricia M. Ball and Mr. Craig Carlson for assistance with my indexes; and to the Exeter City Library for helpful services, now and in the past. I thank Professor Sadhan Kumar Ghosh for allowing me to use my introduction to his recent *Tragedy*.

Before closing I would pay a tribute to my friend and ever-kind supporter, the late Charles B. Purdom. He had agreed that I should use our B.B.C. discussion on his recent *What Happens in Shakespeare*, and his widow, Mrs. Lilian Purdom, has generously confirmed the permission. For many years this thesis had been a burning conviction of his, and that alone should recommend it to our attention. His mind was always vigorous and alert, perceptive both to art and to what lies beyond art. Of his other books, *The Building of Satellite Towns* (1925) was a major contribution, and so was his impressive study *The God-Man* (1964), on the saint and mystic *Meher Baba*. Between the solidities of Town Planning and the higher reaches of the spirit lies drama; and to drama Purdom was devoted. His *Harley Granville Barker* (1955) is a standard biography and source-book, and he has written on Shaw and on stage production. Now that keen intelligence has left our plane for other quests.

G. W. K.

Exeter, January 1967

It seems now that Dr. Van Domelen's Bibliography will not appear in the Bulletin.

Exeter, March 1968

CONTENTS

I

INTRODUCTION

I

THE essays included in this volume constitute a fairly consistent record of my attempts over a period of some forty years to explore the deeper significances of Shakepearian poetry and drama. Once at Oxford, in about the year 1922, my brother, listening to Caliban's lines on music at a performance of *The Tempest*, murmured with deep feeling, 'What does it *mean*?' For many years I have set myself to the answer. Whether it was really that question which prompted me I cannot now be sure; if it was, it was only one example from many of his life-long way of starting by an off-hand remark thought-streams in other minds that afterwards flower independently. One of his favourite tenets was that the quality of a mind was to be assessed rather by the questions it asked than by the answers it provided. But answers are wanted too, so far as we can find them, and that has been my business. These 'answers' inevitably draw close to religion. If the significances discovered were limited to psychology and sociology we could be reasonably certain that they did not correspond to the Shakespearian impact.

My present collection of essays may be distinguished from the more specialized commentaries of my main series of Shakespearian interpretations. In those, having found my way in the technique of what I call 'interpretation', I quite early felt impelled to publish my results with a minimum of discursive explanation. There was, in book after book, so much to say that I had little space available for defences, explanations and reservations. But while these volumes were appearing I also, from time to time, composed short pieces of a more explanatory kind. The essays incorporated into *The Wheel of*

Fire had themselves appeared in a number of religious—not literary—periodicals during the years 1929–30; and before, and often since, there have been occasions for brief pieces, some of what is known as an 'occasional' type. Many were written in response to a request, often with difficulty and sometimes with reluctance. The main volumes after *The Wheel of Fire*, relying as they did on a prepared audience and making no concessions, were comparatively easy to compose; but these other essays had, as it were, to assume nothing, to speak directly and simply to the non-specialized reader; and though harder to write, they are easier to read.

What they had to do was to explore and explain the *religious* significances of what was usually regarded as *entertainment*; high entertainment, of course, but the word 'high' raises a host of awkward questions, and these questions touch religious issues. My Shakespearian work, as I have often enough explained, developed not only from a new view of Shakespearian tragedy but simultaneously, and even more, and *first*, since my first book was the unpublished 1928 *Thaisa* (p. 199), from my view of Shakespeare's last plays as myths of immortality. It will be seen that in my present collection I keep returning to this theme. A second main emphasis, starting in the late thirties, was national. More and more I began to see Shakespeare as a national, and thence a world, prophet. Nearly all these essays, and I have included all, or nearly all, that I can find, are close to one or the other of these two themes. Only one essay is deliberately concerned with my more technical and professional works: the essay 'New Dimensions in Shakespearian Interpretation'. This relies on some knowledge of my main series and their method of 'spatial' analysis. The unprepared reader may gain some idea of my more intensive methods from my essay on the Inca drama, *Apu Ollantay* (pp. 139–80). For the rest, the essays are on a variety of levels, written for different purposes at different times, and some as talks, or lectures.

'Occasional' writing has its own peculiar strength and value. Much that is abstruse and complex has to be avoided; and yet, in so far as the occasion is taken into account, it is possible that more may be received from a popular, even if propagandist, piece than in an academic study. For this reason: to tell the exact and whole truth of Shakespeare's or any other great poet's spiritual meaning is clearly impossible. The commentator is conditioned by his personal temperament and the culture of his period, though generally both writer and reader incline to pretend that he is not: all writing is to this extent 'occasional'. When however a brief piece is *known* to have been composed for a specific purpose, the limits are admitted and accepted, and, as in any work of art, the resultant whole becomes within and in terms of its own limits universal. It is recognized to have been said within a known context, without claiming finality; and, the context recognized, a richer whole, embracing both statement *and* context, is received than would otherwise be possible. Humility brings its reward; by claiming less it achieves more.

Here is an example. It would be easy to dismiss, at a first glance, my 'Lift up your Hearts' talks (p. 227), done on the invitation of the B.B.C. for the Birthday Week of the Shakespeare Quatercentenary, as too slight to deserve permanent attention. But to compose for a vast and unprepared audience six simple talks of $4\frac{1}{2}$ minutes each, giving exact quotations—for such were asked for—on so complex a subject was a pretty task. It was my aim to avoid abstractions and generalities; to pin-point six concrete themes, and support them, all in the simplest possible language. It was vitally important to choose the right themes, and only those. The results are to be read as my response to this challenge. Much of their interest lies in the variety and the selection, the different avenues of approach constituting an admission that in such a matter no simple thesis would be adequate and that what we need is a variety of contacts. Each of the six talks relates to other essays in this book where its theme is more fully developed. They form the *heart* of the collection; that is, the heart of my life's work on Shakespeare.

Much the same applies to 'Four Pillars of Wisdom'. These were not actually composed as talks; I seem to recall that I thought of them first as propaganda leaflets to be dropped from the air; but the principle is the same. Those done for my Westminster Theatre *This Sceptred Isle* in 1941 (p. 113) were written to be read aloud, for the speaking voice, and were read by Henry Ainley during the second and main part of the programme.

In the essays of war-propaganda the occasion is always important, and must be remembered; and if remembered it gives the writing concerned a permanent validity. One can say of it: 'This is the kind of power that can be tapped from Shakespeare at such a crisis.' One must bring to the argument the emotions of the crisis; and if that is done it will be found that they are in Shakespeare too, though they may be emotions which we cannot ourselves so easily feel before or after the crisis.

There is more to be said. My propaganda was from the start far from any facile reliance on the history plays culminating in *Henry V* and the St. Crispin speech before Agincourt.

It relied in part on this sequence, certainly, but even here a new depth was being plumbed in relation especially to royalty, to the crown. I recall what came on me as a sudden illumination like that I experienced when first recognizing the more mystical properties of the Final Plays. I saw that Shakespeare's seemingly out-dated kings and barons with their rivalries and murders were, if we were prepared to see Shakespeare's persons as corresponding to contemporary parties or nations, not out-dated at all, but rather true reflections of the turmoils and tyrannies rampant across Europe. Dangers we had grown used to as stage fictions were now appallingly real, and magnified. What was needed was a power strong enough to oppose tyranny. In Shakespeare that power was in the poetry of kingship, of royalty. Shakespeare's kings, as persons, could be weak or wicked, but the royal essence was in the poetry clear, and never questioned. Our business today was to attune ourselves to this royalty, this poetry.

My first published national piece, except for a brief article on *Timon of Athens* in Canada (p. 117 below, note), was the small brochure *This Sceptred Isle* in 1940, a condensation of a script composed earlier in the same year but not published till 1944 as *The Olive and the Sword* of which the main text was reprinted in *The Sovereign Flower* in 1958 and the opening and concluding chapters appear in my present collection (pp. 91–111). I also gave a number of lecture recitals, culminating in my week at the Westminster Theatre in 1941. I found it easier to get the meaning across in this way, interspersing acting with comment. The acting was a main part of it; the commentary flowered from the acting.

But, as I have said, these recitals and my published writings did not rely solely on the history cycle ending with *Henry V* half-way through Shakespeare's career. There was much more to it than that. If those historical dramas corresponded to the turmoils of contemporary Europe, then Shakespeare's subsequent dramas should surely point towards a solution. The history cycle was followed by the critical approaches to war and government in *Troilus and Cressida* and *Measure for Measure* and by the tragedies plunging into the Dionysian and anarchic underworld of man's earthly drama. Always the ideal of social harmony was remembered and the royal or princely essence, though buffeted, alive. This dark sequence was finally summed up in the Nirvanic mysticism of *Timon of Athens*, a drama deeply relevant to our contemporary discontents and given an especial prominence in my Westminster production.

Nor did we stop there. That would still be merely to leave us among our present discontents. What really made a new understanding of Shakespeare's nationalism possible was my acceptance of *Henry VIII*. Shakespeare passed from the sombre tragedies to the more optimistic balancing of war-heroism and love in *Antony and Cleopatra* and *Coriolanus*, and then on, through the mystical plays *Pericles* and *The Winter's Tale*, to the union of Rome and Britain in *Cymbeline* and to the magician-superman Prospero in *The Tempest*, who is nevertheless a ruler and returns to his governmental office; and finally concludes with *Henry VIII*, a vastly patterned drama crowning his life's work. Now for long *Henry VIII* had been under a cloud; it had seemed to scholars a pageant only, loose and inorganic. Nevertheless the spatial grouping of its themes held profound implications to which the learned had been blind, so that they were driven to suppose that parts of it were composed by some other writer, leaving *The Tempest*, so much more easy to appreciate, as Shakespeare's last play. But I had, as had happened earlier with so many supposedly un-authentic Shakespearian plays or parts of plays—a good early example was the Doctor's speech on the King's Evil in *Macbeth*—found it coherent and meaningful. Under the new approach what had been regarded as disjointed or irrelevent was found significant within a dominating pattern; and arguments for spuriousness melted. My first published remarks on *Henry VIII* appeared in

The Criterion (p. 75 below) and my full study, later, in *The Crown of Life*.[1]

The importance of *Henry VIII* can hardly be over-estimated. It alone renders Shakespeare's dramatic output a single and harmonious whole. For now we have this sequence: Shakespeare moves from a comparatively simple patriotism through anarchic and mystical adventures to, in *Henry VIII*, a purified patriotism of religious tone, culminating in Cranmer's prophecy over Elizabeth (p. 249). This prophecy, Shakespeare's last word to his countrymen, had been unduly neglected. In *Henry VIII* the mighty wheel of Shakespearian drama comes full circle; not only the Histories, but the Tragedies and last mystical works too, being clasped and enclosed within the circle of that 'golden round' (*Macbeth*, I. v. 29), the Crown.

If it were still suspected, despite the arguments set out in *The Crown of Life*, that *Henry VIII* was only in part Shakespeare's, I have today more evidence to draw upon. Among my arguments were the clear facts that the scenes distrusted on metrical and linguistic grounds were nevertheless, in theme, human insight, placing and dramatic treatment, all characteristically and deeply Shakespearian. Now a book has recently appeared drawing attention to a hitherto neglected facet of Shakespeare's artistry: Francis Berry's *The Shakespeare Inset*. This discusses Shakespeare's habit of bringing before us scenes in one way or another outside the main actions and time-schemes of the dramas in which they occur. Mercutio's Queen Mab speech in *Romeo and Juliet*, Horatio's description of old Hamlet's rivalry with old Fortinbras, Othello's account of his travels, are all, in this sense, 'insets'. Insets exist to enrich the drama beyond the surface of temporal sequence; to show depths, and vistas, and visions. The purpose within their use is moreover precisely the purpose within the composition of *Henry VIII* which, more than any previous play, relies on a juxtaposition and patterning of various dramatic themes to show qualities in design and depth; it is less a single story

---

1. My interest in the authenticity of *Henry VIII* was first aroused by a letter of Edgar I. Fripp as recorded in *The Crown of Life*, 30, note; and see also p. 81 below, note. Prof. Peter Alexander has for long been a stalwart supporter of the play, and so has Prof. Frank Kermode. Acceptance has become now fairly general. The story is told and much of the evidence lucidly deployed in Paul Bertram's important volume *Shakespeare and The Two Noble Kinsmen* (Rutgers University Press, New Jersey, 1965).

than an interlacing and intershading of stories, given their unity by the presiding figure of the King. The principle behind Shakespeare's use of insets is to this extent found to be already active within the main action or actions. Since the drama is concerned to handle near-distance historical, and in the main peaceful and in consequence undramatic, substances in terms of patterning and depth, it is natural that the surface interlacing should be yet further enriched, the various themes linked, and the depths shaded in, by various insets of the ordinary kind as well. This is, as it were, a natural world for them, their proper soil, from which they flower in abundance. *Henry VIII* is largely composed of insets. We start with an elaborated description of the Field of the Cloth of Gold and soon afterwards Buckingham's servant is describing his supposedly treasonous words in evidence before the King. Buckingham's great farewell speech is one long narrative inset. The King's account of how his conscience was aroused concerning his marriage to Katharine is another. The Gentleman's description of Queen Anne's coronation is of central imaginative importance; and so is Griffith's narrative of Wolsey's end. Some of these hark back distantly, some are almost contemporary. Two point ahead: Queen Katharine's dream or vision of a future Paradise and Cranmer's prophecy of the reigns of Elizabeth I and James I. These and other insets exist in varying sizes and are of varying importance. Some are among the greatest moments of the drama. It is a drama in which time-streams eddy and interfurl. We are not involved in a single, passionate, story; rather we are emotionally unattached and uninvolved, while enjoying a supreme awareness, which includes an awareness of avenues and depths within simple and real events, seen as from some higher dimension; and this awareness depends very largely on the use of insets.

That Mr. Berry did not himself use *Henry VIII* in his book only makes it more valuable for my purpose. Now that this favourite Shakespearian device is before us all, we find that *Henry VIII* in this matter not only conforms but even, as the nature of its composition and its place in the Shakespearian canon would lead us to expect, surpasses the rest.

II

Throughout the following pages two main emphases predominate: (i) the immortality[1] themes in the last plays, and (ii) the theme of a spiritualized nationalism, its symbol the crown. My collection shows how I have been for forty years labouring to liberate the Ariel powers, the spirit-powers, of Shakespearian drama for our use. There has been need for continual reiteration and continual defence. The liberation of new powers, however salutary those powers, in all ages arouses a bitter opposition; and of that there has been no lack.

It has taken me a long time to realize exactly what *is* the cause of this opposition. The matter was put simply to me many years ago by the poetess, Miss Dallas Kenmare. Speaking primarily of my acting but including my Shakespearian interpretations too, she remarked that what led to opposition was a certain 'spiritual' quality in these engagements. At the time, I found the thought strange; but I now realize the truth of it. That *has* been the trouble.

In all my literary commentaries I have from the start made heavy use of the occult and spiritualistic properties of poetry and drama. My good fortune in being able to reveal new and harmonious patterns in Shakespeare has very largely depended on my being willing to accept without suspicion or softening the more miraculous or 'superstitious' elements in the literature under survey; for all great literature is saturated in these qualities. Again and again I have been involved in what lies beyond death. I have always been aware of, and interested in a general way in, Spiritualism.[2]

1. I here avoid the phrase 'resurrection themes' which, though valuable in pointing a Christian relevance, is also in danger of suggesting too *exact* a relation to the Church's doctrine of the resurrection of the body. The word 'resurrection' was, I think, first applied to one of Shakespeare's last plays (*The Winter's Tale*) by Dr. Hugh Brown, in the *Hibbert Journal*, some time in the thirties. My own original choice was the word 'immortality', which may, in face of current misunderstandings (pp. 293–303) be safer.

2. Direct experience of Spiritualism has not changed, though it may have clarified, my metaphysical opinions. My first published article, 'Poetry and Immortality' in *The Adelphi Magazine* of September 1926 (IV, 3), discussed the problem of human survival with references to both Spiritualism and Wordsworth's *Immortality* ode and a general conclusion in exact accord with my present views. I hope to reprint the article in a future collection.

There is no question but that spiritualism and poetic drama show in all periods an intimate relation and a number of correspondences; and yet there is also a distinction to be made. It would be natural to suppose that the greater writers should show a rational and non-superstitious approach to the spiritualistic. We today would surely respect them the more for a semi-scientific, at least a philosophic, approach, leaving the superstitions to the second or third-rate artists. And yet what we find is precisely the opposite. In Shakespeare's period it is the lesser figures, as I have shown in *The Golden Labyrinth*, such as Chapman and Tourneur, and also the dramatists of the Restoration, who approach psychic phenomena in a scientific fashion, showing occult knowledge and a probing intelligence; whereas Shakespeare, outside the healing theme of *All's Well that Ends Well* (pp. 282-3), offers us something rather different, ranging from popular folk-lore to poetic symbolism. It seems that the greater writers in any period prefer to handle such mysteries in traditional terms, relying on popular superstition and past literature, and making from these newly purposive creations; and somehow their results are more effective than those of writers who depend on their own intelligence. The Ghost in *Hamlet*, made of a hotch-potch of dubious traditional beliefs, is more dramatically alive than the more scientifically made ghost—who scarcely deserves a capital letter—in Tourneur's *The Atheist's Tragedy* (*The Golden Labyrinth*, 103). Though the Cauldron scene in *Macbeth* has elements in common with a séance, yet the three Apparitions and the procession of future Kings are symbolically more potent, and far *tidier*, far more artistically purposeful, than any manifestations likely to be met among twentieth-century, or perhaps any other, psychic phenomena. Instead of trying to express the truths of spiritualism through scientific attention to the evidence, great poets actually prefer to play with crude superstitions as raw material for some new symbolism of their own fabrication. This is because the deeper truths cannot really be transmitted in intellectual terms, however 'true'; all science, as science, is provisional only, and facts of any kind regularly inadequate and often deceptive. The lesser writers flirt with science and fact, and make us *think*; the greater ones, offering drama in place of reporting and leaving the factual for the actual, make us *experience*; and experience depends on

layers of human feeling and belief descending to us from past generations. My favourite example is Antony's

> Where souls do couch on flowers, we'll hand in hand,
> And with our spritely port make the ghosts gaze.
> Dido and her Aeneas shall want troops,
> And all the haunt be ours.
>
> (*Antony and Cleopatra*, IV. xii. 51)

Age-old beliefs in a classic Elysium are used, Vergil's account being
recalled in Dido and Aeneas. The word 'souls' exerts religious, and
'flowers' nature's, authority; 'spritely' keeps us aware of spirits;
'haunt' has overtones of old wives' stories. A cluster of what might
be called *easy* effects is used, and response unmediated by conscious
thought; and in the process a marvel of experience is brought to
focus. We are not expected, nor even allowed, to engage in para-
psychological enquiries; we are already *on the other side*. This may be
trickery; it is the method of greatest art.

We could put it like this:—Spiritualistic messages give us direct
reports of the beyond. Writers of the second order often do much the
same, in vision, fantasy and extravaganza. Other writers of the
second order, concentrating solely on the earth-plane, think in terms
of character, sociology and 'realism'. The greater writers are those
who *mix up* earth-reality, including centuries of human experience,
with the visionary and the imponderable; and it is precisely in this,
in the inter-twisting, in the establishing of a relation, that their
greatness consists (*The Christian Renaissance*, 1962; 27, 37–40, etc.).

To this extent Shakespeare is an earthly rather than an idealistic
poet. The weight of centuries of human psychology is on him and
there is the less emphasis on the abstract and the transcendental. In
Pericles and *The Winter's Tale* he is certainly engaged in making
myths of immortality; but he does it by relying on his own past
play-designs of romance and tragedy, fusing these to make quite
impossible stories through which the great truth, or fact, or whatever
we choose to call it, is dramatically realized. Hermione, who should
have died, is 'warm' (*The Winter's Tale*, V. iii. 109). Many a modern
dramatist, Masefield in *Melloney Holtspur* or Priestley in *Johnson over
Jordan*, gives what for us in our highly intellectualized era seems a far

more trustworthy account of the mysteries in question. But note that
T. S. Eliot is less successful. It is fascinating to watch him in *The
Family Reunion* and *The Cocktail Party* labouring hard to rely on
Greek drama, pagan ritual, modern psychology, and Christian
priestcraft, and only very half-heartedly letting the 'spiritualistic', at
the end of *The Cocktail Party*, seep through.[1] Though the result is not
wholly convincing, we can at least see what is happening: Eliot has
the instincts of a great poet; he is *trying* to compose in the manner of
a great poet; though whether this is the right way for our century
may be questioned. Experience of Spiritualism is now widespread
and there may be new advances, following Masefield, to be made, a
new kind of great poetry to be attempted.

Meanwhile we can align Shakespeare with Christianity in respect
to what might be called his earthy, humanly warm, approach to the
spiritualistic truths. Christianity, like Shakespeare, while *including* all
the spiritualities and among them what we today call 'Spiritualism',
puts a primary emphasis on *incarnation*. The opposition of the Church
to Spiritualism may be supposed to be motivated at the worst by
vested interests and professional rivalry and at the best by a deep-
seated will to make us not merely know, but experience, the spiritual;
or perhaps at all costs to make us experience it *before* we know,
mental knowledge alone, even of authentic spiritualistic facts, being
of little value in itself, and perhaps even for some people dangerous.
The relation of Christianity to Spiritualism is thus as the relation of
Shakespeare to Chapman, Tourneur, and such Restoration dramatists as Dryden, Lee and Settle. Tricks may even seem to be played
on us to inject into us an experience or recognition impossible by
other means. The raising of Lazarus and the empty tomb of Christ,
however hard to accept intellectually, have an ignition and an
impact that no amount of the most convincing esoteric teaching
from spirit-communicators in higher spheres could exert; and so
does the Church's dogma, deliberately contradicting the spiritualistic
St. Paul who insists on a 'spiritual body' (1 Corinthians, XV, 44),

---

1. See my essay 'T. S. Eliot: Some Literary Impressions', one of a collection of
essays on Eliot under the editorship of Allen Tate in *The Sewanee Review*, Winter,
1966 (LXXIV, 1). The collection has now been published in book form (New York
and London) as *T. S. Eliot: The Man and his Work*.

of a physical resurrection. I do not propose to answer these questions here: I have provisionally handled them in *The Christian Renaissance* (1962; Epilogue). One day perhaps these contrasts and conflicts will be resolved, and the Lion of Catholicism and the Lamb of Spiritualism be at peace. It will not be yet, and it may be too late when they are.

III

Here we may engage the questions as to whether Shakespearian drama can be called 'Christian', and whether I myself am responsible for the general assertion that it is.

Some more distinctions are necessary. I have been criticized for suggesting that Shakespeare's tragic heroes may be regarded as 'miniature Christs'. The remark must be read in its context, where some necessary reservations are made (pp. 296-7 and note). We must moreover distinguish between 'Christ' and 'Christianity'. In doctrine there are vivid divergencies. Christ states God's love for man and bird, and sees children as signposts to Heaven, whereas the Church gives central emphasis to the horror of the crucifixion and regards children as sin-tainted before baptism (cp. pp. 185-7). Christ was a romantic, the Church is realistic.

Both aspects appear in Shakespearian tragedy: each hero reflects at least some elements of Christ's powerful course, and each tragic art-form has affinities with the grim logic of the crucifixion. In both the New Testament and Shakespeare we sense a purpose within tragedy and

> let determin'd things to destiny
> Hold, unbewail'd, their way.
> (*Antony and Cleopatra*, III. vi. 84)

My comparison of Shakespearian drama and the New Testament has been developed at length in *The Christian Renaissance* (III and IV). As a tragic protagonist Christ shows qualities of self-assertion and personal claim that would be repudiated by the Church if they appeared in one of his followers; and it is in this unethical, Dionysian, sense, with the accompanying upward thrust and forward drive of their tragic stories, that Shakespeare's heroes, whatever their moral failings, may be said to resemble Christ; but they do not resemble Christians, any more than he did.

I have often drawn attention to the upward lift of Shakespeare's art. Each of his longer speeches shows it, rising in one, or two, waves, and then falling;[1] scenes are so composed, and whole plays. Despite apparent disaster and evil there is a spiritual lift, as in Othello's recapturing, with advantage, his lost dignity for the cosmic splendours of his supreme poetry in the drama's final scene; each protagonist in turn attains a supernal insight (*The Sovereign Flower*, 249; pp. 190–1, 231–2, 247–8 below). Energies are released and values created by the tragic conflict and some high, if undefinable, purpose appears to be achieved. Ethic is part only of the statement which speaks from a more Nietzschean comprehension. The soul-bark of these 'miniature Christs' is tossed but not destroyed, and the transition through *Antony and Cleopatra* to the mystical dramas, in which Shakespeare blends tragedy with romance to make art-forms different from either, was inevitable.

In the tragedies salvation comes not through repentance, but through honesty, self-knowing, and a clear sight of what has been, and is. Macbeth speaks his greatest poetry from a state of being unrepentant but self-condemned; and in this state there is some high achievement (p. 190). The implied doctrine is Byronic and Nietzschean, and in tune with modern psychology, but it has little in common with religious penitence. Its nature is clear in Wolsey's change of heart after his schemes have been unmasked by the King:

> I know myself now, and I feel within me
> A peace above all earthly dignities,
> A still and quiet conscience. The king has cur'd me.
> (*Henry VIII*, III. ii. 379)

He has been 'cured' by no action of his own, but simply by being

1. See *Shakespearian Production*, 1964; 31–3, 122, 256, 276–8; also *The Sovereign Flower*, 246–50. A number of illustrations are given in my tape-recording 'Shakespeare's Rhetoric, now available from the publishers, *Sound Seminars*, 50 East Hollister, Cincinnati, U.S.A. See also p. 248 below.

unmasked. There is less evidence of contrition than of joy in a new freedom maturing from an honest relationship and self-recognition (pp. 100-1, 134-5, 232-3). Such too is the nature of Macbeth's agonized poetic serenities throughout his final scenes.

There is here a clear divergence, even a challenge, in respect to Church doctrine. We should scarcely be surprised. Shakespeare is a writer of the Renaissance era, which gave us Marlowe's challenging *Doctor Faustus*. Marlowe's play has had a number of successors, of which the most famous is Goethe's *Faust*. The story gripped because it responded to a need, like the Don Juan story. The two stories, one from Germany and one from Spain, corresponded to the rising claims for theological and sexual freedoms; and they have become the central myths of Renaissance Europe.

Shakespearian tragedy is part of this movement. It has its probing Nordic dramas, *Hamlet, Macbeth* and *King Lear*, and its Mediterranean love-romances, *Romeo and Juliet, Othello*, and *Antony and Cleopatra*. The challenges are less simple in Shakespeare than in others, but they are there. Sexual freedom was thereafter developed mainly in comedy. The other, Faustian, thrust is apparent in Milton's Satan, the Gothic dramas of the Romantic period and the writings of Blake, Byron and Shelley; and in *Wuthering Heights*. All are within the one tradition, which culminates in Ibsen, Nietzsche and Shaw. It is a tradition of challenge against Church doctrine in attempt to reveal what man *is* before telling him what he ought to be. Within this movement Pope's 'The proper study of Mankind is Man' (*Essay on Man*, II. 2) is a central statement.

Nowhere can we so clearly see the divergence of Shakespearian tragedy from Christian teaching as in *Hamlet*, written at the start of the tragic sequence. I have often urged that there is much that is likeable in Claudius and much that is questionable in Hamlet. Claudius' advice to the mourning Hamlet on acceptance of death as a law of nature, conceived in direct contrast to the strained and over-elaborated speech of Hamlet which it answers, is not merely sensible: his long speech is *the* one indispensable passage in our whole literature for help on such central occasions. He is regarded always as King, and as King he has strong dramatic status. There is more than flattery in these words:

Guildenstern: Most holy and religious fear it is
To keep those many many bodies safe
That live and feed upon your majesty.
Rosencrantz: The single and peculiar life is bound
With all the strength and armour of the mind
To keep itself from noyance; but much more
That spirit upon whose weal depend and rest
The lives of many. The cease of majesty
Dies not alone, but like a gulf doth draw
What's near it with it; it is a massy wheel,
Fix'd on the summit of the highest mount,
To whose huge spokes ten thousand lesser things
Are mortis'd and adjoin'd; which, when it falls,
Each small annexment, petty consequence,
Attends the boisterous ruin. Never alone
Did the king sigh, but with a general groan.

(III. iii. 8)

The convoluted phraseology, so like the style of *Troilus and Cressida*, though scarcely pleasing, suggests less flattery than the intellectual flamboyance of university wits: certainly no audience of Shakespeare's day could fail in response. Respect, even sympathy, is demanded.

Claudius has a crime on his conscience and he tries to deal with it in the traditional way: by prayer and repentance. For our immediate purpose we can observe that he tries hard to repent in the correct, doctrinal sense, his marvellous prayer-speech (p. 228) illustrating simultaneously the will to repentance and the impossibility of attainment; and this 'impossibility' applies to all of us, quite apart from the nature or degree of the sin, for it would be idle to suppose that the great crimes of drama bear no relevance to our own humdrum lives and the more or less wicked societies which they support. The question is, shall we try to get rid of our committed sin or shall we admit serenely that it was a part of ourselves and our destiny? The one seems impossible, the other inexcusable. In discussing one of my many treatments of this dark problem, Mr. R. J. Zwi Werblowsky in *Lucifer and Prometheus* (1952; 100) suggested a happy clarification. Acceptance of evil must be limited to the 'retrospective' and is 'useless' in regard to new decisions. That is, to see one's crime of yesterday as part of a necessary pattern may be salutary; but to plan one for tomorrow is a different matter. We are reminded of Claudius' words 'my fault is past' (III. iii. 51) countered by his inability to choose future good.

Hamlet himself shows a different approach to sin from that of Claudius. When, soon after Claudius' prayer-speech, he has slain Polonius, he is at first callous:

> Thou wretched, rash, intruding fool, farewell!
> I took thee for thy better.
>
> (*Hamlet*, III. iv. 31)

Cooling down, he feels sorry. After starting with a rather glib use of the word 'repent', he passes on to a different and more truly tragic viewpoint:

> For this same lord
> I do repent; but Heaven hath pleased it so
> To punish me with this, and this with me,
> That I must be their scourge and minister.
>
> (*Hamlet*, III. iv. 172)

It is all, he says, part of God's will, and I have to bear my own errors and even crimes, acting as a medium for powers beyond my understanding. This is not far from Richard Duke of York's 'For this, among the rest, was I ordain'd' as he murders Henry VI, adding 'I am myself alone' (*3 Henry VI*, v. vi. 58, 83). Macbeth, so cruelly edged into crime, might have said as much. Marlowe's Tamburlaine saw himself regularly as Heaven's 'scourge'. In Shakespearian terms Claudius is in this matter trammelled by traditional religious doctrine and Hamlet, within the new Renaissance individualistic and psychological ways of thought, is free of it. I say 'in this matter', since in others, as in his thoughts of the Devil and damnation, Hamlet thinks traditionally, and in matters of peaceful diplomacy Claudius is in advance of Hamlet, who accepts and admires the warrior valuations. Values are criss-crossed bafflingly, but this at least is clear. In *Hamlet*, at the start of the tragic sequence, Shakespeare dramatizes in Claudius the inadequacy of repentance as usually understood and touches through the person of Hamlet the prevailing mood, or mode, of the great tragedies to follow (pp. 228-9, 232).

Before moving on, I would point to two strong supports for the Shakespearian way. One is Byron. In both *Manfred* and *Cain* the issues are handled in a manner corresponding to our Shakespearian reading. Manfred, like Macbeth, is unrepentant yet self-condemned, enduring 'remorse without the fear of Hell' (III. i. 71). His hell is within; the mind is its own hell (III. iv. 129-36), and he refuses to submit to the devils who come for him. He is his own judge and scorns lesser spirits like dirt, rather as Macbeth scorns the Weird Sisters. In *Cain* Lucifer tells Cain that he must unravel his ethical conflicts within his own mind or soul, and in that way rise towards the spiritual (II. ii. 463-6; and see p. 193 below). The emphasis is on man; the help he needs is within; we are, presumably, relying on what Alexander Pope called 'the God within the mind' (*Essay on Man*, II. 204), who is the 'god' of Powys's poem *The Ship* (p. 18 below). Cain's 'That which I am, I am' (III. i. 509), spoken after the murder of Abel, follows Shakespeare (Sonnet 121; *3 Henry VI*, v. vi. 83; also p. 24 below. See *Byron and Shakespeare*, 179, 340; for *Manfred*, 176-7, 298-301).

The other support comes in our own time from spirit-communicators speaking through trance-mediumship, who regularly repudiate orthodox doctrines of Hell and Damnation while with an equal insistence asserting that cosmic law cannot be obviated by a vicarious sacrifice. We are what we are and beyond death are open, like Macbeth and Wolsey, to others' sight, and our own too, whence we, like Byron's Manfred, must judge ourselves. Suffering and labour may be involved before release is won (p. 233).

An objection may be raised. If we are to avoid the more conventional type of moralizing in regard to Richard III and Macbeth, what becomes of our national propaganda in the following essays, wherein they are regarded as exponents of evils which it is Great Britain's destiny to overcome? Shall we say simply that such essays are superficial pieces serving an ephemeral purpose, whereas the real truth is to be had only in such pieces as 'The Avenging Mind' (p. 181)? The answer is not simple. At the height of my propaganda I argued that 'the Dragon has his rights' (pp. 110; 123-4). The evil is evil, and must be overcome; but the overcoming is to be won less by repudiation than by self-identification, as is so excellently illustrated in Aeschylus' conclusion to the *Oresteia*, where the evil, which are also the avenging, powers, the Furies or Eumenides, are only placated by being accepted and even honoured as part of the community (p. 38). Their home is to be *below* the city; as though there are forces in man which must be simultaneously honoured and kept from sight.

And what then of Hitler? There seems no logical reason why we should not accord him at least the same degree of sympathy which we accord to Tamburlaine and Richard III. One day such dramas will be written of him: he had certain tragic requisites, seeing himself, like Tamburlaine, as an earth-cleansing scourge of Heaven, and dying by his own hand. But how *can* we sympathize with such appalling evil? This time the answer is simple: by looking inwards, by admission of our own *worst fantasies* ranging from solitary lusts to noblest art. Writing of man, Nietzsche crisply diagnoses his state:

> In gazing on tragedies, bullfights, and crucifixions hath he hitherto found his best happiness on earth; and when he invented hell for himself, lo, hell was his heaven upon earth.
> (*Thus Spake Zarathustra*, 57, 'The Convalescent')

What are we to do about it? Well, for centuries the Crucifix has, as was argued in my *Christ and Nietzsche* (104–5), acted as a sublimation, first hooking the hideous instinct and next raising and transmuting it. Today our best doctrine, forecast by Pope's honouring of instinct in his *Essay on Man*, comes from John Cowper Powys who urges the free use of dangerous fantasies with physiological release in order to confine them within such limits. This doctrine I have discussed, comparing it with Pope's and Nietzsche's, in *The Saturnian Quest* (119–20, 125–6). Powys's poem *The Ship* (*Poems*, ed. Kenneth Hopkins, 1964; 179) is a symbolical description of the process. The technique advocated is a technique for facing the more disreputable instincts, realizing them as constituent elements of ourselves, and rendering them harmless. It induces a salutary humility.

Hitler was ourselves, magnified; he summed centuries of human ruthlessness; but though magnified he was not necessarily, in essence, worse. His gas-chambers were not more cruel, and may have been less, than the burnings of the Inquisition or the public drawings-and-quarterings of our own near-distance history; and the vast scale of his deeds, in accord with modern 'advance', was matched by the Hiroshima bomb.[1] The cruelties rampant among all nations today, inflicted on man and animal, are patent.

If we in Britain can claim any superiority, we can only do so if we admit the truth of ourselves while struggling painfully for the rest. This is precisely how Shakespearian tragedy acts on us. We identify ourselves with the protagonist while simultaneously repudiating not him, not his soul, but the evil with which his soul is in its earth-passage engaged.

Nor is this the whole story. We may remember Pope's marvellous couplet in the *Essay on Man* (II. 183):

> The surest Virtues thus from Passions shoot,
> Wild Nature's vigor working at the root.

Somehow an embedded value is in the satanic theme itself, awaiting release. We need not simply to forgive and avoid, but rather to *use*, the satanic fires. As I once put it: 'goodness without power is quite as dangerous and far less interesting than power in dissociation from goodness' (*Chariot of Wrath*, 1942, see p. 22, note; 147). Within the worst is some indefinable secret. In his introduction to *Gregory VII* the dramatist R. H. Horne wrote:

> Whatever the crime, there is always something grand and solemn in exploring the depths of human nature. The wisest or the shallowest sitter-in-judgement would tremble and be mute were the criminal's thoughts and passions all laid bare to view. In the worst acts, it is probable, we might find within the individual something exculpatory, if not redeeming; something which, *under the circumstances, seemed right*; something, at heart, the very opposite to his one fatal act . . .
>
> (quoted *The Golden Labyrinth*, 227)

As an attempt at rationalization that is well said. In *Morwyn* (III,

---

1. My views on the Bomb were uncompromisingly set down within a fortnight of its use and subsequently published in my *Hiroshima* in 1946.

178) Powys's Taliessin goes further, claiming that in his poetry he touched

> the deepest secret of all in our ancient religion; a secret that bears upon the mystery of good and evil and upon the mystical light that sometimes shines out from the most noisome regions of evil.

For some such reason *Macbeth* is to many, as it is to John Masefield, Shakespeare's most fascinating drama; and that is why I have so often, as in 'The Avenging Mind' (p. 188), insisted on its positive content. It seems that Henry V's words on the grim plight of his army before Agincourt

God Almighty!
There is some soul of goodness in things evil
Would men observingly distil it out

(IV. i. 3)

may be expanded far beyond its context. A metaphysical problem is involved.

Shakespeare and Byron are probably unique among our Renaissance poet-prophets in their uncanny way of preserving a balance of power-quest and ethic. Neither takes quite the fearful course of Wordsworth's *The Borderers* (*The Starlit Dome*, 25–9; *The Golden Labyrinth*, 212–15); nor would Nietzsche himself have gone so far as that. In Shakespeare and Byron ethic is strong, and traditional doctrines are respected, but the more Nietzschean insight pushes through. In Shakespeare's last plays repentance, in the usual sense,[1] reappears. Even so, what there is of it, as indeed happened in *King Lear* too, is repentance more for *wrongs against a human sanctity* than for any against God; though we must not forget Apollo in *The Winter's Tale* and the sense of Providence (I. ii. 159) in *The Tempest*.

It will be clear that Shakespeare's tragedies do not submit to a simple interpretation in terms of Christian orthodoxy. The power-quests beating through them are too strong for that. There are, certainly, contained thoughts subscribing to orthodox doctrine, such

---

1. The reservation is necessary since the New Testament *metanoein* scarcely corresponds to 'repent' as we today use the term. See *The Sovereign Flower*, 249, note; also pp. 185–6 below.

as Othello's crying out for his own damnation (v. ii. 276–9); but the speech is less important than, and cannot dispel, the sublime poetry of his lonely yet cosmic valuations earlier in the scene (pp. 247–8); and he dies in pride. Shakespeare composes from a mind saturated in orthodox tradition; he can call on it whenever he wants to; medievalism is alive in imagery and thought; but in the yet more important matters of dramatic manipulation and human action, and in his major naturalistically conceived or pagan—apart from the Angels in *Henry VIII*—symbolisms, he is a Renaissance poet whose dramatic persons have the drive of Webster's Vittoria Corrombona in *The White Devil*. Like Milton and Byron, Shakespeare writes from a transitionally inclusive view covering two cultural periods; but to reduce Shakespeare to medieval Christianity would be equivalent to writing off Milton as a Renaissance hedonist and no Puritan, or Byron as an Augustan and no Romantic. It is just because of their inclusive qualities that Shakespeare, Milton and Byron stand pre-eminent. In Shakespeare orthodox Christianity may at any moment, if the story allows it, appear with accepted sanction; but though his thought and imagery may tend towards the medieval, in human delineation, plot, action and dramatic conception he is of the Renaissance; and he has much in common with the dramatists of ancient Greece. Like those, he is concerned, as the medieval Church was not, with the Dionysian and erotic energies, with politics and power-quests and dramatic supermen.

IV

What we want is a union of Christianity and these intransigent yet indomitable demands. In *The Christian Renaissance* and *Christ and Nietzsche* I used European literature to establish a blend of the instinctive powers and Christianity. In the one study the eros was felt as power and in the other the power-quest as love. In Shakespeare these twin human attributes are found together, and Ibsen was to present them in careful balance. Shakespeare's valuations are heroic; but the heroism is countered by love. Power and Love: that is the human problem. One could almost say that there is no other, the rest being derivatives.

It cannot be too often emphasized that the New Testament alone, on which the Church's central doctrines are built, does not at all obviously face and minister to those two appallingly insistent problems of the human condition, sex and politics. I say 'obviously' because there are relations not generally recognized. Though heterosexually celibate, Christ himself, in the manner of a Socrates, Michelangelo or Shakespeare, knew love for a youth, the Beloved Disciple, John; and it seems likely that the royal overtones of the titles 'Messiah' and 'Christ' represent a quality and purpose in his life to which we should give a greater attention than is usual. These problems are discussed more fully in my *The Christian Renaissance* (1962, Epilogue; and see pp. 28–9, 238, 259 below).

The New Testament is an esoteric book in contrast to the normality of the Old Testament with all its emphasis on human propagation and heroic war. The Hebrews looked, and still look, for the Messiah, the leader, who is to be the earthly and political lord which Christ, in effect, was not.[1] To Nietzsche Christianity seemed to be a gospel for weaklings. Shakespeare's heroes certainly house primitive and unmoral energies which Christianity had for many centuries done its best to stifle; and our artistic sense of a justification in their protagonist violences is not unrelated to our consciousness of a limitation in Christian ethic; we feel that it does not cover the problem. Christ and Paul had the advantage of living and working in a pacific society under Roman domination, and meanwhile Rome herself was now in process of taking over and incorporating the Messianic dream, as may be felt in the writings of the poet-prophet, Vergil. 'Vergilian Rome', to coin the phrase, had the needed qualities and strength to blend Christianity and Empire; and in the Ages of Faith that followed Rome's fall, there was century by century the will and striving to establish a harmony between the Emperor in Europe and the Pope in Rome. The great voice of this 'will' is Dante, whose *De Monarchia* envisaged a world-order under an Emperor as Christ's vice-gerent in harmony with the Pope as successor of St. Peter. The aim was a harmony in separation; but observe that the higher status is the Emperor's, in direct relation to Christ

---

1. The problem is subtly handled in *Paradise Regained*; see my *Chariot of Wrath*, to be reissued in a volume entitled *Poets of Action*.

(see p. 359 below). Great poets do not remain content with the spiritualities. Their instinct is to assimilate 'Christ' to 'King'.

The balance which Dante looked for came about at the Renaissance not in Europe but in an island on its north-west coast: England. As Prof. Patrick Cruttwell argued in *The Shakespearean Moment* (for my review of it, see Appendix B), a State-Church settlement was realized in England resembling the Emperor-Pope dream of medieval Europe. The scale was small: the territory was limited and the religion was the reformed and narrowed church of Protestantism. Nevertheless time and circumstance conspired to make possible a momentary prefiguring of men's greatest hope on earth. Now we may suppose that this temporarily achieved harmony lay behind the generation in Renaissance England of the organic strength and power of survival seen in (i) the birth of Britain's trade, empire and influence and (ii) the works of Shakespeare. We begin to see *why* Shakespeare remains so universally important and his appeal so wide. Though locally generated, his work has global implications.

The harmony did not last, politically, but after the Civil War a balance was established, and has, if only provisionally, been maintained in our British constitution. Meanwhile our poets and dramatists have consistently laboured for a more perfect integration; human, political, and cosmic. Shakespeare's tumultuous dramas and Dionysian protagonists register an unrest, a striving and a power culminating in the magic of Prospero and the grandeur of *Henry VIII*. Milton in his royalistically loaded prose and poetry wrote from a Hebraic, Old Testament, sense of Britain as a Messiah nation of the Reformation inheriting the throne of David and warring for Christ as King.[1] The weightier dramas of all our periods, Elizabethan,

---

1. This element in Milton's thought is discussed in my *Chariot of Wrath*, to be reissued as part of the new volume *Poets of Action*.

In his valuable study *Jerusalem and Albion* (1964) Harold Fisch sees Milton's patriotism as establishing a 'link with the Hebraic notion of a social community' (124). The Hebraic world-view had a wholeness subsuming politics and religion which we, for the most part, have lost. Of the political societies of our own time he writes:

A little history would show them that they had each laid hold of a fragmented portion of Hebraism and seized upon it as the whole of truth and the whole of salvation for humanity (237).

The argument is, in the main, indisputable, though I should myself claim that

Jacobean, Restoration, Augustan and Victorian, labour to inter-penetrate political tyrannies with softened sensibilities, power with love: the story is set out in *The Golden Labyrinth*, with an especial emphasis on Nathaniel Lee in the seventeenth century and the state dramas of leading poets in the Victorian era. The tradition attains its finest flowering in the life-and-work of Byron which, as I showed in *Lord Byron: Christian Virtues* (289), can be seen as one consistent attempt to 'render unto God the things that are Caesar's, and demand of Caesar the things that are God's'. Our most fully conscious literary statement is Ibsen's. His dramas throughout, as I have shown in my study, *Ibsen*, interweave themes of power and love, the dramatic emphasis, as is usual in drama, falling on the former; and at the heart of his work, at the centre and hinge of it, is the mammoth world-drama *Emperor and Galilean* prophesying the advent of a Messiah as one 'who wills himself'—the 'I am that I am' of Shakespeare and Byron (pp. 16–17 above)—and is accordingly able to bring in the 'Third Empire' in which State and Church will be transmuted within a greater unity. Notice that the communal issue depends on a union within the individual; a blend of ethic with his whole, often disreputable and Dionysian, self; that is what dramas are for. And more may be involved than drama: behind, or within, is the personal sex-life of each and all of us. On this our most important statement is probably that of John Cowper Powys, to which we have already (p. 18) referred, on the use of dangerous sexually located fantasies, for release and health. The Powysian doctrine may be felt subtly hinted also in Nietzsche's *Thus Spake Zarathustra* (*The Christian Renaissance*, 1962, 273–4). Such is the way to Nietzsche's dream of a 'Roman Caesar with the soul of Christ' (*The Will to Power*, 983).

This is our context for the understanding of Shakespeare. The royal dramatist of my interpretations may on certain occasions be called 'Christian', provided that we recognize the all-important difference, which is, very simply, as follows: Shakespeare differs from orthodox Christianity not by being less, nor alien, but by a greater

---

Prof. Fisch's Hebraic totality is implicit within the structure of all our greater dramatic and poetic works from Milton's day to our own.

inclusiveness; as when in *Measure for Measure* he interweaves his themes of sexual instinct, gospel mercy and judicial action. Here and in *The Merchant of Venice* ladies, Isabella and Portia, are Shakespeare's main voices for Christian government (pp. 229–30; also 123, 180); feminine romance has often a Christian aura (*The Imperial Theme*, 11–14). The Crown may have Christian, even Christlike (pp. 101–3, 120–1, 359), implications.

Shakespeare is concerned with love, but also with power; and power and politics converge. He is always 'royal', seldom 'ecclesiastical'. His dramatic supermen, culminating in Prospero, are personal power-bearers who, however ambiguously, recall not Christianity but Christ, pointing on to Byron and to Nietzsche. The trouble is, that few readers can see the electric word 'Christ' in print without assuming a theological and ecclesiastical submission. Few understand that the word may be used as freely as one uses any myth, the Prometheus myth or the Faust myth, as an imaginative and historical force existing in its own right independent of religious commitment; or that one may, like Dante, be looking for the true successor to Christ in Emperor or King, the Church corresponding to St. Peter. This is not to say that the theology of church Christianity is necessarily false, but merely that its truth or falsity need not at every moment be in question. We can talk or think of the Faust story without worrying about the German scholar with whom it started. If the New Testament were proved by some newly found scroll to be an historical fraud, the Christian myth would lose little of its imaginative authority and power over us; nor perhaps its historical, even divine, authority, since it would only the more clearly have come into being in response to a need, and would therefore have to be regarded as part of the Providential scheme. Historic fiction might be cosmic truth. But surely we need not, as students of Shakespeare, be involved in such abstruse disquisitions. Let us keep to the simplicities.

I can hear critics saying that, by calling Shakespeare and other great writers more inclusive than Christianity, I am falling into the error of expecting poetry to replace religion; others will say that I am denying Christ's supremacy. I *might* be doing these things; but I am not *necessarily* doing either. I take these two objections in turn.

Though Shakespeare points towards a greater inclusiveness than Christianity, he does this only in imaginative terms. What we enjoy imaginatively need not lead to a total commitment. We need not *live* by it. Even if imagination attunes us to truths *greater* than those we can live by, it still remains ephemeral, a hint, an influence; it does not saturate our daily life, like a religion. It may do this for the creative artist himself but not, except in rare instances, for his audience.

At the Renaissance dramatic ritual passed from the Church to the play-house. It became public entertainment dependent on the individual's passing mood and choice and his willingness to expend that outward sign and sacrament of the individual's power, money. Money acts as the individual's personal sovereignty and freedom; if he spends money on a show this is because he wants it, and he wants it because it corresponds to a need. The romantic love-interests and royal rituals of Shakespearian drama corresponded to human needs intuitively recognized, which included the need to see mankind as heroic and noble, and which were not covered by the Mystery cycles. The one protagonist of medieval drama was henceforth supplanted by a number of lesser protagonists, nearer to ourselves, and with problems not so very different from our own. Stories and protagonists became various in correspondence to various needs. Man was in this way being helped towards identification with what was akin to, yet higher and more noble than, himself; and to involve himself temporarily in problems that were like his own, and see the outcome. In such dramas man is invited to use his own instincts in order to objectify himself and his problems, learning their nature; and to rise above them, for his protagonist self-reflection will be more noble than himself, and more poetically vocal, and within the poetry ethical valuations are contained. He is being invited less to change himself than to develop, to integrate, himself, and also his society, because in these matters individual and society involve each other. There is however no exploitation, in public drama of this higher order, of raw instinct, as in the public drawings-and-quarterings and bull-baiting shows of Shakespeare's day and the worst indulgences of our own. The place for those is in the secret sexually impelled fantasies which we have already discussed. Instead, imagination is at work; the faculty, that is, of recognizing and enjoying powers which are not quite ourselves and yet find reflections and responses in ourselves; hints of a higher self. But there must be first a degree of contact with our lower selves, or we shall not respond: and if we do not respond, we shall not part with our money: it is all free. The 'I am that I am' and 'I am myself alone' of Shakespeare's sonnets and protagonists (pp. 16–17) is clearly playing its part. It is all done with —in Pope's indispensable phrase—'wild Nature's vigor working at the root'.

We reach this conclusion: good drama and all literature of similar quality differ from religion by inviting a free use of ourselves to surmount ourselves (see 'The Avenging Mind', p. 193). Here we may note the dangers attending any critical authority or educational system that assumes the right to tell us what we ought to respond to. The most that such an authority should say is, 'I have found this valuable. Do you?' The imagination in man is itself, for each of us, our sole authority.

And yet again, the 'let's pretend' of play-acting and other fictions does not claim to exert the appalling authority over our daily life and deepest *being* that characterizes religion. Even the most confirmed bardolater is unlikely to go to the stake or risk leprosy and fever in foreign lands for his poet. Religion exists in the order of being and immediate action, drama and literature in the order of imaginative experience. Religion and literature handle, roughly, the same themes; but even when a dramatist such as Ibsen deliberately makes what I have called 'being', the necessity to live and act from a certain profound level, his reiterated theme, what his audience receives is an imaginative and not a religious experience. All great literature, we may say, is about religion; it may even tell us, make us experience, more than religion does; it may tell us in one period what is to become religion at a later day; but it is not itself religion.

Shakespeare, ranging so widely over human affairs and problems, does, I think, tell us much in the political sphere that will become part of man's religion eventually. We have in our time seen two ideologies exert a religious hold on their followers: Communism and National Socialism. The very facts of these suggest that we cannot remain much longer content with a religion in dissociation from politics and national and international action. Pope's *Essay on Man* is a universal statement opening out, as I argued in *Laureate of Peace* (reissued as *The Poetry of Pope*) to what could be a world religion; and he had planned its expansion to cover ecclesiastical and political government.

As for the second criticism, I do not deny Christ. I go far in regarding him as royally and sexually inclusive (p. 22).

He lived, but did not write, poetry. Living outspaces writing, however great; and it is for this reason that I attribute a pre-eminence to Byron beyond that of other poets. Christ is said to be the perfect, the whole, Man. And yet this can only be true if we are to adopt what is today an unconventional view of him. He appears to have lacked what D. H. Lawrence, bringing him to life in his story *The Escaped Cock* (or *The Man who Died*) after the crucifixion to experience sexual intercourse with a woman, regarded as a human essential. But this is surely to misunderstand. Do we not instinctively feel that a marriage relationship would be for him out of place? Does not a total integration preclude the need for such a completion? And is not the nature of this completion—the 'complete bosom' unhit by Cupid's dart of *Measure for Measure* (I. iii. 3)—fully explained in Shakespeare's Sonnets (e.g. Sonnets 115, 118; see *The Mutual Flame*, 125–6; *Byron and Shakespeare*, 56–67)? If Christ is perfect man that 'perfection' is the 'perfection' of the Phoenix poems of Shakespeare's time (*The Mutual Flame*, Part II, 183–4): the perfection of the artistic state, enjoyed by genius and evident in the love-psychology of Socrates, Michelangelo, Shakespeare and Byron; and with those it would not be hard to align others, such as Milton, Swift and T. E. Lawrence. In such men there is an abnormal sexuality, searching less for difference than for self-reflection, or soul-reflection, found usually in male youth, often accompanied by a parental or educational care; and yet also seeing through the adored one into higher spheres by what I call 'the seraphic intuition'. It is often supposed that such psychological states have been conditioned by a close mother-relationship in childhood leading to an 'Oedipus complex'. They may be regarded as a disease, but if so it is a disease more vital than health, leading to lives and works of deathless quality. Oedipus, we may recall, was first in the *Oedipus Tyrannus* guilty and unclean, but in Sophocles' sequel, the *Oedipus Coloneus*, he becomes a saving power of divine authority given an ascension resembling that recorded of Christ. His story has analogies to Shakespeare's *Timon of Athens* (pp. 215, 221).

Christ, as he is presented by the New Testament and Church tradition, shows a similar sexual divergence. His only close personal love relationships of which we are told are those with (i) his Mother and (ii) the Beloved Disciple, John, the disciple who lay upon his breast at the Last Supper. The matter is discussed in the additional section of the 1962 reissue of *The Christian Renaissance*. Here we need only point its relevance to Shakespeare's Sonnets and other kindred writings. This is a peculiarly clear example of the way in which I am likely to be found supporting Christianity: there is generally something startling, even shocking, but not necessarily unorthodox since it may sometimes be found that I am reviving an important but forgotten tradition, about my approach. I regret having to cause disquiet, perhaps pain, but I am making advances of great importance, and such advances are bought at a cost.

Meanwhile, I am not denying Christ. By comparing his humanity to that of men of greatest genius and finding a close analogy, I am being more reverent than my contemporaries. If the Son of God is to appear in human form, is it likely that he would appear as a normal man? Is it not far more likely that he would appear as a man of genius? That is, in fact, what appears to have happened.

There seems to be a recurring challenge from ancient Greece onwards concerned variously with a newly spiritualized psychology, with the seraphic intuition, and planes beyond death, but also close-bound to man's earthly condition and to the power-quest, lifting us through conceptions of royalty and the superman towards some vast communal purpose transcending religion; in Christian terms, the return of Christ in power and the New Jerusalem as City of God, wherein there will be no temple (Revelation, XXI, 22).

V

The probings and turmoils of Shakespeare's tragedies are part of a single design pointing on to *Henry VIII*. Without that conclusion the wheel would not have come full circle, the labours would lack context and purpose, and the corpus its crown. And yet, might it not be objected that this drama's contents are inadequate to the high themes we have been envisaging? Can so evident a period-piece bear so royal a weight?

Yes, it can. For this contemporaneity, this 'dating', is no weakness but strength. Do we not find a similar contemporaneity at the conclusion to the *Oresteia* of Aeschylus? In Vergil? In Dante? Milton? Yes, and throughout the Bible itself? Just as many of the following essays derive definition and detonation from the reader's knowledge of their 'occasional' origin, so is it with our greater poets. The philosopher and theologian may be content with generalities; the poet prefers the more difficult task of finding the universal in the particular. He labours with the here and now, the actual and the burdensome; he would infuse spirit into the heavy and intransigent. Had Shakespeare, instead of concentrating on King Henry and in Cranmer's prophecy on Elizabeth I and James I, spoken of 'England's destiny' or 'mission', he would have been less the poet. Strangely, too, he would be now out-of-date, since the words are soiled; but what *he* said in *his* day and for *his* purpose of three contemporary sovereigns remains deathless as a symbol and an exemplar. Aeschylus' Athens, Vergil's Rome, Shakespeare's England—all live on as, in my brother's phrase for Vergil's Rome, a 'spiritual city'. Having first their own warm life, they become for later ages immortal. But we shall not suppose that every detail is to be imitated; we shall not start inaugurating a new Council of the Areopagus and we may have different views on Henry, Elizabeth and James. We have first to accept the imaginative statement in its own right with a willing suspension of criticism, and then, assimilating it, re-express it for our own time. And the way to re-express it for our own time is to face the prophetic powers in Aeschylus, Dante, Shakespeare, Milton, Pope, Byron, Tennyson, Ibsen and Nietzsche; for what is needed today is less any new poetry and drama of this order than *an interpretative facing of what we already have*. Among the moderns I know only one British poet who in the interfusion of Christian sensibility with the jungle instincts of communal man can stand beside the great names I have listed: I am thinking of Francis

Berry's *The Iron Christ* and *Murdoch* (in *The Galloping Centaur*), and *Morant Bay*.

Since Shakespeare's Histories and Tragedies show correspondences to our own political and psychological turmoils, his solution, or at least conclusion, demands a careful response.

In *The Tempest* the rejected superman Prospero, matured in wisdom and magic, proves victorious over political wickedness and returns to re-engage his ducal responsibilities. From *The Tempest* we may suppose that the esoteric movements of our time, and especially the greatest of them, Spiritualism, must be faced and incorporated within our seats of learning and councils of state before we can attain to mastery.

Henry VIII is comprehensive. The power-quest assertive in the earlier Histories and the Tragedies is represented by Buckingham and Wolsey, dangerous in life yet noble in their falls; and beside these is the tragedy of Queen Katharine, summing Shakespeare's many heroines, herself perhaps the most wonderful of all and given a vision of Paradise in attunement to the mystic intimations of *Pericles* and *The Winter's Tale*. Countering tragedy is the King's marriage with Anne, in succession to earlier romances; the humility, of traditional Christian quality, of Cranmer; the steady rise of the King, and Cranmer's concluding prophesy at the christening of the child Elizabeth at a ceremonial supported by a raucous and sexually fertile crowd signifying the raw material of human creation of which nations are made. Throughout there is a prevailing peace in which, under the Law and the King, conflicts are serenely contained. King and Church are balanced; balanced in conflict with Wolsey and in harmony with Cranmer. State and Church are, in the final ceremony, the King and Cranmer together central, at one. It is a drama of peace; more, it is poetically peaceful; there are many events, but no prolonged action or passionate movement forcing involvement; time, with the help of many 'insets' (pp. 6–7 above), is subdued to a supervening, eternal, sight.

Properly understood, the task Shakespeare set himself in *Henry VIII* was probably the hardest of his career. To make so expansive and profound a drama in terms of a strict adherence to unsensational events of recent history was a tremendous achievement. The nature of it may perhaps be best seen in King Henry himself. He is wonderfully conceived as a very human man and yet, as such a man and no more, yet also, superbly, King (*The Crown of Life*, 306–7). Earlier monarchs were as men either contrasted with their office or, as in *Henry V*, subdued to it. Henry VIII is man and office in identity; and to convince us of this without rhetoric and with little action and no taint of romanticizing or idealism, is a miracle. We are left in no doubt regarding the part played by Anne Boleyn in his conscientious scruples regarding his marriage with Katharine (II. ii. 17–19; *The Crown of Life*, 309). Indeed, no one actually praises his wisdom, virtue or valour; these are qualities reserved for Cranmer's prophecy on Elizabeth; but even so this 'mighty piece' of 'princely graces' (v. v. 26–7) towers above everyone, a King unquestioned. In the King's person the peculiar quality of *Henry VIII*, its way of being the better as a prophetic document for being a piece of unassertive contemporary realism, is brought to personal focus.[1]

One way of seeing how difficult was the task undertaken is to observe a certain weakness, of a kind met earlier in Vergil and afterwards in Milton.

The dangerous and tragic power-bearers are more poetically attractive than Cranmer, who is almost absurdly humble and utterly dependent on the King's support until the great moment at the end when he suddenly assumes dramatic authority, interrupting the King and speaking his prophecy, not in his own person but, as he explicitly tells us, as a medium for divine inspiration. Until the prophecy he is, in comparison with Buckingham, Wolsey and Queen Katharine, dramatically weak; almost a non-entity. Is this good enough for a key-figure in so massive a play? And yet, can what we call 'Christian' humility ever be expected to make strong

1. Shakespeare's study exactly corresponds to the considered views of the modern Cambridge historian, G. R. Elton, who writes of Henry as 'the very embodiment of personal monarchy' (3); royally symbolic, standing for 'nation and commonwealth', he was yet more than that, receiving a 'personal and direct devotion' approaching 'idolatry', and this is quite irrespective of 'what he did' (11–12); by 'personal magnetism' (12) he was, though 'no statesman' (24) and 'neither a good nor a wise man', yet 'a 'great king' (26). To sum up (12): 'No person was ever more monarchical, no monarchy more personal in this sense, than Henry VIII's' (*Henry VIII: an Essay in Revision*, pubd. for The Historical Association; 1962). See also John Bowle, *Henry VIII*, reviewed *T.L.S.*, 18 March 1965.

drama? As Blake pointed out in *The Everlasting Gospel*, Christ himself was *not* humble.

One rejoinder is obvious: why have dramatic poetry? If drama exists to exploit and direct dangerous passions, then in so far as they remain quiet we can do without it. We nevertheless feel that there should be an equivalent power on the side of the good, and such a power Cranmer only shows under inspiration; and inspiration is always in danger of seeming unreliable because unpredictable. We only feel really *safe* with the King; and the great prophecy itself is all about a Queen and a King, anyway.

A comparison with Vergil may prove helpful. Shakespeare's final emphasis, recalling Christian mythology and Vergil's Messianic Eclogue, is on a child: the child Elizabeth. Vergil and Shakespeare show a number of similarities: in both, at the very heart of their life's work (*Aeneid* VI and *Macbeth*), a hero descends to an underworld, rather as did King Saul at Endor, to receive a prophecy regarding his nation's future. In retrospect I find it interesting that my brother, W. F. Jackson Knight, should have devoted so much of his life to Vergil, and I so much of mine to Shakespeare.[1]

They were certainly akin in what might be called their poetic psychology. Both leave evidences of the homosexual, seraphic, idealism already discussed. Indeed, it was my brother who first, in a single exquisite page of *Roman Vergil* (1944 etc., IV, 113–14; 1966

1. My brother died on 4 December 1964. Official obituary notices appeared in *The Times* on 7 December (with others by Francis Berry and Peter C. L. Phelan on 10 and 11 December); in *Erasmus*, 1965, vol. 16, cols. 641–3, by Prof. J. A. Davison; in the *University of Exeter Gazette*, No. 38, Jan. 1965, by Prof. F. W. Clayton; in the *Easter Bulletin* for 1965 of the *Exeter University Club*, by Keith R. Prowse; in *The Bloxhamist* (magazine of Bloxham School), Spring 1965, by 'D.G.L.' and also by E. A. Christopher Lee, and see issue of May 1936, 289; in the 1964–5 *Proceedings of the Virgil Society*, by Prof. T. J. Haarhoff; in the *Reports of The Royal Society of Literature*, 1965–6, by Dr. E. V. Rieu; in *The Orbilian Society Newsletter*, February 1965; in *Vergilius* (U.S.A.), II, 1965, by Prof. A. G. McKay; in *Le Parole e le Idee* (Naples), VII, 145, by Prof. Giulio Vallese; in the *Rivista di Cultura Classica e Medioevale* (Rome), VIII, 1966, by Prof. Franco Mosino; and in *Psychic News*, 12 and 19 December 1964.

Provisional bibliographies, by John G. Landels and John Glucker respectively, have appeared in the *Proceedings of the Virgil Society*, as above, and in *Pegasus*, 4 and 6, University of Exeter Classical Society, October 1965 and June 1966. Posthumous publications are to appear under the editorship of Mr. John D. Christie, starting with *Vergil: Epic and Anthropology* in 1967 (Messrs. Allen & Unwin Ltd.)

Peregrine, 146; Italian translation, Milan 1949, 169–70), covered the whole range of what I have since grown to call the 'seraphic intuition', noting that Vergil's main poetic affection in the *Aeneid* seems to be given to the ill-fated boys Nisus and Euryalus; to the young Pallas and Lausus; to the bisexually conceived, Amazonian, girl-warrior Camilla; and to Aeneas' divinely-guiding mother, Venus, athletically conceived in huntress disguise (a figure, we may add, neatly identifying in one person the 'Oedipus' and 'seraphic' themes). My brother with a caution perhaps less characteristic of my own writings concluded that Vergil's trust was nevertheless in the home and marriage, since except for Venus these youthful figures end tragically. This remarkable page, which must have influenced my own thinking, maintains a salutary balance; and yet the long tradition of homosexual elegy suggests that tragedy does not invalidate the vision.

Shakespeare has his sonnets in adoration of his 'master-mistress' (Sonnet 20), the Fair Youth; and quite apart from these, the erotic and maternal feeling for slaughtered youth in his early histories (*The Mutual Flame*, 109–10) is clearly Vergilian.

What is most important for our present purpose is that in both we find similar failures in face of a similar, central, problem: the creation of a good and powerful hero. Aeneas strikes us as a deliberately fabricated person less warm and human than Turnus precisely as Prince Hal in *Henry IV*, and even when he becomes King in *Henry V*, is less humanly warm and attractive than Hotspur; as, rather differently, is Cranmer than Buckingham and Wolsey. The same problem recurs in *Paradise Lost* where Satan has a dramatic lustre and wins dramatic honours not enjoyed by the mild and courteously conceived Messiah, Son of God, until his assumption of God's appalling wrath and power, for it is emphasized that he acts as a vice-gerent or medium only, as he ascends the chariot to ride victorious over the rebel hosts. Just as with Cranmer's prophecy, a preliminary mildness is found to be the condition for the inrush of greater powers.

Vergil's Aeneas scarcely exists except as a medium or implement of Destiny, and perhaps that is why the *Aeneid* concludes so sharply with the grim slaying of Turnus: it is as though Vergil is saying that such deeds of blood and war have to be accomplished by the good; we are reminded of Hamlet as Heaven's 'scourge and minister' (p. 16); and since neither Vergil nor we know exactly why it is so ordained, no comment is offered, and the poem ends. It is not really Aeneas who does it; it is not a question of characterization. Aeneas himself claims that it is the slain Pallas, perhaps symbolizing for Vergil the sweeter powers crying in an inhuman universe for revenge; or perhaps this is only Aeneas' rationalization of a deed he *has* to do, without knowing why. Fearful deeds are today being forced on us all, across the world. Vergil did well to conclude like that, refusing comment.

Such *implements* as Aeneas are scarcely, as men, real, and certainly not attractive. In great literature the good people lack power. Where inspiration and poetry alone are concerned, as in Cranmer's prophecy or that of the dying John of Gaunt at the point of death as 'a prophet new inspired' (*Richard II*, II. i. 31–68) and Milton's *description* of God's awful chariot and the Son's use of it, there is power enough; and we may observe that the near-satisfying heroism of *Henry V* is carried largely by descriptive prologues, as though Shakespeare realized that he could not do what he wanted by *dramatic* creation alone. Reliance on poetry and inspiratory or otherwise guiding powers is, of course, the Christian, as it is also the Spiritualistic, way; but against it stands the Byronic and Nietzschean demand for a more human realization. Byron, writing to Francis Hodgson on 12 May 1821, states the problem neatly. He refers to Aristotle, and quotes Dryden from Johnson's *Lives of the Poets:* 'The pity which the poet is to labour for is *for* the criminal. The terror is likewise in the punishment of the said criminal, who, if he be represented too great an offender, will *not be pitied*.' Byron continues:

> In the Greek tragedy innocence is unhappy often, and the offender escapes. I must also ask you is Achilles a *good* character? or is even Aeneas anything but a successful runaway? It is for Turnus men feel and not for the Trojan. Who is the hero of *Paradise Lost?* Why Satan—and Macbeth, and Richard, and Othello, Pierre, and Lothario, and Zanga!
>
> (*Letters and Journals*, v, 284)

The question is, how can we graft, as Pope would have us, virtue onto instinct, identify love with power, fuse sweetness with combat, not only in words and vision but through man, dramatically activated, as we know him? Perhaps, though Byron appears to have come near it (*Lord Byron: Christian Virtues*, VI), it is impossible. Some will say that we should not demand it, but our greater poets try, and when they fail their failure is the measure of the difficulty which it defines.

The works we have been discussing may be impregnated by ephemeral beliefs and much of it, even when supposedly historical, may be fiction. We shall accept them as make-believe, as play-acting; but the experience will be an attunement that goes on subtly influencing our lives and policies and raising questions which we do well to ask. In this way Shakespeare has composed for us his own, royalistic, Bible. Probably the most important single suggestion in the following pages is that where I see Shakespeare's total work as, in structure, another Bible (p. 301). The correspondence is remarkable; and we could add the Sonnets to correspond to the Song of Songs.

VI

We can see why Shakespeare is of so overpowering an importance still and exerts so world-wide an appeal. In his own terms, and writing from a period which in its own limited area and epoch—and this is why he does it better than his successors—actually went far to realize the synthesis, he speaks of that for which the whole world, as Ibsen's *Emperor and Galilean* so vividly explains, is today labouring. He puts before us the human energies, the power in man that, as Nietzsche has it, is 'unburiable and blasteth rocks' (*Thus Spake Zarathustra*, 33, 'The Grave-Song'); driving on and up, despite evil and tragedy, and attaining to what is beyond death and immortal. And this he shows in relation to the wider need of including them, as the stories of Buckingham, Wolsey and Queen Katharine are in the massive patterning of *Henry VIII* included, within some kind of royally conditioned society, he for his day and we for ours. I do not say 'order', an abstraction of deceptive appeal. I say royalty. Once again I quote Gordon Craig's indispensable statement in *On the Art of the Theatre* (1957; 45):

> I use the word 'Kingdom' instinctively in speaking of the land of the Theatre. It explains best what I mean. Maybe in the next three or four thousand years the word Kingdom will have disappeared—Kingdom, Kingship, King—but I doubt it; and if it does go something else equally fine will take its place. It will be the same thing in a different dress. You can't invent anything finer than Kingship, the idea of the King.

Whatever we think of that, it is deeply Shakespearian. In Shakespeare there are two dominating imaginative powers, each in its way serving to unify his work. One is the interplay of thunder-tempests and music, tumult and harmony; the other, more personal, is royalty, the crown. The two converge (p. 111). The crown acts within society as a leavening harmony, a music; it is to that royal harmony that 'the prophetic soul of the wide world dreaming on things to come' (Sonnet 107) invites us.

Democracy is of the earth and religion of the sky; but royalty is as a rainbow, like Shakespeare's definition of poetry in *A Midsummer Night's Dream* (v. i. 12–13), arching from earth to heaven and heaven to earth. In the royal insignia of the Incas the king wore a rainbow head-dress. Now, despite his handling of King Henry VIII, Shakespeare himself had little that could be called perfection in contemporary royalty to feed his dreams; and that is why among our following essays the Inca drama, *Apu Ollantay* (p. 139), fills a gap. It was written from a society that really did feel their Inca-King as divine, and lived and enjoyed the implications of this belief under a ruler who himself went far to live the part. In Shakespeare's last plays there are hints of the same quality, especially in *Pericles* and *The Winter's Tale*, where the mystic insights they carry are brought to bear on royalty, the twin themes of my book converging; for here royal persons are felt *intimately*, and rather wonderfully, as sacred (*The Crown of Life*, 72, 115–16, 121, 158–9). In such passages, person and office are momentarily identified, with an emphasis falling on sanctity; but these gems of poetry are scarcely justified by the human delineations. *Henry VIII* shows, it is true, a fully developed and satisfying coalescence of man and office, but, despite his religious devotions, without radiations of personal sanctity, such categories being left to the play's suffusing religious poetry and the prophecy of Cranmer. To this extent the Inca drama, which is in other respects also closely similar in pattern to the plays of Shakespeare's final period, holds an inclusive conviction which Shakespeare scarcely matches.

It may be that the Shakespearian feeling for royalty in the person is best read on the analogy of our political story. Democracy, as Milton and Ibsen knew, demands a nation of kings; its aim is to spread royalty everywhere. Perhaps, just as we do well to expand Shakespeare's royal nationalism to make it a type or symbol of some world royalty to be, so we may expand his sense of the sacred person in king or queen to a sense of the sacred, the divine, in all men. Great poetry lives by two principles: it is (i) sharply concrete and individualized and (ii) is for ever expanding. It is for us to keep close to the particulars and encourage the expansion.

There is much left unsettled. No mystic or prophet, nor discarnate spirit-guide, has been able to solve the problem of evil, nor explain its fascination. If, as there well may be, there were an answer known to some of them, it could not be communicated in words which we should understand. But, as my brother and I used so often to say—I do not know who said it first—'what cannot be thought out may be lived into'. In Aeschylus' *Oresteia* the Erinyes, or Furies, become under Athena's guidance the Eumenides or 'kindly ones', to be accepted and honoured as constituents to society, their shrines underground. They are within us, secretly but necessarily. This too is the gospel of Pope's *Essay on Man*. Rationally the incompatibles of power-quest and Christianity, of state and church, cannot be harmonized; but the harmony may be striven for and in the individual man may be, almost, lived; and perhaps, eventually, in society also. If we want to watch it incarnated on a grand scale before the eyes of the world, we know where to turn: to the life and works of Byron.

II

BRUTUS AND CASSIUS

My first Shakespeare article, written for a competition set by J. Middleton Murry
The Adelphi, March 1927; IV, 9.

[The quality of the comments upon the problem from *Julius Caesar* was extraordinarily high. Not one of them failed to display some real subtlety of discrimination, and a deep interest in fundamentals of Shakespeare criticism. I regret that it is impossible to print more than one of the essays, and I regret still more that there is no periodical where such absorbing questions of Shakespeare interpretation can be adequately treated.

On the simple issue whether the 'he' of 'He should not humour me' was Brutus or Caesar, opinions were about equally divided. On the more complex question of the characters of Brutus and Cassius, a strikingly large majority were in agreement that Cassius is essentially the finer and more human spirit, and the one with whom Shakespeare himself felt the truer sympathy: which is my own opinion.

For convenience of reference the passage is repeated:

> Well, Brutus, thou art noble: yet I see
> Thy honourable mettle may be wrought
> From that it is dispos'd. Therefore it is meet
> That noble minds keep ever with their likes:
> For who so firm that cannot be seduc'd?
> Caesar doth bear me hard, but he loves Brutus.
> If I were Brutus now, and he were Cassius,
> He should not humour me.

J. M. M.].

'THY honourable metal[1] may be wrought from that it is disposed.' I do not think this contains the idea of honour becoming dishonour. The 'honourable metal' may be *wrought* (cp. *Othello*, v. ii. 344) to substitute a new line of action in the name of honour from the one to which it has been disposed or directed before. A thing cannot well be said to be wrought from its essential nature. And seduce = deflect, without a derogatory sense, i.e., Who cannot be shaken in his convictions of what is right?' Up to this time the speech suggests that men of principle have only to be convinced that an act is morally necessary for them to sacrifice their instincts: exactly what happens here. After generalizing on Brutus' character Cassius turns to his own, contrasting their motives. Two things stand out boldly in Cassius throughout the play: envy, and intense desire for friendship. Darkness and light are intermittent in his soul, and so he walks abroad when 'the cross blue lightning seemed to open the breast of heaven'; and as he early presents himself in 'the aim and very flash of it' (I. iii. 50–2) so later he presents his breast to his own dagger in the loved Brutus' hand (IV. iii. 99–100). Deep, though perhaps unconscious, symbolism. After the Storm scene Shakespeare knew his Cassius. Dark envy is shot with the lightning of love: frustrated, he has vision; he is of the company of lost angels.

I take the 'he' in 'He should not . . .' to be Brutus, and do not think the line 'Caesar doth . . .' therefore dislocated from its successor: rather it is an essential to this reading. By itself, 'If I were . . . humour me' is a weak periphrasis adding nothing to 'I would not be influenced by Brutus.' But if the 'Brutus' in it throws back to the Brutus preceding it means, 'If we were to change places in Caesar's affection.' 'If Caesar loved me I should not be persuaded to betray him.' Cassius would not betray love.

This speech illustrates and is illuminated by Cassius' character which to me dwarfs the other figures. He is not free from the taint of Elizabethan stage villainy. But beside his envy is a heart 'dearer than

1. My spelling varied from Murry's 'mettle': I leave the discrepancy as it stands.

Plutus' mine, richer than gold' (IV. iii. 101). This confession is wrung from him in tears, and, whatever his actions, such things are not said into futility. I see Cassius as a man thwarted by life, embittered, lonely; but with a passionately loving heart. As the play progresses he stands out with increasing humanity and so dignity: in the quarrel the rights and wrongs (Cassius' of course) are forgotten as we watch his darkened soul in agony at Brutus' righteous taunts. Schemes, expert efficiency, are gone: love for the man so coldly aureoled in high principle that he seems of another order, unreachably pinnacled on righteousness—this only is at stake: 'I, that denied thee gold, will give my heart' (IV. iii. 103). When at last he has drunk his fill of Brutus' love, he will not argue about strategy: though on the brink of military disaster, he has another prize.

Brutus is cold. He binds his soul in fetters. His wife compares herself to 'his harlot' (II. i. 287) and after her death (contrast its effect on Cassius), and after Cassius' death, he has so much 'in art' (IV. iii. 193) that he disgusts us. Shakespeare vents an almost personal spite on the Brutus who would not qualify for tragic honours, whose ice would not catch fire. But Pindarus is free 'yet would not so have been . . .' (V. iii. 47). Titinius sobs the greatest poem in the play over Cassius' dead body and then dies for him (V. iii. 59–63). No other personal touch in the play moves me as 'my sight was ever thick' (V. iii. 21). It is right that Cassius, in a scene whose atmosphere trembles between two worlds, dies for friendship.

Julius Caesar is unique in Shakespeare's progress. I once exercised the privilege of an ardent Shakespearian to smile forgivingly at *Henry V*, *Much Ado about Nothing*,[1] and though I now know better and blush at the remembrance I still feel something static in them. Their poetry is facile, with the blazing facility of a Shakespeare. I suggest he reviewed the fact and deliberately tried a new style. Whereas the magnificence of *Henry V* is packed with metaphor, *Julius Caesar* is in *most* speeches almost devoid of it: nowhere else is his language so *thin*, and so amazing a contrast must have been due to deliberation. Did he forgo his chief instrument to see what might

---

1. The text breaks off ungrammatically at the second title. Presumably there should have been a third, possibly *Twelfth Night*.

push itself to the surface? Groping for the new thing, that had not come, but must be made to come? This is what came:

> You are my true and honourable wife,
> As dear to me as are the ruddy drops
> That visit my sad heart.

(II. i. 288)

and,

> O setting Sun,
> As in thy red rays thou dost sink to-night,
> So in his red blood Cassius' day is set;
> The sun of Rome is set.

(v. iii. 60)

There are many more; the organ notes of tragedy; the movement that surges to the final half-line and breaks.[1] The voice is new, if not the form. And with this power Shakespeare no longer refused the metaphor which became the dazzling glory of Cleopatra.

Shakespeare now saw disclosed the riches of human souls as human souls. Cassius the envious, storm-lover, but whose heart *because it is a heart* is dearer than Plutus' mine, in the passage we discuss stops his scheming thought to watch for a moment his own soul-bitterness and then considers that other soul-yearning in himself which no principles could conquer. He has begun to justify himself artistically in Shakespeare's eyes. And though others press chaotically for chief consideration in this tentative transitional play, to me, I think to Shakespeare, the last two acts are Cassius' tragedy pointing Shakespeare to the un-moral poetic humanism of his greatest work. Once the true light of poetry settles on such a character it will not leave him. Nor is it strange. It happened sixty years later to another lost angel.

1. Compare my brother's observation of the 'eloquent Vergilian silence' given by some of Vergil's perhaps intentionally uncompleted lines (W. F. Jackson Knight, *Roman Vergil*, 1944 etc., 297; enlarged 1966 (Peregrine), 360. See also Taraknath Sen, 'Shakespeare's Short Lines', *Shakespeare Commemoration Volume*, Presidency College, Calcutta, 1966.

III

THE POET AND IMMORTALITY

The Shakespeare Review, October 1928; 1, 6.

I T is often assumed that Shakespeare's works have no positive religious meaning. And yet a sincere lover of the plays must be unwilling to let such a statement pass unchallenged. To be moved deeply by that sense of human sublimity that great literature gives us, to have our minds or souls purified by the contemplation of the human spirit in conflict with its fate; to suffer in imagination and yet to treasure that suffering as good rather than ill; to be thus reconciled to the necessity and beauty of the tragic fact—surely all this is to be momentarily at one with the great principle of human creation. This surely is, if not 'a religion', yet certainly Religion in its widest and deepest sense. But if we isolate the separate themes of the greater plays it is, perhaps, a little hard to reconcile some of these with what we are accustomed to call 'religion'.

There is, of course, much definitely and obviously 'religious' and of direct moral value in Shakespeare. But there is also much that is not. We are often told that Shakespeare admired the blunt and honest character: Horatio, Kent, Flavius. No doubt he did, so do we all. We know that he must have loved the fearless innocence of his Desdemona, his Cordelia's strength, and that broken flower of girlhood, Ophelia. Passages of extreme beauty on the Christian Redemption witness at least a fine sensibility to the beauty and truth of Orthodoxy. But beside these things of obvious beauty we must put the nightmare of Macbeth's blood-guilty soul; the grand unbending pathos of his wife, whose dreadful will relaxes only in sleep to reveal the inevitable misery traced by crime upon her soul; the passionate grief of Lear's madness; the volcanic curses of a Timon's hate; the sensuous and shameless fascination of Cleopatra. What of these? They form the greater and more significant part of Shakespeare's grandest plays. And what, too, of Hamlet's and Claudio's terrors at the orthodox teaching of a possible survival in pain after death—their poignant desire that death may be the utter annihilation of consciousness? Is all this religion; and if so, what exactly has it to tell of the meaning and the mysteries of existence?

In a most interesting article contributed to *The Shakespeare Review* of June 1928 Mr. Guy Boas writes of Shakespeare and Christianity, showing points of contact between the two. In writing of Othello he says:

> Before the innocent meekness of Desdemona the huge physical strength of the Moor lies prostrate. Innocence in the end conquers suspicion not by expostulation or complaint, but merely by remaining itself and bearing no malice. Surely it is in such a sense as this that Christ meant that the meek shall inherit the earth?

That is obviously true. But later Mr. Boas asserts that the plays of Shakespeare give us no insight into the mysteries of birth and death; and that I am impelled to deny. After pointing out individual instances of moral beauty in Shakespeare he writes:

> But morals alone do not constitute religion. To all religious teachers we look for an explanation of the mysteries of existence: the miracle of creation, the riddle of death, the hope of immortality. What has Shakespeare to say to these eternal problems?

My answer to this is that between the years 1599 and 1611 Shakespeare was engaged primarily with these very problems; and he has left us as clear an answer as a mind of his depth and imaginative insight can give. Within the compass of this note I cannot do more than indicate very briefly the bare outlines of my meaning, though I hope to deal with the question in more detail later. A careful study of the texts from *Hamlet* to *The Tempest* will show my conclusions to be based on the rock of imaginative fact.

First, consider Mr. Boas' words: 'Morals alone do not constitute religion.' Now if we regard the reference above to Desdemona's

death we see that 'morals' is not the best word. Desdemona's purity
and meekness are not the fruit of 'morals' in the usual sense. Desdemona has even been blamed on 'moral' grounds for the lie with
which, to quote from Mr. Boas' article, she 'tries to shield him from
detection after he has mortally injured her'. 'Morals' will not do; its
associations and derivation degrade it. Mr. Boas writes finely of 'the
unearthly love' with which Desdemona forgives Othello; and I
think the author of this phrase will agree with me that a better word
would be 'values'. The poetic dramatist is not concerned primarily
with morals, in the cruder sense: they are to him no more than the
background, like historical facts or social distinctions, against which
the lightnings of spirit values shoot, evanescent perhaps, yet winged
to immortality. Shakespeare from 1599 onwards is concerned with
the passionate activity of the human spirit, that is with values; of
ambition, of faithfulness, of sorrow, of agony in crime—but above
all with the supreme value, Love: the pangs of its soul-torture, the
ecstasy of its fruition. He is concerned too with death: with death
that opens vistas of possible unending torment worse than the

most loathed earthly life
That age, ache, penury, or imprisonment
(*Measure for Measure*, III. i. 127)

can lay on men; with death, perhaps, if fate is kind, a gentle sleep;
with death the ender of suffering. I think in writing *Macbeth* and
King Lear Shakespeare knew death to be in one sense the ender of life,
and the thought brought him peace: and yet somehow he had
reached another life-truth firm and based in eternity: in the mysterious eternity of value; the value of human aspiration and passion,
unmoral, timeless, indestructible. And at the end—or nearly the
end—of the great sequence of tragedies comes an act of poetic creation
that surpasses all earlier examples of Shakespeare's tragic and poetic
achievement: a vision and revelation of death joyful, immediate, and
final. I refer to the last two acts of *Antony and Cleopatra*. Here all the
threads of obstinate questionings, fears, passions and aspirations of
the earlier great plays are caught up into those supreme moments
where love and death—the two most recurrent of Shakespeare's

problems—are harmonized into one spiritual reality and shown to be mutually relevant and explanatory.

As Mr. Boas convincingly shows us, the duty of the poetic dramatist is the representation of life. He does not press beyond the grave. He works in terms of this life. That is true. But his figures are not copies of life as we ordinarily observe it. Their characters are rather bodies infused with that innermost spirit of being apprehended alone by poetic intuition: and they reveal the basis of human existence, the springs of action, the deep compulsive current of passionate spiritual reality—the substantial fabric of the unseen on which is woven the very pattern of human fate. The plays of Shakespeare, as too the poetry of all great poetic humanists, go deep, for their poetry is rooted in the otherness of the spiritual order. Now these plays, thus created on the analogy of human life, necessarily have human and religious meaning. Especially does the great *Julius Caesar–Tempest* succession have compelling force if regarded as a sequence of life representations. For it shows a clear progression and development. I will shortly outline this sequence.

The three plays, *Hamlet, Troilus and Cressida, Measure for Measure* are all plays of pain. They question the truth of the romantic vision, they suggest horrors beyond the grave. Love in *Troilus and Cressida* is killed by the arch-enemy time:

> Injurious time now with a robber's haste
> Crams his rich thievery up, he knows not how.
>
> (IV. iv. 42)

This thought of time's destroying nature permeates the play and leaves the romantic flower drained of its sap and withered to the root. So too in *Hamlet* and *Measure for Measure* is death horrible when viewed through the mists of time. Immortality in time is a state to be dreaded: the time-processes of bodily disintegration and personal survival are hateful to Hamlet and Claudio, who would both welcome death if death were all. Now the supreme tragedies *Macbeth, King Lear* and *Timon of Athens* contain answers to the foregoing problems. They are, of course, more than that, for great poetry is always more than an answer to any intellectual problem. But the fact remains that they do contain within their total significance answers to the earlier questions. In them we have a representation primarily of human passion: passion which reaches outward and upward stretching the limits of personality. There is no time-thinking about the matter of death and immortality. All three great figures at last cry out for death which comes blessedly, the ender of crime and suffering, surest balm of hurt minds. Macbeth (v. iii. 22) cries: 'I have lived long enough.' And Kent in *King Lear*:

> Vex not his ghost! O let him pass! He hates him
> That would upon the rack of this tough world
> Stretch him out longer.
>
> (v. iii. 315)

And Timon:

> My long sickness
> Of health and living now begins to mend,
> And nothing brings me all things.
>
> (v. i. 191)

There is no thought of individual persistence in *Macbeth*, *King Lear*[1] and *Timon of Athens*, and yet there is a grandeur which makes death shadowy and unreal. In great tragedy we are, in fact, faced with the expression of a spiritual value which carries its own conviction of immortality; but the immortality of tragedy's revelation is not a temporal process. In *Macbeth*, in *King Lear*, we watch a reality beyond the analysis of reason, something independent of the limits of time. The immortality expressed by tragedy is a timeless immortality in the realm of value.

And then we have the final vision of *Antony and Cleopatra*. Here death is extolled as the supreme good:

> I will be
> A bridegroom in my death, and run into 't
> As to a lover's bed.
>
> (IV. xii. 99)

Cleopatra and Antony die for love: more, they die into love. The

---

1. Perhaps, as Miss Stella Williams once reminded me, this statement is not quite accurate. Kent also (v. iii. 323) thinks of death as a 'journey' and of the dead king calling him. **[1966]**

delicate and romantic flower of love was killed by time in *Troilus and Cressida*: immortality in time was terrible to Hamlet and Claudio. But here death is

> that thing that ends all other deeds,
> Which shackles accidents and bolts up change.
>
> (v. ii. 5)

Death the ender—the death of *Macbeth* and *King Lear*—here kills time the slayer of romantic sight at the moment when that romantic sight is crystal clear. The supreme value Love, at a supreme moment, is thus synchronized with the time-destroying act of death; and its immortality is then apparent, immediate and indisputable. This is how those last two acts answer at the same moment the love-misery and the death-misery of the earlier plays. *Antony and Cleopatra* asserts the timeless Immortality of Value.

'Morals alone,' says Mr. Boas, 'do not constitute religion.' No—but values do. The tendency of the best modern religious thought (e.g., W. R. Inge, *Outspoken Essays*, Second Series, 1927, 33–44; B. H. Streeter, *Reality*, 1927, 311–12) is clearly to assert that the truth of immortality is to be read in terms not of quantity but of quality; not of time, but of value. Canon Streeter, in his *Reality*, suggests that the truth of this timeless immortality can only be expressed 'by metaphor or myth'. Now what form should such a myth take? Values appear to be killed by time: they have so often immediate and unquestionable significance, only to fade, like sweet dreams in cold day-light, blurred, forgotten and unreal. The true myth of immortality should then assert that the intuitive perception of value is to be trusted and that all other evidences are to be regarded as false. That which inspires love cannot die, although it seems to die; the beautiful thing which is lost, is not lost but is in safe keeping and will be restored. Hermione and Thaisa thus wake from seeming death to the sound of music, and are restored to Leontes and Pericles. Pericles finds Marina to 'the music of the spheres' (v. i. 231). For *Pericles, The Winter's Tale, Cymbeline*, are to be read as parables or myths. We must cease to assert that Shakespeare throws no light on these eternal facts and that the final plays are inartistically 'unreal'. Rather should we see that the unreality of these creations is a purely symbolic reflection of that truth of the immortality of Value which was touched by direct representation at the end of *Antony and Cleopatra*. In these last plays the loved and lost one is found, restored to the mystic sounds of music. As in *Antony and Cleopatra* the love and death revelations are one: since we are shown a representation of immortality in terms not of time, but of quality and value which is Love.

I think in *Cymbeline*—which I would put later than *The Winter's Tale*—Shakespeare tries to body forth his hard-won religious conviction in personal symbols. The Vision of Jupiter, with its fine poetry but rather strained artistic reality, though often considered an interpolation, is authentic enough: the crux, in fact, of the play, as is at once apparent when one realizes the symbolic nature of the final myths. Perhaps it is unsatisfying. Anthropomorphic symbols of God always are. Probably, too, Shakespeare thought it so himself, and that is why his last[1] play is written in terms of pure poetic rather than religious symbols—yet the pure poetry of a poet become mystic. In *The Tempest* Shakespeare's art and religious symbolism are perfectly harmonized; hence its superiority over the cruder anthropomorphism of *Cymbeline*.

Mr. Boas refers to 'the miracle of creation' as one of the 'mysteries of existence' untouched by Shakespeare. But what of the birth symbolism in *Pericles*, *The Winter's Tale*, and *Cymbeline*? I cannot analyse it here—nor, indeed, can I see its full significance—but the birth theme is recurrent, and has meaning: Marina, Perdita, Posthumus—all are thrown helpless at birth into the stormy turbulence of temporal existence, but are yet guarded by heaven and, though lost, restored.

The poet does not search for what is normally termed religious truth. He writes of life, but unconsciously he writes not alone of life as we see it but of the spiritual and poetic basis of life, the Shakespearian 'nothing' which is both the soul of man and the very stuff of airy poetry (*The Sovereign Flower*, General Index, B, VI 'Miscellaneous', 317). He creates symbols and fashions plots which seem to reveal to him the deepest significance of life: such are the plots of Greek and Shakespearian tragedy. And the great poet knows, better

---

1. 'Last' was an error: see p. 81, note.

probably than his critics, that he is revealing a profound and glorious truth: that there is no pessimism in high tragedy. Sometimes the Greek tragic poets made use of a *deus ex machina* solution—leaving direct representation of life for religious symbols and merging thus the two forms to create at once tragedy and the interpretation of tragedy. At the end of Euripides' *Alcestis* we have, in Gilbert Murray's translation, lines that speak the significance of tragic creation:

> There be many shapes of mystery;
> And many things God brings to be,
>   Past hope or fear.
> And the end men look'd for cometh not,
> And a path is there where no man thought.
>   So hath it fallen here.

That is implicit, though unspoken, in *Macbeth* and *Lear*. 'With God all things are possible.' It is the lesson of tragedy. It is the lesson of the Cross. God will not have the cup of tragedy pass from man. The soul's triumph must be wrested out of the very darkness and the misery of absolute failure. But the appearances of life are not true of life's spiritual significance, they are not true of the tragic poetry of man's aspiring and thwarted soul. It is exactly this mysterious and transcendent mystic truth of tragedy that is the very basis of the curious plot texture of the final plays of Shakespeare. Everyone has noted the mystic and religious atmosphere of the mythical succession: we have the *deus ex machina* theme in the persons of Diana in *Pericles* and Jupiter in *Cymbeline*; we have the Delphic Oracle in *The Winter's Tale*; we have chapels, temples, dreams and visions; we have, in fact, plays whose 'unreality' is due to an attempt to body into five acts of drama the purely spiritual and mystic truth of tragedy— *the immortality of value.*

One more point before concluding these scattered remarks. It does not matter whether Shakespeare was deliberately and consciously creating immortality myths or whether they came, to use Keats' words on poetry, 'as naturally as the leaves to a tree' (to John Taylor, 27 February 1818). We do not worry as to whether Shakespeare meant *Macbeth* and *King Lear* to be grand rather than pessi-

mistic. Nor need we worry whether Shakespeare meant the final plays
to be myth and parable rather than unreal and unconvincing, though
beautiful, romance. We should, in the interpretation of Shakespeare,
always concentrate on what he has done—not on what this or that
critic, or the recorded events of his material life, would have us
believe that he meant to do. The great poet may well be greater than
he knows. Shelley writes in his *Defence of Poetry*:

> Poets are the hierophants of an unapprehended inspiration;
> the mirrors of the gigantic shadows which futurity casts upon the
> present; the words which express what they understand not;
> the trumpets which sing to battle and feel not what they inspire;
> the influence which is moved not, but moves. Poets are the
> unacknowledged legislators of the world.

It is time we believed it.

IV

ROMANTIC FRIENDSHIP

The Holborn Review, October 1929; New Series, xx.

SHAKESPEARE'S Sonnets are often regarded as a fascinating revelation of a unique personality. And yet, as a revelation, they will continue to baffle us, since they ring the changes on so many moods of love that they become universal and varied as are the love themes of his plays. Much has been written about the identity of 'Mr. W. H.' (i.e. Master W. H.), the mysterious fair boy of the Sonnets, to whom, it seems, Shakespeare at one time gave a lover's devotion. Sir Sidney Lee favours Henry Wriothesley, Earl of Southampton; Prof. T. G. Tucker, in his admirable edition of the Sonnets, inclines to William Herbert, Earl of Pembroke, whose initials do, at least, make 'W. H.'; and Samuel Butler, in his delightful and stimulating, though not wholly trustworthy, *Shakespeare's Sonnets Reconsidered* (1927; first published 1899) assures us that neither of these were the right ones: that 'Mr. W. H.' cannot, in fact, have been a man of noble birth at all. Personally, I think George Saintsbury has here, as often elsewhere, given us the best advice when he tells us (in his *Short History of English Literature*) that the matter is irrelevant: 'What is important is that Shakespeare has here caught up the sum of love and uttered it as no poet has before or since, and that in so doing he carried poetry . . . to a pitch which it had never previously reached in English, and which it has never outstepped since.' One can say no more than that Shakespeare had probably at one time experienced a passionate love for some friend: perhaps for more than one. Expressions of such friendships were common enough, and fashionable in Elizabethan society: I say 'expressions', since human nature does not change, if manners do. The man who is not, potentially at least, capable of an extreme admiration of young masculine beauty may be many things, but he certainly is not a poet.

Shakespeare returns to this love-theme often throughout the plays. We find it first implicit at the opening of *Venus and Adonis*:

> Rose-cheek'd Adonis hied him to the chase;
> Hunting he lov'd, but love he laugh'd to scorn.

Venus' protestations of love are often very close to the Sonnets. But this does not prove that Southampton, to whom the poem was dedicated, was 'the only begetter' of the Sonnets. Anyway, that is not important. This delightful inverted romance is Shakespeare's first poem: to use his own words, 'the first child' of his 'invention'; sensuous, if you like, but naïvely, poetically sensuous; human, warmly human, tingling with physical life. Here is Shakespeare's youngest poetry alight with passion, and shooting its first exquisite flames.

The Elizabethan manner of friendly protestations is shown poetically in *The Two Gentlemen of Verona*:

> Proteus: Wilt thou be gone? Sweet Valentine, adieu!
> Think on thy Proteus, when thou haply seest
> Some rare noteworthy object in thy travel.
> Wish me partaker in thy happiness
> When thou dost meet good hap; and in thy danger,
> If ever danger do environ thee,
> Command thy grievance to my holy prayers,
> For I will be thy beadsman, Valentine.
>
> (1. i. 11)

At the end of the play, after discovering the inconstancy and treachery with which Proteus leaves his own love Julia and seeks to win Silvia from Valentine, Valentine forgives Proteus at his first word of repentance and not only forgives him, but shows himself immediately willing to hand over Silvia to his unreliable friend:

> And that my love may appear plain and free,
> All that was mine in Silvia I give thee.
>
> (v. iv. 82)

Silvia is treated merely as a possession: of infinitely less importance to

Valentine than is his friend Proteus. It is, perhaps, a little hard to feel enthusiastic over the various love interests of these two 'gentlemen'.

The next instance of this friendship-theme in Shakespeare is more moving. Antonio's love for Bassanio in *The Merchant of Venice* is a deep and true affection: albeit, perhaps, a little self-centred and sentimentalized like his habitual melancholy—Gratiano did not always talk nonsense. I never think the end of Antonio's letter to Bassanio was quite kind:

> ... Notwithstanding, use your pleasure. If your love do not persuade you to come, let not my letter.
>
> (III. ii. 321)

Nor, perhaps, his words:

> Pray God, Bassanio come
> To see me pay his debt, and then I care not!
>
> (III. iii. 35)

After all, Antonio had insisted on accepting Shylock's conditions against Bassanio's better judgement. The thought of Bassanio watching his sacrifice ought not to be a pleasure, or even a desire. But there is a fine description of the friends' parting:

> Salarino: And even there, his eye being big with tears,
> Turning his face, he put his hand behind him,
> And with affection wondrous sensible
> He wrung Bassanio's hand; and so they parted.
> Salanio: I think he only loves the world for him.
>
> (II. viii. 46)

It is certain that Bassanio, youthful and thoughtless though he was, saw more in Antonio than a convenient source of income:

> Portia: Is it your dear friend that is thus in trouble?
> Bassanio: The dearest friend to me, the kindest man,
> The best condition'd and unwearied spirit
> In doing courtesies, and one in whom
> The ancient Roman honour more appears
> Than any that draws breath in Italy.
>
> (III. ii. 292)

I feel more admiration for the other Antonio's love for Sebastian in *Twelfth Night*: it is more passionate and fiery, virile, a love of reckless adventure and noble anger. Love makes him follow Sebastian into the town where he himself runs great personal risk from the authorities.

> Antonio: The gentleness of all the gods go with thee!
> I have many enemies in Orsino's court,
> Else would I very shortly see thee there;
> But come what may, I do adore thee so,
> That danger shall seem sport, and I will go.
>
> (II. i. 47)

Or again:

> I could not stay behind you: my desire,
> More sharp than filed steel, did spur me forth.
>
> (III. iii. 4)

His love is an instinctive passion. Though it be largely selfish, he seems, unlike the first Antonio, to be at no pains to hide the fact from himself or anyone else: he does not sentimentalize his love. And so we believe him when he adds:

> And not all love to see you, though so much
> As might have drawn one to a longer voyage,
> But jealousy what might befall your travel,
> Being skilless in these parts. . . .
>
> (III. iii. 6)

His parting with his purse is a delightful little piece of thoughtful affection:

> Haply your eye shall light upon some toy
> You have desire to purchase.
>
> (III. iii. 44)

True, we see the other side of his nature when he thinks he has been scorned with base ingratitude: like Othello and Timon, his nature swerves from one extreme to another. He neither loves nor hates by halves, and he is always passionately sincere. This is one of the most interesting, and yet often overlooked, love-themes in all the golden romance of *Twelfth Night*.

From these we may pass on to the deeper notes with which the same theme is touched in *Julius Caesar*. *Julius Caesar* is a play of friendship and love, but not sexual love. Even Portia's love for Brutus is rather one of gentle companionship. The atmosphere of the play is charged with eroticism, but not passion. Though the stage may be set for an action 'most bloody, fiery, and most terrible' (I. iii. 130), though the action be fine, spirited and adventurous, and noble blood be magnificently spilt in the third act, yet the human element is nearly everywhere one of gentle sentiment, melting hearts, tears and the soft fire of love. I doubt if in any other of Shakespeare's plays the words 'love' and 'lover' occur so often. There is 'love' mentioned between Ligarius and Brutus, Decius and Caesar, Cassius and Lucius Pella, Volumnius and Brutus, Cassius and Titinius, Artemidorus and Caesar—to name some of the minor ones: no doubt there are others. And then there are the major love-themes: that of Antony for Caesar, of Portia for Brutus, of Brutus for Caesar—above all, poetically, the love of Brutus for the boy Lucius, and Cassius for Brutus.

Brutus' nature, so often outwardly cold and reserved—though inwardly enduring the mental conflict and anguish of a Macbeth—so unresponsive, though courteous, to Portia and Cassius, shows its true flower of natural sweetness to Lucius alone. If we want to love Brutus in spite of his many hardnesses, we should watch him with Lucius. Herein lies a deep truth. The hardest of mankind—and Brutus is only superficially 'hard'—may be softened by the melting fire of love. To Brutus, Lucius is the symbol of that unsullied innocency and peace of soul with which he has been forced to part. Lucius, but not Brutus, may 'enjoy the honey-heavy dew of slumber' (II. i. 230). That, perhaps, is ever the way of love: by means of its strength the lover irradiates another with all those dream-qualities unrealized and unrealizable in himself; so that the loved one is always a symbol, an image lit by the candles of aspiration, before which the lover kneels with instinctive faith, at worship of a divine impossibility.

And there is Cassius' love for Brutus. Cassius is the supreme lover in this play of lovers. From the first his love of Brutus is apparent:

> Brutus, I do observe you now of late:
> I have not from your eyes that gentleness
> And show of love as I was wont to have.
> You bear too stubborn and too strange a hand
> Over your friend that loves you.
>
> (I. ii. 32)

'Eyes' in Shakespeare, the 'most pure spirit of sense' (*Troilus and Cressida*, III. iii. 106), are always the ambassadors of love. Cassius, the lover, dominates the last two acts. His love lights the quarrel scene with an unearthly fire; it makes of the bowl of wine a sacrament of the wine of love; it lends a tragic harmony to the parting on the plains of Philippi, so much deeper, nobler, and more beautiful than the sentimental farewell of Antonio from his Bassanio by the blue waters of Venice:

> Brutus: ... But this same day
> Must end that work the Ides of March begun;
> And whether we shall meet again I know not.
> Therefore our everlasting farewell take:
> For ever, and for ever, farewell, Cassius!
> If we do meet again, why, we shall smile:
> If not, why then, this parting was well made.
> Cassius: For ever, and for ever, farewell, Brutus!
> If we do meet again, we'll smile indeed;
> If not, 'tis true this parting was well made.
> Brutus: Why, then, lead on. O, that a man might know
> The end of this day's business, ere it come!
> But it sufficeth that the day will end,
> And then the end is known.
>
> (v. i. 113)

This particular chord of tragedy, the deep tones of the spirit forced to echo the approaching end, has been touched with so exquisite a perception by one other English poet alone: Webster. But how far off all this is from the first love tragedy, *Venus and Adonis*.

The death of Cassius forecasts the death of Cleopatra. Both die, as it were, into the spirit of love. Cassius cries:

> O coward that I am to live so long,
> To see my best friend ta'en before my face!
>
> (v. iii. 34)

Titinius momentarily takes Brutus' place as the symbol of love; but somehow that is not at all strange at this moment in this play. The love is the same, though I do not quite know how to explain it. It is the something not altogether of this world in the light of which Cassius walks from the Quarrel scene onward—something that makes him say:

> For I am fresh of spirit, and resolv'd
> To meet all trials very constantly.
>
> (v. i. 91)

His death, followed by the choric words of Titinius, with their grand blood and fire imagery, is, poetically, one of the finest things in the play:

> . . . O setting Sun,
> As in thy red rays thou dost sink to-night,
> So in his red blood Cassius' day is set;
> The sun of Rome is set.
>
> (v. iii. 60)

The death of Cassius contains that positive and dynamic life-in-death poetically apprehended which we meet again in *Antony and Cleopatra*: something which we do not find in the deaths of Brutus and Macbeth, something connected with love. Titinius crowns the dead Cassius with the wreath of victory:

> Titinius: But, hold thee, take this garland on thy brow;
> Thy Brutus bid me give it thee, and I
> Will do his bidding. Brutus, come apace,
> And see how I regarded Caius Cassius.
>
> (v. iii. 85)

'Thy Brutus' . . . it was once pointed out to me that Iras and Charmian seem so curiously to understand the nature and necessity of the love-sacrifice of their queen. Priestesses at the altar of her death. So, too, Titinius understands. At a moment like this we must, poet-like, think in symbols. It is significant that both Cassius and Cleopatra die thus aureoled in love: and they alone are crowned in death.

Julius Caesar is a play of pure idealism and unsullied spiritual vision: and it is followed by three plays that appear to be, as Mr. Masefield in *Shakespeare and Spiritual Life* (p. 201 below) has said of *Hamlet*, 'a questioning of vision'. In *Hamlet, Troilus and Cressida* and *Measure for Measure*, the higher values are continually questioned and sometimes satirized. In *Troilus and Cressida* especially, things of beauty are dissected, analysed, and not seldom cursed, for their inadequacy, frailty and futility. It is not surprising that the theme of romantic friendship should be withered by the general blighting breath of intellectual criticism. Achilles and Patroclus are fast friends. 'My sweet Patroclus', is Achilles' term of address (v. i. 42). Whilst the others are engaged in battle or counsel, they stay apart, jesting with each other, making fun of the Greek leaders:

Ulysses: The great Achilles, whom opinion crowns
        The sinew and the forehand of our host,
        Having his ear full of his airy fame,
        Grows dainty of his worth, and in his tent
        Lies mocking our designs. With him Patroclus
        Upon a lazy bed the livelong day
        Breaks scurril jests,
        And with ridiculous and awkward action,
        Which, slanderer, he imitation calls,
        He pageants us.

                                              (I. iii. 142)

A friendship of laziness, of 'scurril jests': the polar opposites of creative action and romantic faith. The antithesis between this friendship and the high adventure of the friendship of Brutus and Cassius is the antithesis of two opposite views of human existence on the part of the creating mind of the poet. One burning with the ardour and the faith of spiritual vision and high romance: the other, intellectual, coldly and harshly intellectual; uninspired with the life-force of love, and so only capable of seeing uncleanness and bestiality within the compass of its horizon. The friendship of Achilles and

Patroclus is typical of this play, and typical comment is made on it by the embodiment of visionless intellect, Thersites:

> Thersites: Prithee, be silent boy; I profit not by thy talk. Thou art thought to be Achilles' male varlet.[1]
>
> (v. i. 16)

And soon after he heaps the following terms of abuse on Patroclus:

> . . . thou idle immaterial skein of sleeve-silk, thou green sarcenet flap for a sore eye, thou tassel of a prodigal's purse, thou? Ah, how the poor world is pestered with such water flies, diminutives of nature.
>
> (v. i. 35)

Compare this view of a friendship with the picturesque and senti-mental love of Antonio and Bassanio, or the plane of heroic action on which is set the loves of Brutus and Cassius, and you have the measure of the difference of *Troilus and Cressida* from former plays. In this play we are constantly brought up against the foul and bestial potentialities of human existence: Thersites is ever at our elbow, with a chorus of curses and snarls. It is the recurrent hate-theme, which we get again in Apemantus, in Timon, in parts of Lear's madness, and finally bodied into the purely poetic conception of Caliban; the view of humanity as something unclean, coarsely material, the view of the Iago-intellect undirected and unimpelled by the infusing quality of love. *Troilus and Cressida* is in parts an exquisitely beautiful play: but we are constantly forced to an awareness that the flame of romance is out, and then the odour is of oil and smoke.

The hate-theme of Thersites is later given a supreme and massive tragic form in *Timon of Athens*. Timon is a grand and uni-versal lover; generous, free-hearted and noble. And he is disillusioned. I have seen it objected that Timon's hate is altogether out of propor-tion to his grievance, and although that may be true, and the play may be thus not a perfect work of art—which should always carry conviction in itself—yet the other love-themes in Shakespeare will help us to understand the agony of a Timon's soul. We should

---

1. Thersites subsequently (v. i. 20) explains the term 'male varlet' as 'masculine whore'.

remember the many themes of friendship in the plays, the stress laid on the love of man for man, and read something of this into the love of Timon for his friends, into his superb and aristocratic and oriental joy in rich display, open hospitality, and extreme and noble, if unwise, generosity. We should remember, too, Shakespeare's continual recurrence to the hated thought of ingratitude. It is finely denounced in *Henry V*, in the King's speech to the traitor Scroop, his former close friend (II. ii. 93–142). I have noticed the hot passion of Sebastian's Antonio at the thought of the boy's ingratitude; and we find Timon's retirement to the woods forecast in *The Two Gentlemen of Verona* and *As You Like It*. Says Valentine:

> How use doth breed a habit in a man!
> This shadowy desert, unfrequented woods,
> I better brook than flourishing, peopled towns:
> Here can I sit alone, unseen of any,
> And to the nightingale's complaining notes
> Tune my distresses and record my woes.
>
> (v. iv. 1)

This thought is repeated in *As You Like It* continually, in speech and song. Timon is a personification of the same theme raised to its highest possible human limit: universalized, titanic, like Macbeth and Lear. So Timon cries:

> Timon will to the woods: where he shall find
> The unkindest beast more kinder than mankind.
>
> (IV. i. 35)

Timon is the embodiment of the aspiring and loving soul that finds the world unworthy. The light of romance and beauty is quenched, and the world of men becomes a barren colony of filth and vice. But every one of his volcanic curses echoes the measure of his titanic and disillusioned love. The spirit of man challenges the world of men to draw level with itself, and finding it less noble, scorns it with the uttermost of scorn. Now, even if death be annihilation, it has positive meaning for man: since life at best is the negation of his proud and aristocratic nature. Though death be nothing, it cannot, as life, be less than nothing; therefore

> My long sickness
> Of health and living now begins to mend,
> And nothing brings me all things.

(v. i. 191)

We have passed into a world beyond the world of *Julius Caesar*: the world of *Macbeth*, *King Lear* and *Antony and Cleopatra*, where the hero is as a giant and the giant strength is the strength of the spirit, and the forms and shapes of other images of life are as puny dolls and saw-dust puppets, and Death alone the last antagonist against which the force of human passion deigns to measure its strength.

V

MYSTIC SYMBOLISM

The Aryan Path, April 1931; II, 4. Reprinted October 1964; XXXV, 10.

THE criticism of Shakespeare has in the past been too strictly limited. Confining itself almost wholly to 'common-sense' analysis of the plays, it has noticed the clash of character with character, the human interest of poignant dramatic situation, and the firm ethical sanity that is everywhere apparent in Shakespeare. Such criticism has done valuable service; yet that which is of even greater significance has been left almost unnoticed. The more imaginative qualities have been too often forgotten. Throughout Shakespeare there is a subtle use of atmospheric effect; as, for instance, the murk and evil that muffle the Scotland of *Macbeth* or the bright imagery and sensuous magnificence that scintillate in *Antony and Cleopatra*: and this can be analysed, can be and should be related to the metaphysical and ethical significances of the plays concerned. Nor have the varied uses of poetic symbolism been adequately noticed: such as the use of animal-symbolism in *Julius Caesar* and *Macbeth*, where an essentially *unnatural* act is accompanied by unnatural behaviour in the animal world; or the recurrent stress throughout Shakespeare on 'storms' or 'tempests' as symbols of tragedy. Now a careful attention to such poetic and imaginative effects produces striking results: for it illuminates the significance of those final plays whose curious plots have never been properly explained.

Elsewhere (in *Myth and Miracle: An Essay on the Mystic Symbolism of Shakespeare*, 1929) I have shown that Shakespeare's later plays fall naturally into three groups: first, plays of pain and intellectual despair, such as *Hamlet*; second, plays of tragic grandeur, superficially sad, it is true, yet inwardly strong with the mystic optimism of poetic tragedy—of these I would quote *King Lear* as a typical example; and third, a curious group of plays where the tragic theme is reversed, and a happy ending is brought about contrary to the natural logic of human life and to the canons of realistic art. *Pericles* and *The Winter's Tale* are not plays of any usual type. The poet who designs a happy ending naturally attempts to clothe his plot with some outward probability. Shakespeare does not do this here. There is no attempt at realism. Therefore, having regard to the succession which these plays continue, and, moreover, to the fact that they are strongly impregnated with an atmosphere of religious mysticism—dreams, oracles, and divine appearances—I regard them essentially as mystical resolutions of those difficulties and despairs which are the theme of earlier plays, which are definitely painful in the first group and recognized intuitively as things of necessity and beauty in the great tragedies. They do in fact definitely and decisively contradict the earlier humanistic logic. They explicate the irrational optimism of tragedy in the form of myths or parables. Shakespeare's greater tragedies turn nearly all on the same theme: the failure of Love to body itself into any earthly symbol. Sometimes the loved ones prove actually false, as Queen Gertrude or Cressida, or Goneril and Regan, or the friends of Timon; sometimes the lover suspects falsely, as Hamlet seems to distrust Ophelia, as Othello distrusts Desdemona. But the difference is superficial: all these plays equally suggest that the human soul finds love too delicate a reality to weather the stormy voyage of temporal existence.

The Final Plays of Shakespeare, however, reverse this theme. In them the story is pursued to the brink of tragedy: and then tragedy is curiously averted. Thaisa, the wife of Pericles, is cast apparently dead into the stormy waters; yet she and his lost daughter Marina are restored to him after a passage of years. Cerimon, the hermit, raises Thaisa to life in a scene which recalls the raising of Lazarus in the Gospels. In so far as we admit a universal tragic significance in earlier plays, we are, I think, forced to recognize a universal mystic significance in these final plays. They represent symbolically the resurrection of that which *seems to die*, but is yet alive; the conquest of love over those stormy waters of temporal existence which appear to engulf it. It is significant that tempests, Shakespeare's percurrent symbol of tragedy, recur in these two plays. But there is not only loss in the tempest: there is revival, resurrection, to the sounds of music. Pericles, finding his long-lost Marina, hears a mysterious 'music of the spheres' (v. i. 231) just before his vision of Diana. In *The Winter's Tale* (v. iii. 98) Hermione, too, is awakened to the sounds of music.

As though some insistent truth was yet striving for fuller expression, we have these same themes amazingly multiplied within the compact plot-texture of *Cymbeline*. Bellarius, Arviragus and Guiderius, long lost to Cymbeline through his mistrust, are yet restored to him at the end; and both Posthumus and Imogen think each other dead, only to be joyed at their loved one's miraculous survival. Most interesting of all, in this play we have the Vision of Jupiter which has baffled past commentators; yet it is a natural attempt on the poet's part to explain in some degree, through an anthropomorphic theism, this mystic realization of the ineffable which is beating in his mind.

Shakespeare found the perfect form at last. Let me again emphasize the importance of the tempest-symbol which is ubiquitous throughout the plays of Shakespeare. *The Tempest* is well named. Here the whole sequence of past plays is, as it were, caught up into one supreme moment of vision. More exquisitely compact than *Cymbeline*, *The Tempest* is a record of Shakespeare's spiritual progress and, simultaneously, a vision of mankind tossed on the turbulent waters of this life. Therefore Prospero is both the Supreme Being from one point of view, and from the other Shakespeare, the poet. The story is simply this: a magician draws to him, by means of a tempest, a ship-load of men—good, evil, wise and ignorant: them he both wrecks and saves. The mystic melodies of Ariel's pipe sing the travellers to the yellow sands where all is forgiven and all restored. *The Tempest* is the most perfect work of mystic vision in English literature.

A detailed interpretation of *The Tempest* involves many references and many subtleties. I cannot note them here. My view is most interestingly corroborated by a remarkable and profound book by Mr. Colin Still, *Shakespeare's Mystery Play: A Study of The Tempest* (1921). This book the publication of my essay *Myth and Miracle* brought to my notice (but see p. 201 below). Mr. Still analyses The

Tempest as a work of mystic vision, and shows that it abounds in parallels with the ancient mystery cults and works of symbolic religious significance throughout the ages. Especially illuminating are his references to Vergil (*Aeneid*, VI) and Dante. His reading of *The Tempest* depends on references outside Shakespeare, whereas my interpretation depends entirely on references to the succession of plays which *The Tempest* concludes. We thus reach our results by quite different routes: those results are strangely—and yet, after all, I believe, not strangely—similar. To the sceptic, this may suggest that mystical interpretation of great poetry may be something other than Horatio's (*Hamlet*, I. v. 133) 'wild and whirling words'. It is not without its dangers, yet it is the only adequate and relevent interpretation of Shakespeare that exists; since, if the vision of the poet and that of the mystic are utterly and finally and in essence incommensurable, where are we to search for unity? And yet if the art of poetry has its share of divine sanction and transcendent truth, then what limit can we place to the authentic inspiration of so transcendent and measureless a poet as Shakespeare?

VI

JESUS AND SHAKESPEARE

The Aryan Path, January 1934; V, 1.

I do not consider Shakespeare as a 'teacher' in any usual sense. He is the most inclusive of poets. What is true of him is, usually, true of Western poetry as a whole. His work is therefore a pointer indicating fundamental tendencies of the Western mind; the great poet being not merely an entertainer but rather one who gives concrete and symbolic embodiment to those dark or bright impulses which mould the later history of the race. Great poetry is thus intrinsically prophetic. For these reasons I consider Shakespeare important.

In his early work we have two kinds of play: histories and the romantic comedies. The first analyse closely the intricacies of national life, the calls of king or party, the stress and turbulence of civil war, the glitter of martial honour and the glamour of royalty; the epic nobility of England's troubled and blood-stained story. These plays are concerned primarily with the body politic, and the concept of 'order' is fundamental throughout. Within their plots, however, we have frequent reminder of the individual's spiritual longing, and this is, in Shakespeare, usually a matter of human love. This is the dominant theme of the other group, the romantic comedies. In them the fleeting dreams of romantic happiness that torture and deceive the tragic destinies of mankind are endued with a more than kingly authority and assurance. The history plays are realistic, the comedies romantic. The one group shows life as it is; the other, as we might well wish it to be.

The second half of Shakespeare's work marks a change in style. Henceforward he blends the two modes, relating the individual's pain and frustration, his romantic desire, his conflicting allegiances, to the body of which he forms part. Though the stress is on the individual, the relative importance of state-order is never neglected. In *Hamlet*, in the problem plays *Troilus and Cressida* and *Measure for Measure*, in *Othello*, *Macbeth*, *King Lear*, *Timon of Athens* and *Coriolanus* the protagonists are shown as at odds with their environment; all, in various ways, fail to project their passionate instincts into harmonious action; but with all we feel the conflict is itself of some mysterious creative significance. Herein, by close understanding, we may penetrate the mystery of suffering and evil, their necessity and creative strength. Crowning the tragedies we have *Antony and Cleopatra*. This is scarcely a tragedy in the usual sense. The protagonists, it is true, are again at odds with their environment; but they accomplish, poetically, an apocalyptic love-union with each other in their dying. The play is toned brightly to harmonize with this revelation as we are lifted to a height where human desire and failure radiate outwards a conquering brilliance, a light which is immortality. This play is probably the closest approach the human mind has ever made to revealing the mystic riches of death.

Beyond this no poet can well be expected to advance. But in his final plays Shakespeare creates a series of love-parables whose plots of loss in tempest and reunion to music correspond, as I have shown in *Myth and Miracle*, to the vision of immortality more directly exposed in *Antony and Cleopatra*. In these last plays from *Pericles* to *The Tempest* the interest is almost entirely concentrated on personal love, loss and reunion. *Cymbeline*, it is true, has a complex plot involving national issues and warfare: but even there the most vital effects tend towards the transcendental and mystical. In Shakespeare's former work we saw two main themes: personal love and state-order. The final plays reveal a spiritual rather than political salvation. Here we are concerned primarily with love, birth, death and resurrection.

What are we to make of this conclusion? Chiefly this, I think; that the ultimate realities for humanity are matters not of statecraft but rather the vast simplicities of life, love and death. For through love alone can life become significant and death a positive, not a negative, experience. So in Shakespeare love at the last is divinely guarded. Tossed by jealousy, wrecked by unfaithfulness, it yet reaches the magic island in whose music all is restored and forgiven. National problems have ceased, it would seem, to weigh down and impede the poet's personal aspiration and visionary wisdom.

Yet this love is not a tranquil emotion: nor is it only spiritual. Rather it is a warm, passionate, unrestful, very human love. Let us call it Eros. Now Jesus also preaches love: love universal. This is to be distinguished from the Shakespearian Eros in that it is not limited to individual persons. Jesus repudiates those who are not prepared to leave their families for the sake of the Realm of God. To him mankind in general is the only true family. Yet this love is vastly beyond the comprehension of most of us since it is not only a matter of dutiful sacrifice but properly understood is itself rich with romantic splendours and romantic pain: not transcendental merely but instinctive; not merely divine but natural. We must pay exact regard to Jesus' imagery. Continually he embodies his teaching in concrete poetic figures: the vine, fig-tree, harvest; flocks of the field and birds of the air; food, drink, clothing, money; and the marriage-banquet. Here is a symbolism suggesting life, growth, richness and all creative excellence.[1] Therefore the love to which he calls us is the consummation and direction, in no sense the negation, of the richest instincts in man; as though the Realm of God were the natural and instinctive goal of the human race and Jesus came, not to demand a sacrificial and other-worldly pilgrimage, but to point the way to fulfilment of our deepest and most universal desires; to reveal, not only God, but Man, to mankind.

Therefore the New Testament can be shown to solve the Shakespearian antinomy of state-order and the individual's romantic pain. In terms of the Gospel of Love—and only in such terms—the two converge. It is significant that Shakespeare continually sees the community as a 'body', an organism, of which the individual is as a limb: whereas St. Paul, too, sees the brotherhood of man as a 'body', the Body of Christ. Perfect love thus fulfils the creative purposes of individual and state alike. And, like the Shakespearian Eros, Christian love is, in St. Paul's writings, the very gateway to immortality.

Throughout Shakespeare the direct influence of Christianity is powerful. Not only are there passages—the most beautiful in English

1. This reading I had recently developed in *The Christian Renaissance*, 1933; revised and enlarged, 1962.

religious literature—of direct Christian sentiment; but one play in particular, as I show in *The Wheel of Fire*, is almost a thesis on Christian ethics. Numerous single persons are, in their contexts, Christ-figures of a sort. That is, they express an inclusive love, a universal wisdom: such are King Henry VI, the Friar in *Romeo and Juliet*, Theseus in *A Midsummer Night's Dream*, the Duke in *Measure for Measure*, Cerimon in *Pericles*, Prospero in *The Tempest*. These saintly[1] figures are not quite so richly conceived as, say, Cleopatra or Hamlet. Shakespeare does not, perhaps cannot, create a universal love as glamorous and compelling as a purely human romance. It is as though he is intellectually aware of the saintly consciousness while not having experienced it with the strongest emotional fervour. He knows however that, at its best, the saintly ideal can reconcile the conflict of personal desire and state-order: observe how his Henry VI, the Duke in *Measure for Measure* and Prospero are all studious characters to whom government is painful; but how the two latter, after sacrificing political duty to personal aspiration, eventually undertake again with deeper insight the responsibilities of ducal authority. Perhaps this is why Shakespeare wrote one more play after *The Tempest*. For long he had been engaged on spiritual and personal problems: perhaps his own problems. What religion there is in the tragedies and final plays is more or less the result of his own religious speculation. But in *The Tempest* he sees the convergence of human charity and state-order, as Prospero leaves his magic island and returns to the world of men. Therefore in *Henry VIII* Christian orthodoxy floods in to possess for the first time a Shakespearian play with assertive splendour and transcendental statement. Here angelic figures tread the stage, and England's futurity is shown in terms of prophetic wonder. The grand sequence of plays ending in *The Tempest* has driven the greatest poet of the modern world through the agonies and paradisal ecstasy of Eros to a self-forgetting nationalism and the peace of Christ.

But Shakespeare's saints, such as Prospero, remain austere, a little colourless. Put them beside Cleopatra, and they show, like Octavia, 'a body rather than a life' (*Antony and Cleopatra*, III. iii. 20). We

---

1. Theseus, if not exactly saintly, is comprehensive: see *The Shakespearian Tempest*, 167–8; also p. 136 below. [1966]

have yet unresolved our antinomy of Christ-love and Eros. It presses hard on us to-day. Either we give our allegiance to Eros; most artists do this, and also the philosophers and scientists, since under 'art' all such studies may be subsumed; and each and all are subject to Eros. Or we may give our allegiance to Jesus, sacrificing the urge of instinctive desire to an ethical purpose which we have never vitally experienced, rigidly subduing our aspirations to the limits of communal morality. Neither ideal is complete.

Many—indeed most—suffer inward tension and torment, divided between these directions; yet only in so far as we can see, feel, and make them to converge do we help onward the great purposes of incarnate life. Every such attempt itself involves a conflict; and yet this is fundamentally the only true Christianity. Jesus is not finally to be equated with Shakespeare's saintly persons: rather in him we find a blending of saintly peace and universal assurance with the unrestful propulsive quality of Eros. He is as it were driven on by a mighty power that leaves him no rest, driving him from his family and home into the romantic drama of his tragic ministry. He is a God-tormented lover, suffering from Eros like Desdemona or Troilus. Thus to follow him is no peaceful task. It involves conflict, unreachable desire, agony: for without the throes of continual birth there can be no truly creative life. Herein, as I see it, is the strength of creative Christianity, the partiality of all wisdom-religions and the fallacy of passive mysticism. So the Eros and the Christ are one; and whenever we forget that Jesus calls us not only to a mystic tranquillity but also to an impassioned adventure; to a love which is bitter-sweet as Eros, as life-giving and yet as ruthless as he; to a surrender as final and irrevocable as the surrender of the most passionate love; until we include the myriad complex passions of Shakespeare's tragic and romantic world in a richly passionate Christianity—until then, we talk of matters we do not understand and offer up incense to an abstraction.

VII

ON *HENRY VIII*

(For *Henry VIII* see also pp. 5-7, 31-3, 37-8 above.)

The Criterion, January 1936; xv, 59.

ERHAPS no other Shakespearian play presents so queer a case of academic disintegration and uncritical popularity. Scholars have for long written off the most important scenes as the work of Fletcher, while asserting that the whole lacks unity. This position has been left unchallenged (but see p. 6, note). Actors have, however, generally recognized the greatness at least of individual scenes and persons in the play. Irving played Wolsey with Forbes-Robertson as a famous Buckingham.[1] *Henry VIII* was one of Tree's most successful productions, and Wolsey one of his best parts. Since the war Dame Sybil Thorndike has played Queen Katharine, and Charles Laughton, more recently still, Henry himself. The play appeals to the profession. The general public have mainly followed the actor's rather than the professorial lead. They have not been unduly disquieted about 'feminine' endings; and, I think, rightly. Here I wish to plot out a short interpretation maturing from acceptance of the play's artistic and organic validity. Afterwards, I return to the question of authorship.

The King here is not the middle-aged, sensual, robustious, goodhearted but expeditious wife-killer whose successful promiscuity

1. There is a gramophone record easily obtainable of Forbes-Robertson's speaking of Buckingham's great speech, which Mr. Granville Barker, in his lecture *From Henry V to Hamlet* (*Aspects of Shakespeare*, see p. vi above, note) has called 'the most beautiful piece of speaking I ever heard'. I understand Mr. Granville Barker's aspersion on 'such creaking methods'; but I nevertheless suggest that anyone who thinks the speech is by Fletcher should buy the record and play it from time to time.

1966: The record may not be so 'easily obtainable' now, though a copy is lodged at the British Institute of Recorded Sound. My own reading is obtainable on a tape 'Shakespeare's Rhetoric' published by Sound Seminars, Cincinnati (p. 13, note).

has endeared him to the hearts of the British public. He can be best placed by considering the response we make to such a stage-direction as: 'Flourish: Enter King and Attendants.' He is not primarily a character study and should certainly not be performed as a 'character' part. Primarily he is King of England; dignified, still young, honourable, and every inch a King. We should not let our sympathy for Katharine and our knowledge of a certain self-deception within Henry's supposedly conscience-stricken desire to divorce her—both have undoubted support in the play—prevent our recognition of his central position and sacred office. This is recognized and stressed by all the persons. The others do not blame him; nor should we. Certainly, during the early acts he is a little insecure, deceiving himself once, deceived by others often, and distraught by troublesome rivalries and ambitions. But at the end he is a king of power and a peace-maker, overruling all turbulent and envious discontents: which brings us to another important thought.

The play is epic rather than dramatic in structure; or perhaps an epic which includes a succession of single dramatic movements. Three of these show an important similarity. Buckingham opposes Wolsey's ambitious scheming and quickly falls under an apparently false charge of treason. He was formerly haughty, aristocratic, intolerant, but he goes to his death already 'half in heaven' (II. i. 88), forgiving all his enemies, praying for the King, a martyr of Christ-like strength[1]: a sudden reversal, but more than paralleled by the fall of Wolsey. Wolsey is a crafty, unprincipled and ambitious schemer and statesman. His indirect methods are exposed, the King's displeasure falls on him, and he next embraces a religious humility and poverty with only his robe and his 'integrity to heaven' (III. ii. 453) in place of his former glories. He preaches what is almost a sermon at his fall, urging Cromwell to serve the King without ambition, thus forgiving and honouring to the last the master who he nevertheless feels has been unjust and ungrateful to himself. He dies, as Griffeth tells us, in religious peace. Third, we have the tragedy of Katharine. She is shown first as a strong, almost domineering woman who hampers Wolsey's policy. At her trial she

---

1. The speech's 'Christ-like strength' is not maintained to the end; see *The Crown of Life*, 277; also p. 300 below. [1966]

excels in innocent and wronged dignity, and shows scathing scorn of what she considers Wolsey's injustice and hypocrisy, a theme developed further in her subsequent scene with the two Cardinals. Her story closes too in religious light. She hears of Wolsey's death, prays for his rest, though showing that she is not yet free from bitterness towards him; next listens to Griffeth's noble eulogy—which is perhaps necessary to stimulate our forgiveness too—and at last attains to perfect charity towards her wronger. Whereupon follows her Vision, in which angelic figures, to solemn music, offer her the garland of immortality from the land of 'that celestial harmony' (IV. ii. 80) that awaits her. She dies blessing the King, like the rest, without resentment.

Notice how with all these we are never quite clear as to faults and virtues, the exact rights and wrongs of it all, but the rhythm from personal pride and sense of injustice and unkindness—each endures the typical Shakespearian sense of betrayal by friend or lover—to Christian humility, absolute forgiveness, and religious peace is found in each. It must be observed too how service to the King is uppermost in the thoughts of all at their end and is inextricably twined with the thought of duty toward God. Thus is unrolled the sequence of individual tragic movements. The play is rich with both a grand royalism and a thrilling but solemn Christianity; orthodox religious colouring being present and powerful throughout far in excess of any previous play.

There is more, of less tragic impact. Countering and interwoven with these we have the rise of Anne Bullen. The King meets her in a scene of revelry and dance, and she has a gorgeous coronation, staged for us by direction and description. She is presented as a lovable and beautiful woman, and we are pointed by choric passages to rejoice in the King's good fortune. The play culminates in the christening of her child and the striking prophecy of Cranmer. These happier elements are mostly associated with the future Protestantism of England—hence the importance of Cranmer—whereas the tragic elements are entwined rather with the Cardinals, the Pope and Roman Catholicism generally. The movement from Queen Katharine to Anne Bullen is, partly at least, a religious movement. Nor can the play be properly understood without a clear sight of its amazing conclusion, to which the whole surge of the epic advances. Cranmer's prophecy is the justification and explanation of all that precedes it.

All these themes radiate from the central figure of the King. He is like a rock, the others are waves breaking round him; and he grows in dignity and power. Towards the end he dismisses the third trial in our story, that of Cranmer, enforcing peace and goodwill, and silencing the fiery Gardiner: all which is of course to be contrasted with the earlier unhappy trials of Buckingham and Katharine. So we have a most involved story-pattern in terms of a few years of one King's reign which nevertheless suggests a vast history and universal movement: the rise and fall of noble men and women, whose individual sufferings and deaths are in some way necessary to the structure of a greater than themselves, here the religious independence and national glory of England; and whose troubled stories, and the King's too, including his lapse from strict honesty with himself, are shown as necessary, or at all events preliminary, to their final flowering, justification and perfection in the child Elizabeth. In producing the play[1] it is perhaps best to mark it into three act-divisions: two mainly tragic, the third optimistic. The first ends with the execution of Buckingham and the second with the fall of Wolsey; the third presenting a rising action with the coronation of Anne Bullen, Katharine's Vision—which may be allowed to suggest the peace in eternity that has also received Buckingham and Wolsey—Cranmer's trial and re-instatement, the final christening, and the prophetic conclusion forecasting the happy reigns of Elizabeth and James I.

The mystic riches of that eternity which bounds human tragedy here alternate with the more temporal glories of successful kingship, and both contribute to the inspired words of Cranmer over the new-christened Elizabeth, foretelling a divinely ordered prosperity, worship and peace. That such a blending of national and religious prophecy should be centred on a child is nothing strange: Isaiah and Vergil offer interesting correspondences.[2] The final scene of *Henry*

1. Details of my staging of *Henry VIII* are given in *Principles of Shakespearian Production*, 1936; enlarged as *Shakespearian Production*, 1964.

2. See T. F. Royds, *Virgil and Isaiah*, 1918: an admirable short study of that very entwining of spiritual prophecy with national affairs which I find in *Henry VIII*. This book has helped my general understanding.

VIII is in essence close to a medieval, or modern, nativity play: and as such should it be rendered in the theatre.

I shall now briefly notice *Henry VIII* in relation to Shakespeare's other work. I need not recapitulate in any detail what I have elsewhere written on Shakespeare's final plays; but it may be as well to repeat that they are saturated in religious transcendentalism and present plots mainly concerned with loss in tempest, jealousy, misfortune and all evils, balanced against divine appearances and the resurrection of lost loves to music, with a general stress on oracles, dreams, prophecies and chapels. These plays, following the sombre plays, seem to represent a certain inward progress of the poet's informing genius from tragedy to religious light. They and the tragedies may all be called 'personal' in comparison with the earlier histories. *The Tempest* presents a final and comprehensive synthesis of the poet's main intuitions, Prospero's farewell to his art resembling, inevitably and with no necessary trick of conscious allegory, what Shakespeare the man might be supposed to feel on looking back over his completed work. Prospero leaves his island to embrace again the community of men; and Shakespeare the artist writes another play with a theme national rather than personal and philosophic, an impregnating mythology Christian rather than pseudo-Hellenic or elsewise pagan, and a prophetic finale referring primarily to the two sovereigns under whose reign he has lived.

It is a logical conclusion enough. There is something almost inevitable about this play coming at this time. It is crammed, too, with reminders of the other final plays. Queen Katharine on trial before her own husband is almost a reincarnation of Hermione; as later, listening to music to solace her marital distress, she reminds us of Desdemona. Her Vision repeats in Christian terms the theophanies to which the others have accustomed us, the oracle of Delphi and the appearance of Apollo described in *The Winter's Tale*, Diana in *Pericles*, Jupiter in *Cymbeline*; and, of course, much of the same sort in *The Tempest*. In close connexion with each of these, except only the examples from *The Tempest*, occurs the rare word 'celestial', used too by Katharine just before her visionary sleep (III. i. 4; v. i. 251; v. iv. 114; IV. ii. 80. 1966: and see *The Tempest*, II. ii. 126). The recurrent forgiveness-motif in *Henry VIII* presents exactly the quality and depth of Prospero's forgiveness.[1] Most important of all, the birth and child themes of the other final plays are reflected here in the glorification of the baptized child Elizabeth. I have elsewhere claimed that the restoration of Hermione and Thaisa to their husbands may be said to correspond to an intuition of a paradisal eternity such as that which lies behind, or may be said to lie behind, the restoration of Beatrice to Dante or Gretchen to Faust; whereas the finding of the lost child, Perdita or Marina, and I might add the importance given to the various children's happiness and success at the last moments of all the final plays, suggests rather the onward progress of creation within time; the words 'time' and 'eternity' being here deliberately used as metaphysical concepts arbitrarily applied to a poetic creation to bridge the gap between art and thought. In *Henry VIII* we find a similar contrast. Queen Katharine's vision of eternal bliss is set directly beside the more humanly joyous coronation of Anne Bullen, and not long after we have the baptismal ceremony of the infant Elizabeth. Notice how much happier this contrast is than the more cruel juxtaposition earlier of the King's revelling in Wolsey's Palace immediately before Buckingham's execution. It is as though time and eternity were seen converging as the play unfurls, to meet in exquisite union at Cranmer's prophecy: which again may remind us of the soothsayer and the prophetic conclusion of *Cymbeline*.

If in *The Tempest* Shakespeare gives us a comprehensive and inclusive statement of his furthest spiritual adventures, in *Henry VIII* he has gone yet further, directly relating those adventures to the religion of his day and the nation of his birth. In the prophecy of Cranmer I see the culmination not only of the epic movement of *Henry VIII* as a whole but the point where the vast tributary of Shakespeare's work from *Hamlet* to *The Tempest* enters the wider waters of a nation's historic and religious advance, to swell 'the state of floods' (*2 Henry IV*, v. ii. 132) to England's glory and through her the establishment of the peace of Christ on earth.

All this, I shall be told, would be well enough, if there were ten syllables in each line of the great speeches here and not eleven.

---

1. The statement is inaccurate. Prospero's forgiveness has not the warmth and humility found in *Henry VIII*. See *The Crown of Life*, 252, note; 253; 297. [**1966**]

Frankly, I do not know how satisfactorily to answer this objection: because I do not understand it. I believe such pseudo-scientific theorizing is again here, as elsewhere, merely an unconscious projection of our sense of organic incoherence within the play due to failure in focus and understanding. *Henry VIII* is generally divided into scenes of what is usually considered 'ordinary' Shakespearian verse, and those where there is a high percentage of eleven-syllable lines. If these latter are by Fletcher,[1] we certainly have not an instance of Fletcher spoiling the Shakespearian art-form by weak collaboration, but rather, if we cannot because of variation in style see the play as an organic whole, we must observe Shakespeare trying in vain to spoil a Fletcherian masterpiece, since it is the best scenes that are considered un-Shakespearian; a masterpiece in some ways, in a certain selfless and Christian nobility and finality of restrained power, greater than anything Shakespeare had done himself outside *The Tempest*. There is surely no necessity for all this. Shakespeare had for long, in the latter acts of *Timon of Athens* for example, been finding the extra syllable a means, when he wanted it, to verbal mastery of an especially grand but reserved strength of statement. In *The Tempest* it is continual: Act V alone provides all the examples anyone should want. In *Henry VIII* this style is finely used to mark the solemn cadences of the grandest scenes: Buckingham's Farewell, Katharine's Trial, her interview with Wolsey and Campeius, Wolsey's Fall, Katharine's Vision, Cranmer's Prophecy. I find on reinspection that the admittedly Shakespearian scenes have a goodly sprinkling of it too. Shakespeare has only here carried a certain technical effect, which he had for some time been progressively and increasingly developing and had brought to a climax in *The Tempest*, just a little further than before, emphasizing it especially in the most important scenes according to the quality of the occasion.

These noble speeches are rich in the cadences of typical Shakespearian emotion and Shakespearian thought; and though the expression is restrained, as in *The Tempest*, the metaphors are likewise

---

1. The late Edgar I. Fripp once strongly opposed the Fletcherian theory in a letter written to me about my first Shakespearian publication, *Myth and Miracle*, suggesting, if I remember right, that I should incorporate *Henry VIII* in my general thesis. His letter re-directed my attention to a play I had not then read for some years.

Shakespearian,[1] and the general power is such that, if Fletcher wrote them, he was clearly one of the two greatest poets in our literature, sharing that honour alone with the author of *Timon of Athens* and *The Tempest*, to whom he bears so striking and uncanny a resemblance.

1. Miss Spurgeon certainly notes that a single typical strand of Shakespearian imagery is not found in the suspected scenes, while it is found elsewhere. But imagery and rhythm both naturally vary with scenic tone. It is pleasant to find Miss Spurgeon writing that the evidence of imagery 'by no means all points one way', and expressing her belief that Shakespeare 'wrote the greater part of the play'. (*Shakespeare's Iterative Imagery*, 1931; included in *Aspects of Shakespeare*, as above, p. vi note).

VIII

THE MAKING OF *MACBETH*

Principles of Shakespearian Production, 1936 and 1949, 1. A section omitted from the revised *Shakespearian Production*, 1964.

WHAT we mean by Shakespeare's *Macbeth* was not caused solely by Elizabethan stage conditions, by Shakespeare's own experience of the terrors of a guilty conscience, by any one person or any number of persons he had met and observed; by a story, or stories, from Holinshed; nor by a desire for box-office receipts, nor in order to please Burbage with a good part. Probably all contributed. There is nothing strange in that: there are as many contributory causes for the writing of this book. Any act, artistic or otherwise, is poised into existence on a scaffolding of numberless convergences.

Shakespeare was a literary and dramatic artist working in terms of stage technique. He was moreover a man of spiritual sensibility with a keen and able mind. By the time he wrote *Macbeth* he was fairly sure of his public. Lately he had been turning out tragedies and writing more powerfully than ever. He now feels like attempting a darker tragedy than any before.

Turning over some favourite authors he comes across an old Scottish story. The name 'Macbeth' thrills him. It rhymes with death. Another play will be needed shortly to act before the new King of Scotland. A Scottish play would be apt. Moreover, the Scottish setting, with its weird and Gaelic associations, the deep-sunk legends and superstitions that cling to lonely glens and mist-scarfed hills, all appeal to him. He begins to feel his play as a quality; it takes colour and some vague proportion in the womb of his mind. This play will deal with black, abysmal, and supernatural evil.

But for the very setting it suggests the story of Macbeth is unsuitable. Macbeth killed the King of Scotland openly, a declared rebel; whereas what is wanted is a central act essentially dishonourable, dastardly and unforgivable. Something that would keep you awake at night. He turns over the pages of Holinshed and decides to borrow the crime of Donwald and fuse it to his story.[1] Then why not call the play 'Donwald'? No, that would never sound so well. The play is to be 'Macbeth': he is sure of it; and it is to be more intense, more soaked in horror of blood, more abysmal in its soundings, than any play his public has seen. They are still drawn to tragedies of blood: which is fortunate, since his tragic genius has more work to do. Even if they were not, at this stage in his career, he would not care. His imagination is now powerfully at work, a hound at the scent.

There is one difficulty. Julius Caesar was killed grandly on the stage, and the scene was a great success. This murder must be more powerful still, yet somehow no sort of open and active assassination will be so sickeningly evil and nightmarish as his vague idea demands. But action is his usual medium; visible action. His idea demands, it would seem, a dramatic loss: which, he has long ago discovered, must be impossible, since the two are not properly distinct. There must be a solution. He remembers how heavy the atmosphere of evil is to be; the Scottish and Celtic twilight of it, the mystery and supernature, the very mystery of evil; and then sees how the crime will be ten times more powerful with a mysterious and spiritual darkness if done off stage. Vague impressions float before him: an air-drawn dagger; questions, fear, the shrieking owl; knocking at the gate. Why, the thing is half-way toward completion. He has the central act and dominant tone: something like those nightmares that racked him ten years ago when he was writing happy plays and everybody thought him so merry. He can still hardly bear the memory; even now sometimes corpses nod over his bed at midnight. Yes, but he will have his revenge; make the action

1. For Macbeth's dastardly murder of Duncan Shakespeare drew mainly on Donwald's murder of an earlier king, Duffe. The historical Macbeth appears to have been deliberately blackened by Shakespeare for his purpose. Does this account for the stage tradition that the play is *unlucky*? Is the real Macbeth still active behind the scenes? [1966]

of his new play present a living nightmare; and once and for all pillory those tortures of the mind in poetry.

As he writes, old images and thoughts from *The Spanish Tragedy* and his own *Henry VI* and *The Rape of Lucrece* cluster in his mind.[1] He uses all past impressions that fit. He doesn't search for them, but knows that they will come, racing like filings to a magnet; all he has ever seen or heard that fits the *Macbeth* idea. *Richard III* is built into his new play, and the Queen's forebodings in *Richard II*. The pattern of *Julius Caesar* is closely followed. And all the time he is drawing, too, on past emotional experiences of his private life. His Elizabethan sense of kingship and the necessity of order in the state, his terror of anarchy, play their part. Unconscious and conscious elements bind and fuse together. As for stage-technique, this is instinctive and mostly unconscious: he thinks and creates inevitably in terms of it. He will not forget so to arrange his short and long scenes that one can be played while the other is being set. He hears Burbage's voice, and stage thunder crashes in his mind: drums, alarums, hautboys sound. These are his merest grammar. But two things trouble him.

He has never gone in much for flattery: but this is a special occasion. The newly crowned King James was King of Scotland before coming to England. And he is, as it happens, an authority on witchcraft. Holinshed's three Weird Sisters[2] had therefore better be developed. Yes, they will be important as the Ghost in *Hamlet*. Creatures of evil, the Greek Furies. Just what he wants, anyway: how curiously it all works in together. But how to please King James with some more obvious flattery? He certainly mustn't be allowed to think this play a satire on Scottish monarchs, which would never do. And there's another point: How in so tense and whirling a drama as this, to give Burbage a rest after the middle action? He is beginning to insist on this nowadays and made a great fuss about *Othello*, in spite of Desdemona's Willow-song. But how?

---

1. See my 1927 essay '2 *Henry VI* and *Macbeth*', reprinted in *The Sovereign Flower*, App. D; also my letter 'A Shakespeare Problem', *T.L.S.*, 2 August 1928.

2. The term is in Holinshed, where they are also called 'goddesses of destiny'. Shakespeare blended the conception with contemporary beliefs regarding witchcraft. [1966]

To have another king somewhere, and a change of scene. England, necessarily. They can go there for aid, and give Burbage his rest. Without knowing precisely why, he suddenly recalls Holinshed's description of Edward the Confessor's miraculous powers. The very thing to contrast with the evil-tormented Macbeth, tone with other suggestions of divine grace, and give him a chance of flattery about the powers of healing to be handed down to future kings of England. How strangely to the point these things turn out. And what was that about future kings? The phrase worries him, crying for attention. Future kings? Yes, of course, he will make it very clear that Macbeth is not ancestor to a line of Scottish Kings. Banquo's descendants will be glorified. Another fine philosophic and poetic contrast, and a reference to the future union of the two realms. Two-fold balls and treble sceptres . . .

His artistic conscience, however, is never for one moment relaxed. He alters, selects, blends, copies, borrows, and so on; and for divers reasons; but each and all are, in the very instant of adoption, coloured and moulded by a single dominant and unwavering purpose. Possibly he can't say exactly what that purpose is. The manager perhaps tells him that a certain long passage by a gentlewoman describing Lady Macbeth's mental disintegration isn't fair on the boy who acts the leading lady. Why not show Lady Macbeth's pain in action? Shakespeare thinks for a second or two. You might observe perhaps a quiver cross his face, a clouding anguish that passes. Then he smiles, and agrees. He has vaguely as to details, and yet precisely as to quality, conceived a scene that will be an interim of deathly peace before the tragic conclusion; like Richard II in prison listening to music; or the Graveyard scene in *Hamlet*; or the Scholars' conversation with Faustus in Marlowe's play. Yes, like those two latter, in prose. Implicit in his conception is a glimpse of an all but ineffable guiltlessness within guilt, where, in Tchekov's words, 'all is forgiven and it would be strange not to forgive'. Following this moment of spiritual illumination his artistic pride sees also a fine opportunity of attacking the apparently impossible: directly after the murder of Macduff's children and Macduff's receipt of the news, to recapture an audience's sympathy for Lady Macbeth: 'God, God, forgive us all' (v. i. 82). In a flash, the quiver passes, and he smiles. And they think: 'He's no highbrow artist like Ben Jonson. You can't tell Ben anything about his work.' Which marks the difference between a mind of quivering creative sensibility and receptivity and one of formalized and rigidly dogmatic intelligence.

During the writing of *Macbeth* everything would to Shakespeare have seemed expressive of *Macbeth*. The most amazing things happened: he couldn't enter a tavern without hearing an invaluable piece of crime psychology; nor read a book that wasn't crammed with helpful imagery or philosophic or historic suggestions. And every limitation of the Elizabethan stage seemed to force him into new infinities. The play was writing itself. Then one day in the street he saw a child all covered with blood. At another time he wouldn't have thought twice about it. Now it beats and beats in his mind.

And when they were congratulating themselves on Shakespeare's docility concerning Lady Macbeth, someone would perhaps raise carelessly another, and minor, point. 'By the way, that Bloody Child of yours will have to go. The stage-manager says he can't possibly arrange that. Your other apparitions are all right. But the Bloody Child's just impossible.' Suddenly Shakespeare becomes adamant. 'What's it for, anyway?' they ask. 'That born-of-woman business isn't very effective, you know.' That may be. He can't explain what it's all for. But the Apparition stays as it is: 'It's the very heart of the whole play. No—I can't say why, but it is.' He can't, or won't, explain. They can delete his Bloody Sergeant if they like, but if he can't have his Bloody Child he will tear the manuscript to pieces and never write another line. How strangely powerful the mild little man has become. His eyes flash like Burbage's. These poets . . . To give way on so many points and then flare up over a triviality. You can get no more out of him. He is already concentrated on something else . . . 'Here's the smell of the blood still . . .' (v. i. 55).

This is the point I wish to make. Shakespeare will go to great care to suit everyone and meet all conditions. But for no one, not for King James himself, will he sacrifice an imaginative essential. The poetic intuition is, in every last resort, the one and only arbiter. He welcomes difficulties, colours and moulds and shapes intractable material, and finds obstacles continually and most mysteriously turning into assets by the time he's done with them. They help him to build, give him a tangible start. After all, the heart must have a body; but he never once gives us a body without a heart and by the time his play's finished every fingertip, every hair and toe-nail, tingles with life shooting from that heart.

The resulting play, *Macbeth*, becomes a work of true imaginative literature: it has a quality common to Aeschylus, the Book of Job, Dante, Milton, Dostoievsky, Melville, Hardy. Its medium of dramatic structure—if we make the distinction at all—is merely a medium: a good, probably the best, kind of medium, but still a medium, not the essence. The artistic intuition is always the only final cause of the art-form in its totality, which includes the controlled inter-activity of all its parts. That is why, in my interpretations, I examine only a play's direct and final imaginative significance, rejecting all oblique and subsidiary causes. I do not stop at every moment to observe that *Macbeth* and *King Lear* were meant to be acted. Not that I am ignorant of this, but that I was never in doubt of it. It is the same with a producer: concentration on the 'dramatic construction' is not enough. Unless he gets the idea behind the construction, he is impotent. Certainly, you must always read with an eye for necessary compression of action and character-condensation; which is also often true of an epic or novel. But the dramatic medium need never preclude our sight of an intellectual profundity: rather it should assist. So we will not be put off our stroke because a play, Shakespearian or otherwise, was meant to be acted. You might as well hold up the interpretation of *Paradise Lost* by saying that it was meant to be read.

In the final artistic meaning only such things exist for attention as an ideal spectator may be supposed to receive from an ideal performance. In such a spectator's mind issues will not be raised concerning the play's composition. He will not be busy subtracting passages from Plutarch from the completed *Antony and Cleopatra* while giving the remainder an extra degree of interest as being 'Shakespeare's own'. To use again my favourite analogy: a man in the wings of the theatre, though he may see more of the works, cannot get the producer's precise message as well as a spectator in the dress circle. He views from a wrong angle, fine effects are masked, grouping becomes meaningless, and a host of irrelevances interrupt attention—an anxious stage-manager, a bored prompter, a phlegmatically chewing stage-hand watching Cleopatra die, the wires and spare flats and hanging floods: all distract. Similarly, to know that Shakespeare had to get bodies off the stage at the end is not constituent to a refined spectator's artistic pleasure, which includes intellectual sensibility, during the grand ceremonial of a Shakespearian conclusion. Or rather it ought not to be. It may before now have made a university professor happy to think of this while listening to Fortinbras or Caesar, but if so it was, I fear, an illegitimate and naughty enjoyment.

IX

ST. GEORGE AND THE DRAGON

The opening and concluding sections, under a new title, of *The Olive and the Sword*, a book composed in 1940, published in 1944, and reprinted in the volume *The Sovereign Flower* in 1958. Our present sections were omitted from the 1958 volume.

I

FOUR years ago the sudden fusion of parties into a single united British front gave confidence and purpose to a nation in peril. Only when all parties are felt as, in the depths, at one, can the soul of a nation be revealed; as in a human life, when different attributes, body, heart and mind pulse together, the soul is known. So sudden a birth is perhaps embarrassing. A new thing has been hatched and blinks dazedly at the world around; and the soul of England has yet to find, or rather hear, its voice.

We are seriously hampered by old inertias and many indecisions. For what are we fighting? No doubt, to shield ourselves, and therefore many other peoples, from German domination: that is, we fight a negative and defensive war to preserve from worse evils a society which our own most incisive thinkers have continually condemned. We can of course point to our Christian tradition; but to what lukewarm conventionality, half-belief, and impotence had that tradition fallen! 'Tradition' is, by the way, too vague a word to provide a proper test. Dare we say, for example, that we are fighting for Christ? Today a positive and personal imitation of—I do not say allegiance to—Christ will lead as often as not to some theory of pacifism; and though such pacifism must prove unsound while its holder supports a civil order based on ultimate force, for the difference is superficial only, a difficulty remains. Nor should we lay too great an emphasis on abstract concepts of 'justice' and 'law' (those

91

self-righteous catchwords at which our continental critics scoff) without recognizing that, though 'right' and 'wrong' may be ultimate, resting between man and God, 'justice' and 'law' exist properly only in terms of an ordered society to which our world cannot as yet lay claim. Even such a society is not inherently pacific, since it usually comes into being and always maintains itself through some play of force; and all its civil ordinances are tainted with murder. If enough people join in crime, that crime becomes a revolution; and every war is an extension of civil revolution, which if it be successful next imposes its own law; and whether that law is good or bad must be settled on other than legal grounds.

Why then are we at war? Many different answers might be with some show of reason offered. But Great Britain was, in its essence, its soul, forced sooner or later to oppose the tyrannic brutalities of the Hitlerian challenge. This is a simple human opposition in the realm of eternal values independent of any 'justice' as to territorial boundaries, any League of Nations agreements, or any possible responsibility of our own statesmen for the rise of Hitler; and it is an opposition looking not back, but forward. When Mr. Chamberlain spoke of 'this wild beast that has sprung at us out of his lair', his very phrase was symptomatic of our uncertainties. For it was not, strictly speaking, true. I am reminded of St. George, who went out to slay a dragon, and has been honoured for it ever since. Let us admit frankly that, when the hour struck, we declared war on Hitler.

A preacher in Canterbury Cathedral once observed that Hitler's young armies were driven on by a fanatic belief which we might envy; but their faith, though powerful and sincere, remains wholly pagan. Germany appears deliberately to have fostered and used the beast within man, while dark presences, like the Weird Women in Shakespeare's *Macbeth*, have attended the adventure, lending it for a while their aid. But have we, on our side, no comparable strength? No purer magic to set against those dark and blood-stained demons? Germany reiterates the rights of her future. Have we, in our turn, no destiny? Some new creative faith is needed.

Perhaps we are right not to assert that we are fighting directly and only for Christ. We are, I think, sometimes too ready to acknowledge former errors and failings, though that very willingness holds a value nations of lesser experience misunderstand. Let us however be rightly humble, with a humility Christ himself, knowing the baffling contradictions of our existence, would respect. He did not legislate directly for nations; but nevertheless on England, as nowhere else, falls the burden, though as yet dimly recognized, of tuning nations to His will. Moreover—and this appears to be even harder—on us eventually will be laid the compulsion of confessing among ourselves and before the world that this appointed task is ours, whatever dangers, hatred or ridicule may be incurred. Meanwhile we fight[1] the reptilian dragon-forces of unregenerate, and therefore unshaped and inhuman, instinct, energies breathing fire and slaughter across Europe, because such is our destiny, asserted by our own time-honoured national symbol, St. George, the dragon-slayer, whose name our present sovereign bears; and we should first search out that destiny not in platitudes of half-belief nor any reasonings of our own fabrication, but where alone it rests authentic, in the great heritage we possess of English letters, the greatest accumulation of national prophecy outside the Old Testament that the world has seen; where the soul of England, which is her essential sovereignty, speaks clearly—in Shakespeare, Milton, Pope, Byron, Blake, Wordsworth, Tennyson, Hardy and many more.[2] I offer no new analysis, but a new source of power; no historic reminder, but a prophetic insight. If ever a new Messiah is to come, he will come, says the greatest of all American writers, Herman Melville, in the name of Shakespeare. We need expect no Messiah, but we might at this hour turn to Shakespeare, a national prophet if ever there was one, concerned deeply with the royal soul of England. That royalty has direct Christian and chivalric affinities. Shakespeare's life-work might be characterized as expanding through a series of great plays the one central legend of St. George and the Dragon. It would be

---

1. Though composed in 1940 the text had been revised for publication in 1944. I adjust this tense for the original version. [1966]

2. My study of Milton as a national prophet appeared in *Chariot of Wrath*, 1942 (to be included in my forthcoming volume, *Poets of Action*). I wrote similarly on Tennyson in *The Times Literary Supplement* of 10 October 1942, and the essay was reprinted in *Hiroshima*, 1946. *Hiroshima* also included (89–98, 108–14, 120–4) brief commentaries from a national viewpoint on Pope, Burke, Hardy, Kipling and Francis Berry. [1966]

well to face and accept our destiny in the names both of Shakespeare and of St. George, the patron saint of our literature and nation.

II

It is interesting to observe how thinkers, whether as individuals, parties, or nations, are, under the stress of the present conflict, being forced back beyond their recent lines of defence. Pacifism is, unless very deeply held, repudiated, it would seem, in wartime; many have put aside, temporarily, their communism; while the capitalist sees that big business itself depends finally on a national strength no money can buy. One can watch clouds of superficial reasonings being puffed away to reveal facts; but the facing of facts is not in itself enough.

In a time of multiplying confusions our record has been mainly creditable, if only because we have, not unlike Hamlet, lived through those confusions whilst holding in tension and variously articulating and putting into practice a greater variety of critical thinking than any other of the great powers. But we must now advance, as Shakespeare advanced beyond *Hamlet* and *King Lear*, through *Timon of Athens*, to *Henry VIII*.

In this war, we say, we fight in the cause of international justice; but 'justice' will be construed differently by the interested parties in any dispute. 'Law', and in its normal semi-legal sense 'right', only exist as such within an ordered community with some central authority; and to render our claims reasonable we must feel at least in vague outline the already forming existence of such an order, with Great Britain, if not its central authority, certainly in view of her historic past and geographical position its keypoint. The German challenge exceeds any purely national assertion and is far closer to world-revolution, attacking the root-principles of that growing imperial and international structure or organism which Britain consciously or unconsciously fosters. Therefore when the rumble of a risen Germany grew more menacing it inevitably fell to Great Britain as a nation, and not to communism, democracy or the Christian church, to oppose it. Russia and the United States quite naturally thought first of themselves; while the main emphasis of established religion, Catholic or Protestant, remains transcendental, with as things are slight political influence.

Great Britain too was thinking of herself, and did her best to circumnavigate the vortex; but nevertheless *she cannot, however much she wishes it, think of herself without thinking of the whole world*. She, or Providence, has worked herself into a position from which there is no escape. She must, and it is an extremely awkward destiny, either fall or lead; must, much as she may scorn, hate, or—and perhaps this is the deeper truth—fear the thought, reaffirm her power and purpose across the world.

This will be to continue more self-consciously what has already led to her imperial greatness; to increase rather than decrease it, aiming, and it is not easy, to expand, without dissipating, her strength. A recent leading article in *The Times* drew a valuable distinction between 'imperialism' and 'domination', seeing both the Roman and the British empires as characterized by a will to inclusion, not only of peoples, but of their peculiar individualities and ways of thought; while also suggesting that such imperial control was properly a temporary, but of course very long range, expedient, willing finally its own loss, or self-realization, in a yet greater totality.

It is surely foolish to expect any such total order to come about by a planned co-operation of supposedly reasonable entities. Great things are never so created, nor are human entities, particularly as groups, reasonable. Nor will unity be created by the iron force of Germanic domination. No. Organic existence can only mature from what already has organic life. It is far too usual an error to start planning from above, from the rationalizing centres, while neglecting some already living attempt that stands in need of encouragement and nurture. What is to survive must grow naturally, like poetry, which, says Keats (to John Taylor, 27 February 1818), if it does not come as naturally as the leaves to a tree, those branching cedars of *Cymbeline* and *Henry VIII*, had better not come at all:

> Our poesy is as a gum which oozes
> From whence 'tis nourish'd. The fire i' the flint
> Shows not till it be struck; our gentle flame

Provokes itself, and like the current flies
Each bound it chafes.

(*Timon of Athens*, I. i. 21)

So Shakespeare's poet distinguishes the mechanical and fiery from the more instinctive process. Keats' words are quite as true of empire as of poetry, and probably no empire has grown more spontaneously than the British. Trade, the primary medium of England's expansion, is certainly rooted in the soil of personal initiative as mass military aggression can never be. Nevertheless to Keats poetry is also 'might half slumbering on its own right arm' and, since it relies on inexhaustible sources of energy beyond rational understanding and control, the 'supreme of power' (*Sleep and Poetry*, 236–7). Likewise the organic growth of our empire has been accompanied by, whilst never exactly subservient to, the exercise of strong action; such strength being one constituent, not the aim, of the creative purpose; which purpose is, in its own way, itself a supreme power, there being no greater or more masterly powers than those of Shakespeare's 'great creating nature' (*The Winter's Tale*, IV. iii. 88).

We must therefore expect and work for a more self-conscious extension and expansion of Britain's already formed imperial growth, yet not planning from any rigid imperialistic design but rather getting back at all costs to that central core from which her imperial strength has hitherto branched, and re-nurturing that. Therefore it is that I urge the incomparable necessity of re-awakening the national imagination, which means a renewed respect for our poetic, and particularly our Shakespearian, heritage; since in a vital understanding of Shakespeare's work lie the seed and germ of a greater Britain. Shakespeare speaks moreover to nations beyond the Empire, especially to the United States of America, related to us by the greatest of all bonds, the bond of language and therefore of great poetry; and also, since his work has already 'put a girdle round about the earth' (*A Midsummer Night's Dream*, II. i. 175) to encompass in spite of linguistic barriers the whole of civilization, it may be felt now as a rainbow arch above the flooding fields of war promising, in the fine phrase of Sonnet 107, 'olives of endless age' to mankind.

In order to serve such a world-wide purpose our own social and political system must be newly understood and purged of all rottenness, regaining direct contact with sources of strength. Why has the National-Socialist movement in Germany had so strong a hold over its youth? Have we nothing to learn from it? I think we have, but only in order to repenetrate, re-express and fulfil our own national destiny, which is potentially one certainly no less great, and probably far more inclusive, than that of Germany. There must be many changes bearing heavily on the shallow purposes of big business and the equally shallow criticism which it has spawned on all sides; but no party, as such, must be allowed exclusive rights in our thinking. As in Shakespeare warrior idealization and its obverse of ironic criticism, revolutionary fervour and governmental authority, justice and mercy, worldly ambition and religious humility, masculine strength and feminine love, are all balanced, harmonized and integrated, so our British constitution has room for capitalist initiative as well as socialist reform, for armed strength as well as pacifist counsel; but our sole final allegiance is to that whole of which all these are parts and whose symbol is the Crown.

Capitalism has a bad name today, and much of the mud flung at it is deserved. But not all. In two Shakespearian plays, *The Merchant of Venice* and *Timon of Athens*, riches are a primary theme, and in both they are contrasted with a greater value. In the one we have three caskets, of gold, silver and lead, the prize of love housed within the meaner metal to drive home the deceptiveness of a superficial brilliance; and in the Trial scene laws made for money-transactions are subtly shown to be unsuitable, indeed illogical, where the supreme good of life itself is at stake.[1] In *Timon of Athens* all worldly riches are felt as either insubstantial or definitely evil once they cease to serve a sacramental purpose as the outward sign and symbol of an inward communion between man and man. But, and the 'but' is most important, the gold-essence is never repudiated.

1. The economic implications of the Trial scene were pointed out by Max Plowman in 'Money and the Merchant', *The Adelphi*, September 1931; New Series II, 6; and by Lt.-Col. A. Hanbury-Sparrow in *Gilt-Edged Insecurity*, 1934. See also my *Principles of Shakespearian Production*, 1936; enlarged as *Shakespearian Production*, 1964.

Portia, figure of grace and love, is herself rich; and the once princely and generous Timon, at his story's end, digs gold from his wild retreat and is still sought after, remaining in savage nakedness a spiritual aristocrat if ever there was one, concentrating yet on his gold however he may curse it, obeying his old compulsion to give and handing it to all who come with imprecations that turn, like those of the Hebrew prophet, to blessings as we read them; while even reforming a bandit by urging him to wholesale destruction and theft. Timon treasures the richer values in himself: they are to Shakespeare themselves indestructible however widely they may be falsified. Therefore the gold of human virtue, of love, of life itself, must be safeguarded, and the essence of capitalism, which is merely individual responsibility, freedom, enterprise and power, is not necessarily at fault. It needs only subjection to that other gold of the community's life, the Crown, wherein not only the general good but also that sum of the human personality on whose rights capitalism bases its own structure is richly maintained.

It is the same with socialism. The bubble of communist revolution under a proletariat dictator Shakespeare pricked finally as far as he was concerned in the comedy of Jack Cade's rebellion in *2 Henry VI*, with comic reflections in the citizen riot in *Julius Caesar* and Gonzalo's Utopian dreams in *The Tempest*. But when the socialist advances his indictment of a nation selling its soul for cash in terms splendid as John of Gaunt's denunciation in *Richard II* (II. i. 31–68), he will be newly empowered; while to let any 'dictatorship of the proletariat', to borrow a communist phrase, usurp the throne of sovereignty is to insult intelligence and alienate sympathy. Lord Byron's two greatest plays, *Marino Faliero* and *Sardanapalus*, are pertinent to the advancing social consciousness of Europe. Unwilling to sever contact with traditional allegiances, and possessing a Shakespearian feeling for sovereignty, the poet dramatizes tales of (i) a revolutionary 'doge', or duke, that is very nearly king, of medieval Venice, who is infuriated by a decadent nobility; and (ii) a socialist and pacifically inclined king of Assyria in the ancient world, who is likewise sickened by a meaningless waste of military bloodshed and a crude imperialism. Both rulers have their faults, and one must not draw any simple conclusions and father them on the poet; but most urgent contemporary issues are contained with a dramatic vigour of high importance relying on a fusion of qualities usually opposed. Byron himself, the revolutionary aristocrat, may be taken as symbolic of the more nobly conceived socialism that we need, a socialism speaking in terms not merely of remedial legislation covering the bodily welfare of a certain class but crying out against the wrongs done against not only the body but the soul of the nation as a whole by class selfishness and suicidal incompetence. The Crown is as much a possession of the poorest as of the richest; it should function like the sun, soaking up and next redistributing as a heart the fluidities of wealth, whilst radiating also warmth and divine joy throughout the nation; and therefore those who have just complaints and a vital social message may claim its fullest sanction. If they will not or cannot do this, or regard such allegiance as either puerile or shameful, we shall suspect them to be half-consciously aware that their message does not pierce beyond a transient and brittle welfare, and even fear lest their socialism serves a destructive rather than a creative end.

As for that much-bandied and much-abused word 'democracy', what of it? No one, I suppose, desires a pure democracy, government by the people alone being scarcely desirable and certainly impossible; at least 'the people' must be taken to include those long dead and those not yet born to render such a system worthy, for the present is directly answerable to both. Many honourable traditions and a subtle sense of future direction must play their part in any government which is not to be ephemeral and undisciplined. The people can, as Shakespeare suggests in *Julius Caesar*, be easily manipulated by a master-mind, and in our day of mass propaganda the dangers are great. Except in *Julius Caesar* Shakespeare's greater persons are not involved in any fight for freedom: being kings or nobles they already have it, and the dramatist is concerned rather with their use of it. Freedom is never an end in itself: or rather true freedom as opposed to licence is not easily come by without some degree of discipline and education. A perfect democracy must refuse to educate its children; for education presupposes certain more or less unchanging values and principles and an aristocracy, as well in Soviet Russia as democratic Britain, to give them life and expression.

Such an aristocracy need not remain one of blood-descent, nor should it, I think, be either intellectual or capitalist. Both in Henry V's 'Crispin' speech (*Henry V*, IV. iii. 18–67) and Cranmer's prophecy at the conclusion of *Henry VIII* (V. v. 15–56), the aristocratic essence is to be distinguished from birth; and so is the 'cunning' (i.e. wisdom) and 'virtue' of Cerimon in *Pericles* (III. ii. 27), words in which a magical power is being suggested. Self-deception and a thousand dangers wait round the corner, I know; and a democratic liberalism must necessarily function as a vital constituent, as one main aid towards realization of that greater and exceedingly complex whole of past, present and future, historic tradition and prophetic destiny, of which the Crown itself, and nothing else, is symbol.

If Great Britain has uniquely succeeded in preserving her royalistic tradition while incorporating also a high degree of democratic freedom, that is because her people can on the whole be trusted not to falsify their heritage. There is accordingly tension without internal conflict, and a deep-seated if unformulated faith that all must be well 'if England to itself do rest but true' (*King John*, V. vii. 118); if, that is, she remains true to the Shakespearian world, where any one person—as opposed to crowds—is, however low his social status, given by the artist something of a royal integrity. There remains the danger that she will not preserve this truth:

> That England that was wont to conquer others
> Hath made a shameful conquest of itself.
>
> (*Richard II*, II. i. 65)

Hero after hero in Shakespeare works through inward conflict to self-recognition: Katharine the Shrew, Benedick and Beatrice, Richard II, all the great tragic heroes, Cleopatra who is 'noble' to herself (V. ii. 191) in her dying, Leontes, Coriolanus, Wolsey with his 'I know myself now' (III. ii. 379)—all follow the one pattern towards self-realization. Shakespeare's broader thinking sees nations, and in particular England, as suffering, like single persons, from self-deception and self-conflict, even the comedies working generally across a background of civil disunity. But there is always the greater compulsion, as when in *King John* the revolted Salisbury returns to loyalty:

We will untread the steps of damned flight,
And like a bated and retired flood,
Leaving our rankness and irregular course,
Stoop low within those bounds we have o'erlook'd,
And calmly run on in obedience
Even to our ocean, to our great King John.

(v. iv. 52)

The barons of Shakespeare's historical plays are the various parties
of today, but the same truth holds, now as then. Liberty is not
licence; man obeys a destiny greater than his own understanding;
and that destiny is discovered not by Macbeth's occultist agonies
but by a loyalty which is self-discovery and self-realization. Shakespeare ultimately has a greater trust in man as man than many a more
obviously daring interpreter; and likewise Great Britain, in trusting
her own people with wide political rights and expecting other
nations to do the same, shows a faith in human nature, in the basic
goodness of human instinct, which the Germanic ideal of forceful
domination with a view to further violent action contradicts.
Shakespeare trusts in an ultimate unity and believes, like Wordsworth in his great ode on immortality, in the *royal* destinies of
mankind.

The balance of man and office in *Richard II*, *King John* and
Henry VIII[1] reflects at once an acknowledgement of discrepancy and
a foresight, the story of Richard II actually prefiguring that of
Charles I and the political development in which his life and death
are crucial (see p. vi). Shakespeare's plays, historical or otherwise,
owe their tough persistence and ever-yielding richness to a realization
of personal and communal complexities as forcibly projected into
imagery and symbol as into the plot-story and its hero-king; and his
steady reservations, whether humorous or tragic, concerning power-
values are very precisely reflected in our constitution.

The present function of the Crown is a super-rational function,

1. I have since written: 'King Henry is the one king in Shakespeare in whom you
cannot dissociate man from office' (*The Crown of Life*, 306). That is probably true,
and although the delineation is with great skill not too far developed, he may be
supposed to include the royal qualities discussed in this and my next paragraph.
See p. 32 above, and note.

with a reliance on the imagination where logical reasoning fails and a trust in paradox akin to that of Christian symbolism. The conception touches both humour and tragic insight. The nation's ruler is utterly dependent on his ministers' advice, at once semi-divine in office and yet less powerful than his lowest subject on election-days, being the one man in the nation without political power. Shakespeare's Prince Hal and Byron's Sardanapalus, both conceived as attractive, ideal, though unconventional, sovereign types who embarrass their respective societies (and bear, perhaps, an important relation to our own Edward VIII), are humorous types also. These are men who as living individuals embody rather than symbolize the semi-mystic properties of kingship, and are therefore the less obviously suitable for their constitutional position, and will be either super-kings or failures, or both at once. The baffling paradox of the Crown witnesses, as do all great humour and great tragedy alike, a salutary recognition of ultimate failure, of ultimate human impossibilities; while, in its turn, conditioning a host of positives. A personal centre is needed to safeguard the sanctity of personality, dramatize the greater self of each subject, and deliver the nation from the paralysis of the abstract concept. The Crown preserves the more magical radiations of the hero-leader without the attendant risks; for the one final essential of a personal centre is that he should not remain, as a person, final.

The design of a Shakespearian play is—and in this Shakespeare follows Lyly—closely related to the queen-centred society of Tudor England; but the king himself, and there is nearly always a king or duke, is not necessarily the hero, nor is the hero himself always or indeed often the play's true centre. The king or hero tries to identify himself with something that almost necessarily eludes personification and may be felt as hinted rather by poetic imagery and certain out-standing symbolisms (1966: in the Histories the crown and symbols of royalty; p. 308) such as the magical handkerchief in *Othello*, the weirdly-wild tempest in *King Lear*, the crowned and tree-bearing child in *Macbeth*, or the mysterious music in *Antony and Cleopatra*. These, which utter deep, non-rational truths obscure to the persons themselves, correspond more directly to the Crown in our modern system. They focus the whole drama; just as Richard II when added to his necessary failure, but not Richard alone, points towards a constitutional monarchy. Such symbols bind and redistribute the action, fuse and direct disparate energies, opening vistas of the eternal which the thinking hero does not see. Similarly the Crown today is the heart of the nation's body as the prime-minister, or parliament, its rationalizing head; drawing to it and redistributing the life-fluid, as London is the heart of our country's economic life with roads and railways as arteries. The heart beats and functions silently, but it is always there and always awake, as the mind is not, conditioning the activities of limb, of eye and of thought, imitating that sovereign power of nature which, says Pope in writing of poetry, 'works without show, and without pomp presides' (*Essay on Criticism*, 75); a phrase recalling the 'mild majesty and sober pomp' of Burke's characterization of the British state in his *Reflections on the Revolution in France*. Certainly the greatest creative work is accomplished when the mind is sunk within the whole act being performed; a nation may be slowly fulfilling a destiny which its best leaders themselves do not always understand; and many an action of minister or party raising sharpest criticism may also be felt as working within, and as part of, a whole not to be subjected to a facile judgement.

Of this whole the Crown is itself a symbol, and being in essence an holistic conception serves as the one bond of unity in an empire otherwise mainly composed of autonomous states. The Crown is both heart and whole of the nation or empire; and therefore reflects at once its historic heritage, present soul-potentiality, and future destiny. Today many a thinker urges that man's religious consciousness must necessarily be confined to the social organism, while others put sole trust in the established church, but what is best in both tendencies will be subsumed under a vital royalism pointing towards both a new social order and a newly empowered and authoritative Christianity. The Crown is a dynamic and inexhaustible symbol piercing into realms of the infinite and the eternal; it shadows more even than a 'destiny', touching that higher otherness and its purposes *for which the nation exists on earth*; and 'God save the King' asks something vaster than national preservation.

Shakespeare does not stand alone: he is father to a line of poets who in the mass balance that one massive life-work. They in turn accentuate this or that side of it, but he only, unless perhaps we may set beside him Lord Byron, is comprehensive. My exposition of Byron's work appears in *The Burning Oracle*,[1] and I can here do no justice to it, nor to the many other writers deserving our attention. Two important emphases drive through our literature: nature, and especially English nature, as in Pope's *Windsor Forest*, Wordsworth's *Tintern Abbey* and *The Prelude*, and Hardy's Wessex; and the sea, so powerful in Byron, Wordsworth and Tennyson. All this is deeply Shakespearian. The Histories are rich, however violent the argument or action, in reminders of that English countryside such turbulences deface. Shakespeare's more gentle, lyric and pastoral understanding roots from the Warwickshire of his birth, taking poetic form in woodland fairies and forest glades; and I wonder what the subdued yet rich and fertile luxuriance of what Blake in *Jerusalem* called 'England's green and pleasant land', together with its wide variety, has had to do with her widespread and enduringly creative work throughout the last three centuries, expanding from this tiny island to make, as Shakespeare's Cranmer says, 'new nations' (*Henry VIII*, v. v. 53). I am reminded of an exquisite miniature in *Macbeth* condensing wide areas of the Shakespearian gospel. As they press towards victory, the saving forces swear they will pour out, if needed for their 'country's purge', each drop of themselves

> To dew the sovereign flower and drown the weeds.
> (v. ii. 30)

That is, to plant young Malcolm on Scotland's throne. 'Sovereign flower': a magical excellence is hinted, as in 'sovereign remedy', yet nature is preserved. Shakespeare's nature-feeling is one in kind with his royalistic doctrine; hence his equation of kingship with the sun as in *Richard II* (III. ii. 36–52), and with love in *The Merchant of Venice* (III. ii. 178–84) and *Troilus and Cressida* (III. ii. 35–9), and the fusion of all three in the Sonnets, preserving throughout the royalty of the romantic imagination.

1. This essay, together with other parts of *The Burning Oracle*, will be included in my volume *Poets of Action*. For Byron's royalism, see pp. 98, 128–9, 180. [**1966**]

As for the sea, it thunders in passage after Shakespearian passage, and is Shakespeare's main poetic symbol, its roughness especially being used over and over again to impress on us a sense of man's turbulent existence, with a storm-tossed boat as a recurrent symbol for man's buffeted soul. Naturally enough his last play but one, planned to capture the essence of his total poetry, is called *The Tempest*. Britain's power has been pre-eminently a sea-power and her political story one of a semi-nautical skill, a veering to the winds, her immediate goal often unknown, but trusting, with a navigator's instinct, to the stars. Germany's assertion is a land-assertion, up-standing and jagged, like a mountain rock, and thickly clustered with armed might as the massive tree-legions of the Black Forest. I feel a relation between the sea and the vaster powers; and in the present war it seems proper enough that England should be out-numbered on land, and yet, if a wider space and longer period be taken, should expect to gain, in her turn, from a strength due to imperial expansion and sea-mastery.

On our coins we have pictured Britannia, with shield and helmet and a trident to signify control of the sea. She resembles Pallas Athene, goddess of wisdom, and on our latest pound notes we have two such persons, one bearing an olive branch, for peace, and another, as a water-mark, helmeted and with a Greek profile. The sea is the great realm of subconscious pre-animal life, and its mas-tery may be equated with mastery of instinct and therefore highest wisdom. Great Britain has been for long at pains to train and humanize the savage and bestial instincts, spurning their attack:

> England bound in with the triumphant sea,
> Whose rocky shore beats back the envious siege
> Of watery Neptune . . .
>
> (*Richard II*, II. i. 61)

Browning in *Caliban upon Setebos* talks of the 'snaky sea', and the association of sea and reptile life is normal enough; and I once, in *Atlantic Crossing* (x, 332), suggested that Nelson was set towering over all London's heroes because he was 'master of the great dragon', and a 'reincarnated St. George'. Our pound notes picture not only Britannia, but also St. George slaying the Dragon.

A rough sea in Shakespeare's poetry is over and over again associated with wild beasts, dangerous instincts being said to make man bestial, as in *The Merchant of Venice*, where Gratiano suggests that a wolf's soul has found its way into the human form of Shylock (IV. i. 130–8). Bears, wolves and boars I have in *The Shakespearian Tempest* (19, 230) termed Shakespeare's 'tempest-beasts'; Coriolanus (V. iv. 14) is compared to a dragon, so is Lear in his first wrath (I. i. 124); and Richard III is compared to numerous beasts and called a 'cacodemon' (I. iii. 144); and so on. Last comes Caliban, the fish-monster, at once beast, savage and semi-devil.

Against Caliban is Ariel, air and fire as against earth and water, angelic and swift; and so against Shakespeare's tempest-beasts are his hounds, especially greyhounds, and horses. These are swift and graceful; and we may remember both the musical hounds on which Theseus, the perfection of knighthood, rhapsodizes in *A Midsummer Night's Dream* (IV. i. 125–32), and the fine horses of good King Duncan, 'beauteous and swift, the minions of their race', in *Macbeth* (II. iv. 15). Both hounds and horses are highly honoured in *Henry V* (I. chorus, 7; III. vii. 11–49), and in Shakespeare's first poem, *Venus and Adonis*, we have two animals, good and bad: Adonis' finely described horse and the ugly, murderous, boar. It is a hunting poem, and hounds are sympathetically described; hunting often in literature serving to suggest virility without inhumanity, as in the imagery of *Henry V*, and with Theseus and Timon, the 'princely boys' in *Cymbeline* (IV. ii. 171), and Coleridge's remarkable play *Zapolya*. Such poetry aspires to the symbolism of St. George. Shakespeare's warrior kings cry regularly on St. George in battle (*The Sovereign Flower*, 23, 40; and see below, p. 311, note.)

We have various images of angelic grace athletically perceived, as when Hamlet sees his father's poise as

> A station like the herald Mercury
> New lighted on a heaven-kissing hill
>
> (III. iv. 58)

or Romeo sees his love as a 'winged messenger of Heaven' bestriding the clouds (II. ii. 28); or Macbeth imagines 'Heaven's cherubin hors'd upon the sightless couriers of the air' (I. vii. 22). These are riding figures, and athletic; and so, in characterizing man's semi-divine nature, Hamlet says of him 'in action how like an angel', but 'in apprehension, how like a god' (II. ii. 325–6).[1] One is not surprised that Prince Hal in *Henry IV* should be described in terms of a mercurial horsemanship:

> I saw young Harry with his beaver on,
> His cuisses on his thighs, gallantly arm'd,
> Rise from the ground like feather'd Mercury,
> And vaulted with such ease into his seat,
> As if an angel dropp'd down from the clouds,
> To turn and wind a fiery Pegasus
> And witch the world with noble horsemanship.
>
> (*1 Henry IV*, IV. i. 104)

Pegasus was the mythical flying horse on which Bellerophon, a dragon-slayer like Perseus, the angel Michael (see Revelation, XII, 7–9) and St. George, was mounted. 'Young Harry' is Shakespeare's picturization of ideal English youth; and Shakespeare's athletic and mercurial imagery certainly fits that aerial skill and heroism of our own day likely to prove as important henceforth in our national story as sea-adventure in the past. This speech is throughout light, volatile, aerial, with bird-references and cleverly used i-vowels in the lines preceding my quotation—'estridges', 'eagles', 'glittering', 'spirit'—as well as thoughts of bathing and comparison with 'May' and young animals. But against it the more Germanic Hotspur next speaks, using rounded o-sounds, anxious to offer his opponents 'all hot and bleeding' to the 'fire-eye'd maid of smoky war', visualizing the 'mailéd Mars' sitting 'up to the ears in blood'. Hotspur's 'horse' is to bear him like a 'thunderbolt' against 'the bosom of the Prince of Wales'. He ends with a fine couplet:

> Harry to Harry shall, hot horse to horse,
> Meet and ne'er part till one drop down a corse.
>
> (IV. i. 122)

Heavy, thudding, impactuous sounds and cruel imagery are balanced against aerial brilliance and an almost sportive military excellence.

---

1. We must beware of the clearly inaccurate punctuation of the Quarto sometimes followed, which makes the passage relate 'apprehension' to 'angel'. See *The Wheel of Fire*, enlarged, App. B. [1966]

The more violent energies are, however, to be respected, and on occasion the lion or tiger is used to figure a noble ferocity, but the St. George symbol, if not too precisely urged, holds good: even when he writes a pure farce, Shakespeare calls it *The Taming of the Shrew*. Similarly Great Britain's story has been one of a steady humanizing, both in her traditional, somewhat puritanical, ethic at home and her civilizing mission abroad, playing Prospero to beast Caliban. On our pound notes, as once on our golden sovereigns, we have St. George on his prancing charger with Roman helmet and sword, slaying his dragon. He is, like so much in Shakespeare, a compound of the Roman and the Christian, and his job the quelling of those dragon-forces that so easily disrupt human existence. He is chivalric: that is, he symbolizes strength without brutality, as is suggested by the name 'Shakespeare' itself. A quatrain from Dryden's *King Arthur* (v. 1) describes him:

> Saint George, the Patron of our Isle,
> A soldier and a saint,
> On that auspicious order smile,
> Which love and arms will plant.

He figures, dragon-crested and wearing a red cross, as 'Guardian' of our land in Wordsworth's *Ode: 1814*, written in celebration of an English victory. He appears in G. K. Chesterton's (see p. vii)

> I am Saint George, whose cross in scutcheon scor'd
> Red as the Rose of England on me glows.
> The Dragon who would pluck it found this sword
> Which is the thorn upon the English Rose.

Shakespeare's reputed birthday is 23rd April, St. George's Day; which seems natural enough, and if it be by design the more significant for that.

What do these symbols mean to us? To draw attention to them at this hour will seem perhaps a trifle silly to many of my readers. Yet they are on every note we spend, stamped on the golden currency of our social life, the elixirs of private wealth. I am urging no new discoveries or new readings. I can truly say with Antony in *Julius Caesar* (III. ii. 228), 'I tell you that which you yourselves do know'. I merely interpret for us our own national myth, and my remarks are in the main highway and central tradition of our literature. Poetry is the only true wisdom, and it is not widely enough recognized how it affects, or should affect, as our philosophical theologies and political theorizings do not, the seats of action.

But, you may say, neither the works of Shakespeare, nor our Britannia and St. George symbolisms, no, nor the Crown, need necessarily possess those meanings I attribute to them, nor exert those compulsions I urge. No—they need not. Poetic perception, like religious faith, is no passive acquiescence but rather an active co-operation, the very truth concerned being dynamic and needing as does the actor's art a lively response for its realization. While we remain sluggish in our reception of literature and the national myth we fail necessarily to respond to the Crown itself which is an essentially poetic and dramatic conception, a make-believe utterly dependent—and therein lies its supreme value—on our creative participation: it is more than a safeguard of our freedom; it is a means of forcing it. Why do we append 'God Save the King' to our musical and dramatic and cinema performances? Surely because all such ritual—for ritual it is, however popular the entertainment offered—is an approach to the high drama of the Crown. Our national life does not rise above the dramatic, but aspires to it; and the faculty of the dramatic imagination is not, as so often supposed, secondary, but sovereign. Today we have slight national imagination, except in times of peril, which is like having no religion except when ill; and where there is no imagination, the people, sooner or later, perish.

Therefore I reassert the necessity of understanding afresh our national symbolisms in crown, in patron emblems and in literature. All these we must know as dynamic, not merely historic; must feel them not only as they are, but as they might be to an awakened comprehension. The great poetry of our past is a treasure-casket laid by for the hour of need, charged accumulators awaiting contact. Maybe we cannot feel glamorously, as does Germany, about our own destiny. We have risen beyond cheap and destructive nationalisms; but we must now rise further to a new national faith, nobler than any yet known on earth. We cannot go back.

We must press on, and up. We can moreover do what Germany cannot, search within our own literature for authoritative inspiration and re-infection with those powers which we so sorely need.[1] True, Shakespeare is probably more widely loved in Germany than in England; and I confess that certain Shakespearian depths of the metaphysical imagination are more sensitively received in Germany than by us. But such a response is surely potential in us too, for we, not Germany, produced Shakespeare, just as we, not Germany, invented aeroplanes, and even tanks. Shakespeare's total impact is, moreover, apart from any explicit nationalism, superbly British: with its greater comprehensiveness and balancing of opposites, its respect to the softer values, and use of those two integrating factors so important as unifiers of instinctive energy and the rationalizing consciousness, the sense of sin and the sense of humour, both of which the Germanic temperament lacks.

Today two ways of life are opposed. As in Shakespearian tragedy the psychic conflict of the middle action expresses itself in outward military opposition towards the end, so, reversing the process, we can see, beneath our present armed contest, an ancient, if somewhat rusty, pseudo-Christian culture challenged by keen forces that have steadily gathered in Europe since the Renaissance. This is no mere question of national boundaries or possessions: rather the powers grouped against each other, as, to borrow a phrase from *Hamlet* (v. ii. 62), 'mighty opposites' of causes stretching beyond themselves and their own time, wrestle for the mastery of man's soul. Our joint destiny must, I think, involve a fusion of the very powers now seemingly engaged in death-grapple: 'the red rose and the white are on his face . . .' (*3 Henry VI*, II. v. 97). The Dragon—as Nietzsche knew[2]—has his rights. The demonic energies

1. I intended no slight to German literature. Goethe and Nietzsche are, as I have made abundantly clear in *The Christian Renaissance* and *Christ and Nietzsche*, among my own greatest influences. All I meant was, that Germany has no *national* literature of the kind being discussed. [1966]

2. So did Richard III:

Our ancient word of courage, fair Saint George,
Inspire us with the spleen of fiery dragons!

Those two lines contain a world of meaning beyond their context (v. iii. 350. Cp. *Henry V*, III. i. 3–17, also 'dragon' applied to Henry V in *1 Henry VI*, I. i. 11–14. Many normal examples of the symbolism occur in *1* and *2 Henry VI*). [1966]

which Shakespeare's art so beautifully controls are yet the raw stuff of his greatest poetry, his music. Each play is a ritual whereby internal discord is objectified in war, and war transmuted into peace, until the whole succession culminates in that vision of British peace outlined by Cranmer's prophecy in *Henry VIII*. So the two principles of unity in Shakespeare—his tempests and his nationalism—converge; and since his day Great Britain has worked, in the wider context, to make harmony of discords. This task Englishmen must henceforth continue with a will to the service of not merely a nation, nor even an empire, but a world. This will be the task of a Great Britain which, if it does not claim to be, as a nation, or empire, purely Christian, is yet a nation long chosen and self-dedicated to creative labour across the globe, and which, through a sovereign henceforth not only defender but also advancer of the Faith, may approach, without shame, the throne of Christ.

X

FROM *THIS SCEPTRED ISLE*

Three introductory pieces composed to be spoken in the second part of *This Sceptred Isle* at the Westminster Theatre, London, July 1941. Particulars are given in *Shakespearian Production*, 1964, and the prompter's text is included among my *Dramatic Papers* at the Shakespeare Memorial Library, The Reference Library, Birmingham. A facsimile of the programme appears on p. 114 (the final line was wrongly spaced).

I. *HAMLET*

SHAKESPEARE'S genius takes on a sombre tone. After vivid dramas of action, we sound the depths of philosophic speculation. This mood is introduced by Shakespeare's most famous play, *Hamlet*.

Here we have a hero of sensitive temperament, shadowed by consciousness of death. From beginning to end, Death rules his story. Hamlet learns from a Ghost that his father's untimely end was caused by the treacherous act of his own uncle, his father's brother, now himself King. To Hamlet, the world is henceforth darkened, and society diseased. Honour demands that he execute revenge, but his will is paralysed. He typifies all great men whose depth of insight and emotion prevents them from obeying the calls of action in a disordered world.

The play therefore touches many aspects of our own national thinking during recent years. Instinctive abhorrence of warfare and realization of its absurdity have put us at a disadvantage beside less responsible, and more thoughtless, nations, just as Hamlet is at a disadvantage beside Laertes and Fortinbras, ardent young men for whom his problems just do not exist.

We present two extracts. The first is Hamlet's famous 'To be or not to be . . .' soliloquy. In this he wonders whether endurance or

This Sceptred Isle

PART I.—"ST. GEORGE FOR ENGLAND"

Faulconbridge's lines from the conclusion of " King John "

John of Gaunt's speech on England from " Richard II "

Richard III before the battle of Bosworth

Henry V before and during the battle of Agincourt

(INTERVAL OF TEN MINUTES)

PART II.—PATRIOTISM IS NOT ENOUGH

Two Soliloquies from " Hamlet "

Macbeth's vision of Great Britain's expanding royalty

Three scenes from " Timon of Athens," showing Timon's meeting with—

(1) Alcibiades and his army

(2) Some bandits

(3) The Senators of Athens

(INTERVAL OF FIVE MINUTES)

PART III.—THE ROYAL PHOENIX

From " Henry VIII " :

Buckingham's farewell

Cranmer's prophecy

Queen Elizabeth's Prayer before the Armada

action be the nobler course. He next lets his mind wander over the trials and tribulations of human existence, asking why men do not cast off all burdens by self-destruction. Our second extract presents Hamlet's other soliloquy spoken after watching a stage-player lash himself into an unreal passion. Why, asks Hamlet, does he himself, with so much greater cause for passion, do nothing to avenge his father? Finally he decides to get the players to act before the king his father's murder. He would touch the king's *conscience*.

Hamlet now becomes a dramatic artist, aiming to purify society from *within*. Like all great poets and prophets he endeavours, when complexities become intolerable, to penetrate *below the surface*. His last words in this soliloquy

> The play's the thing
> Wherein I'll catch the conscience of the king
>
> (II. ii. 641)

have thus a universal meaning; and we may apply them in our own day to the paramount necessity of enlisting the purifying powers of great drama, and especially Shakespeare, as a means to national re-birth and social guidance.

II. *MACBETH*

In the profounder mood of these greater plays Shakespeare returns to study of his root-evil, the criminal urge to unrightful power. Against this Shakespeare's England is always opposed. In *Macbeth* Shakespeare sees this evil thing as a *mysterious force* getting a grip on man unsuspected and leading him from one act of blood to another. The three 'weird women', or witches, prophesy that Macbeth, already a successful general, will eventually be king; and so tempt him to murder Duncan, the reigning king of Scotland. Circumstances conspire to make the murder easy; and, despite his own horror of the deed, Macbeth commits the crime.

But the crown brings him no peace. He is tortured by nightmare fears. Especially he fears Banquo, a Scottish noble who, according to the witches' prophecy, was to be ancestor of many future kings; whereas Macbeth was to be king only himself. Macbeth's royalty is lustful, selfish, and must soon die; but Banquo's is unself-seeking and therefore creative, and so inexhaustible and immortal. Here we see the difference between destructive and creative forces. The guilt-stricken Macbeth necessarily hates and fears Banquo.

About the world today are clear examples of those dark forces Shakespeare analyses in *Macbeth*, piling destruction on destruction, as Macbeth himself commits murder after murder. Once you start on such a course you cannot stop yourself. It was so with Macbeth; it is so in Europe at this hour. *Fear* drives you on.

We select two scenes, played as one. In the first, Macbeth meditates on his fears of Banquo. In the second, he re-visits the Witches, half-way through his career of blood, to learn from them his fate. This latter incident we show as a delirious dream.[1] Imagine that Macbeth sees the Witches busy at their evil charms over a cauldron, brewing trouble for mankind. He demands their aid. They show him three deceptive visions which bring him some comfort and assurance. He next asks if Banquo's descendants shall really possess the throne; and a line of splendid kings passes before his horror-struck gaze. They are the divinely guarded descendants of Banquo; symbols of the God-appointed creative scheme whose harmony no tyrannous crimes can for long disturb or interrupt.

There is something more to say. Banquo's descendants are to be kings of England as well as Scotland. The play was written during the reign of King James I, under whom the three realms of England, Scotland and Wales were first unified. That is why Banquo's descendants hold 'two-fold balls' and 'treble sceptres'. They are kings of *Great Britain*. Therefore this procession celebrates once again the victory of Great Britain's destiny over that power-lust always, from century to century, so eager to strangle its growth. In slaying Banquo Macbeth attempted to cut off this creative destiny at its root; but Providence was not to be cheated, and Banquo's son escaped. Such are the national issues twined into the structure of Shakespeare's greatest study of evil.

1. Since, though off-stage voices were used freely, I was the only visible performer, the arrangement was forced. The formal commentaries here printed were read by Henry Ainley. In Parts I and III of the programme, where changes of costume were slight, I gave my own informal talks before each recital.

III. *TIMON OF ATHENS*

We pass now to one of Shakespeare's very greatest plays, which has not had the attention it deserves: *Timon of Athens*. We are shown a rich, generous and princely-hearted hero, a universal lover and benefactor of mankind. His wealth once exhausted, the friends on whom he relied prove grossly ungrateful, and deny him all assistance. In fierce anger he casts from him the trappings of civilization and returns to a state of savagery by the wild sea-shore. Here he lives on what he can find and, in digging for roots, discovers gold. All who visit him he answers now with curses.

He is far more than a savage. He is like the old Hebrew prophets. He denounces wholesale the decadence and miserly greed of man's so-called civilization. The next three centuries of undisciplined commercial rivalry seem to have presented themselves before Shakespeare's ranging vision; and Timon prophesies (IV. iii. 393–5) *war* as the inevitable result.[1]

Here we have a play that touches all of us. Though its meaning be limited to no particular time or place, it will do us no harm to apply its medicine to ourselves. We might remember John of Gaunt's prophecy attacking England's king for selling his country's soul. To Shakespeare the vices of peace—lack of generosity, insincerity, self-satisfaction and greed—are no less reprehensible than the cruder, more war-like, lust for power analysed in *Macbeth*. From this play we can see that, though Shakespeare returns at the end of his career to supreme faith in Great Britain's destiny, he has certainly shirked none of the criticisms levelled against society in our time by communist or pacifist.

And Timon is more than a critic of society. He is the soul of great poetry voyaging on a lonely quest, most truly at home with sun and moon and earth, and all elements of nature, and listening from time to time to the sob and surge of the great seas into which his story fades. From the depths of eternity he pronounces judgement on the pettiness of man.

1. In an article 'Shakespeare on the Gold Standard' in *Saturday Night* (Toronto) of 17 February 1940 I had stated: 'Shakespeare writes at a period when the feudal order was disintegrating before a rising commercialism'. [1966]

We present three scenes from the later acts, arranging them according to the lights of Heaven: first, dawn; second, moonlight; and third, sunset.[1]

In the first Timon finds gold while digging for food, and ruminates on its powers for evil; and, visited by the commander of an army marching to invade his native land, gives him gold to assist his enterprise, praying him to loose destruction on a wicked civilization, with the additional and characteristic charge that he be next himself 'confounded' (IV. iii. 129).

After this we watch Timon visited by poverty-stricken bandits, whose voices are as the cry of poverty in any age or place. To these, too, Timon gives gold, charging them in a speech of fantastic imagination to thieve as freely as they wish, since thieving is the one law of man and nature.

Lastly, the governors of his native land visit him, confessing their sins and imploring him to return and bring back his own great virtues to save them from the invader while there is yet time. His bitterness is not relaxed, and he refuses.

Our scenes are presented as a series of impressions in the hero's mind; almost as remembrances of the world he has left. The gold he gives may be allowed to symbolize the golden wisdom which burns alike in his early love and later hatred. Timon stands for something very close to the heart of Shakespeare; something of saving power which we ought not to reject.

1. The conclusion in sunset differed from the scheme used in my two full-length presentations of *Timon of Athens*: see *Shakespearian Production*.

XI

FOUR PILLARS OF WISDOM

The Wind and the Rain, Winter, 1941–42; I, 3.

I. A ROYAL PROPAGANDA

COMPLAINTS regarding the absence of a 'programme' in our national propaganda are not all captious. Psychologically and socially we are still, as on the field of battle, fighting a defensive war. There is some truth in Mussolini's recent statement that Nazi Germany and Fascist Italy are fighting for victory, but we for safety. Before us looms the fear of tyranny; before our enemies rises a highly desirable goal demanding supreme sacrifices. They are consequently the more empowered, not only in military action but also in thought and plan: their plans all point somewhere. They think less of freedom and more of service, and no one is so alive with power as a thinker whose mind is dedicated to some supreme end.

The grip totalitarianism exerts on Europe is seriously underrated by the British mind. Except for an unfortunate minority the people, especially the younger people, in a totalitarian state are not necessarily unhappy. Nor do they necessarily feel less 'free'. It is possible to barter political freedom for other freedoms more instinctive and more enjoyable. German youth has certainly been encouraged to express instincts common to mankind which would not be allowed by us. It is probable that many in England today feel freer under our present restrictions with all the attendant opportunities for purposeful service than they did before the war. Again, a sense of service acts as a release of power.

There is an undeniable fascination about the Nazi programme for state, continent, or world, offering as it does a place for everything and everything in its place. Though it be attained at the cost of hideous suffering and manifold injustices, yet one might argue that suffering and injustice are anyway the stuff of human existence always; and certainly our pre-war world was a chaos. Hence pan-Germanism is in places infectious. It thrives upon outward success. It is a flame that spreads, and may well spread even more rapidly in the near future. That is a danger we must recognize. We must realize the true nature and strength of what we oppose. The old cry of democracy against tyranny, right enough as far as it goes, does not go far enough. The world today demands strong leadership and Germany's strength lies in her willingness, indeed her consuming passion, to assume that leadership. Leadership cannot gain a response without an authority born of self-confidence and a sense of vocation; but our own propaganda, pounding on the democratic monotone, offers neither. Our cause lacks the necessary radiations.

We know well enough that we stand for something greater than Nazi Germany, but that 'something' we are extremely loath to define. It is more Christian, giving greater respect to the individual personality, more comprehensive, more creative and enduring. It is not however to a superficial view either more efficient or more attractive. The difference is that between a work of great literature, say *Hamlet* or *Paradise Lost*, and a best-seller. Both the German and Russian programmes are in their fashion best-sellers, whereas our own system holds the greater dignity and richer worth of some noble classic. That is what our propaganda must put across. Admittedly it is not easy, but unless we do that we put across nothing of any real value at all. Any other programme must be partly insincere and its insincerity half-consciously detected and distrusted.

Our system is Christian because with us the body politic is crowned by a sovereign conception raising it to divine stature; it safeguards the dignity of the individual by keeping at its heart no political theory nor inhuman 'state', but a royal personality; it is comprehensive because it believes in opposing parties with full rights of speech finding their own fulfilment in joint subjection to the throne; and it is enduringly creative because its varying political changes are all as beads strung on the one golden thread, traditional yet always developing, of a national imagination finely crystallized in our hereditary and constitutional monarchy.

Yet in all the spate of pamphlets and articles one reads today the Crown is generally neglected. The mistake lies not in our system but in our own lack of imaginative understanding; and until we awake that imagination in ourselves our international propaganda will remain sterile.

Meanwhile, we spend our time hashing up and half-promising weak imitations of the German or Russian schemes. For those who want either, surely their spontaneous originators are the ones to trust. Besides, anything we are forced into because of the war is likely to be third-rate. Instead, we might learn to know, and trust, ourselves. We have for long had something of golden worth to offer, which has room for all the best that can be devised by man for man; within which a nobler socialism and a truer aristocracy than any hitherto known might find place and purpose. The British Crown is a dream, a myth, a poetic creation, a mighty symbol. It is our one bond of Empire. More—it is fast becoming the central hope of Christian mankind. That is the truth we should blazon across the world.

II. SHAKESPEARE AND THE NAZI DICTATORSHIP

Shakespeare alone unites Germany and England. The German nation responds to his rich, almost Wagnerian, humanism, and mighty word-music. Probably Shakespeare is more widely honoured in Germany than in England.

But he is England's national prophet, with splendid passages on the invincibility of our island-fortress. The history plays present various types of English royalty—the weak Richard II, the villainous Richard III, the baffled Henry IV, and, to crown the sequence, the God-fearing patriot-warrior, 'mirror of all Christian kings', Henry V (*Henry V*, II. chorus, 6).

Shakespeare's greater work may, however, be characterized by that famous phrase, *Patriotism is not enough*. All problems of righteous action and just rule are profoundly reconsidered; they converge pitilessly on Hamlet. The great tragedies explore those passionate riches and daemonic powers in man's soul that Germany perhaps understands better than England. The Nazi revolution has unleased such energies on a nation-wide scale.

Richard III is a miniature of Nazi Germany, with the same unbounded ambition, subtle propaganda, and scorn of weakness; but *Macbeth*, with its dark embodiment of the supernatural, is the profounder study. Reckless blood-adventure brings the protagonist to disaster as a confessed tyrant:

> Those he commands move only in command,
> Nothing in love.
>
> (v. ii. 19)

This is the reverse of England's reliance on an empire of free peoples. Beside Macbeth stands Banquo, in whom England's future burns, saying:

> In the great hand of God I stand, and thence
> Against the undivulg'd pretence I fight
> Of treasonous malice.
>
> (II. iii. 137)

Banquo is ancestor of those future English kings who in vision enfuriate Macbeth:

> What, will the line stretch out to the crack of doom?
>
> (IV. i. 117)

Macbeth tried, vainly, to cut off Great Britain's destiny at its root. To Shakespeare this was all-important; and, since his time, England has regularly opposed tyranny.

The main issues contending for mastery today are precisely those deepest-rooted in Shakespearian drama. Coriolanus, like Hitler, thinks to pursue an ice-cold policy, crushing softer instincts. He is an iron dictator:

Menenius: He wants nothing of a god but eternity and a heaven to throne in.
Sicinius: Yes, mercy, if you report him truly.

> (v. iv. 25)

The criticism of Nazi Germany is clear: what 'mercy' did Hitler show Poland? Or the Jews? 'Hath not a Jew eyes . . .' (*The Merchant of Venice*, III. i. 63).

To Shakespeare power is only half the highest good. The other half is love, or 'mercy', which in Portia's famous speech becomes

> The throned monarch better than his crown.
>
> (IV. i. 189)

Towards that ideal Shakespeare's whole work marches, concluding with Cranmer's prophecy over the child Elizabeth in *Henry VIII*, wherein are listed those things for which England must always fight:

> Good grows with her.
> In her days every man shall eat in safety
> Under his own vine what he plants, and sing
> The merry songs of peace to all his neighbours.
> God shall be truly known; and those about her
> From her shall read the perfect ways of honour,
> And by those claim their greatness, not by blood.
>
> (V. v. 33)

England's sovereignty is handed on:

> Peace, plenty, love, truth, terror,
> That were the servants to this chosen infant,
> Shall then be his, and like a vine grow to him.
> Wherever the bright sun of heaven shall shine,
> His honour and the greatness of his name
> Shall be, and make new nations . . . Our children's children
> Shall see this, and bless Heaven.
>
> (V. v. 48)

So Shakespeare's last word prophesies England's greatness; and England still labours to fulfil this inclusive, Shakespearian, destiny.

Hitler is a genius; but Richard III too was an intellectual giant. Criminality and genius are, as Nietzsche saw, akin. *Macbeth* is Shakespeare's most powerful tragedy. There is a fascination—this is the secret of Hitler's success—about such heroes of blood. More, they actually serve as high a purpose within the drama of human history as in Shakespeare's. The Hitlerian challenge will have jerked humanity up to a higher level. But—and my authority is Shakespeare—that cannot happen if England be defeated: Macbeth is great, but to have him victorious would be to invert Shakespeare. Under a Nazi victory there could be no collaboration. What humanity craves is the union of power with goodness, of the Germanic and the British ideals, to create some new, more deeply Shakespearian, manhood.

III. GOETHE IN THE TWENTIETH CENTURY

Goethe's *Faust* is an epic of the Germanic spirit characteristic of its author's mammoth genius. This vast lyrical drama, Goethe's life-song, lifts on massive wings. It is at once a great poet's spiritual autobiography and the recorded soul-history of Renaissance Europe.

In Part 1 we watch man's eternal inability to seize paradisal satisfaction from romantic love-experience.

Part 2 ranges more widely. Here Goethe condenses the past, present and future history of Europe.

Faust, the hero, is a medieval conception, but he now visits the Emperor's court and assumes the function of a Renaissance artist, assisting in production of a 'masque' and introducing Helen, spirit of ancient Greece. Later we have dramatized his union with Helen, symbolizing the blend of medieval Christianity with Hellenic humanism which underlies Renaissance culture. Faust and Helen have a child, Euphorion, supposed to represent Lord Byron and more generally suggesting the next stage of European development called the Romantic Revival, that upspring of an aspiring idealism sweeping across Europe in the early nineteenth century, and closing as swiftly as it began. The boy Euphorion meets premature disaster while too impetuously scaling mountain-heights.

We have now reached Goethe's own day. What shall come next? Undaunted, he proceeds to penetrate the future; perhaps the boldest prophetic adventure on record. Such is the true significance of those hitherto baffling scenes that follow. Though poor stuff dramatically, they are when recognized as prophecy amazing.

Goethe sees the Emperor (i.e. the ruling classes of Europe in our time) growing decadent and greedily licentious, letting the realm (i.e. Europe) become a riot:

> How he enjoyed, good lack!
> While went the realm in anarchy to wrack.
>
> (2. IV. 363)[1]

A rival Emperor (i.e. contemporary dictators) starts up, christening himself 'our army's Duke' and 'our barons' liege' (2. IV. 371), and wins the masses, since he at least has a crisp programme and promises order. Things have grown 'too mad' and so

> That man is lord who peace bestows.
> The Emperor cannot, will not. Come then, choose we
> A new Lord, into the Realm new soul infuse we. . . .
>
> (2. IV. 364)

The masses follow their new, and false, Emperor 'in sheepish kind' (2. IV. 369). The diagnosis is acute. We have watched it all happen.

Faust (i.e. the soul of Europe) sides with the *real* Emperor and shows him a vision of a griffin, called a purely 'fabulous' beast, in conflict with the imperial eagle:

> Him how could his conceit inveigle
> To pit him with a genuine eagle?
>
> (2. IV. 376)

The fight queerly forecasts the 'war of nerves' and aerial attacks of Germany and Great Britain today:

> Each about each with menace gruesome
> In circles wide they wheel, then stoop
> Each upon each with furious swoop,
> And tear and mangle neck and bosom.
>
> (2. IV. 376)

The griffin falls, its 'lion's tail all limp', lost from sight. Next the actual war is fought out and, with the help of Faust and Mephistopheles, the Emperor wins.

1. My quotations are drawn from Albert G. Latham's admirable translation in the old Everyman edition. Numerals indicate Part, Act and Page. Acts III, IV and V of Part 2 start on pages 306, 356, and 390.

However, he returns to his former weaknesses. Faust, the soul of Europe, struggles manfully on, and dies battling creatively for humanity against vast nature-forces, dedicated to civilizing effort. At death he is raised to a Christian paradise, where he is received by his first love, Gretchen.

Though the poem, with its mountains and torrents and primary symbolisms of fire and water, is thoroughly Germanic and more than a little pagan, yet it ends in Christian mysticism. So did Wagner (Hitler's favourite) in *Parsifal*. Both Goethe and Wagner are Germanic prophets, in whom those volcanic energies so terrifying today are transformed, as Nietzsche taught, to 'heavenly children' (pp. 130, 193 below). *Faust* once pictures a luscious nature-paradise as setting for a race of supermen:

> We stand amaz'd, and still the question holdeth
> If men, if haply Gods, are they?
>
> (2. III. 339)

Beside it we must place the poem's concluding lines:

> All things corruptible
> Are but reflection.
> Earth's insufficiency
> Here finds perfection.
> Here the ineffable
> Wrought is with love.
> The Eternal-Womanly
> Draws us above.
>
> (2. V. 422)

Pagan strength is crowned by Christian grace: both are necessary.

This mighty prophetic voice of Germany has found deaf ears among the Nazi leaders. Perhaps they recognize in themselves Goethe's ill-fated 'griffin', vainly fighting against the eagle-soul of their nation's destiny; and in Britain the upholder of true royalty, battling to preserve the traditions of Europe.

IV. BYRON—THE VOICE OF EUROPE

Lord Byron is often a sharp critic of Britain's puritanical insularity. Perhaps that is why England has failed to appreciate his stature.

He is a virile poet, with colourful stories of spectacular deeds, hot-blooded passions, revenge and chivalry. Historic Europe thrills him with memories of fine action. With these co-exists sympathy for the sufferings of ordinary men. He curses tyrants who 'dare to pave their way with human hearts' (*Childe Harold*, I. 42). 'Conquerors and kings' are as 'madmen who have made men mad by their contagion' (*Childe Harold*, III. 43). He admires martial heroism whilst pressing beyond it. He recognizes the lion in Napoleon, but despises wolves; he would not deny the rights of power but instead would 'teach all kings true sovereignty' (*Childe Harold*, III. 19).

Such balancing of opposites many minds find impossible. Byron is himself tugged diversely by his own distended comprehension. His early heroes are guilt-burdened men of proud, darkly-mysterious, suffering, at once satanic and chivalrous. He would resolve the deep antagonism of *power* and *love*.

In the mountainous setting of *Manfred* this conflict reaches cosmic proportions. The spiritual agony demanding resolution prefigures our contemporary world-conflict:

> It is an awful chaos—light and darkness,
> And mind and dust, and passions and pure thoughts,
> Mix'd, and contending without end or order. . . .
> (III. i. 164)

In Hell's despite the hero battles for the rights of human instinct. *Manfred* is an archetypal drama, endured for the regeneration of mankind.

This trust in man widens to a fervent passion for political freedom:

> Yet, Freedom! yet thy banner, torn, but flying,
> Streams like the thunder-storm *against* the wind.
> (*Childe Harold*, IV. 98)

Beside this we find an almost superstitious reverence for religious tradition, and even for

> The dead, but sceptred, Sovereigns, who still rule
> Our spirits from their urns.
>
> *(Manfred,* III. iv. 40)

The golden mean is Byron's solution: 'I wish men to be free as much from mobs as kings' *(Don Juan,* IX. 25). He is an *aristocratic revolutionary*.

He wrote two great political plays. *Marino Faliero* tells of a Venetian sovereign who, despite an instinctive, traditional abhorrence, joins a popular revolution against a decadent upper-class. He would 'share' his 'sovereignty' with his people (I. ii. 419)—feeling royalty, in true British fashion, as a communal possession—and so 'free the groaning nations' (v. i. 398). This complex action outlines the finer social artistry to which our world travails:

> We will renew the times of Truth and Justice,
> Condensing in a fair free commonwealth
> Not rash equality but equal rights. . . .
>
> (III. ii. 168)

At such organic symmetry the British constitution has for long aimed.

Sardanapalus attacks a similar problem: that of a pacifist king, who, like Shakespeare's duke in *Measure for Measure,* is too spiritually profound to be an efficient ruler. He sees his conqueror-ancestress Semiramis as 'a sort of semi-glorious human monster' (I. ii. 181):

> Enough
> For me, if I can make my subjects feel
> The weight of human misery less, and glide
> Ungroaning to the tomb.
>
> (I. ii. 262)

King of a great empire, he yet has no desire to 'go on multiplying empires' (I. ii. 550). He is however brave, and when forced to, fights royally. He does not enjoy it:

I am content: and, trusting in my cause,
Think we may yet be victors and return
To peace—the only victory I covet.
To me war is no glory—conquest no
Renown.   (IV. i. 502)

Here Byron is again English. No other nation has so blended power
with the will-to-peace. When Europe finds our pacifism strange, it
should read *Sardanapalus*; just as we should study Byron's (perhaps
unjust) attack on Wellington in *Don Juan* for not using Britain's great
power after the Napoleonic wars to organize the liberty of nations.

Much of Byron the German mind will respect. His transmutation of satanic energies towards a radiant strength forecasts Nietzsche.
Nietzsche admired Byron. But the only *political* order approaching
the Byronic ideal is the British. There only you have power with
pacific intention; empire held in trust, but not feverishly desired;
and democratic freedom existing, as does our king himself, in vassalage to that nameless royalty which is the soul of empire. Byron's
international popularity should help to expand this British idea
across Europe.

He died, aptly, fighting for the liberation of Greece—Greece, the
early inspirer of our arts and sciences, inaugurator of democratic
freedom, and spiritual ancestor of the civilized world.

V. A BRITISH VIEW OF NIETZSCHE

We have all misunderstood Nietzsche. To the English he is part-
instigator of Germany's more ruthless actions across Europe; to the
Nazis an accepted prophet of their iron regime. He certainly called
himself 'dynamite'—but that is metaphoric. His real aim is to blast
a way for man's advance to a higher state of being.

For this words are scarcely adequate and so his most carefully
considered work, *Thus Spake Zarathustra*, speaks mainly through
poetic symbolism. His gospel is best studied here.

His quest is spiritual freedom: 'the Golden Wonder, the boat of
free-will and its Master' (58).[1] This is *not* license. He emphasizes

1. I use the Everyman translation, 1933, by A. Tille and M. M. Bozman.
Numerals designate sections, the Introductory Discourse not being counted.

creative good-living as opposed to conventional morality, attacking social rottenness and religious decadence like Christ. All half-hearted and therefore powerless virtues anger him. Psychic power he rates higher than charity, as Christ puts God before man.

He is the supreme individualist of literature as Christ of life. His trust is in man's central instincts:

> Many an one can command himself, but falleth far short in obeying himself.
>
> (56)

He sees himself as a *creative* teacher:

> My burning will to create driveth me ever and again unto man as the mallet is driven unto the stone.
>
> (24)

He recognizes as basic the will-to-power, but confronts with a stern challenge all eminent men, such as Napoleon or Hitler. Such a man

> must yet unlearn his hero will ... he must yet resolve his monsters and his riddles, he must change them to heavenly children.
>
> Not yet hath his knowledge learned how to smile and to be without jealousy; not yet hath his torrent passion grown still in beauty ...
>
> But chiefly to the hero the beautiful is hardest of all things. Unattainable is beauty by the vehement will. ...
>
> And of none demand I beauty so eagerly as of thee, thou man of power: let thy gentleness be thy last surmounting.
>
> (35)

Nietzsche's imagined super-hero is half in eternity; for 'the world revolveth not about the inventors of new noise, but about the inventors of new values; inaudibly it turneth' (40).

Nietzsche's superman doctrine demands a democratic order allowing for originality; whereas a totalitarian state stifles creative living. Nietzsche hates 'the state'; to call it equivalent to the people is a 'lie', it is born of destroyers, not 'creators':

Destroyers are they which lay snares for the many and call them States: they impose on them a sword and an hundred lusts. . . .

A confounding of the languages of good and evil: this sign give I unto you as a sign of the State. Verily, it is a sign of the will to death! Verily, it beckoneth to the preachers of death!

(11)

We are instead pointed to the arduous quest of *individualist freedom*, for

a thousand paths there are that none hath yet trod, a thousand healths and hidden isles of life. (22)

Democracy alone, nevertheless, cannot satisfy the royalty of the individual soul and keep alight the superman-faith. In the British Constitution the Crown, a mystic, super-personal symbol, preserves us from the dangers of dictatorship, bureaucracy, and the herd-instinct. Our constitution correctly expands Nietzsche's psychological doctrine.

His assertion of psychic power is clearly related to the great upsurge of power-will throughout Germany. No other culture could have produced him. But, just as he teaches the *transmutation* of lusts, so Germany herself must re-direct her national energies in a greater cause:

It is power, this new virtue: a master-thought it is, and round about it a subtle soul: a golden sun, and round about it the serpent of knowledge. (22)

Is this the 'power' of storm-troopers tormenting Jews?—of mass executions in Poland?—of the machine-gunning of civilian refugees in Belgium? The thought wrongs Nietzsche's shining gospel, which points us rather to the creative powers of great music, such as Germany before all other nations has given to mankind; to the poetic power of Shakespearian drama, which Germany so justly appreciates; and, finally, though Nietzsche did not himself fully recognize the kinship, the power of Christ, death-vanquisher. That is what *Zarathustra* means; and in a true understanding of her greatest teacher lies the best chance of a new Germany lending her gigantic spiritual powers to the creation of a new and greater world.

A purer insight into the royal powers of great literature is demanded. Therein lies wisdom and guidance towards a strong political faith supporting the domed splendour of a new Christendom.

XII

SHAKESPEARE'S WORLD

A broadcast on the North American Service of the B.B.C., January 1942; subsequently printed in *Hiroshima*, 1946.

THE British Empire and the United States of America are united in the most far-reaching adventure of peoples that this world has seen; and I am to speak of Shakespeare, the greatest master of our joint language.

Shakespeare wrote soon after the structure of medieval Christendom had collapsed. The intellectual language of medieval culture had been Latin, which now gave way to a new use of the vernacular throughout Europe. The language of Shakespeare's England was, however, a strange concoction, of various origins; and with this molten fluid Shakespeare worked, pressing rich stories into his service from the wealth of many ages and many peoples, and often coining, with a splendid ease, new treasures of speech.

So too, the strength of Great Britain herself has proved no strength of isolation, of pure breed, but rather a strength of inclusion. Throughout history invaders, emigrants and refugees have contributed variously to the body of our islanded way of life; and that is why Britain's influence has also expanded, and an empire grown able to include the cultures of other races. Such is the inclusive nature of the British genius.

Something similar has happened in the United States of America, whose vast population is only in part Anglo-Saxon. Language does more than descent to determine character; and the varied racial stocks of Great Britain and North America are one in their vassalage to Shakespeare's language.

It is always hard to select from Shakespeare's world, but I

should like to draw attention to just three things which seem, at the moment, important.

The first is the sea. Shakespeare continually compares human turmoils to stormy voyages over dangerous waters. Tragedy is a 'shipwreck', and his comic action is regularly played out across a background of maritime adventure and merchandise. Britain's world-influence derives from the personal initiative of brave men to whom the ocean was no hostile barrier but a way to be opened up; to America and other lands. Shakespeare wrote in that greatest age of our sea-adventure, of which the United States of America is the child.

Here he is writing of sea-tempest in *Pericles*:

> Thou God of this great vast, rebuke these surges,
> Which wash both heaven and hell; and thou, that hast
> Upon the winds command, bind them in brass,
> Having call'd them from the deep . . . Thou stormest
>   venomously;
> Wilt thou spit all thy self? The seaman's whistle
> Is as a whisper in the ears of death,
> Unheard.
>
> (III. i. 1)

His last play but one, *The Tempest*, is a mystic parable telling of sea-loss and resurrection:

> Full fathom five thy father lies;
>   Of his bones are coral made.
> Those are pearls that were his eyes;
>   Nothing of him that doth fade
> But doth suffer a sea-change
> Into something rich and strange. . . .
>
> (I. ii. 394)

In the ocean-volume of Shakespeare's poetry we may feel the English-speaking races bound on ever-greater voyages of discovery.

Second, I speak of Shakespeare's human interest. His persons too are shown gradually discovering their true selves. This happens with Katharine the Shrew, Benedick, Orsino; with Lear, Coriolanus

and Leontes, and all the tragic heroes; and with Cardinal Wolsey.
Truth to oneself is truth to others:

> This above all: to thine own self be true,
> And it must follow, as the night the day,
> Thou canst not then be false to any man.
>
> *(Hamlet*, I. iii. 78)

Honesty involves loyalty, and we have a long list of faithful retainers
and friends: Horatio in *Hamlet*, Kent and the Fool in *King Lear*,
Flavius in *Timon of Athens*; all descendants of Faulconbridge in
King John, whose loyalty is a loyalty to England. And there is a
corresponding horror at treachery and ingratitude, as in Henry V's
tirade at what we should call a group of 'fifth-columnists'. Both
aspects recur in Enobarbus, Antony's faithful follower, who plays
at last a Judas role, only to realize that he has offended most deeply
against, not his master, but himself.

Yet basic rectitude may, as in *King Lear*, demand that a servant
oppose his master's wickedness:

> Hold your hand, my lord.
> I have serv'd you ever since I was a child,
> But better service have I never done you
> Than now to bid you hold.
>
> (III. vii. 72)

At the end of *Othello* the rough, insensitive Emilia towers suddenly
to grand proportions in denunciation of her husband's villainy.
Though his stage be filled with fine aristocracy, the virtues Shakespeare rates most highly are those basic to human nature, the rough
uncut diamonds of human nobility and courage. Or, if these are
absent, honesty at least may remain. No obvious virtue is set higher
than courage. In *All's Well that Ends Well* a braggart, comically
revealed as a coward, admits that, if his heart were great, it would
'burst' with shame; but it is not, so—'Simply the thing I am shall
make me live' (IV. iii. 370–4). Such honesty is brave in its own
despite.

The humour of Falstaff is dependent, as best humour must be,
on honesty. He goes to the wars whilst deriding military honour.
Can honour 'set to a limb' or 'heal a wound' (*1 Henry IV*, v. i.

133–4)? He will not be led from common-sense by a flashy phrase. Falstaff is surely alive today. We may have to fight like Henry V, but we need not deny that Falstaff's humour derives from a pre-eminently British common-sense.

And what of Shakespeare's bad people? There are the subtle, Machiavellian types, in whom wickedness is also duplicity: Iago, Iachimo, 'slight thing of Italy' (*Cymbeline*, v. iv. 64); the impostor Claudius; the evil persons in *King Lear*, whose swift degradation and descent to sadistic cruelty appear, unfortunately, so eminently modern; the grand-style protagonists of crime, Richard III and Macbeth, whom lust for power drives to self-destruction; and the would-be iron soldiers, Hotspur and Coriolanus, though the one has some attractive qualities and the other cannot live up to his harsh intentions.

So Shakespeare's drama defines our world-conflict, expressing, in the only way possible, those qualities so difficult to label, summed up by the words 'integrity' and 'humour', You might say that it is an 'honest' world and a 'good-humoured' world for which the English-speaking nations fight.

Our third heading must lead us just a little further. We are, I think, rather diffident about claiming our cause as purely Christian. That very fact witnesses an honesty Shakespeare would approve.

He has, of course, many passages directly religious. But I would point rather to those tendencies in which human nature is felt as reaching up to, without claiming, Christ-likeness. One of the best examples is Duke Theseus, in *A Midsummer Night's Dream*,[1] who refuses to scorn the simple efforts of the rustics who come to entertain him. They mean well and he accepts them for their intentions. Though men have often hesitated and stammered before him in their nervousness, nevertheless, says Theseus,

> Out of this silence yet I pick'd a welcome. . . .
> Love, therefore, and tongue-tied simplicity
> In least speak most, to my capacity.
>
> (v. i. 100)

---

[1] My extended interpretation of *A Midsummer Night's Dream* is given in *The Shakespearian Tempest*, 141–68.

Such instinctive charity rises in *The Merchant of Venice* to the great assertion of mercy as a universal power over-arching the dignity of monarchs:

> It is twice bless'd:
> It blesseth him that gives and him that takes.
> 'Tis mightiest in the mightiest: it becomes
> The throned monarch better than his crown.
> His sceptre shows the force of temporal power,
> The attribute to awe and majesty
> Wherein doth sit the dread and fear of kings;
> But mercy is above this sceptred sway,
> It is enthroned in the hearts of kings,
> It is an attribute to God himself;
> And earthly power doth then show likest God's
> When mercy seasons justice.
>
> (IV. i. 186)

Such are the high moments of Shakespeare's earlier work. After the succession of great tragedies, so deeply concerned with the agonies and the blessedness of human existence, we need not wonder at those strangely mystic plots of his last plays leading to *Henry VIII*, a work rich in Christian feeling and ending with Cranmer's prophecy over the child Elizabeth, outlining those things for which the English-speaking nations are today at war:

> Good grows with her.
> In her days every man shall eat in safety
> Under his own vine what he plants, and sing
> The merry songs of peace to all his neighbours.
> God shall be truly known; and those about her
> From her shall read the perfect ways of honour,
> And by those claim their greatness, not by blood.
>
> (V. v. 33)

A greater destiny is next foretold, as Britain's influence expands across the earth:

> Peace, plenty, love, truth, terror,
> That were the servants to this chosen infant,
> Shall then be his, and like a vine grow to him.

Wherever the bright sun of heaven shall shine,
His honour and the greatness of his name
Shall be, and make new nations; he shall flourish,
And, like a mountain cedar, reach his branches
To all the plains about him. Our children's children
Shall see this, and bless Heaven.

(v. v. 48)

That is Shakespeare's last word.

This, then, is Shakespeare's world; a world of sea adventure and spiritual adventure; of simple honesty and of humour; and of Christian affinities; a single but richly inclusive world, determined by the integral strength and wealth of the English tongue. So Wordsworth wrote in his sonnet 'It is not to be thought of . . .':

We must be free or die who speak the tongue
That Shakespeare spake; the faith and morals hold
That Milton held.

And yet Shakespeare has, outside *Julius Caesar*, little to say of freedom. Freedom is the natural cry of slaves rather than of free men; whereas Shakespeare himself, with his eye on the innate royalty of man, is more at home phrasing the noble rights of service in the language of kings; and that thought takes us yet farther.

It may soon fall to the English-speaking nations to create something never yet seen on earth. For such a task, where can guidance be sought? The seas are not quite uncharted. Precise schemes and programmes fail before the vast unknowns of human instinct and economic complexity. But something may be discovered in the delicate apprehensions, the noble sympathies and majestic rhythms, the profundities and the wisdom and the glories, of Shakespeare's world.

XIII

SHAKESPEARE AND THE INCAS: A STUDY OF *APU OLLANTAY*

An interpretative study composed as part of a composite volume, completed in 1947, on the Incas, of which my play *The Last of the Incas* was a constituent. Though the collection remained unpublished, its circulation in typescript may have led to the broadcast of *Apu Ollantay* some years later. Parts of the opening section of the essay here printed, including my references to E. C. Hills and more recent books, contain new writing. Except for the occasional new sentence or note and some technical adjustments the rest is as originally devised.[1]

I

OUR one complete Inca drama *Apu Ollantay*, or *Ollantay the Great*, was translated from the Quichua language by Sir Clements Markham and his text included, with introduction and notes, in his comprehensive work *The Incas of Peru* (1910). Of this drama I here present an interpretation with, in particular, a view to discovering how far it bears out the

1. The only part of my 1947 collection hitherto published is *The Last of the Incas*, which was brought out by myself in 1954 on the occasion of its first presentation by Mr. Arnold Freeman at the Sheffield Educational Settlement in October of that year. Subsequent presentations have been given by The New Era Players, Stoke-on-Trent, produced by Mr. Roy Holland, in 1955; by the Leyton County High School for Boys, produced by Mr. B. G. Brown, in 1955; by The Leeds University Union Theatre Group, produced by Mr. Steve Evans, in 1956; and by the Keighley Boys Grammar School, produced by Mr. Arthur Cockerill, in 1959. I have heard of a production in Kashmir, but have no details.

The Conquest of Peru by William H. Prescott, 1847, is available in an Everyman edition. *The Ayar-Incas* by Miles Poindexter, New York, 1930, has a coloured picture of Inca regalia.

The early authorities, Cieza de Leon, Garcilasso de la Vega, and others, are available in translation, under the editorship of Sir Clements Markham, among the handsome Hakluyt volumes published by the Hakluyt Society.

reading of Inca civilization put forward by Garcilasso de la Vega and other early authorities. We have good reason to suppose that the Inca and his clan—the term 'Inca' may denote variously the ruling sovereign, the royal family and the race from which that family sprang—were beneficent rulers of a wide empire, showing a remarkable and most un-European incorporation of humane values into their political and imperial activities. What we in Europe tend to regard as the peculiar contribution of our Church acting as no more than a leaven in matters political, they seem to have regarded as a natural element of government.

Our early authorities however do not all tell the same story, and there is much about which we cannot be sure. Has an element of sentimentalization been active in some of our accounts? It is my purpose to argue that *Apu Ollantay* may go some way towards resolving our doubts.

A drama of quality is evidence of a peculiar kind. We shall not expect from such a work a one-way, propagandist, statement. It is likely to contain a conflict and contrasts; both sides will have their rights, and we shall expect the drama's meaning to exist in the way the conflict is handled and our sympathies directed. Many subtleties may be involved; we must be as interested in the tonal qualities of atmosphere and imagery as we are in the story; and if we listen in to these while also involving ourselves in the action, we shall uncover evidence more convincing than the explicit paragraphs of the historian. A good drama is a living work, hot from the mintage and bearing on it, to borrow a phrase from *Richard III* (I. iii. 256), its 'fire-new stamp' untarnished by the centuries. In it we have a close-up of at least the more sensitive elements in the culture that gave it birth.

I shall first quote from Markham's account of the play given in *The Incas of Peru* at pages 143–56 and 323–36. The drama's authenticity as an Inca creation he regards as indisputable. In the last century, he says, it had been suspected, since in showing the Inca Pachacuti as succeeded by the Inca Tupac Yupanqui it conflicted with Garcilasso's account, then the accepted authority; but since it has now become known that Garcilasso was wrong, our drama's historicity is on this central point found to be correct after all (Markham, 153, note). Markham dates its composition about 1470;

that is, not long after the events it describes, though the written text is much later.

Inca, or Quichua, drama was allowed after the Spanish conquest, presumably at first handed down by memory with perhaps support from records on the *quipu*, the system of coloured strands used by the Incas instead of writing. In the year 1781, however, following the rebellion and execution of José Gabriel Condorcanqui, who had for his purposes taken the name of his ancestor, calling himself the Inca Tupac Amaru, all native plays and festivals commemorating the Incas were suppressed. The official sentence prohibiting 'the representation of dramas as well as all other festivals which the Indians celebrate in memory of their Incas' is adduced by Markham as 'a clear proof that before 1781 these Quichua dramas were acted' (Markham, 326; and see 147). Garcilasso in his vast compendium of history and personal reminiscence entitled *The Royal Commentaries of Peru* (presumably the first part, on the history of the Incas prior to the conquest, completed 1604; Markham, 279) stated that 'both tragedies and comedies . . . were represented before the Inca and his court on solemn occasions' (Markham, 147).

Following the prohibition in 1781 the text of *Ollantay* was set on paper in Quichua by a friend of the unfortunate Inca, Dr. Don Antonio Valdez, who died in old age in 1816.[1] His copy was transcribed by his friend Don Justo Pastor Justiniani, a man of illustrious ancestry with claims to descent from both the Emperor Justinian and the Inca Pachacuti, whose son Pablo, Cura of Laris, inherited the script and allowed Markham to make a copy. A full account, together with notice of the various MSS, occurs in Markham's *Incas of Peru*, though there seems (145) to be some confusion between the father Justiniani and his son in the story of Markham's visit in 1853 to Laris to get his copy (Markham, 144–8; 326–7).

In asserting that the Incaic authenticity of *Ollantay* has been established Markham may have been overconfident. In his *The Quechua Drama, Ollanta* (reprinted from *The Romanic Review*, v. 2, April–June 1914; B.M. Catalogue 11851 tt 33), Elijah Clarence Hills (of Colorado College) is more sceptical. He reviews the whole

[1]. It had apparently been set down in writing before, in 1735, and in other versions of the seventeenth century (Markham, citing 'Von Tschudi', 148).

matter, giving valuable references and citing in some detail E. W. Middendorf's *Ollanta, ein Drama der Keshuasprache, etc.* (Leipzig, 1890) in support of his conclusion that the drama cannot be regarded as an indigenous creation. J. Alden Mason's *The Ancient Civilizations of Peru* (Penguin-Pelican, 1957, revised 1964) remains non-committal, stating that in pre-Conquest days 'there was probably no true drama', but that subsequently dramas were composed embodying 'old legends and songs', *Ollantay* being 'the most famous' (XIV, 232). In his *Incas and Other Men* (London 1959) George Woodcock acknowledges the dramatist's historical equipment while regarding the form and love-interest as Spanish. Louis Baudin in *Daily Life in Peru* (tr. Winifred Bradfield, 1961; orig. Paris 1955) asserts (177) the drama's basic authenticity as of ancient, Inca, origin and refers (citing J. G. Cosio in *Revista Universitaria de Cuzco*, 1941; II, 3) to a certain Espinoza Medrano (of Indian blood; 1632–1688) as probably its first transcriber.

Whatever the truth, whether in composition mainly Inca or from a fusion of Inca and Spanish, the drama is clearly *conceived* as Incaic. It bears the full impress of a culture unlike that of Europe, speaking of a way of life alien to, and in some respects superior to, our own. If the author were a Spaniard he was one at home with the older native language in its pre-Conquest diction and both anxious and able to tune in to native tradition. Markham states (325–6) that about 1775, a little before the prohibition of patriot native drama, it had been acted before the revolutionary Condorcanqui, whose subsequent revolution caused the banning of native plays, killed the living tradition, and led to the recording of the text of *Ollantay* as literature.

In plot-construction and emotional tone *Apu Ollantay* bears a remarkable similarity to the dramas of Shakespeare's final period.

II

This is the story. Prince Ollantay, vice-roy over the mountain tribe of Anti-suyu, loves Cusi Coyllur Ñusta, meaning Princess (Ñusta) Joyful Star (Markham, 340; 360, note), daughter of the great Inca Pachacuti, now an old man. His suit is rejected with fury and, though already secretly married, he is forced to retire to the mountains where he repulses the Inca's army and installs himself as lord in his own right over the mountain people, successfully resisting all attempt at subjection. Years pass and Ollantay's daughter, Yma Sumac, the name meaning 'How Beautiful', a child of ten who knows nothing of her parentage, is being forced against her will into the convent of the Sun-Virgins. Here, in the temple grounds, she hears the laments of a mysterious prisoner shut in a stone cavern, whom she discovers to be her mother, Cusi Coyllur, cruelly put there by the late Inca; for by now Pachacuti's son, Tupac Yupanqui, has succeeded to the throne. The new Inca allows Rumi-ñaui, his father's general, to try once more to break the rebels' power, and the old warrior, ashamed of his former failure, plans and successfully carries through a peculiarly treacherous attack, Ollantay and his generals being captured. The new Inca forgives Ollantay and even instates him as his own vice-roy at Cuzco with his second-in-command as vice-roy over the Anti-suyu. Finally Yma Sumac reveals the plight of her mother, Ollantay recognizes his long-lost wife and daughter, and all ends in forgiveness and peace.

The play is carefully wrought and highly though not crudely dramatic. It was divided into acts and scenes by Dr. Valdez, and the stage directions, which relate so well to the text and the action that I shall for my present purpose accept them as authentic, are his (Markham, 148). There is throughout an undersong of deep feeling. The range of dramatic tone is wide. The at first sight loose structure of its event-sequence would rank it as a romance. There are a number of pleasing pastoral touches. Yet there is, too, a weight of tragic emotion. As a political play, its thought is careful and its revelations, to us, interesting. Comedy is provided by the hero's page, Piqui Chaqui, a humorous character typical of drama the world over. Finally, the concluding scenes hold a pathos and serenity that outdistance all normal dramatic concepts of the conventional 'happy ending'. The work is, like the plays of Shakespeare's final period, in turn heroic, romantic, humorous, pastoral, tragical and mystical.

Ollantay in dialogue with Piqui Chaqui introduces the romantic theme using vigorous poetry of sun and star to characterize his love (1. i). The scene is 'an open space' in the mountains 'just outside the

gardens of the Sun' at Cuzco, the Temple of the Sun beyond and
the Sacsahuaman Hill and fortress in the distance. The High Priest
enters, speaking in high religious fashion of the Sun and Moon and
an approaching sacrifice. Ollantay is disturbed by his entry, and
with reason, for we find that the priest has already discovered our
hero's love:

> I read thy secret on the Moon,
> As if upon the quipu knots . . .[1]
>
> (I. i)

He proceeds to remind Ollantay how well he stands in the old Inca's
favour and how mad it would be to wound his sovereign to the
heart by so lawless and presumptuous a suit. Mortals, he remarks,
are only too ready to drink death from a golden cup, being stubborn
of heart. Our hero is clearly warned: we are not to regard his actions
as blameless.

The Priest, asked by the despairing Ollantay on his knees to cut
out his broken heart, tells Piqui Chaqui to bring him a withered
flower, and, holding it, remarks:

> Behold, it is quite dead and dry.
> Once more behold! E'en now it weeps,
> It weeps. The water flows from it.
>
> (I. i)

Water streams from the plant. The meaning is, Let your broken
heart be revived by tears. But Ollantay will not resign his claims:
it were more easy, he says, for the rocks to bring forth water than for
him to renounce his love. Once more the Priest warns him in a
pastoral vein characteristic of the play:

> Put a seed into the ground,
> It multiplies a hundredfold;
> The more thy crime shall grow and swell,
> The greater far thy sudden fall.
>
> (I. i)

---

1. The Incas had no writing but used instead a system of coloured strands variously
interthreaded on a rope called the 'quipu'. Markham uses the plural 'quipus' for the
collection of strands.

But now Ollantay reveals that he is already secretly married. He knows his danger:

> The lasso to tie me is long,
> 'Tis ready to twist round my throat;
> Yet its threads are woven with gold,
> It avenges a brilliant crime.
>
> (I. i)

That is, he exults, glories, in the thrill of his grand sin. He asks the Priest for help and advice. The honourable 'record' of his many battles, he says, is 'carved' on his club. Uillac Uma, the priest, is grave:

> Young Prince! thy words are too bold,
> Thou hast twisted the thread of thy fate . . .
>
> (I. i)

Ollantay's presumption is underlined. The Priest's advice is to confess before it is too late; and, with assurances of his remembrance, he goes. It is a grave and moving scene, beautifully handled. Left alone, Ollantay establishes himself in determination, praying: 'Cusi Coyllur, surround me with light.' The idealization is semi-transcendental.

The next scene is set in the Colcampata, the Queen's palace. Cusi Coyllur confesses her pangs to her mother:

> Since the day when I last saw my love
> The moon has been hidden from view;
> The sun shines no more as of old,
> In rising it rolls among mist;
> At night the stars are all dim,
> All nature seems sad and distress'd;
> The comet with fiery tail
> Announces my sorrow and grief;
> Surrounded by darkness and tears,
> Evil auguries fill me with fears.
>
> (I. ii)

Now her father, the Inca Pachacuti, enters and addresses her as his 'symbol of parental love', an awkward but revealing phrase, for his

love is felt to be almost dangerously parental and possessive as he
assures her that she is 'all' his 'happiness', and lover-like endues her
beauty with magical properties, even comparing her to his own
supposed father, the Sun, and continuing:

> Without thee thy father would pine,
> Life to him would be dreary and waste.
> He seeks for thy happiness, child,
> Thy welfare is ever his care.
>
> (I. ii)

One doubts the last couplet. He reminds one insistently of the old
King in Shakespeare's *King Lear*. The characterization is neat.

There is a dance of boys and girls, who sing a fascinating song
addressing the 'tuya', a small finch, in the diminutive 'tuyallay',
meaning 'my little tuya', and warning it of the dangers that await it:

> Thou must not rob,
> O Tuyallay,
> The harvest maize,
> O Tuyallay.
> The grains are white,
> O Tuyallay,
> So sweet for food,
> O Tuyallay.
> The fruit is sweet,
> O Tuyallay,
> The leaves are green,
> O Tuyallay;
> But the trap is set,
> O Tuyallay.
>
> (I. ii)

The song tells next of the fate of a *piscaca* (a larger bird), dead and
nailed to a tree as a warning, and ends with 'See the fate ... of
robber birds'. In its place, the song holds strong dramatic point in
reference to Ollantay's presumption; as a pastoral, it has charm; but
notice too its peculiarly sympathetic quality; it is *inside* the little bird
and its doings and longings, in a fashion that D. H. Lawrence
would have appreciated. There is a quality unique and un-Euro-

pean about it. Cusi Coyllur recognizes its omen and asks for a
different song. She is now alone, and hears a mournful elegy sung
by a solitary girl, about a bereaved bird, resembling Shelley's 'A
widow bird sate mourning for her love ...' It forecasts the love-
tragedy to follow. Markham notes that the song belongs to an
elegiac type well known in the Quichua language.

The suffusing tone so far has done much to bring before us the
lost world of Inca civilization. Its imagery alone is significant,
especially imagery from textiles, as when Ollantay sees his fate as a
lasso whose 'threads are woven with gold' and the Priest carries on
the metaphor with 'thou hast twisted the thread of thy fate' (I. i); or
Cusi Coyllur, after embracing her father, is told to 'unwind' herself
as 'a thread of gold within the woof' (I. ii). The many references to
the Sun as god are, naturally, to be expected. Valdez' stage-directions
are well attuned to the action. The first scene has its view of the
Sacsahuaman Hill and the Palace of Colcampata and the second, in
the palace itself, a view of gardens with beyond the 'snowy peak' of
Vilcañota. Especially impressive is the first appearance of Uillac
Uma, up-stage, with his 'arms raised to the sun' (I. i). We shall meet
other impressive directions. The interiors are equally well imagined
and described and the costumes and regalia all set down in order. As
one reads, the old civilization springs to life.

Our next scene introduces a new theme: war. Ollantay, as the
Inca's chief commander, is given his commission to lead the imperial
troops in a new campaign. References to martial music, drum and
fife work up the dramatic atmosphere, weighting it with a sense of
impending power. 'Every detail', says Ollantay (a phrase probably
typical enough, if we are to believe the historians, of Inca thorough-
ness), is 'prepared and in place'. Equally characteristic is the King's
reminder:

> But first you must give them a chance
> To surrender, retiring in peace,
> So that blood may not flow without cause,
> That no deaths of my soldiers befall.

(I. iii)

The accounts of the early historians, Cieza de Leon and Garcilasso, with their emphasis on the humane qualities of the Inca imperialism, may be remembered.

Before setting out Ollantay makes his personal appeal, asking the hand of the Princess. Markham's translation throughout aims to give the metre of the original and here he follows the Quichua with quatrains rhyming abba as in *In Memoriam*, a form in which Garcilasso tells us that the Incas were proficient (Markham, 358, note). By a rather daring piece of unhistorical dramatic anachronism (Markham, 358, note) Ollantay claims to have subdued the rival empire of the Chancas himself:

> Now every tribe bows down to thee—
> Some nations peacefully were led,
> Those that resist, their blood is shed—
> But all, O King, was due to me.
>
> O Sovereign Inca, great and brave,
> Rewards I know were also mine,
> My gratitude and thanks are thine,
> To me the golden axe you gave.
>
> Inca! thou gavest me command
> And rule o'er all the Anti race,
> To me they ever yield with grace,
> And thine, great King, is all their land.
>
> (I. iii)

Notice the two references to peaceful submission: they are valuable. So Ollantay leads up to his request for the hand of Cusi Coyllur, which meets a violent rebuttal. The old Inca is blind with fury. The climax is perhaps too sudden, and the burden on the actor heavy. Ollantay is dismissed.

The old man is, in the manner of Shakespeare's irascible fathers, unreasonably extreme in anger. The action is however in character and must be directly related to his equally excessive and egocentric speech of possessive and paternal love. Royal parents throughout the ages have shown unreason in such matters, and we may remember with advantage that Pachacuti was the first Inca to inaugurate the rule that royal blood must not be mixed with an inferior stock

(Markham, 336). Ollantay was, according to Inca standards, though a prince of dignity, yet an alien, and so inferior. The play is, it seems, a play about this particular innovation; at least, it is likely enough that it was originally so conceived.

Now follows our second movement. A new impetus is, just as in Shakespeare, released through conflict, and the action grows violent. Ollantay is shown on a rocky height above Cuzco. Like Coriolanus, he swears enmity against an ungrateful people; like Timon, Manfred and many another, he leaves a hated civilization for the wilds; like Timon, he pauses, to look back on the city he has left and brand it with his curse. Here is Timon:

> Let me look back upon thee. O thou wall,
> That girdlest in those wolves, dive in the earth,
> And fence not Athens!
>
> *(Timon of Athens,* IV. i. 1)

And here Ollantay:

> Cuzco! O thou beautiful city!
> Henceforth behold thine enemy.
> I'll bare thy breast to stab thy heart,
> And throw it as food for condors;
> Thy cruel Inca I will slay,
> I will call my men in thousands,
> The Antis will be assembled,
> Collected as with a lasso.
> All will be train'd, all fully arm'd,
> I will guide them to Sacsahuaman.
> They will be as a cloud of curses
> When flames rise to the heavens.
> Cuzco shall sleep on a bloody couch,
> The King shall perish in its fall.
>
> (I. iv)

His pride is wounded by his being thought 'too base' for the Princess' hand. Dramatically we sympathize, but we are not necessarily expected wholly to approve. It is perhaps strange to find such criticism of the greatest of the Incas allowed so strong a dramatic sanction as it here receives. Ollantay is our hero, and a fine one; but he has already been reproved by the Priest, and the guilt of his *hubris* is a major theme in our drama. At this moment he enjoys the kind of half-guilty approval we admit for Coriolanus, while falling short of Timon's prophetic justification. The balances are carefully preserved, and the soliloquy in its setting remains a piece of towering drama, a magnificent *peripeteia*.

More remarkable still is the sudden and lovely sequel. Ollantay's egotistic fury is interrupted by a mysterious song coming from the rocks. This song recalls us poignantly to remembrance of Cusi Coyllur, comparing her physical excellences in detail to sun, moon, star, rainbows and dawn; to pearls and crystal, snow, icicles; a sheaf of corn and flowers. She is associated with—the words are important —'mercy' and 'grace' as well as 'laughter'. Ollantay listens, tranced, to the wondrous song. He is deeply moved and, jerked out of his egotism and wounded pride, thinks, like Goethe's Faust beside his mountain cataract, of the suffering girl he has left behind:

> O Princess! O loveliest Star,
> I alone am the cause of thy death . . .

> (I. iv)

Piqui Chaqui answers with a poignant little couplet:

> Perhaps thy star has passed away,
> For the heavens are sombre and grey.

> (I. iv)

In his bitterness Ollantay feels sure that all the people must rise in his cause and leave the 'tyrant'. The scene closes with comic relief provided by Piqui Chaqui, who assures Ollantay that his generosity, his kindness and hand 'always open'—like Timon's—'with gifts', win all men's love, though he himself, he says, could do with a little more of such opportunities:

Ollantay:	Of what hast thou need?
Piqui Chaqui:	What? the means to get this and that,
	To offer a gift to my girl,
	To let others see what I have,
	So that I may be held in esteem.
Ollantay:	Be as brave as thou art covetous,
	And all the world will fear thee.

Piqui Chaqui: My face is not suited for that;
                  Always gay and ready to laugh,
                  My features are not shap'd that way . . .

                                                      (I. iv)

Sounds of war are heard and Ollantay decides to move on. Says Piqui Chaqui: 'When flight is the word, I am here.' The comedy is well placed.

We return to Cuzco, to Pachacuti's palace (I. v). The Inca is in high wrath, demanding the whereabouts of the 'infamous wretch' who dared to love his daughter. A messenger enters, announcing that Ollantay has retreated to the hills, has actually assumed the royal fringe and is supported by 'all the Anti host'. The general Rumi-ñaui, the name meaning 'Stone-Eye', is dispatched with a great army, boasting with—in view of the sequel—a certain dramatic irony that he will 'drive them flying down the rocks'. The old Inca, in this his last appearance, is far from likeable; there is much of the tyrant in his rage. Markham comments (381, note) that 'the Inca Pachacuti does not appear to advantage in the drama'.

We move (II. i) to the hall of the fortress-palace of Ollantay-tampu. Before 'seven immense stone slabs' surmounted by a monolith stands a golden throne. In this rugged setting we watch Ollantay's installation. We have already felt Pachacuti's anger as tyrannous; the play appears not quite to uphold our view of the Incas as a benevolent monarchy; and now we hear our criticisms worded. Ollantay's chief supporter, Urco Huaranca, or 'Mountain Chief', levels a direct charge against the Inca imperialism:

                  The women weep, as you will see—
                  They lose their husbands and their sons,
                  Ordered to the Chayanta war.
                  When will there be a final stop
                  To distant wars? Year after year
                  They send us all to far-off lands,
                  Where blood is made to flow like rain.
                  The King himself is well supplied
                  With *coca* and all kinds of foods.
                  What cares he that his people starve?
                  Crossing the wilds our llamas die,

Our feet are wounded by the thorns,
And if we would not die of thirst
We carry water on our backs.

(II. i)

The speech is capped by Ollantay's:

Gallant friends! Ye hear those words,
Ye listen to the mountain chief.
Fill'd with compassion for my men,
I thus, with sore and heavy heart,
Have spoken to the cruel king:
'The Anti-suyu must have rest;
All her best men shan't die for thee,
By battle, fire, and disease—
They die in numbers terrible.
How many men have ne'er return'd,
How many chiefs have met their death
For enterprises far away?'
For this I left the Inca's court,
Saying that we must rest in peace;
Let none of us forsake our hearths,
And if the Inca still persists,
Proclaim with him a mortal feud.

(II. i)

The incident bristles with interest. Dramatically it adds new weight, exactly at the right time. The plot, so to speak, thickens; it accumulates new excitement and reveals new, unsuspected depth, as personal antagonism becomes communal revolution. One feels that more than a particular person's interest is at stake. As in Shakespeare's Cassius and Byron's Marino Faliero, the two strands, personal and communal, are closely inwoven. Ollantay is surely not being quite honest, since he was all for leading the Inca's troops until his own suit was rejected. This, in view of our new scene's impact, may be the kind of thing we should, in drama, be willing to forget; in the theatre we would be looking forward, not back at such a moment. Besides, we can say, as with Shakespeare's and Byron's revolutionaries, that personal antagonisms may well direct a man towards a truth; though Markham's note suggests that Ollantay's complaint

152

does scant justice to the Inca system, since the recruiting was so equitably divided that no great strain was felt.

Then follows the installation as Ollantay receives the royal fringe from Hanco Huayllu, himself a chief of distinction. This is our central act of *hubris*, which must have struck an Inca audience with no less violent an impact than Agamemnon's walking on the red carpet in Aeschylus' drama excited in ancient Athens:

> Receive from me the royal fringe,
> 'Tis given by the people's will.
>
> (II. i)

Here royalty claims democratic status. Next Ollantay appoints Urco Huaranca chief of the Anti-suyu, giving him the insignia of arrows and plume; and tells Hanco Huayllu, 'most venerable and wise' of his supporters and 'kin to the august High Priest', to present to the Mountain Chief (his name's meaning) a symbolic ring, which he does, with these words:

> This ring around thy finger's plac'd
> That thou may'st feel, and ne'er forget,
> That, when in fight thou art engag'd,
> Clemency becomes a hero chief.
>
> (II. i)

A strange reminder, at such a moment, in such a warlike scene; and one which would scarcely be expected to occur outside the Inca tradition. The ceremonial is developed till Urco is positively 'bristling like the *quiscahuan*' (i.e. he is stuck full of thorns; a paraphrase might put 'like the porcupine').

The rebel army prepares now to meet the troops approaching from Cuzco. Ollantay charges Urco Huaranca with the arrangements, suggesting surprise and a ruse. The chief gives orders for the deployment of his forces with exact reference to the various hills and gorges: the play is geographically meticulous throughout. The scene works up to a martial enthusiasm, with cheers and military music.

The battle—and for this the producer will be duly thankful—is not actually staged. In view of its nature it could not have been, since there is strictly speaking no battle at all, the rebels winning by hurling down rocks on their attackers. The music is probably intended to work up to appropriate sound-effects and we next (II. ii) find Rumiñaui, the opposing general, wounded and blood-drenched, lamenting in soliloquy the hideous slaughter of his army. Soliloquy is a second time used to gripping effect:

> Holding that traitor to be brave,
> I sought to meet him face to face—
> Rushing to seek him with my mace,
> I nearly found a warrior's grave.
>
> My army then was near the hill,
> When suddenly the massive stones
> Came crashing down, with cries and moans,
> While clarions sounded loud and shrill.
>
> (II. ii)

He feels that he has been fooled. Later he is to have his revenge.

III

This is a convenient place to pause and take stock of our findings. How far, we may ask, does this drama, considered as our one dramatic record of values and virtues, support the reading of Inca culture that we have gained from Garcilasso and other writers? The drama's balances are carefully maintained; the rights and wrongs are as indeterminate as in Shakespeare. The reigning Inca does not seem always to have been a superman of kindly virtue, since it is clear that stern criticism of his rule was historically conceivable and dramatically natural. But the criticism cuts both ways: we note an enlightened tendency to regard imperial wars as, after the manner of Byron's *Sardanapalus*, a wicked waste of life; and the claim of our revolutionary party to stand for a democratic, or 'constitutional', monarchy. The central, ritualistic, injunction on Ollantay's mountain chief to blend clemency with victory, and also the old Inca's original command that Ollantay should seek to spare the lives of his soldiers, fall into line with our historians.

It remains true that the action shows a fierce and rugged people, as well in the Inca himself as in his violent adversaries. There are, moreover, some especially awkward lines to be faced concerning the High Priest, Uillac Uma, on his first entry (I. i).

Here Ollantay certainly regards the Priest with fear and suspicion:

Ollantay: Who comes hither, Piqui Chaqui?
Yes, 'tis the holy Uillac Uma;
He brings his tools of augury.
No puma more astute and wise—
I hate that ancient conjurer
Who prophesies of evil things,
I feel the evils he foretells;
'Tis he who ever brings ill-luck.

Piqui Chaqui: Silence, master, do not speak.
The old man doubly is inform'd;
Fore-knowing every word you say,
Already he has guess'd it all.

(I. i)

Ollantay has, it is true, his own reasons for suspicion and hostility; this passage by itself is no criticism of the priesthood, though it certainly suggests that the national religion was in part a religion of fear. The Priest refers to a coming sacrifice to the Sun, saying a thousand llamas await the knife; and such sacrifices we expect. But Ollantay appears to associate the Priest with *human* sacrifice too:

Old man! thine aspect causes fear,
Thy presence here some ill forbodes;
All round thee dead men's bones appear,
Baskets, flowers, sacrifice.
All men, when they see thy face,
Are filled with terror and alarm.

(I. i)

The lines, which indicate human sacrifices such as those so extensive among the Aztecs, seem to constitute a contradiction to Markham's ably argued contention that human sacrifice was not customary among the Incas.[1] The poetry is weighted with sense of witchery:

> . . . the Sun's great day,
> The Moon's libations, are not yet . . .   (I. i)

In that lies surely a shiver of fear. It is possible that human sacrifices, as both Prescott and Markham agree, were on rare occasions made. There is nothing peculiarly evil, and certainly nothing decadent or innately savage, in spite of our conventional beliefs, in such occasional sacrifices: the cruelty involved would be less, since the victim would probably feel himself honoured, and the creative pointing far clearer, than those, in our own history, of European, communal, executions. Or again, we may be faced by a sophisticated poet in an enlightened Inca society dreaming back to a time when such rites were a daily threat. The tribes the Incas conquered were probably before conquest accustomed to cruel sacrifices: and these may have been in everyone's mind. Whatever the exact truth, the drama uses for its purpose this particular fear of the priest; in all times and places, until recently, a peculiarly frightening person.

We are very similarly impressed by the House of the Virgins of the Sun (II. iii) in which Ollantay's daughter, Yma Sumac, is to be shut away. To this House we are introduced after Rumi-ñaui's defeat; a lapse of ten years, presumably, being understood, though the act numbering, which could be improved, does nothing to mark the division. The orphan child is assured by her companion, Pitu Salla, that her life will be pleasant enough:

> Thou art belov'd by every one,
> E'en Virgins of the royal blood.
> The Mothers love to carry thee,
> They give thee kisses and caress—
> You they prefer to all the rest.
>
> (II. iii)

The lines serve to lend Yma Sumac, whose very name means 'How Beautiful', a mysterious charm like that radiated by Shakespeare's

---

1. Prescott, with less knowledge on which to base his conclusions, states that such sacrifices were known, but very rare. Anyone interested should carefully study Markham's arguments (108–9).

girl heroines in his latest plays. Though assured that there is 'peace'
in contemplation of the Sun, the child insists that the House is a
gloomy prison, characterizing its atmosphere in the manner of Pope's
Eloisa to Abelard:

> The place oppresses—frightens me—
> Each day I curse my destiny.
> The faces of all the *Mama Cuna*
> Fill me with hatred and disgust,
> And from the place they make me sit,
> Nothing else is visible.
> Around me there is nothing bright,
> All are weeping and ne'er cease;
> If I could ever have my way,
> No person should remain within.

(II. iii)

Outside, she says, are people moving and laughing, the real world;
inside, gloom, misery, prison. More: she has become aware of a
mysterious creature suffering in the grounds:

> Last night I could not get to sleep,
> I wander'd down a garden walk;
> In the dead silence of the night
> I heard one mourn. A bitter cry,
> As one who sought and pray'd for death.
> On every side I look'd about,
> My hair almost on end with fright,
> Trembling, I cried, 'Who canst thou be?'
> Then the voice murmur'd these sad words:
> 'O Sun, release me from this place!'
> And this amidst such sighs and groans!
> I search'd about, but nothing found—
> The grass was rustling in the wind.
> I join'd my tears to that sad sound,
> My heart was torn with trembling fear.
> When now the recollection comes,
> I'm fill'd with sorrow and with dread.
> You know now why I hate this place.

(II. iii)

She has, it is true, a precise reason for her hatred, but even so it is clear that these convents were in part, or could at least on occasion be considered, places of gloom and suffering. We must beware of any temptation to suggest a later interpolation satirizing the new, Christian, religion and its monasteries and convents: in conception the play, whatever its date, reads as an Inca record from start to finish. Mama Ccacca, the Mother in charge of Yma Sumac, dressed in grey and black, is drawn as a cold and cruel woman, telling Pitu Salla that Yma Sumac, being an orphan, should be thankful for any refuge:

> Tell her plainly, very plainly,
> That these walls offer her a home,
> Suited for outcasts such as she,
> And here no light is seen.
>
> (II. iii)

She stamps out. Pitu Salla, alone, cries:

> Ay, my Sumac! Yma Sumac!
> These walls will be cruel indeed,
> To hide thy surpassing beauty.
> What a serpent! What a puma!
>
> (II. iii)

On those words the scene uncompromisingly closes.

What sort of society, then, do we find? A society where priests are feared and associated with grim sacrifices; where orphan girls are shut from the light of day in a convent ironically sacred to the Sun; where the Inca himself is a cruelly harsh father imprisoning his own daughter (for it is she Yma Sumac had heard groaning in the convent grounds) for the sin of loving an unwelcome suitor; where the expanding imperial system is denounced for its continual drain on the blood of subject nations; where the romantic hero revenges his dismissal by revolution. The picture appears disturbing enough, and far from the idyllic society we might be expecting. We must nevertheless remember the countering effects of pastoral reference and poetry, the animal sympathy of the bird-lyric, the mysterious song-music invading our harsh action with a mystic melody. We must also keep in mind those key-passages concerning war where the old

Inca impresses on Ollantay the obligation of attempting to win over the foe without needless waste of his soldiers' lives and the ritual presentation of the ring of clemency to Ollantay's field-marshal, Urco Huaranca ('clemency becomes a hero chief'). These two speeches, together with the equating of Cusi Coyllur in the rock-song with mercy and grace, flower directly from the world of Garcilasso's account; while the criticism of a wasteful imperialism is itself significant of an enlightened conscience. The world of *Ollantay* is much like the world of our own experience and that of the various dramas, from ancient Greece onwards, that reflect it. The good and evil are balanced. But the amount of good shown is really less important to us than the *nature* of that good which does indeed appear; and our drama is the more convincing in that it does not present, nor show the least sign of wishing to present, a Utopian society.

It must be remembered that all works of history and political philosophy tend to select and emphasize to elaborate a thesis. Drama may not do this; its nature demands variety and conflict. Here our moments of generosity and pathos, the exquisite lyrics, the humour, can only properly exist in contrast to the stern and cruel action. Dramatic conflict generates a field where everything is seen exactly as it is, only more intensely so than normally appears. We are accordingly jerked back from Markham, Prescott and Garcilasso to a society sharing most of the evils of Europe; and this may be near the truth. It might be argued, since without such conflicts there could be no drama, since if evils were absent it would be necessary for the dramatist to invent them, that therefore the darker elements here may be considered an artistic device merely; but this will not do. Why have any drama? In a perfect society drama of any quality could scarcely appear; and during the Middle Ages, when the culture of Christendom at least aspired to an all but complete intellectual harmony, drama as such was necessarily silent. Dante is logically the typifying poet of a period that had no room for an Aeschylus or a Shakespeare, their place being taken and the stature of all such dwarfed, by the central drama of the Mass. Drama blooms from the growing pains of a creative society aiming to transmute its own particular evil through its own peculiar and home-made ritual. This is precisely what we find in *Ollantay*. And what is the creative direction shown? Exactly what Cieza de Leon and Garcilasso have asserted it to be. Garcilasso's account may be overdrawn; but its mythical element is not therefore irrelevant, since at the very lowest it shows the kind of halo that the Inca tradition loved to place on its heroes; a halo not of great conquest so much as of an almost excessive altruism and clemency.

With a strong dramatic realism and a subtle handling of fine distinctions *Ollantay* now proceeds to drive home this very statement, powerfully witnessing the will not merely towards justice, which remains an earth-bound and political concept, but towards an amazing clemency. Its conclusion accordingly draws near to the divine unreason of Jesus' parables; to Portia's 'Mercy' speech in *The Merchant of Venice*; and Byron's Sonnet to the Prince Regent *On The Repeal of Lord Edward Fitzgerald's Forfeiture* (p. 180 below).

IV

Pachacuti is dead, and Tupac Yupanqui reigns:

> All Cuzco has elected him,
> For the late king chose him,
> Giving him the royal fringe;
> We could elect no other. (III. i)

Again, observe the emphasis on a popular election; even though following the old sovereign's will, it remains significant. Markham observes, and the text of *Ollantay* further asserts, that Pachacuti's eldest son was, with his own approval, passed over in favour of his younger brother.[1] The new, and young, sovereign is to be characterized by generosity, as a contrast to his stern father. Markham writes (381, note):

The Inca Pachacuti does not appear to advantage in the drama. But he was the greatest man of his dynasty, indeed the greatest

---

1. According to Piqui Chaqui in our text (III. i; Markham, 381) Tupac Yupanqui was the youngest of a number of sons. Markham simply notes that the eldest, Amaru Tupac, 'was passed over by his father with his own consent, and was ever faithful to his younger brother' (Markham, 381, note).

that the red race has produced. He was a hero in his youth, a most able administrator in mature age. As a very old man some needless cruelties are reported of him which annoyed his son.

No doubt these cruelties form the basis of our present portraiture. Pachacuti exists in the play mainly in order that his tyrannic actions may be reversed by his son.

The new Inca appears as King, giving his 'benison' to all:

> The realm, rejoicing, hails me king;
> From deep recesses of my heart
> I swear to seek the good of all.

(III. ii)

The High Priest continues with description of the national sacrifices, in a speech recalling the conclusion to *Cymbeline*:

> Today the smoke of many beasts
> Ascends on high towards the Sun;
> The Deity with joy accepts
> The sacrifice of prayer and praise.

(III. ii)

The beasts are llamas; but there was also a mysterious eagle—the text at this point is not very clear—which when opened was found to possess no entrails, and considered therefore as an omen, the superstition recalling the auguries of Greece and Rome, and Shakespeare's *Julius Caesar*:

> Plucking the entrails of an offering forth
> They could not find a heart within the beast.

(II. ii. 39)

The Priest equates the eagle with the Anti-suyu, and prophesies that they will renew their allegiance to the Inca.

Rumi-ñaui, remembering his defeat and the hideous massacre in the mountains, determines to make a new attempt to wipe off his disgrace and reinstate himself in trust and honour. His commission granted, he plans to succeed this time by cunning. He visits Ollantay (III. iii), wounded and besmeared with blood. Ollantay receives his old enemy chivalrously, embracing him and promising hospitality (the incident reminds us of the meeting of Coriolanus and Aufidius in Shakespeare). We have a noble magnanimity underlined for us, the more impressive for the dastardly plot that is in hand. Rumi-ñaui pretends that the new Inca has risen 'against the universal wish' on a 'wave of blood', and asserts that he himself has been wounded in the course of a wholesale massacre. Again, we note that such tyrannies are at least envisaged by our dramatist, even though in this instance the story is false. Ollantay welcomes his visitor, referring to the coming festival, and receives from Rumi-ñaui an answer loaded with dramatic irony:

> Those three days of festival
> To me will be a time of joy . . .
>
> (III. iii)

When everyone inside the fortress is relaxed by heavy feasting and drinking, Rumi-ñaui, like the Greeks in the wooden horse, lets in his waiting army. There is a general massacre, though Ollantay and his commanders are captured.

Now starts our long final and resolving movement. Yma Sumac implores Pitu Salla to reveal the mystery of the convent grounds:

> Within these hard and cruel bounds
> Does someone suffer for my sins?
> My sweet companion, do not hide
> From me, who 'tis that mourns and weeps
> Somewhere within the garden walls.
>
> (III. iv)

They meet in the garden by night. Yma Sumac is tense with a nameless expectance:

> A thousand strange presentiments
> Crowd on me now, I scarce know what—
> Perhaps I shall see that mournful one
> Whose fate already breaks my heart.
>
> (III. v)

Yma Sumac is depicted as preeminent in (i) beauty and (ii) sympathy. Pitu Salla discovers to her a stone door behind some bushes and within we see the prisoner, a woman with a snake twined about

her. 'Behold,' says the girl, 'the princess for whom you seek.' Yma
Sumac thinks it a 'corpse' in 'a dungeon for the dead', and faints, but
Pitu Salla assists her 'lovely flower' to recover and, in phrases
recalling the amazing discoveries in Shakespeare's last plays, assures
her that it is not a corpse but the living, though unhappy, princess.
Cusi Coyllur is given food and, after the 'long and dismal years', is
refreshed by sight of this 'new and lovely face'. Yma Sumac is
distraught with sympathy:

> O my princess, my sister dear,
> Sweet bird, with bosom of pure gold,
> What crime can they accuse thee of
> That they can make thee suffer thus?
> What cruel fate has placed thee here
> With death on watch in serpent's form?
>
> (III. v)

There seems to have been a puma too in the prison (p. 173 below).

In contrast to the cruelty, notice the delicate comparison of Yma
Sumac to a 'flower' and Cusi Coyllur, in our recent speech, to a
'sweet bird'. Though normal enough, yet there is in them, and in
other such, a sweetness recalling both the 'tuyallay' harvest-song here
and the lovely phrase 'the bird is dead' spoken of Imogen by one of
the royal boys in *Cymbeline* (IV. ii. 197). There the mountain-setting
somehow lends poignancy to the phrase, as here too the mountains,
perhaps through their height, perhaps by rocky contrast, give the
bird-image a peculiar precision. Certainly the sweet feminine
persons—Cusi Coyllur was in the Rock-song a symbol of 'grace'
and 'mercy'—are contrasted with all that is rock-like and cruel.

Cusi Coyllur tells her sorrowful story of love and cruel punishment within a stony dungeon, culminating in this sudden promise
of liberation, this irruption of innocence and youth as against harsh
injustice:

> But who art thou, my dear, my love,
> So young, so fresh, so pitiful?
>
> (III. v)

The recognition that follows reads as a rescript—or if we decide to follow Markham's dating, prescript—of Pericles' reunion with Marina:

Yma Sumac: I too, like thee, am full of grief,
For long I've wished to see and love
My poor forlorn and sad princess.
No father, no mother are mine,
And there are none to care for me.

Cusi Coyllur: What age art thou?

Yma Sumac: I ought to number many years,
For I detest this dreadful house,
And as it is a dreary place,
The time in it seems very long.

Pitu Salla: She ought to number just ten years
According to the account I've kept.

Cusi Coyllur: And what is thy name?

Yma Sumac: They call me Yma Sumac now,
But to give it me is a mistake.

Cusi Coyllur: O my daughter! O my lost love,
Come to thy mother's yearning heart.
Thou art all my happiness,
My daughter, come, O come to me;
This joy quite inundates my soul,
It is the name I gave to thee.

(III. v)

For 'what age art thou?' compare the reunion of Viola and Sebastian at *Twelfth Night*, v. i. 236–68; but the closest analogy is clearly *Pericles*, v. i. There is the same play on the girl's name to bring recognition; and the same overwhelming joy. Compare 'This joy quite inundates my soul' with

> Give me a gash, put me to present pain,
> Lest this great sea of joys rushing upon me
> O'erbear the shores of my mortality,
> And drown me with their sweetness.
>
> (*Pericles*, v. i. 193)

Of the original Quichua I cannot speak; Markham's version is poetically incommensurable with Shakespeare; but the feeling behind the treatment, and for the most part the treatment itself, is of the same *genre*. So Yma Sumac and Pitu Salla go for help.

Meanwhile we return to state affairs. The scene that follows is truly great. The Inca in full regalia hears from Uillac Uma, the High Priest, that the rebels are defeated and, he thinks, everyone slain. The Inca had hoped that Ollantay's life would be spared; he now appears a little uneasy, but, quite unnecessarily one would think, reminds us all of his responsible position and the compulsions of law and order:

> The Sun, my Father, is my shield,
> I am my father's chosen child.
> We must subdue the rebel host,
> For that I am appointed here.
>
> (III. vi)

The little speech delicately witnesses a remarkable soft-heartedness and forms a precise introduction to the complex dramatic situation to follow. A runner enters with a quipu and a full account. The quipu is read by the priest:

> This knot, coloured burnt *ahuarancu*,
> Tells us that Tampu too is burnt;
> This triple knot to which is hung
> Another which is quintuple,
> In all of quintuples are three,
> Denotes that Anti-suyu's thine,
> Its ruler prisoner of war.
>
> (III. vi)

'And thou', says the Inca to the messenger, 'where wert thou?' He is speaking curtly, suspiciously:

> The Chasqui: Sole King and Lord! Child of the Sun!
> I am the first to bring the news,
> That thou may'st trample on the foe,
> And in thine anger drink their blood.
> Tupac Yupanqui: Did I not reiterate commands
> To spare—and not to shed their blood?
> Not anger, but pity, is my rule.
>
> (III. vi)

In our old accounts we are pointed both to (i) the Incas' habit of treading ritualistically on captives and spoils and (ii) their clemency. Here, as throughout our drama, we see how both are true; that is, the insistence on clemency was not an overruling custom but a continual ideal countering the normal state of human affairs, in all their ruggedness and cruelty. It was a tendency, shall we say, almost a compulsion, towards an enlightenment not as yet attainable by warfaring mankind. Of this tendency our new Inca is shown as a noble exponent.

There follows a series of rapid and extremely complex developments. The messenger answers that no blood has actually been shed, that all were taken off-guard, saying how 'arrows came on them like rain', and most died 'in their sleep, without pain', knowing nothing of the disaster. He thus recognizes the value of avoiding suffering but returns to boasting of how the Antis are slain by thousands and the leaders captive. It appears that the Inca's command 'to spare' (if Markham's translation is exact) has been misunderstood; the letter obeyed but not the spirit. Bloodshed has been avoided by the use of arrows.

Clearly the Inca cannot exactly be pleased. He answers noncommittally, with what may be a touch of sarcasm in reference to the treachery:

> As witness of what has occurred
> On Vilcamayu's storied banks
> No doubt thou hast told me the truth.
> It was a well designed attack.
>
> (III. vi)

Officially he must approve, since we cannot suppose that avoidance of slaughter was the primary aim of Inca warfare. The messenger is probably surprised by his coldness and thinks him ungrateful. The Inca shows no signs of triumph.

The treacherous but victorious Rumi-ñaui enters, kneels, and proud of his success asks that he be reinstated in honour and trust. The Inca formally congratulates him in a short speech and Rumi-ñaui, with remembrance in the last line of his former defeat, boasts:

Our enemies perished in crowds,
Their chiefs were captur'd and bound,
Overwhelm'd by my terrible force,
Like a rock detach'd from the heights.

(III. vi)

The Inca asks, pointedly, in one line: 'Was much blood shed in the assault?' and Rumi-ñaui answers:

No, Lord, not a drop has been shed,
To thine orders I strictly adher'd,
Those Antis were strangled in sleep . . .

(III. vi)

This is not what the messenger told us, but we may let that pass. Is Rumi-ñaui a blockhead, who only understands the words, but not the meaning, of the Inca's commands? Or does he speak—in view of what follows, the more likely, and certainly more dramatic, reading—with a triumphant smile, as though he, bent on revenge, has tricked the Inca? Almost certainly the latter. The young Inca, I think, pauses. Again he is non-committal and asks simply 'Where are the rebels?' Eagerly Rumi-ñaui answers:

They are waiting with agonis'd fear,
For their fate, to perish by cords.
The people are sending up cries,
Demanding their deaths without fail.
Their women are now in their midst,
The children raise hideous cries;
It is well that thine order should pass
To finish their traitorous lives.

(III. vi)

The Inca seems convinced. 'It must be so, without any doubt,' he says: all must perish that Cuzco may recover her 'peace'. Rumi-ñaui, no doubt, registers delight. The 'traitors' are brought in. The Inca demands of Hanco Huayllu why he has allied himself with Ollantay. But Ollantay takes on himself to answer, simply:

O father, we have nought to say,
Our crimes are overwhelming us.

(III. vi)

He admits his *hubris*; he makes no defence; he says nothing of the old Inca's harshness and ingratitude; and for this very reason he is, at last, as never before—for he is *not* a simple romantic hero—guiltless.

The tension is already great, but it grows greater. Instead of pronouncing doom, the young Inca, rather like Duke Vincentio in *Measure for Measure*, withholds judgement, asking for the voice of another:

Tupac Yupanqui: Pronounce their sentence, great High Priest.
Uillac Uma: The light that fills me from the Sun
                Brings mercy and pardon to my heart.
(III. vi)

This complication, our first direct suggestion of mercy, is sudden and probably unexpected. Now the Inca speaks to, and probably looks pointedly at, Rumi-ñaui, behaving rather like Portia in *The Merchant of Venice*:

Tupac Yupanqui: Now thy sentence, Rumi-ñaui.
Rumi-ñaui: For crimes enormous such as these
                Death should ever be the doom;
                It is the only way, O King!
                To warn all others from such guilt.
                To stout *tocarpus* they should be
                Secur'd and bound with toughest rope,
                Then should the warriors freely shoot
                Their arrows until death is caus'd.
(III. vi)

Rumi-ñaui has all natural justice on his side. He also has in him a burning desire for revenge. At this tense moment we are reminded of the presence of Ollantay's clownish servant Piqui Chaqui, who takes on himself to lament the proposed execution of the Antis, while cunningly making a most pointed reference which no one but he, who as a semi-comic figure need lay no claim to courage (p. 151 above), could have made: 'What pouring out of blood is here!' Piqui Chaqui is reminding the Inca of his original command. Rumi-ñaui shouts:

Silence, rash man, nor dare to speak.   (III. vi)

We are reminded of Falstaff's interruption of a war council and
Prince Hal's rebuff in *1 Henry IV* (v. i. 28–9); and Enobarbus'
similar interruption and rebuff on a like occasion in *Antony and
Cleopatra* (ii. ii. 107–16).

Sounds of lamentation are heard outside. Rumi-ñaui, probably
in soliloquy, punning on his own name (rumi = stone) and
remembering his first defeat, mutters:

> Having been roll'd just like a stone,
> My heart has now become a stone.
>
> (III. vi)

The old bitterness burns in him still and inspires his advice. He is
sinning against our play's primary virtue: magnanimity. The Inca
commands that the traitors be led to their death and Rumi-ñaui, like
Shakespeare's Gratiano only in this instance to his own undoing
since he is piling retribution on himself, cries exultantly, unashamed
in his triumph:

> Take these three men without delay
> To the dreaded execution stakes;
> Secure them with unyielding ropes,
> And hurl them from the lofty rocks.
>
> (III. vi)

He is *enjoying* his victim's suffering. We are at this moment seriously
repelled by him and all, including the justice, for which he stands.
The Inca's reaction has remained in doubt, but our own has begun
to demand mercy. At this climax, like Richard II when he throws
down his warder, and still more like Duke Vincentio in *Measure for
Measure*, when after seeming adamant he reverses his earlier decision
and forgives Angelo, the Inca cries: 'Stop! Cast off their bonds.'
They are unbound. They approach, and kneel. In a kindly voice the
Inca tells Ollantay to rise and come to him. Then, in a graver tone:

> Now thou hast seen death very near,
> You that have shown ingratitude,
> Learn how mercy flows from my heart.
>
> (III. vi)

The Inca's withholding of his decision is not merely a stage trick to keep the audience guessing, nor merely a means of making Rumi-ñaui an example. It is in addition a way of ritualistically *satisfying justice*, acting the condemnation, before justice is surpassed in clemency.

Tupac Yupanqui now proceeds to raise Ollantay 'higher than before'. Instead of being merely chief of the Anti-suyu he is appointed the Inca's first general, given the plume and arrows of command. Markham's note (397), in manner typical of Edwardian literary criticism, reads:

> Rather a staggerer for Rumi-ñaui! Perhaps, too, the change is too sudden, and infringes the probabilities. Tupac Yupanqui may have thought that his father had been unjust and that there were excuses. It is known that the young Inca was indignant at some other cruelties of his father. As a magnanimous warrior he may have despised the treacherous methods of Rumi-ñaui. He may have valued Ollantay's known valour and ability, and have been loth to lose his services. All these considerations may have influenced him more or less. The rebels were the best men he had.

Such evidence from outside the drama, though sometimes interesting and not totally irrelevant, is yet likely to be misleading and only really needed when all else fails. We do not need it here. The Inca has not himself shown any 'change' according to my interpretation; and if such an interpretation was not in Markham's mind, so much the better, since his translation is cleared of special pleading. True, the Inca's behaviour is quixotic; but is not that precisely what we are led to expect by the old historians? Dramatically, we are meant to receive a shock, an excitement, a happy sense of reversal, as in the sequence of forgivenesses by the king in *Cymbeline*; or again, as at the conclusion of *Measure for Measure*. The forgiveness in *Ollantay* is more clearly prepared for than in either of those plays; for it is precisely this conclusion that has been demanded all along. The whole play's impact is behind it. We have been reminded before (p. 153) that 'clemency becomes a hero chief'; in spite of Ollantay's *hubris*, the rights and wrongs of the original conflict were highly disputable; much of Ollantay's story, and especially the magnanimity and open-heartedness of his reception of his old enemy, charmed our sympathies; Rumi-ñaui has become thoroughly ugly, first in his treachery in betrayal of Ollantay's hospitality and second in his vengeful enjoyment of his own triumph. The 'staggerer' for Rumi-ñaui is thus quite in order, for he has in every way offended—this is his dramatic office and that is why he is called Rumi-ñaui, 'Stone-eye'—against our supreme value: magnanimity. Beside that one virtue, the finest flower of Inca idealism, Rumi-ñaui's 'justice' is malodorous. This *dénouement* may be staggering, but it is a staggering *relief*; it is what the audience have been subtly trained to want. Throughout our stern action has been countered by gleams of a sweeter—and once, in the rock-music, a mysterious—world; our sympathies have been wrung by pathos; and mercy from the seat of power is now felt to be a resolver of human interactions and antagonisms, in all their complexity and incertitude. Ollantay has put in no word whatsoever for himself; that is his final justification. I do not know a drama, or any other work of literature, more skilfully designed than this to drive home, and in strict relation moreover to politics and the throne, the truth behind the parables of the New Testament.

Like those parables the action now grows definitely paradoxical. The Inca cannot stop. He behaves like the magnanimous princes of Garcilasso de la Vega, the early historian who did so much to establish the Incas' reputation for such behaviour. The 'mighty Pontiff of the Sun' is told to robe Ollantay in the regal dress. He does so, saying:

> Ollantay, learn to recognise
> Tupac Yupanqui's generous mind;
> From this day forth be thou his friend,
> And bless his magnanimity.

> (III. vi)

The Priest next gives Ollantay the sacred ring, called a 'potent charm', like the ring of clemency handed earlier by the High Priest's relative to Ollantay's general; and, as from the King, the mace. Ollantay, by now almost in tears, protests that he is 'tenfold the great Inca's slave', belonging to him 'body and soul'. We find dramatized a remarkable exhibition of clemency, breaking down the barriers of the soul and establishing a union of lord and servant, in exact accord with Byron's *Fitzgerald* Sonnet (p. 180 below) and not unlike the action of the Christian Cross on a convert. Urco Huaranca, the Mountain Chief, is next given the arrow and plume of generalship over the mountain tribe and similarly protests his utter slavery from now on. As for Rumi-ñaui, he puts in one weak couplet only, asking if there are to be two generals, and is told that Urco is to rule the Antis, and Ollantay to preside at Cuzco, as the Inca's viceroy; he is even given the royal fringe (*llautu*) to wear. Finally, as a neat way of leading up to our concluding scene, he is urged to settle down and take a wife; but he answers that his one love is gone for ever. The populace outside are told of the new viceroy, but their sounds of acclamation are suddenly interrupted; someone is pleading for entrance, the guards shouting 'Go back!' Through the raucous noises comes a little girl's voice, crying for the King and threatening to die rather than to give way; a typical effect, like that of the rock-song following Ollantay's fury; and Tupac Yupanqui, hearing who it is, asks her to enter. The ten years old little girl comes onto the scene of royal ritual and warrior chieftains; and from now on she dominates.

Yma Sumac enters in tears and, seeing two royal figures, asks which is the King. When she hears, her words pour out:

> O my King! be thou my father,
> Snatch from evil thy poor servant,
> Extend thy royal hand to me.
> O merciful child of the Sun,
> My mother is dying at this hour
> In a foul and loathsome cave . . .
>
> (III. vi)

Hearing of her mother's plight the Inca is deeply moved by such 'inhumanity', and gives the 'case' to Ollantay. The little girl looks at him. 'For you,' she says, 'I know not who you are'—a lovely piece of half-humorous dramatic irony—and then turns again to the Inca, Tupac Yupanqui murmuring:

> In midst of reconciliations
> This young maid assaults my heart.
>
> (III. vi)

The second line again suggests insistently the effect of Marina on her father in Shakespeare's *Pericles* (v. i).

The final scene, by the dungeon, is given throughout an atmosphere of wonder. Tupac Yupanqui is surprised at being taken to the House of the Virgins, and Mama Ccacca asks whether his sudden appearance is 'a dream or reality'. Cusi Coyllur is discovered, unconscious, chained, with the snake and now a puma too. Markham (404, note) comments: 'The puma would not have hurt his fellow-prisoner. Unpleasant animals were occasionally put into the prisons of criminals. The Incas kept pumas as pets.' Even so, it was a poor custom; especially the snake. The Inca is shocked, asking what 'wretch' is responsible, and is told by Mama Ccacca that it was his own father, the late Inca, who commanded this 'punishment for lawless love' (III. vii). The excuse does not prevent the Inca's wrath: 'Be gone! be gone!' he cries, 'harder than rock' (ccacca = rock), a phrase recalling Rumi-ñaui's heart turned to stone (p. 169 above). He commands them to 'Break down that door of carved stone' and adds: 'The child has brought it all to light' (III. vii). The agent of victory by which mercy triumphs over stony cruelty is a little child, even younger than those similar heroines of Shakespeare, and playing a more active and decisive role than they. Youth is here emphatic. The Inca Tupac Yupanqui, though the youngest of Pachacuti's sons, had been deliberately chosen by his father, presumably in view of outstanding merit, for the succession (p. 160 above, note). As in Shakespeare's last plays, we feel the new generation, here the young Inca and the little girl, redeeming the errors and sins of the old.

Cusi Coyllur recognizes her daughter but is dazed by the others. Yma Sumac tells her that it is the new king and urges her to 'awake from thy trance'. Tupac Yupanqui is dazed too, grieved by this sight of deathly gloom and anguish, till the little girl, who is running the whole show, calls him to order with:

> Father! Inca! Clement Prince!
> Have those cruel bonds remov'd.
>
> (III. vii)

That first line sums the meaning of our play. The sufferer's name, she tells them, is Cusi Coyllur (= Joyful Star), adding wistfully 'but it seems a mistake'. Ollantay recognizes his long-lost wife, while Tupac Yupanqui reinforces our sense of an almost mystic state, suggested already by 'dream' and 'trance', by saying, 'It all appears a dream to me.' Even so Shakespeare's Pericles too, when confronted by Marina, thinks himself dreaming (*Pericles*, v. i. 163). Tupac Yupanqui embraces the Star, his sister. The drama of recognition and reunion concludes, formally, with music, though for the music of Shakespeare's final plays our best comparison is the mysterious music (p. 150) coming from the rocks above Cuzco.

Well, it may be said, there is nothing strange in all this; the happy ending is no new thing. But this is no more a normal 'happy ending' than the similar conclusions to *Pericles* and *The Winter's Tale*. Resemblances abound. Cusi Coyllur is discovered in a convent, just as Aemilia in *The Comedy of Errors* and Thaisa in *Pericles* are respectively discovered by their husbands in a convent and a temple; though in Shakespeare the lost wife is herself the Abbess or Priestess. In Shakespeare, despite the similarities in pattern, there is, as I have argued at length in *The Crown of Life*, a new depth in the last plays not found in the early comedies; for they contain, and as it were transmute, the whole burden of tragedy. The reunions and resurrections are soaked in tragic feeling. This is precisely what we find in *Ollantay*: there is no facile happy ending whatsoever; just the reverse. In *The Winter's Tale* it is noted expressly that Hermione looks much older; and throughout the statue scene Leontes' own sin-born suffering is extreme. These emphases are even stronger in *Ollantay*:

Tupac Yupanqui: Thy face is worn, thy beauty gone,
Thy looks as one risen from death.

(III. vii)

She was first (III. v) discovered in a sort of tomb, approached with torches by night, as in *Romeo and Juliet*, and Yma Sumac thought her a 'corpse' in 'a dungeon for the dead' (III. v). Both there and in our present scene she is shown as half-dead; she faints and has to be lifted up. The child Yma Sumac, who controls the scene, tells her mother to 'awake from thy trance' (III. vii). The words 'one risen from death' and 'trance' are loaded with weighty suggestion. They recall the revivals in *Pericles* and *The Winter's Tale*. There there was a certainty of death that turned out to be false; here there is less discrepancy, the blend of tragedy and reunion is less jarring. Cusi Coyllur has suffered agonies and is returned half-dead from a tomb-like prison. Her husband, like Leontes, suffers as he greets her:

> Cusi Coyllur, I had lost thee,
> Thou wast quite hidden from my sight,
> But thou art brought again to life—
> Thy father should have killed us both.
> My whole heart is torn with sorrow.
> Star of Joy, where is now thy joy?
> Where now thy beauty as a star?
> Art thou under thy father's curse?
>
> (III. vii)

There is little of the happy ending in that. She answers in a similar, though slightly more hopeful, vein:

> Ollantay, for ten dreary years
> That dungeon has kept us apart;
> But now, united for new life,
> Some happiness may yet be ours.
>
> (III. vii)

'New life': the phrase sounds, faintly, yet insistently; for 'Yupanqui', she says, 'makes joy succeed grief'; notice that the credit for it all is given to the Inca. Pericles, after his years of penitential dress, calls for new clothes; and here the priest asks for new robes for the princess, and when she is royally dressed the Inca hands her to Ollantay, calling her in a phrase reminiscent of Shakespeare's later heroines and perhaps with a reference to the purgatory of her suffering, 'the pure essence of Coyllur'.

Ollantay addresses the Inca:

> Thou art our protector, great King,
> Thy noble hands disperse our grief;
> Thou art our faith and only hope—
> Thou workest by virtue's force.   (III. vii)

Yupanqui promises that joy 'new born' will replace sorrow. The diverging strands and interests of the plot all meet, are knotted, under the control and blessing of the Inca.

V

There is no work of my reading which so closely resembles that of Shakespeare's final period. Though no doubt falling short of these in language, it might well be said to surpass them in clarity of organization. The mysterious beauty of the close is prepared for, it flowers from its soil without strain or surprise. The stage directions were, it seems, composed by Dr. Valdez who transcribed the spoken text 'from the mouths of Indians' (Markham, 148). They are nevertheless so obviously organic to the drama that they may be accepted as part of it. From the Temple of the Sun in the first setting onwards, the Sun, in Inca theology twin deity to Viracocha, balancing nature and spirit, dominates. For the rest, the drama shows two main sets of impressions. First there are those pastoral and bird-like: the garden settings, the 'gardens of the Sun' (I. i), the flowers (I. i), the mysterious dead flower that pours forth water (I. i); the Colcampata with view of its gardens (I. ii), the golden household gods in the shape of maize-cobs and llamas (I. ii), the *tuyallay* harvest-song (I. ii), the elegiac song of 'two loving birds' (I. ii); the garden of the House of the Virgins of the Sun with 'chilca shrubs and mulli trees' and 'panicles of red berries' (II. iii), the other 'secluded' part of the garden with 'a thicket of mulli and chilca' and 'flowers' (III. v). In contrast we have things rocky, hard and gigantic: the Sacsahuaman Hill surmounted by its fortress (I. i), the 'snowy peak of Vilcañota' seen from the Colcampata (I. ii), the 'rocky height above Cuzco' whence Ollantay denounces the city that has rejected him (I. iv), the fortress palace of Ollantay-Tampu with its 'seven immense stone slabs' and horizontal 'monolith' (II. i); the 'wild place in the mountains' (II. ii) where Rumi-ñaui laments his army's slaughter, the 'great terrace entrance to Ollantay-tampu' with a 'long masonry wall', descending terraces and a 'view of valley and mountains' (III. iii). These impressions, which build what we call the play's 'atmosphere', are natural; they are forced by the play's nature and the thought-forms of the land. The softer sort may be precisely used to contribute meaning, as when Yma Sumac and Cusi Coyllur are compared to birds or to other natural excellences, clearly in extension of our *tuyallay* harvest-song and the elegiac song on lover-birds, both of which relate directly to the plot. Yma Sumac's

> Sweet bird, with bosom of pure gold,
> What crime can they accuse thee of. . . ?   (III. v)

are characteristic of a prevailing sweetness. It is the same with the rocky impressionism: sometimes it is a majestic framework, and no more: sometimes, as the rocky-settings for Ollantay's denunciation, the monoliths of the rebels' headquarters and the victory won by hurling rocks down on the attackers, it is something more than that. In Rumi-ñaui's punning on his name (rumi = stone) and his assertion that his heart is turned to stone (III. vi), and in the other unsympathetic person Mama Ccacca aptly called a rock (ccacca = rock), the human reference is explicit. We have an imaginative opposition of gentle emotions, whose images are corn, flowers and birds, against hardened hearts, whose image is rock or stone. There is the stone slab of Cusi Coyllur's prison, removed by the Inca, exponent of the softer virtues: 'Break down that door of carved stone.' Such is the dramatic conflict imprinted on the poetry, drawn, as such equivalents must be, from the poet's own geographic setting. The Inca civilization grew up in a fertile valley surrounded by vast mountains; and to this setting our imaginative structure conforms. There were also numerous relics of a megalithic culture, vast fortresses made of slabs seemingly impossible to move, and of these our play makes fine use. They must have acted on the people of the valley as symbols of gigantic power, at once inspiring and fearsome. The play is finely organic; more so perhaps than the equivalents in Shakespeare, since, this opposition understood, we see that the end is no sudden reversal; rather is it implicit already to the subtler understanding, heralded by many an earlier hint, especially by the remarkable dramatic conception of the mysterious song-music chanting in terms of 'grace' and 'mercy' the praise of our heroine, which, sounding even from the rocks themselves, interrupts our most intense moment of human bitterness.

Ollantay is an inclusive work. It has the communal or national interest of *Cymbeline*; both conclude with a royal clemency, though the Inca is more important, as King, than is Cymbeline; he more nearly recalls the over-ruling wisdom and benevolence of Henry in *Henry VIII*. Ollantay's retirement to his mountain stronghold to muster forces against the Inca is balanced by Belarius' retreat with the royal boys to the Welsh mountains in *Cymbeline*; both men have reason to regard their meritorious generalship as ill-requited by their respective sovereigns. But *Ollantay* also includes the mysterious reunions of *Pericles* and *The Winter's Tale*, with their sense of purgatorial suffering, of error and recognition, their balance of age and youth. Though the dark powers are not forgotten the drama uses them to give point, through the Inca and the little girl, to an excellence equal to or surpassing the highest reaches of our own Renaissance wit. In Shakespeare's work there is sometimes a certain discrepancy between his dramatic form and his informing genius; as in *The Merchant of Venice*, where the depth of meaning behind the trial scene and the height of Christian phrasing in Portia's speech are both incompatible with the lighter, romantic action. It has been argued by D. G. James that Shakespeare in his last plays had not a myth or plot adequate to his conception; especially that he tried to infuse into royal images more spiritual content than they could bear; as though the social and religious thought-forms he was forced to use were lagging behind his inspiration. Whether this be so or not, we need not pause to argue; but in so far as one does feel any such dissatisfaction, it is worth observing that the criticism cannot apply to *Ollantay*. In Shakespeare the final revelations and valuations come as surprises; in *Ollantay* they are natural, almost inevitable. Whatever spiritual stature the Inca is given by the poet he wins not by the poet's artistry but by his own dramatic behaviour; while the nobly spiritualized action is throughout coherent, felt in full relation to human affairs, and in close historic regard. The great Pachacuti did in fact institute new and strict laws to preserve the royal family from marriage with subjects, however eminent (Markham, 336); and he was tyrannic in his old age, and to be contrasted, as he is in our drama, with the more kindly young prince, his son, who disapproved of his cruelties (see pp. 160-1 above) and succeeded him on the throne. For the name 'Ollantay' in relation to the Anta people, there is, though details are lacking, historical evidence (Markham, 335; 148, note). The drama's valuations are, as we have seen, more

Inca than European. Even if the play's Shakespearian affinities were in part derived from a knowledge of Shakespeare in some seventeenth or eighteenth century writer, we should still be faced by the remarkable aptitude of the grafting. One could almost define the civilization of the Incas as one wherein the furthest reach of the Shakespearian imagination is found to be no lonely and fantastic poetic adventure, but rather flowers organically and without strain as a natural off-shoot of the nation's life.

The play is striking for its similarities to other dramas of the more esoteric sort. Besides the Shakespearian comparisons, we might place the Hindu drama *Sakuntala* and Coleridge's *Zapolya* (where the hero, like Yma Sumac, finds his lost mother in a cave); while a reference to the Eleusinian mysteries, and Greek drama, is natural. This kinship does something to support Miles Poindexter's conviction (*The Ayar-Incas*, New York 1930) of the Incas' Aryan descent. But a reservation must be made: though *Ollantay* certainly resembles such Asiatic and European drama, and though its strong action holds other reminiscences of Shakespeare, yet its quality remains unique; it is preeminently a creation of its own land, as our notice of its impressionism shows; and of its own religion, too, using constant reference, too obvious to need emphasis, to the Sun. The action is closely pinned to geographical and historical exactitude. It may seem strange that Markham does not use these arguments—especially the play's impressionism—to support his conviction that the play is wholly a Quichua product; it is still stranger that, given the play's authenticity, which on general scientific grounds he asserts to be established beyond doubt, he did not use its dramatic statement as evidence for the benevolence and enlightenment of the Incas. But then such an interpretative study as we have here given to the drama is a product of our own time. The ability to see drama, or any poetry, as imaginative statement is new; and it is interesting to observe how such an interpretative technique may on occasion be of service to the quest of historical fact. In our early authorities the Incas figure as supermen of an almost unbelievable magnanimity; and though we may suppose such accounts to be in part exaggerations, the value of those assertions takes on an added lustre once we realize that this remarkable civilization has left as its one surviving imaginative record what is perhaps the greatest dramatic parable on the subject of clemency in the literatures of the world.

ADDITIONAL NOTE, 1966

I would emphasize that the unique value of *Apu Ollantay* lies in its dramatization of clemency flowing from political power. Portia's 'Mercy' speech in *The Merchant of Venice* strove for an attunement of temporal royalty to inward grace, but it sticks out a little strangely and Shakespeare composed no full-length drama, apart from the psychological *Measure for Measure*, around this centre. Byron came nearer it in his *Sardanapalus*, though only in a tragic drama, showing the ineffectuality of its hero. Our Inca theme is compactly and perfectly stated in Byron's Sonnet addressed to the Prince Regent *On the Repeal of Lord Edward Fitzgerald's Forfeiture*:

> To be the father of the fatherless,
>> To stretch the hand from the throne's height, and raise
>> *His* offspring, who expir'd in other days
> To make thy Sire's sway by a kingdom less—
> *This* is to be a monarch, and repress
>> Envy into unutterable praise.
>> Dismiss thy guard, and trust thee to such traits,
> For who would lift a hand, except to bless?
>
> Were it not easy, Sir, and is't not sweet
>> To make thyself belovéd? and to be
>> Omnipotent by Mercy's means? for thus
> Thy sovereignty would grow but more complete:
>> A despot thou, and yet thy people free,
>> And by the heart, not hand, enslaving us.

It cannot however be too uncompromisingly insisted that to create a convincing dramatic action may be harder, and in such a matter as this of greater value and consequence, than direct poetic statements, however fine. Mastery in dramatic action is a step towards mastery in life. Such a mastery on this greatest of themes, the fusion of power and love, of state and grace, our drama shows.

XIV

THE AVENGING MIND

A lecture recorded at the Present Question Conference in Birmingham in 1947 and published in *Question*, July 1948; I, I.

I would ask you to think of a ball-room and many people dancing. Imagine them, like myself, very moderate dancers. And in
addition, please, think of the rather paradoxical picture of
people trying to dance without a band or perhaps with a band
which they are too deaf to hear; trying to get their rhythm; perhaps
trying to get it from their partners; or perhaps one pair looking at
other pairs, and trying to get their rhythm that way. Their will to
co-operate is excellent. But all act on the same level; they are trying
to get hints from each other, and the study of each other's behaviour.
The result is that the dance does not go right; because there is no
band, no orchestra.

I want you to turn your minds to the thought of this dance
orchestra; and let me talk to you, even at the risk of speaking in an
esoteric manner, about the mysterious poetic rhythm behind our
existence, which dictates, which creates, the drama of our lives.

I am not going to talk in general terms but rather in precise terms;
about precise works of poetry and about religion. Poetry, you must
remember, is born of rhythm. It is rhythm that gives the poet his
thought. He does not necessarily write in poetry merely because he
likes the idea of rhyme or rhythm. He might even prefer to do
without them. Sometimes you may even get a poem where they are
definitely irritating, but the poem may yet be so full of such rich
thoughts that you forgive the poet, knowing that he could not
perhaps do it in any other way; perhaps he had to speak in rhymed
couplets in order to speak at all.

That is the reverse of our usual way of thinking about poetry, but
I would like you to be prepared to see with me some of the meanings

in poetry. I shall not talk about rhythm as such, but rather about these meanings; the deep meanings that are born from rhythm. For some twenty years now I have been very busy at what I have called poetic interpretation, as opposed to poetic criticism, attempting to listen-in to the rhythmic patterns of great literature and discover their latent meanings. I claim that it all has meaning; meaning of a great sort, meaning which it is not always easy for our minds to understand. Hence the danger of a criticism which dominates, and says of a great poet: 'Here is a subject for my own critical approach. I will pronounce judgement on it.' That to my mind is not, once the poem has been ratified by the imagination, the line to take. Let me give an example of the kind of work I have been doing, work which I may claim as basic to what I am to say to you today and which is a legitimate and necessary extension in our time of our literary consciousness, parallel and analogous to the recent extensions of our understanding in physics; for it is a new method of looking afresh at well-known poems of the past, a new seeing of dynamic design and meaning. My example is Coleridge's poem, *Kubla Khan*, hitherto dismissed as a grand succession of rich images with fine music to it, but a meaningless fragment, supposedly unfinished, which the poet only received from a dream. Let us look at it more carefully.

You will, if you look carefully into it, or better still draw picture diagrams of what it says, see a strange river, a meandering river, coming from a strange place, flowing among trees, and sinking to a dark sea. It is not difficult to see that this river flowing through nature is in some sense a symbol of life; the river of life. Above that is Kubla Khan's pleasure-dome, whatever that may be. It is certainly mysterious. 'It was a miracle of rare device', says the poet, 'a sunny pleasure-dome with caves of ice.' I take this dome to be a poetic image or symbol of some higher dimension over-arching our life; not at the other end of the life-stream but above the life-stream; or even interpenetrating it. We may call it transcendent as opposed to nature, and yet not distinct altogether from nature. It lies half-way along the life-stream, dropping its shadow or reflection in the water.

You may say that this is a rash interpretation.[1] There are many

---

1. A more detailed analysis will be found in my study of the 'romantic' poets, *The Starlit Dome*.

reasons why I think that it is the correct one and not least because it makes sense of the end of the poem. The poet himself goes into an ecstasy about this extraordinary dome. He says: If only I could recapture some weird and wonderful music I once heard, 'I would build that dome in air, that sunny dome, those caves of ice!' And more than that, if I did this, he says, everyone would be struck with amazement and cry:

> Beware! Beware!
> His flashing eyes, his floating hair!
> Weave a circle round him thrice,
> And close your eyes with holy dread,
> For he on honey-dew hath fed,
> And drunk the milk of Paradise.

The dome therefore is in some sense a transcendent reality.

So much for Coleridge's *Kubla Khan*. Coleridge himself had not the faintest idea what it was about; he did not think it was any good; and if it had not been for Lord Byron it might never have been published. At the risk of offending the poets in my audience I must urge you never to trust a poet on his own poetry. He may know nothing about it. It was said of Rudyard Kipling (in a recent letter in *The Times*, by Sir Roderick Jones) that he threw aside his *Recessional*, put it into a wastepaper-basket. It was probably the best poem he ever wrote, but he was not going to publish it; perhaps he did not understand it. The poet, we must always remember, does not think thoughts; he makes them; and he may himself be incapable of thinking the thoughts which he has made.

There seems to have been some suggestion of this new dimension —Coleridge's dome—in all great literature. I say 'all' advisedly, but I cannot talk about it all now. Instead, I shall say a word about tragedy and drama; particularly about tragedy, because great tragedy is always facing this 'Present Question' of ours. From the time of the Greeks to our own time tragic drama has posed the deepest problems and tried to resolve them. It is a ritual in which the darkest themes of blood and sin are transmuted, are in a way transcended, in the art-form itself.

Take as an example of Greek tragedy Aeschylus' *Oresteia*, with murder leading to murder, vengeance to vengeance, and no way out of the long chain of blood and hate, till we are led up to that sublime ritual at the end where the old blood-stained theme is brought to the bar of contemporary Athens, the life of Aeschylus' own day; and the creatures of bloodshed in the ritual are stilled and taken to their home beneath the earth, where, mind you, they are to be given their due of respect and worship. The Athenian audience watched the insoluble problem acted out in terms of their own time, in the ritual.

Tragic dramas are concerned with this question of sin and evil, and are always trying to give it a creative pattern and resolution. The problem of justice beats throughout the great works of Greek drama. It may be a question of justice between man and man; or it may be a question of justice between man and God; as in the *Prometheus Bound* or the Book of Job, the great dramatic work of the Bible.

When we come to modern times, in the Elizabethan drama, we again find the old revenge-theme cropping up; in Shakespeare, in Webster, in others. Do not regard it as an old-world concept, an old temptation. What Nietzsche calls in a pregnant phrase 'The Avenging Mind' (*Thus Spake Zarathustra*, 42, 'Of Redemption') is at work in all our thinking and in many of our actions, though we should wish to get rid of it. Drama, by creatively expressing it, is one attempt to get rid of it. *Hamlet* therefore is an archetypal play, where Shakespeare watched his hero trying, sometimes successfully, more often unsuccessfully, to transmute this dark thing through his own dramatic personality.

Today drama is more popular than ever before, and it is especially interesting to observe the amateur dramatic movement; that is, the attempt not only to watch solutions being worked out in great public performances, but to let everybody have a share in doing something about it, to let every little community have its dramatic group to live out the solutions; because that is just what drama is—a living it out.

In the great ages of faith, in the middle ages, there was no great drama. I think you can see that there could not have been. The central drama of the Mass left no room for lesser ritual. The one great and dominating drama of Christ himself, from which the Mass descends, outdistanced and over-shadowed all lesser dramatic ritual. There was accordingly no great drama and the great poet of the period was necessarily a non-dramatic poet, Dante. We should consider this carefully and ask what it means. Before the ages of faith there was great drama; during the ages of faith there was not. At the Renaissance, at the time of the Reformation, there was a split; and drama again came into its own. Was that good or was it bad?

It means that the one great drama had ceased to dominate. Poets and others were thus thrown back on their own resources. They had to work out their own individual ways of transmuting the evil, according to their time and place and according to various theories of their own. It seems that there has been less and less reliance on what might be called a 'vicarious' sacrifice and a more stern attempt to deal with these things by man himself.

And here, I am afraid, I must make some remarks which are a little bold. I suggest that perhaps our traditional Christianity leaves today a want—I will not say for us all, because for the real devotee obviously it does not—but for many of us. I am speaking for those of us whom the Church tradition does not quite satisfy. I suggest that the more creative forces have gone into poetry and art and science; whereas in our Protestant tradition—I speak of Protestantism only, for I know little of the Roman Catholic Church—the Church's teaching has allowed itself to be dominated by negatives.

By these negatives, I mean this. Deep in the Christian tradition, the Christian life, it has been for ages supposed that a sense of sin is the necessary beginning; that the Cross is the one centre; and, as it was thought quite recently but not so much today, though there is still authority in the tradition, that the end is only too likely to be that grand-scale symptom of the 'Avenging Mind', Hell. That will seem an overstatement; it is a matter of emphasis; but I do suggest that those negatives have bulked largely and in a negative fashion. To St. Paul the Cross of Christ was a great positive, not a negative; I am aware of that. It is the way these things are presented and the way these things are received by the average person, that matter. We are today quite used to the word 'repent', and we think we know what it means. If I remember rightly, the New Testament word was the Greek *metanoeite* meaning 'change your mental direction'. 'Change your mental direction' has a positive ring, it opens out great spaces to the imagination, whereas 'repent' suggests a backward-looking, un-creative, stifling sense of one's own personal sin. I am suggesting that we have let that kind of concept, that kind of mental attitude, dominate our religious thinking (cp. pp. 15–21, 228–9).

You will say, and rightly, that the greatest positive of all is presented by the Church in the life of Christ. And here I dare to be even more bold. The life of Christ, though to the true thinking Chris-tian an ever-present reality, must yet be to a great extent a historical reality too, and to many people a historical reality only. There is a danger in making the centre of our teaching a looking back. Think for a moment of the worker in a school, the producer of a play, or the professional psychologist and his patient. What do they try to do? At all costs they try to enlist the co-operation, the impulses of power, in the pupil or the patient. What hope would there be for a creative teaching if the teacher told his pupil: 'There is little good in you. You are helpless. Rely on me.' Or even worse: 'There is little good in me. Rely only on the founder of your school.' Such a backward-looking technique will not awaken a creative response.

What we want is not imitation but re-creation. What would we think of the producer of a play who demands this or that gesture instead of letting the gestures grow? Are we perhaps too dominated by a rigid sense of morality in our Christian teaching? St. Paul himself claimed to have advanced beyond the Law; the Law of the Old Testament, which we may say corresponds roughly to a rigid sense of good and evil as final opposites.

I am aware that in our own difficulties, where practical matters are concerned, we can none of us claim to be beyond the Law. The Church would be right in not claiming to have advanced beyond the Law. But the one vital point I would emphasize is this: our teachers should be consciously aware, and sermon after sermon should assert it, that we are all at present sunk back into the world of the Law and are not living as individuals or communities in what St. Paul called the freedom of the Gospel. We have lost contact with the positives of St. Paul's Epistles.

That is the emphasis I wish to make; and whenever I find those positives expressed in great poetry I may be forgiven for suggesting that they are offering us something which our church tradition lacks.

How true it is that a consciousness of ignorance is necessary in the pupil, only those who have taught really know. Ignorance, yes; a reliance on the teacher; but never, at our peril, impotence.

What then of the doctrine of the Fall? We could complain, perhaps rightly, perhaps wrongly, that our religious tradition bases its wisdom on a great cosmic blunder. That may be a matter of fact and if there was such a blunder, then blunder there was. I do not know; but I am trying to point out why things are so difficult for the Church today. There are other thinkers who do not base their wisdom on a great cosmic blunder. I do not think that Christ himself did. His attitude to children and to nature was very definitely romantic. There would be heroism in battling if there had been such a blunder, if the creative forces, the Divine Purpose, had in some way made a mistake. It would be a truly heroic business to help to put it right; but too often we are told that we ourselves can do little to put it right; that we have to stand aside as Milton's angels stood aside when the Messiah's chariot advanced to battle, and watch the blunder put right for us. Are the instincts, are the powers of the individual, being channelled in this way? I think not. I think too that though we may fully believe the New Testament and its wonderful story, the possibility of one miracle ahead of us has more creative leverage than numberless well-authenticated miracles of the past. Christ himself looked ahead. St. Paul looked ahead. Too often we seem to look back. The One Revelation has been offered, the One Life lived.

Let me now speak of the other tradition, the tradition of Renaissance literature. How does it diverge? We are thinking primarily of drama. In the middle ages there were the Mass, the Mysteries, and the Moralities. Then in the age of Shakespeare the ordinary love affair became a dominating dramatic theme, and we have the romantic drama of Shakespeare, the novels of a later generation, and so on to the novels, plays and films of today. Drama becomes secular and humanistic.

I shall not speak here of that more romantic literature, but I would like to suggest a point or two about the poetic attempt to deal with sin and evil. I see a single tradition, running from Marlowe's

Doctor Faustus to works of our own day. Doctor Faustus, a typical Renaissance figure, challenges the Church, sells his soul to the Devil, and goes to Hell. The opposition is stark and rigid, though in later works the dark hero gradually seems to gain repute, as do Shakespeare's Macbeth, Milton's Satan, Byron's Manfred and Cain, Goethe's Faust, Shelley's Prometheus and a wide range of Satanic persons later on. Relevant figures occur in Wordsworth's *The Borderers*, Coleridge's *Remorse*, Shelley's *The Cenci*, Emily Brontë's *Wuthering Heights*, Melville's *Moby Dick*; in the plays of Ibsen and the novels of Dostoievsky and John Cowper Powys.

What is such literature about? It seems to be trying to sound into the problem in a new way, to distinguish, shall we say, a purpose in the evil itself.

Renaissance literature with few exceptions tends to face the human problem in this new fashion; especially to give greater rights to human instinct. In order to give a short illustration of how what at first seems quite mad may yet hold a truth, I shall speak for a moment or two about Shakespeare's *Macbeth*. There is a challenge in *Macbeth*. What I am to say may serve as another example of my poetic interpretation, though I would urge that this is a peculiarly daring variation, and not quite characteristic.

Macbeth at first seems a very moral play. The sin is punished; we have a fine reading of how crime leads to disintegration; and in it are embodied a large number of subtle Christian tonings which we might miss, and which make it a first-class morality play. But in this very work, against this rigid structure, there is a countering movement in the manipulation of the poetry itself; we find that the poetry contains another story. Think of Macbeth's early speeches, the movement of them, the nerviness of them:

> This supernatural soliciting
> Cannot be ill; cannot be good;—if ill,
> Why hath it given me earnest of success,
> Commencing in a truth?

(I. iii. 130)

The words come out in jerks, spasms, almost gasps. He describes his breathless state:

> If good, why do I yield to that suggestion
> Whose horrid image doth unfix my hair
> And make my seated heart knock at my ribs,
> Against the use of nature?
>
> (I. iii. 134)

He is all nervy and dithery. Later on, again talking of the murder:

> If it were done, when 'tis done, then 'twere well
> It were done quickly: if the assassination
> Could trammel up the consequence, and catch,
> With his surcease, success . . .
>
> (I. vii. 1)

You cannot speak it smoothly; you get tied up with the dentals and sibilants; it is all neurotic. It continues in a hesitant, jerky, unnatural manner till the great image is reached of Pity riding the winds.

How does Macbeth talk when he has committed his first murder? The lines flow out with greater resonance. He is thinking of Banquo, and whether he had not better murder Banquo too, for his safety. This is how he talks now:

> He chid the sisters,
> When first they put the name of king upon me,
> And bade them speak to him. Then, prophet-like,
> They hail'd him father to a line of kings.
> Upon my head they plac'd a fruitless crown,
> And put a barren sceptre in my gripe,
> Thence to be wrench'd with an unlineal hand,
> No son of mine succeeding. If't be so,
> For Banquo's issue have I fil'd my mind;
> For them the gracious Duncan have I murder'd;
> Put rancours in the vessel of my peace
> Only for them; and mine eternal jewel
> Given to the common enemy of man
> To make them kings, the seed of Banquo kings!
> Rather than so, come, fate, into the list,
> And champion me to the utterance.
>
> (III. i. 57)

We are almost driven to the thought that Macbeth is, to use a current phrase, 'breaking down his inhibitions'.[1] He now goes ahead boldly, and commits more murders.

In one sense he disintegrates; but what about those great scenes at the end? He has established an honest relationship with the community. He knows what he has done, and knows that other people know it; and then he speaks his greatest passages of philosophic poetry, no longer resonant and flamboyant, but rather ennobled, spiritualized, by suffering. Though he is talking of his own failure, he is yet speaking from a pinnacle of experience. There are three wonderful passages of a sublimely confessional, yet unrepentant, tone:

> My way of life
> Is fall'n into the sere, the yellow leaf;
> And that which should accompany old age,
> As honour, love, obedience, troops of friends,
> I must not look to have; but, in their stead,
> Curses, not loud, but deep, mouth-honour, breath,
> Which the poor heart would fain deny, and dare not.
>
> (v. iii. 22)

Then, later, even more famous:

> She should have died hereafter.
> There would have been a time for such a word.
> Tomorrow, and tomorrow, and tomorrow,
> Creeps in this petty pace from day to day,
> To the last syllable of recorded time;
> And all our yesterdays have lighted fools
> The way to dusty death. Out, out, brief candle!
> Life's but a walking shadow, a poor player
> That struts and frets his hour upon the stage,
> And then is heard no more—it is a tale
> Told by an idiot, full of sound and fury,
> Signifying nothing.
>
> (v. v. 17)

1. Compare Richard Moulton, *Shakespeare as a Dramatic Artist* (3rd edn. 1901), VII: 'Macbeth's spirits always rise with evil deeds', crime raising him to 'the loftiest tone'. Even more uncompromising is John Marston's handling of a similar psychological turn in *Antonio's Revenge*. See my quotations in *The Golden Labyrinth*, 98. [1966]

Or again, talking to the Doctor about Lady Macbeth:

Macbeth: How does your patient, doctor?
Doctor: Not so sick, my lord,
          As she is troubled with thick-coming fancies,
          That keep her from her rest.
Macbeth: Cure her of that.
          Can'st thou not minister to a mind diseas'd,
          Pluck from the memory a rooted sorrow,
          Raze out the written troubles of the brain,
          And with some sweet oblivious antidote
          Cleanse the stuff'd bosom of that perilous stuff
          Which weighs upon the heart?
Doctor: Therein the patient
          Must minister to himself.

                                        (v. iii. 37)

They did not know about psychologists in Shakespeare's day.[1]

I maintain that Macbeth at the end of the play is on a pinnacle of spiritual experience of some kind. Perhaps he ought not to have got there, but got there he has. It was all prophesied at the beginning by the Weird Women, who say in lines clearly intended to serve as a pointer:

          Though his bark cannot be lost,
          Yet it shall be tempest-toss'd.

                                        (I. iii. 24)

Macbeth endures a rough passage, but the adventure has not been valueless; he seems at the end to have accomplished something.

Can we make any sense of what appears as mad as this? We can, if we remember Pope's lines, always recalled to me by Coleridge's 'dome', concerning that other mysterious dimension:

          So Man, who here seems principal alone,
          Perhaps acts second to some sphere unknown,
          Touches some wheel, or verges to some goal;
          'Tis but a part we see, and not a whole.
                              (*An Essay on Man*, I. 57)

1. My placing of this speech out of its natural order as an amusing climax was prompted by the psychiatrical nature of the conference to which the talk was addressed. [1966]

Consider *Macbeth* and *Hamlet*, two of Shakespeare's darkest tragedies. At the beginning those supernatural figures that seem to prompt the bloodshed are seen by more than the hero; later the supernatural figures are seen only by the hero; at the end the supernatural figures that prompted the bloodshed do not exist. Is it possible that something is being dramatized here that has to do with the outer universe as well as with our earthly life; that there are forces crying for expression that have got somehow to be expressed; that Macbeth is a vehicle for that expression; and that, although in human terms he must be condemned as a criminal, yet in wider, greater, vaster cosmic or divine terms he is part of a pattern?[1] That is the kind of thought which it may be salutary to hold in reserve; and that is the kind of challenge which I read throughout Renaissance literature, particularly in Byron's *Manfred*, which depicts so beautifully a Faust-figure who knows he has been evil (although we are not told what the evil is), and yet refuses to be damned. He just *won't* go to Hell! He asserts his own integrity. He does not deny that he has sinned. He feels remorse and no devil's torments could make it worse; but he will not surrender his human integrity.

It may be said that in these works there is no solution, that literature is not read by many people, and that in any case literature and poetry are not a cult, not a religion. That is true. Nevertheless we must remember that great drama is very close to religion; the two are interdependent, and always have been. Even at the lowest, even if these great works do not themselves hold a solution, are they not perhaps a symptom of what is happening? I think they are. I say unequivocally that great poetic thinkers like Pope or Byron are great seers, great prophets. Why are they not read as such? Possibly there is a kind of fear in us all of what they are expressing; some purpose, some compulsion, concerning our own instincts, that we would avoid. That is how they are symptomatic, not merely in their own

1. When the criminal young hero of Edward Young's *Busiris* remarks that so many accidents have concurred to work

> My passions up to this unheard of crime
> As if the gods design'd it [III]

we have an exact analogy to *Macbeth*. For *Busiris*, see *The Golden Labyrinth*, 193.
[1966]

statements, but also in our persistent unwillingness to face those statements honestly.

My final conclusion is this; that this great succession of wisdom is summed up by Nietzsche.[1] I believe that his book *Thus Spake Zarathustra*—I shall refer here to this book alone—has a positive gospel of the greatest importance. He is trying to fashion out for us a purpose of the future, a christology, if you like; yet one which in its main emphasis strongly counters our traditional Christianity. Nietzsche is very easily misunderstood. If he says that his super-being, the 'over-man', must conquer sympathy, it is not that he is to be unsympathetic but rather because sympathy—'suffering with'—is a lowering of yourself to the sufferer, a surrender to the negative. Rather must the great soul lift the sufferer to his own joy. That is an excellent example of the way in which Nietzsche's creative doctrine can be totally misunderstood. It is a book that needs the most careful study; which has in it, I think, the germ of a new positive and creative faith. It is concerned throughout with the facing of instincts, the using of them, the creating from them, the seeing good where you saw evil before. That is why Nietzsche so often seems to talk dangerously in terms of evil; he only means that you have to make friends with these dark energies, as you do with a child or an animal before you can properly train them. The book is a laboratory for the integration of those great principles, the Dionysian and the Apollonian, formulated in his early work, *The Birth of Tragedy. Thus Spake Zarathustra* is positive, forward-looking and creative. There may be dangers in it, but, if there are, so there are dangers in the New Testament. In reading all such supremely difficult and subtle works of higher doctrine we do well to preserve two things: our faith in God, preferably a simple faith, a childlike faith; and common-sense. Sometimes these two may conflict; the reducing of the conflict is the art of life.

What do I mean by faith in God? I would again point you to a Renaissance thinker, a precursor of Nietszche, Pope, to whom I have already referred; a poet far greater as a thinker than is generally recognized. I will read you a few lines from his *Essay on Man* on life in

---

1. A considered interpretation of Nietzsche's position is set out in my *Christ and Nietzsche*, 1948. I hope for its reissue at not too distant a date. [1966]

general, on seeing the pattern and design, the creative pattern, in any situation:

> Submit.—In this, or any other sphere,
> Secure to be as blest as thou canst bear:
> Safe in the hand of one disposing Pow'r,
> Or in the natal, or the mortal hour.
> All Nature is but Art, unknown to thee;
> All Chance, Direction, which thou canst not see;
> All Discord, Harmony not understood;
> All partial Evil, universal Good:
> And spite of Pride, in erring Reason's spite,
> One truth is clear, Whatever is, is right.

(I. 285)

This doctrine should be read in its context, as part of Pope's whole work, *An Essay on Man*.[1]

As my quotation stands, the doctrine had best perhaps be called provisional; even so it is a doctrine which, the more you live it, the more truth you will find in it; it is the only way to live if one is to preserve one's sense of purpose. In any given situation, surely, we want first to interpret rather than to criticize. We want to maintain our sense of mystery, a sense of listening-in; and the more we have that sense, the more we shall feel that Nietzsche's vision of great super-beings ahead is no less than a rationalization of purpose itself. He has listened in to the nature of the creative process. Do not make the mistake of thinking that Nietzsche's statement is a simple evolutionary humanism. The superman is a transcendent creation in whom masculine and feminine are angelically blended; a Christ-figure; a glimpse of what the human race is *for*. It seems that in any discussion of any situation we must at all costs have that one positive, or an equivalent, before us; that which we may call the golden reality must take precedence over all our thinking. We must see, even in our last great war, a mighty drama, and be interested in the contestants on each side, and try to find out what it was all about, and without hating, without the use of the 'Avenging Mind', try to see it as a conflict creating something new. In any discussion, in reading the pattern of a poem, in discussing a psychological situation or

1. Studied in my *Laureate of Peace*, 1954; as *The Poetry of Pope*, 1965.

world affairs, or anything of yet vaster implications, we should try to keep the Nietzschean positive before us. There, very clearly, is our key.

I will end by saying that in this time of confusion and doubt we must learn to listen afresh to the orchestra of all our doings if we are to regain a positive vision and a positive faith. I have tried to show how we have missed them in our day and where hints of such a positive may be found.

XV

NEW DIMENSIONS IN SHAKESPEARIAN INTERPRETATION

Composed for publication in French as 'Nouvelles Dimensions' in vol. V of
Œuvres Complètes de Shakespeare, ed. Pierre Leyris and H. G. Evans, Paris,
1959.

MORE than a quarter of a century has passed since I started my work on the interpretation of Shakespeare. I am now to describe how it happened and where, in my opinion, lies its importance.

The main interest of my schooldays lay in the theatre, and in particular the presentation of Shakespeare. Before the first world war I saw many of the rich productions done by Sir Herbert Beerbohm Tree at His Majesty's Theatre; Sir Johnston Forbes-Robertson's farewell season at Drury Lane; and Harley Granville Barker's three notable productions at the Savoy.

On returning from the war, I read for a degree in English at Oxford, and after graduating felt impelled to make some contribution to Shakespearian commentary. I had grown dissatisfied with the usual division of Shakespeare's art into 'characters' and 'poetry': surely the dramatic people were themselves poetic, and if so they should be understood in that light. Shakespearian study in the 1920's was clouded by what has become known as 'realistic' criticism, a term which covered some fine scholarly virtues and a yet greater number of scholarly vices. By 'vices' I refer to the kind of study which appeared to believe, and made wide sections of the public believe, that a proper understanding of the Elizabethan stage and Elizabethan prompt books and printing would serve if driven far enough to render up the Shakespearian secret. Under this heading we might group the then highly influential work of J. M. Robertson, who was steadily proving to us that a large part of the Shakespearian canon was not by Shakespeare at all. From an imaginative, and also from a common-sense, stand-point Shakespearian studies were in a state of chaos.

Apart from a brief[1] academic training at Oxford, my knowledge of the contemporary literary situation was slight: I was not in touch with current trends in criticism until I came across Middleton Murry's periodical *The Adelphi*, about the year 1926. This acted as a release mechanism to my dissatisfied and enquiring thought.[2] Here, in Middleton Murry, was a writer who saw what might be called the 'spiritual' values in great literature, and that was clearly what was wanted. My first Shakespearian article, on *Julius Caesar*, appeared in *The Adelphi* in March 1927. I was particularly interested in Murry's reading of the conclusion of *Antony and Cleopatra* as a positive statement, beyond tragedy;[3] and it seemed to me that we should be able to approach the last plays from a similar viewpoint. These plays had hitherto received a poor response: it was sometimes suggested that Shakespeare might be taking a hint from the work of his younger contemporary, Fletcher; the Victorians had seen no more in them than such 'romances', tempered for a mood of serenity; and Lytton Strachey had recently attacked such sentimental readings with a rather disruptive essay which advanced us little farther. I had for long been struggling with an interpretation of *The Tempest*; and surely, I thought, all this last group of plays should be susceptible to a coherent reading?

Today it appears strange that there should have been any difficulty; and yet there was. Somewhere about the year 1927 the answer came, in a flash. There was nothing spectacular about it; it merely became obvious that these plays should be taken seriously; as seriously

1. Five terms (1922–3) only, under a shortened war-course scheme, though I was advised, and decided, to read the full course.

2. My relations with Middleton Murry at this period have been described in an essay contributed to *Of Books and Humankind*, Essays and Poems presented to Bonamy Dobrée, ed. John Butt, 1964.

3. I cannot now recall which of Murry's comments on *Antony and Cleopatra* I had at that time read: perhaps those in the essay 'The Nature of Poetry', included in *Discoveries* in 1924: and there were probably others. The phrase 'die into love' used in my *Myth and Miracle* was his. [1966]

in their own particular fashion as the tragedies in theirs. When in *Pericles* Thaisa is restored from the dead by the saintly Cerimon and when at the conclusion to *The Winter's Tale* the statue of the supposedly dead Hermione warms to life, what was needed was a simple, child-like, response to the miraculous, such as we accord to similar events in the New Testament. We were to see a mystical or miraculous statement pushing through the form and structure of a conventional play. Everything at once fell into place: questions of authorship settled themselves. We had no reason to suppose that the greater part of *Pericles*[1] or the Vision of Jupiter in *Cymbeline* was spurious; on the contrary, the new reading made it highly probable that these were purposive and coherent.

The new understanding was tentatively set out, with many academic reservations and a number of appendix-notes on the mystic intuitions recurring throughout poetry, in a study called *Thaisa*. During the early months of 1928 the typescript went to a number of publishers and to some literary authorities, but nothing came of it.[2] Being convinced that the argument was one of importance, I stated the gist of it in an article 'The Poet and Immortality' which appeared in *The Shakespeare Review* of October 1928. This was followed by a booklet, published at my own expense and necessarily condensed, called *Myth and Miracle*, in 1929, with a preface containing a general acknowledgement to the work of Middleton Murry, though simultaneously claiming that the main thesis on the Final Plays—I have always refused the designation 'Romances'—was new. This small booklet, later reprinted in *The Crown of Life*, received some kindly attention from men of academic standing and some interesting reviews, among them one in *The Times Literary Supplement* by Middleton Murry, who was unable to accept the new reading. Despite his insight into the spiritual properties of poetry, there was a clear divergence when it came to so uncompromising a statement. His own view of the Final Plays remained, roughly, that of the

1. I say 'the greater part'. I have never urged the complete authenticity of *Pericles*, though I have regarded it as throughout dominated by Shakespeare's mind. See my study in *The Crown of Life*.

2. The typescript of *Thaisa* is now lodged in The Shakespeare Memorial Library at the City Reference Library in Birmingham.

orthodox tradition; and he followed Dowden in rejecting the Vision in *Cymbeline* as spurious. It was clear that Middleton Murry's more mystical insights were liable to be countered on occasion by a readiness to accept the tenets of 'realistic' criticism which I found rather disconcerting; and when my first large book, *The Wheel of Fire*, came out in 1930 it was introduced by Mr. T. S. Eliot, whose own critical tendencies might have been expected to leave him unsympathetic to my interpretative approach, and who only, or so it seemed to me, supported my work by an act of impersonal judgement for which I have always remained most deeply grateful.[1]

The Wheel of Fire was not concerned with the Final Plays, but with the Problem Plays and Tragedies. I had simultaneously been at work on these, and had found that what might be called a new 'dimension' of meaning was lying hidden in them. How exactly this happened it is not easy to explain, since it came naturally and without effort. I recall best the excitement of working on *Troilus and Cressida*: instead of being merely the record of a rather awkward story with flashes of superb poetry, the text became—I can think of no better word—fiery. It now sparkled with a number of intellectual significances peculiar to this particular play and indicating a kind of unity hitherto unsuspected. It was obvious that if this was true of one play it was likely to be true of others. I cannot for certain recall whether *Troilus and Cressida* was the first play to reveal such a unity; but whichever was the first, I was soon finding a number of similar significances made variously of recurring thoughts, images, or major symbols, in all the greater works.

The discovery was not wholly new, since A. C. Bradley's discussion of the poetic 'atmospheres' of *Macbeth* and *King Lear* was of the same type. Bradley was not in my field of conscious thinking when the new approach sprang to life, but I had probably read him at Oxford and knew enough of his work to acknowledge his right of priority in my first published 'manifesto' in *The Shakespeare Review* of September 1928 (reprinted in *The Sovereign Flower*, Appendix E), where my own principles were explicitly related to his. It is the more necessary to record this, since it has so often been supposed that I was

---

1. The literary relationship is discussed in my essay 'T. S. Eliot: Some Literary Impressions' (p. 11 above, note).

reacting against Bradley. The truth is, that that element in his work which I was consciously or unconsciously following has not been adequately faced: he has been known mainly as an expert on 'character' analysis, and against that, as it was in those days practised, I was, certainly, reacting.

An influence at this time which certainly helped me was John Masefield's 1924 Romanes Lecture *Shakespeare and Spiritual Life* (1924; reprinted in *Recent Prose*, 1932) with its imaginative response to the portents of *Julius Caesar*. This was just what was needed, the ability to respond to the whole work and accept its happenings without writing off some of them as irrelevant, archaic, superstitious or for any other reason to be passed over. Here I should also mention another important landmark, Colin Still's *Shakespeare's Mystery Play* which appeared in 1921 (expanded and reprinted under the title *The Timeless Theme* in 1936), a work developing an interpretation of *The Tempest* in terms of ancient myth and ritual. This I did not read until my attention was drawn to it after the publication of *Myth and Miracle*, but the thesis had apparently been known to me before, since a note on an early review of it turned up later among my papers.

Looking back, I can see that the time was ripe for the new interpretation of Shakespeare. In the same year, 1930, that saw the publication of *The Wheel of Fire*, there appeared both Monsignor F. C. Kolbe's *Shakespeare's Way* and Caroline Spurgeon's *Leading Motives in the Imagery of Shakespeare's Tragedies*, the first arguing that each play turned on some distinctive and characterizing idea or word and the other doing the same with imagery. The findings were necessarily partial and have been superseded by a richer understanding of the complexities. Neither attempted, as did Bradley, to possess the whole colouring, the atmosphere, the peculiar world made of thought, imagery, persons and events, but they did serve to indicate, as I had myself indicated in my 1928 *Shakespeare Review* 'manifesto' and have illustrated throughout *The Wheel of Fire* and subsequent books, that what Bradley had done for a few plays might be done in greater detail and on a wider scale.

My own first advances had not met with an easy reception in literary circles. None of the essays eventually collected in *The Wheel of Fire* had found a home in any specifically literary periodical. One had come out in *The Fortnightly Review*, and the rest, together with one not included in my book,[1] in religious journals of various denominations: Catholic, Anglo-Catholic, Evangelical, Methodist, Unitarian and Occult. It was clear that many accepted academic and literary tenets would have to be countered and in my *Shakespeare Review* 'manifesto' and again in *The Wheel of Fire* and subsequent volumes the main difficulties were set out and argued.

It was necessary to counter objections in terms of the following concepts: 'intentions', 'sources', 'authenticity', 'characters' and dramatic purpose. I was aware that I should be asked whether this or that effect was 'intended' by Shakespeare. I should also be told that some of the most exciting discoveries were in Shakespeare's 'sources'; that scholars had decided that much of Shakespeare's supposed work was by other writers; that to stress the symbolic and poetic meanings was to play havoc with Shakespeare's characters; and that anyway such philosophic speculations could bear little relevance to the labours of a practising dramatist working for his living. Such objections were based on a wrong-headed view of literary and dramatic art, and in the main quite illogical. It was accordingly none too easy to meet them on their own terms.

Here roughly are the answers that were given. You can no more say whether Shakespeare 'intended' a certain detail, whether he had it in full consciousness just before he wrote it, than you can say what he was thinking at, say, the moment just before he decided to retire to Stratford. What you can say, is that the work of art itself 'intends' the effect in question; and whether you are right or not must be settled on imaginative rather than biographical grounds. As for 'sources', if we once rule out an effect in the finished art-form because it was in some discoverable source, we are on a road that leads to chaos, since to regard the rest of the work of art as interpretable in dissociation from this effect is equivalent to denying its unity, and therefore its artistry; and since moreover we can never know what other undiscovered sources may exist, and may suspect a source of *some* kind for everything, we shall eventually be left with nothing to study. Arguments against authenticity could again and again be shown as

1. This was the essay on 'Romantic Friendship' included in my present collection, p. 53 above.

untenable, since the new readings, by revealing pattern where previous readings had found chaos—the description of the English King in *Macbeth* (IV. iii. 146–59) is a good example—had removed those grounds of suspicion on which the arguments against authenticity had originally been based: in such matters it was generally unnecessary to face or even refer to the old arguments, the new reading by itself doing all that was needed. 'Character' raises a more subtle problem. I decided not to use the term, preferring 'person'. When the plays were split into characters and poetry it served well enough, but for poetically realized persons it was inadequate. Besides, the moral connotations of the word tended towards the type of moralistic commentary that I wished to avoid. The change had a good stage tradition: 'personae' is the Latin term for the people of drama and the term 'character part' is today in stage use for a specific and limited purpose to describe the very kind of creation, such as the nurse in *Romeo and Juliet*, that Hamlet and Macbeth are not. My arguments on 'character' might be compared with Strindberg's very similar discussion in his preface to *Lady Julia*. As to the dramatic quality of Shakespeare's work, all one could say was, that though the dramatic form is unquestionably Shakespeare's medium of expression, yet this does not preclude his having something to express through that medium.

It was from the start emphasized that these interpretations were to be positive in direction. They were to be distinguished from a moral criticism by seeing the persons as interesting and dynamic for good or ill and as working out a destiny which entrances rather than repels us. This peculiarly dynamic acceptance nevertheless depended on an approach which I called 'spatial'. The term was needed to distinguish the new analysis of pattern, symbol and atmosphere from what had become an excessive concentration on temporal links, on narrative considerations within the play and 'causes', 'sources' and historical conditioning outside it. But the term 'spatial' must not be allowed to suggest the static: what I have called the 'fiery' significances starting up from the page were anything but that. The truth is, they had a vertical rather than a horizontal activity; and here we can see how my two main contributions, the reading of the Final Plays as immortality myths and the revealing of imaginative patterns within other plays were both results of a single, spiritualized, perception, depending on the rejection of irrelevances and a simple attention to the thing-in-itself, leading on to an understanding of it in depth.

To focus the new groupings of thought, symbol and imagery that constitute the various patternings we have first to accept the various effects in and as themselves, in their own right, irrespective of the narrative. Though each has its part in the story, it may simultaneously be playing another part in the pattern, and to see this other part we must be aware of it in itself in distinction from the story. Only so can we become aware also of the clustering similarities. A reference to the sea in *Antony and Cleopatra* may well be demanded by the Mediterranean setting and imperial theme of the story; but if we respond to it also as an interesting 'sea-reference', and then to another, and another, we begin to find very many; and we shall next begin to realize that the sea here acts within the art-form as an imaginative power; and next that this power, this meaning, is of a particular kind of optimistic suggestion, since these sea-references suggest calm in contrast to the normal use elsewhere in Shakespearian tragedy suggesting turmoil. A valuable insight matures which could never have matured had we let our first interest in a sea-reference be negated by knowledge that it was demanded by the plot. But it must be remembered that in seeing these effects 'in themselves' we are, in effect, seeing them as more than themselves, as usually understood: anything isolated from irrelevances becomes more than it was before; we inevitably begin to see or feel it *in depth*, as symbolic, as spiritualized and of universal import. It is often a matter of semi-visualization. The insight is to this extent dramatic: we are *staging* these various effects in the mind's eye instead of letting them pass across the surface of our thought; they have the depth and atmosphere of a stage setting. More, by refusing to let them be clouded by the story, we are being responsive to that first principle of dramatic art which lives and acts less in the narrative sequence than in a succession of immediacies, a succession of 'now ... now ... now', corresponding to what Nietzsche meant by the Dionysian activity, as from another dimension, on which the normal action, the Apollonian events and people, depend. There is less a causation along the horizontal level than a creation from below, or above; from, we may say, the vertical dimension.

It was precisely such a faculty as this which made it possible to focus the visionary qualities of the Final Plays. Once you forgot the received academic reasons previously current to account for these strange works—copying Fletcher's romances, trying to please the public, the work of an ageing and wearied man—once you forgot all this and let yourself be passive to what actually happens, then the resurrection of Hermione and similar events in other plays hit you, dramatically and inevitably, with an impact of mystic affinities. We do, in fact, thrill to the experience of watching a supposedly dead person come to life, in a chapel, to the sound of music. There is no getting away from it. It happens in any, even a mediocre, stage representation. That is why I have always felt so secure against the criticism of the learned. No great learning was needed for so simple an insight, and no learning could possible disprove it. All that the scholars said might be true. These plays might be the work of a tired man copying Fletcher in order to make money; but even so, that had nothing whatsoever to do with the matter under discussion.

A peculiarly good example of the new understanding in depth was my reading of the three Apparitions, 'Armed Head', 'Bloody Child' and 'Child crowned with a Tree in his Hand', in *Macbeth*, as given in *The Imperial Theme* (150–1), *The Shakespearian Tempest* (192–3), and *The Christian Renaissance* (enlarged 1962, 45–7). Hitherto they had been related simply to the story: to Macbeth's death, Macduff's birth and Malcolm's use of Birnam Wood. Without denying these story-references it was possible to see the three apparitions as powerfully symbolic in their own right: as murderous slaughter self-defeated; as life struggling for reassertion from out of the bloody horror; and as life triumphant with all natural, human and transcendental, because crowned, authority. We were faced by a symbolism far more metaphysically interesting than the comparatively superficial matter of the three prophecies' fulfilment in the fifth act; by a little symbolic drama lying at the heart of the action which it was simultaneously interpreting for us. This is followed by the show of future kings in assured royalty, passing to music in firm contrast to the thunderous impact of the symbolism it succeeds. Here we touch the very essence of Shakespeare's artistry, revealing a precision in symbolic statement of an order not previously suspected.

The advance made was not only an advance in the understanding of Shakespeare; it was also an advance in the understanding of poetry, of literary genius, in general; and the method has since been applied to a number of other poets, English and foreign, including Goethe's *Faust* and Nietzsche's *Thus Spake Zarathustra*. Perhaps the most striking single result was the interpretation of Coleridge's *Kubla Khan* offered in *The Starlit Dome* (1941; see pp. 182–3 above).

The word 'interpretation' has often aroused disquietude. Some new term was needed. 'Criticism' could not be used, since it was so often writing of a specifically critical sort that was being opposed. Criticism suggests judging, the awarding of praise and blame, and this had little enough to do with a new dimension of understanding. It is true that criticism and interpretation must always be to some extent interwoven; it is a question of which dominates; but when one dominates very obviously it is important to use the correct term. Many misunderstandings still exist. I find myself sometimes grouped with what is known as the 'Cambridge' school of 'criticism', whose aims are surely of a different kind, though followers of this and other schools of contemporary criticism have on their part from time to time followed up some of the new interpretative trails that have been opened out. My own influences, so far as I can trace them, have already been recorded; and it must be remembered that my direction was set, and my first 'manifesto' printed, in 1928.

These Shakespearian investigations are now completed. They have been published, between 1930 and 1958, in the following works: *The Wheel of Fire, The Imperial Theme, The Crown of Life, The Shakespearian Tempest, The Sovereign Flower, The Mutual Flame,* and *Principles of Shakespearian Production* (1966: now enlarged as *Shakespearian Production*). Of these the first three are mainly devoted to studies of separate plays; the next two are of more general interest, though the first of them contains my full analysis of *A Midsummer Night's Dream* and the second my interpretation of *All's Well that Ends Well. The Mutual Flame* is devoted to the Sonnets and *The Phoenix and the Turtle. The Shakespearian Tempest* takes a 'spatial' view of the whole Shakespearian universe, exploring the opposition of 'tempests' and 'music' throughout, as contrasted and complementary symbolisms binding the whole. *The Sovereign Flower* discusses mainly the royal and specifically British themes in Shakespeare, parts of it deriving from my work on Shakespeare during the second world war.

Principles of Shakespearian Production was the only work to concentrate on the stage; and yet the stage has from my earliest years been my main personal interest. My other interpretations did not speak directly in stage terms, but they certainly grew from a stage awareness.[1] It has always seemed to me that to discuss the more profound meanings of a great dramatist in terms of stage technique advances us little, if at all. My stage interests have accordingly been confined to theatre-going, production and acting. During my years at Toronto between the wars I produced, and acted in, the greater Shakespearian plays, and set down some of my conclusions in the book *Principles of Shakespearian Production*, wherein I tried to show how a modern production might attempt to do justice, in strict terms of stage technique, to the more profound meanings of the dramatic poetry and construction. There should be no real antagonism. After all, we have argued that 'interpretation' is itself a kind of 'staging' in the mind's eye, an attempt to see and feel, in depth, the more powerful significances; to sense their atmospheres, their colour, their aura. This is precisely what stage-production can do, with its atmospheric lighting, its depth, its almost uncanny realization of a new dimension, its peculiar magic. Clearly, what we have called the 'spatial' element in the plays will roughly correspond to the stage-setting, costuming and lighting: and some blending of the tenets of Gordon Craig with my own published interpretations and my own book on production, should give us the direction, as I see it, that is needed.[2]

And what, now, of the results? What effect have these various works of interpretation had? Their effect on stage production is difficult to assess; they have certainly had a greater effect on the little

1. For the necessity of this awareness in the interpretation of Shakespeare's symbolic effects see pp. 305–16 below. I may sometimes have been at fault in assuming its presence for students for whom it was not instinctive. [1966]

2. A discussion of Gordon Craig's work has now been included in the enlarged version of my book entitled *Shakespearian Production*, 1964.

theatres than on the commercial theatre, where nevertheless some results have been sporadically observable. Probably such new findings have necessarily to go through the process of academic assimilation before any widespread effect on the stage can be expected. Their strictly academic influence has already been considerable. Most modern Shakespearian studies and works of literary criticism, both in England and in America, in so far as they are working interpretatively, take the 'spatial' approach into consideration. Most of our best literary scholars in English assume as valid the various attacks and defences (e.g. on 'intentions', 'sources', historical conditions etc.) which were put forward in my early books; the ground then won has been colonized for wider purposes. The authenticity of Shakespeare's works, which could never have been proved but was demonstrated by showing the coherences of suspected plays and the relevance of suspected scenes, is now established: *Measure for Measure*, *Troilus and Cressida* and *Timon of Athens* are safe; so is the Vision in *Cymbeline*; and the complete authenticity of *Henry VIII* is less and less disputed. The campaign has on every front been victorious. This is generally understood; and yet, despite some notable exceptions, there has also been a pervasive reluctance to acknowledge it. There is even a tendency in some quarters to pretend that these are peculiarly personal or esoteric works standing apart from the main stream of academic investigation which is nevertheless following the channel first made available by them. It is seldom nowadays remembered how chaotic was the state of Shakespearian studies before the new interpretations came to reveal the unsuspected harmonies. Why is this?

There is fortunately no need to level any complaint in terms of discourtesy since a far more deep-seated and interesting reason is available. The new interpretation of poetic genius, if honestly followed, leads to difficulties, and some would say to dangers. We are invited to see great works as modern, with contemporary impact; to find living meanings in them without the blurring and blunting of the usual academic devices arranged to keep them distanced, if not dead. It is as though a whole succession of martyred saints—for others besides Shakespeare are involved—were to be suddenly revived with all those attendant embarrassments so excellently indicated at the conclusion to Bernard Shaw's *Saint Joan*.

Here are some of the dangers. Morals appear to be threatened. It is not difficult to detect a Nietzschean quality or colouring about these interpretations; and indeed the interpretation of *Hamlet* offered independently in *The Wheel of Fire* was found later to correspond closely to that offered by Nietzsche in *The Birth of Tragedy*. A just interpretation of Shakespeare's art will inevitably thrill to, and may seem in danger of approving, essences which are, or appear, evil. There is accordingly a tendency to accept the new findings and follow the new techniques up to a point, and yet to reclothe, or reclog, them in some of the more respectable academic accoutrements; to see it all, once again, as aspects of Elizabethan thought; to relate the work of genius to lesser works, as though the one were merely copying the other; to assure us that the more disturbing challenges are accountable in terms of out-worn traditions and superstitions. There is still insufficient recognition of Shakespeare as the transmitter of a truth or truths beyond Elizabethan learning and out-spacing our best thoughts of today. The positive direction of Shakespearian tragedy, its sense of accomplishment, almost of victory, countering the superficial story of failure and distress, is negated: its movement is not seen as rising, expanding, flowering, but as drooping and sapless; and the age-old escape is found yet again by turning tragedy into a moral tract. The beyond-good-and-evil impact of the Shakespearian art, which nevertheless contains many moral judgements within it and itself points us towards a higher good to be won through a state of being rather than a set of precepts, is reduced to a simple and obvious lesson telling us that socially disorderly actions meet with social retribution. The eternal insight is missed; the visionary statement clouded; and the ground won in danger of being rendered sterile.

Nor is it only a question of morality. This 'eternal insight' cannot be confined to the ordinary stock-in-trade of normal sense-perception; of, shall we say, the world of 'common-sense'; for this world it deliberately and definitely aims to transcend. Again and again my interpretations have matured from the willingness to face and emphasize elements in Shakespeare's drama that might be regarded as superstitious: the startling phenomena of *Julius Caesar*, the Ghost in *Hamlet*, the occult powers of *Macbeth*, the preternatural storms and thunderings in play after play, the mysterious music in *Antony and Cleopatra*; the oracles, visions, resurrections and divine appearances of the last period. All these have been accepted; more, they have been used as keys; and any interpretation which ignores or slights them will be both dishonest and deceptive. Now once we see that this is true of Shakespeare, we shall find that it is true of all great drama; and of all fine poetry too, from the ancients down to Yeats, Masefield and Eliot.[1] There is always the mysterious symbol, choric voice or numinous atmosphere which invites us to enjoy some supernormal, esoteric or occult, perception. This the settled world-view of our twentieth century prefers to forget. It is afraid of being tormented, like Hamlet (*Hamlet*, I, iv. 56), 'with thoughts beyond the reaches of our souls'.

As for politics, Shakespeare's is a royal world, and his primary human symbol is the Crown, the King. In an age which sees its choice as one between democratic liberty and totalitarian domination, there seems to be no place for royalty; and yet, in truth, it is this which properly understood as an imaginative and dramatic conception simultaneously safeguarding our freedom and pointing us to self-transcendence, holds the very key which we most need. If it did not, we should not respond as we do to the royalistic dramas of Shakespeare.

Such are the problems which confront us in these interpretations. By drawing from Shakespearian tragedy a sense of man's unmoral but indomitable essence; by their emphasis on occult powers interested for good or ill—and that depends on us—in the human drama; and by their royalistic assertions; in all this our interpretations are offering a challenge to the prevailingly negative and defeatist tendencies of contemporary thought.

1. For Masefield, see my 'Appreciation' in *John Masefield*, O.M., ed. Geoffrey Handley-Taylor, 1960, and my expanded account 'Masefield and Spiritualism' in *Mansions of the Spirit*, ed. George A. Panichas, New York 1967; for Eliot, my essay 'T. S. Eliot: Some Literary Impressions' (p. 11 above, note).

XVI

TIMON OF ATHENS AND ITS DRAMATIC DESCENDANTS

A Review of English Literature, October 1961; II, 4; included in *Stratford Papers on Shakespeare, 1963*, ed. Berners W. Jackson; Toronto, 1964.

DURING many years of concern with *Timon of Athens* both in literary commentary and on the stage, my respect for this remarkable drama has been maintained. Of all Shakespeare's plays it is the most obviously prophetic. Like Ben Jonson's *Volpone* and *The Alchemist* it is a money-play, though its effect has been far greater. It has had many descendants.

Timon of Athens shows its noble hero: (i) as a rich, warm-hearted and generous patron within a glittering society, but when his resources are gone and he is refused assistance by his former friends, as a man deeply angered by human ingratitude; (ii) as a naked prophet of social denunciation and cosmic speculation in the wilds by the sea into which, as into a vast 'nothing' or Nirvana, his story dissolves; and (iii) after becoming the possessor during the final acts of gold dug from the earth, as a being sought after for this and for other more personal reasons by visitants from his native city, which is being threatened with destruction. These themes are reworked by later dramatists.

The first is Richard Brome. In *The City Wit* a formerly generous but now penurious hero is confronted by ingratitude and employs a variety of intrigues to turn the tables on his society. Phrases are redolent of Shakespeare: Are 'open hands' and 'bounty' to be 'rewarded thus'? 'Is, to be honest, term'd to be a fool?' (I. ii). As in Shakespeare we are reminded that all things, in both nature and human society, 'rob each other' (IV. i). That may be, but for man there should be better ways:

> Now they all shall feel
> When honest men revenge, their whips are steel. (v.i)

In *A Jovial Crew* Brome attacks society from a vagabond and nature-planted viewpoint thoroughly Shakespearian. He covers much of *Timon of Athens*; subsequent dramatists usually concentrate on a part.

In the eighteenth century interest falls on the social and financial aspects. Gay's *Beggar's Opera* attacks a society made of people who, when your wealth is gone, are ready with advice but 'shift you for money from friend to friend' (III. iv; Air 44). Fielding's plays are nearly all on a *Timon* wave-length. Lord Richly in *The Modern Husband* holds a Timon-like levee and we are duly warned as in Shakespeare against flatterers and false friends; Boncour in *The Fathers* pretends to be ruined in order to test his faith in human nature; and the poet Spatter in *Eurydice Hiss'd* has composed a drama on the *Timon* pattern of flattery, disaster and desertion of friends. There is a levee just like Timon's.

The concentration grows. Society in the eighteenth century was deeply concerned with the handling of money and its attendant temptations and risks; gambling in play after play is a major problem. We have next a number of warmly conceived but extravagant young men who are brought up sharply against the facts of human nature, especially friends who vary with the winds of fortune, as in George Colman the Elder's *The Man of Business*. In Richard Cumberland's *The Fashionable Lover* the extravagant hero is criticized by the Apemantus-like Mortimer and *The West Indian* introduces us to a brilliantly conceived young colonial from warm Jamaica whose generous and uninhibited instincts are comically at a loss in puritanical and money-greedy London. The generosity of Young Honeywood in Goldsmith's *The Good-Natured Man* meets a sterner judgement. Sheridan's *The School for Scandal* follows the central tradition, the hypocritical Joseph's stinginess when he is tested like Timon's friends being placed in vivid contrast to Charles's instinctive generosity. Such callous refusals are the theme of Mrs. Inchbald's *Everyone has his Fault*. In Thomas Holcroft's *The Road to Ruin* the good-hearted gambling hero when trying to save his father's firm from the ruin to which his extravagance has contributed is shamelessly turned down by one whom he had formerly helped to make a fortune. Holcroft's *The Man of Ten Thousand* reads like a deliberate rewriting in modern terms of Shakespeare's opening acts. Dorington's extravagance is criticized, his ruin follows, friends, as he was warned by his Apemantus-equivalent Curfew, prove false. All this he accepts with a delicate irony. He has all the time known what he was doing on the principle 'do good and receive good' (II. vi). The play might have been composed to demonstrate that Shakespeare's hero was not so foolish as he looks. We are glad when Dorington gets his fortune back.

The formula grows tedious. However, George Colman the Younger's *The Heir at Law* and *John Bull* offer interesting variations on greed, false friends and ingratitude, with an emphasis on goodness of heart among simple people and its absence among the sophisticated; and *The Law of Java* contains strong satire against an avaricious imperialism. During the nineteenth century Dion Boucicault's satire on money in *The School for Scheming* has pith and originality, but D. W. Jerrold's *The Golden Calf* is mainly a *Timon* rehash, and despite its reputation and some technical brilliance much the same might be said of Lord Lytton's *Money*. Wealth, ruin—pretended or real—flatteries, and false friends: it becomes hard not to regard these as a worn coinage, if not a false currency. James Albery's *Two Roses* is saved by its wit.

None of these dramas contests the social system itself. They are concerned simply with an individual's use of his money. The kindly Sheva in Cumberland's *The Jew* prefers the helping on of two young people to leaving his money to any institution, believing that it is better placed with an individual of proved worth. This does not render them out of date; money means power and whatever our social system there will always be opportunities for the individual to choose between selfishness and generosity.

We turn next to plays corresponding to Shakespeare's final acts, wherein his hero assumes what might be called a 'Promethean' stature. If our last mainly satiric group may be labelled 'Augustan', our new group will be 'Romantic'. Timon in his natural retreat forecasts many heroes of the Romantic movement. There are a few earlier links. In the seventeenth century the embittered hero of John Crowne's *The Ambitious Statesman* rejects the court with a Timon-like scorn of contemporary, and especially militaristic, valuations, and imagines himself growing into a scarcely human creature of lonely anguish in the wilderness (IV); as does Molière's Alceste in *Le Misanthrope*. In the Augustan period John Home's *The Fatal Discovery* has in the remorse-stricken recluse Orellan a figure closely corresponding to Crowne's suggestion, living like Timon among howling winds by the angry sea: 'The coot, the cormorant, are his companions' (IV). The severence from society may be impelled either by guilt or by a sense of superiority; sometimes we have a com-plex of both. Among the dramas of the Romantics M. G. Lewis's *Alfonso, King of Castile* has in Orsino a fine descendant of Timon, wrongly suspected of treachery by his friend the King and now living in a rugged setting of rocks and waterfalls. His first speech, moving from social repudiation to an embracing of wild nature, follows a speech of Timon's closely, and like Timon he is implac-able to persuasion. Hate is now his only consolation:

> And would'st thou rob me
> E'en of this last poor pleasure? Go, Sir, go,
> Regain your court! resume your pomp and splendour!
> Drink deep of luxury's cup! be gay, be flatter'd,
> Pamper'd and proud, and if thou can'st, be happy.
> I'll to my cave and curse thee!
>
> (II. ii)

George Colman the Younger's *The Law of Java* has another em-bittered recluse, once wronged by a friend and now living among great mountains:

> Well—let our globe of peopled perfidy
> Roll on, while here I ruminate.
>
> (III. i)

Mary Russell Mitford in *Otto of Wittelsbach* has another. So has Matthew Arnold in *Empedocles on Aetna* with its hero ruminating on society's persecution of great men in a 'fierce man-hating mood' (I. i. 106) before plunging into the volcano. Protagonists die, but the theme is undying; it recurs in Bernard Shaw's old sea-captain, Shotover, in *Heartbreak House* condemning a derelict and vicious society in the name of sea and sky; and in James Bridie's medical genius in *The Switchback* who, after being unjustly thwarted by the vested interests of the British Medical Association, when their attitude changes refuses like Timon all compromise, and sets out for the desert to find eternal life.

The theme may be handled less sensationally, as in the great-hearted Cumberland's *The Wheel of Fortune*, wherein the wronged and misanthropic Penruddock, after years as a Timon-recluse living close to nature, comes into a fortune with power over his wronger's family; is tempted to act coldly; but after a severe self-conflict proves, unlike Shakespeare's Timon, magnanimous, though he rejects the garish falsities of his inheritance and returns to his cottage and nature.

The young Byron acted the part of Penruddock. As we might expect, Byron's own dramas are both relevant and inclusive. *Werner* (III. i. 328–42) has a speech like Timon's (IV. iii, 384–95) on riches; *Sardanapalus* is a grand-scale development of trust and generosity brought up against base ingratitude; and *Manfred* is our supreme dramatic document of romantic severance, having a hero, like Sophocles' Oedipus in the *Oedipus Coloneus*, at once more guilty and more righteous than the society above which he towers, playing out his destiny on the mountain heights; though, taking Byron's life and work as a whole, we shall regard the sea as his more instinctive retreat. T. L. Beddoes left two unfinished dramas, *The Second Brother* and *Torrismond*, in each of which there is a figure of riotous indulgence like Sardanapalus and Charles Surface, and in one of them an embittered person, like Penruddock; the two aspects of *Timon of Athens*, bright and sombre, Augustan and Romantic, being to this extent covered. Our whole story is given a visionary pointing in Nietzsche's *Thus Spake Zarathustra*: Zarathustra on his mountain with his loved beasts delivers a gospel that goes far towards interpreting our succession of subversive dramas.

We come now to our third *Timon* theme: the gold Timon digs from earth. Just as such seemingly dissolute heroes as Shakespeare's Hal or Byron's Sardanapalus must when tested prove themselves better soldiers than their antagonists, so the great-souled bankrupt must regain his gold; either by a normally devised happy ending or symbolically. In Shakespeare the gold has strong symbolic radiations: it maintains and even increases the protagonist's stature; he is still sought after and despite his scorn of it this 'yellow, glittering, precious gold' (IV. iii. 26), if the stage nuggets are properly devised, casts over Timon's retreat a semi-magical lustre.

The lonely Timon with his new gold corresponds to that other outcast in Shakespeare's other money-drama, Shylock in *The Merchant of Venice*. Shylock's wealth is as his soul, Antonio all but pays his friend's debt with his 'heart' (IV. i. 254, 282), and Portia's status as fantasy queen is supported by her possession of infinite riches. Both *The Merchant of Venice* and *Timon of Athens* revolve on the relation of wealth to more emotional, or spiritual, issues. Sometimes money-gold may be used to symbolize what we may call 'the gold essence'. Such gold may function dramatically as the individual's stronghold, one with his lonely integrity and furthest quest, like the symbolic 'gold' of Flecker's Golden Journey to Samarkand in *Hassan*.

That is why miserliness can have so powerful a stage impact. Molière's *L'Avare* touches a serio-comic sympathy deeper than satire; and in the nineteenth century we have two peculiarly interesting studies. The semi-Christian Jew Reuben in Tom Taylor's *Payable on Demand* is a financial genius with a passionate love of his coins:

> Gold, Lina—gold of all countries and coinages—doubloons—pillar dollars—spade guineas—louis d'or—Napoleons. The pretty goldfinches—they all fly London way, Lina. Dip thy hand in, child—isn't it pleasant? I love to feel their smooth, hard, glossy faces under my fingers.
>
> (II. i)

Reuben is forced to an agonizing sacrifice; the conception is noble, and its nobility in part depends on what is sacrificed, for our stage sense of Reuben's worth has lustre from this glittering hoard. Our second study is W. S. Gilbert's *Dan'l Druce, Blacksmith*. The embittered Dan'l, whose love has been poisoned by treachery, rejects

the 'hollow lying world' and its 'den of thieves', lives like Timon by
the sea, refuses compromise with those who come to reclaim him and
concentrates in pathetic miserliness on his winnings as a mender of
nets:

> Ay, brother, I love my gold as other men love their bairns;
> it's of my making, and I love it, I love it . . . See, here's another
> day to thy life, another inch to thy height; grow as thou growest,
> child, and thou'lt be a golden beauty ere long. Gold, the best
> thing in the world; 'as good as gold'—why, it's a saying; the
> best thing on earth to make a bairn of . . .

(1)

It is 'my beautiful golden bairn'. Shakespeare is clearly behind the
conception and this particular speech may assist our understanding
of Timon's new-found gold. Such lonely possessions act on our
minds as imaginative projections, or symbols, of the protagonist's
integral power.

In medieval alchemy the quest of the Philosopher's Stone was
associated closely with the Elixir of Life. The alchemists sought as
fact what we believe as metaphor. Riches are certainly in economic
terms a way to health and life; but far more universal, and independent of systems and currencies, is the metaphoric use of gold or jewels
to point some transcendental, as against the biological, order, or
reality. What is this higher 'reality'? It may be called 'power', in the
Nietzschean sense (p. 131 above); a power as yet only glimpsed, and
that fitfully.

Goethe's *Faust* traces a development from medieval alchemy
through Renaissance art and avarice to capitalism and a war made
lurid by the mountain mine-folk, gnomes who have been earlier in
the Masque described as digging gold and iron from earth and as
kindly to the good while tempting bad men to crime and slaughter
(Part 2; 1). The industrialist's power-quest in Ibsen's *John Gabriel
Borkman* is related to the prisoned metals crying to be mined and
singing for joy when released (11). Minerals mean power, expansion,
rivalry and conquest of nature. Modern industrialization is a gigantic
and living metaphor expressing man's will-to-power in all its glory
and its danger. Both the excellence and the glory are active in
Wagner's cycle *The Ring of the Nibelungs*.

In Shakespeare the metallic wealth is dug from the earth close by the sea; in Goethe and Ibsen it is dug simply from the earth; in Wagner it comes from a river. The Rhine-Gold is stolen by the dwarf Alberich who makes from it a ring which is to give its owner world domination if he renounce love. It passes from the dwarf to gods and from gods to giants, stirring rivalry, a symbol of modern communities in greed-begotten strife, following Timon's

> O thou touch of hearts!
> Think thy slave man rebels, and by thy virtue
> Set them into confounding odds, that beasts
> May have the world in empire.
>
> (IV. iii. 392)

The gold is finally returned to the Rhine, as Timon at one point means to return his gold to the earth. What is our general conclusion? The gold-essence is itself sacred; in myth and legend, as in Wagner too, gold may be guarded by a serpent or dragon; its effect on man is intoxicating and arouses conflicts, though exactly what it is and what is its proper use and purpose remain dark. Our best way to elucidation will be through a close study of the gold-symbolism in *Thus Spake Zarathustra*; or of the ambivalences in Oscar Wilde's extraordinarily subtle use of jewels, on which he is our greatest literary expert, in *The Young King*, *The Happy Prince*, *The Picture of Dorian Gray* and *Salome*.[1]

A striking use of gold in its dual aspects occurs in John Masefield's *The Tragedy of Nan*, which develops a strong contrast of greed and sordid money—'little yellow rounds of metal' (III)—as against emotional integrity and the angelic 'Gold Rider' (III) who impinges victoriously on the tragic action. Though the story has no precise correspondences, *The Tragedy of Nan* might yet be called our most deeply Shakespearian drama in the tradition. Clemence Dane's *Adam's Opera* is impressionistically on a *Timon* wavelength. In O'Casey's dramatic coat of many colours, gold signalizes his best.

Our confusions may be forgiven since, though love of money can be evil, the gold-essence, the 'golden secret' of *Manfred* (III. i. 13), is the goal of all that is best in man; and yet we cannot quite say that

---

1. Discussed in *The Christian Renaissance*, enlarged 1962; 287–300.

the two are independent of each other. Bernard Shaw's acute diagnosis of human economics never forgets that under our present system money exists as a positive, demanding respect. The outward and material forms, or mechanisms, of human traffic must somehow be attuned to an inward and spiritual, but intensely *individualistic*, grace; the individual's integrity, his gold-essence or sovereignty, must at all costs remain undesecrated. This is the theme of Wilde's *The Soul of Man under Socialism*. In it we are close to the meaning of *Timon of Athens*, to the reason why Timon's society implores his return, and to the answer to all our social discontents. Only so can our earthly existence become truly symbolic, or sacramental.

Shakespeare's drama has exerted a strong appeal on creative writers. It was adapted by Thomas Shadwell in the seventeenth century and by Richard Cumberland in the eighteenth. Pope used, or rather misused, the name 'Timon' in one of his *Moral Essays* (IV. 99). Timon was, not surprisingly, in the mind of Swift (letter to Alexander Pope, 29 September 1725). Kean played the part, aptly enough, in 1816, the year Byron left England. Hazlitt in his *Characters of Shakespeare's Plays* thought that *Timon of Athens* was written 'with as intense a feeling of his subject' as any of Shakespeare's plays. Herman Melville for his own purposes coined the terms 'Timonism' and 'Timonized' (*Pierre*, XVII, iii; Lewis Mumford, *Herman Melville*, IX). Dostoievsky, I have been told, regarded it as his favourite Shakespearian play. What the gloomy Tennyson thought of it I do not know, but the bitter passages of *Maud* are in the direct line:

> Arise, my God, and strike, for we hold Thee just,
> Strike dead the whole weak race of venomous worms,
> That sting each other here in the dust;
> We are not worthy to live.
>
> (2. I. ii)

Lytton composed a verse-narrative of some weight entitled *The New Timon*. Today the American poet Robinson Jeffers lives out the destiny of Shakespeare's hero in his rock-built stronghold on the California coast.

Byron's life, with its fierce currents of genius and generosity forced to expend themselves in exile, has a *Timon* structure. He sensed his destiny from youth. In the original text of his *Childish Recollections* he was already seeing himself as a Timon 'not nineteen'; in his 1813 preface to *Childe Harold* he defined the poem's original intention as 'the sketch of a modern Timon'. After a period of social adulation he suffered financial collapse with bankruptcy followed by ignominy and rejection, and left England to find solace among the mountains of Europe and a haven by the ocean in the sea-city, Venice; and he planned to be buried, as was Timon, by the sea. In his *Detached Thoughts* (1821) he includes Timon among the famous figures to whom he has been compared, and when he writes of a young American 'approaching me in my cavern' Timon is being assumed (*Letters and Journals*, v, 408, 421). In Italy he took a new, at times almost miserly, interest in money, which had become for him a spiritual force, to be expended for Greece.[1]

Not unlike Byron's, the drama of Oscar Wilde falls into two parts corresponding to the two halves of *Timon of Athens*. From flamboyance, social dominance, generosity and conviviality he passed to the endurance of ostracism and ingratitude. Lavish expenditure and bankruptcy are part of his story. While in prison he surveyed, bitterly, his financial entanglements, the insincerities of friendship, the shams of civilization and the tragic meanings of his severance; being now, as he tells us near the end of *De Profundis*, more at home—like Timon—with 'the great simple primeval things, such as the sea'.

Timon of Athens is written as from the heart of Shakespeare's genius. Its very roughnesses are the signature of a too-personal sincerity. In W. B. Yeats's *The King's Threshold* the poet Seanchan, denied his place on the Council, refuses, like Timon, to come to terms with the authorities when they, like Shakespeare's Senators, are brought to realize the state's need of the virtue it had slighted. Seanchan is Timon in a modern context. For, deeply understood, Shakespeare's play is far more than an economic extravaganza. Writing in an aristocratic age when patronage was one with poetry and great men aureoled with splendours hard for us to focus, Shakespeare has transmitted through Timon his most cherished dream of

1. For other correspondences of Byron to Shakespeare's Timon, see my recent *Byron and Shakespeare*. [1966]

human worth, stating that Promethean theme for which poetic genius, in every age, exists; recording that generous and golden overflow which meets in every age, or seems to meet, disaster. *Timon of Athens* measures the disparity between the great soul and his fellows. The human link proves false, snaps, and projects the superman on his way, friended by vast nature and the unknown. Too late society abases itself, wooing and cherishing what it had previously scorned, as Oedipus and Timon and Seanchan are wooed, in tardy recognition of the magic, the salvation.

ADDITIONAL NOTE, 1966

Earlier discussions of *Timon of Athens* have appeared in *The Wheel of Fire*, 1930; *Christ and Nietzsche*, 1948; and *The Sovereign Flower*, 1958. For the staging, see *Shakespearian Production*, 1964, and my 'Dramatic Papers' at the Shakespeare Memorial Library, City Reference Library, Birmingham.

My views on this drama have been criticized. It is easy to see the hero's generosity as egocentric and his bitterness as unbalanced; but if allowed to dominate, such a reading remains untrue to the artistic structure and choric pointing, dislocates the movement of the whole, and makes the concluding scenes absurd. Details of response must, if a difficulty occurs, be adjusted to fit the whole, and not the whole to fit certain chosen details. There may be discrepancies awaiting a surface smoothing that never matured; and if so it is our business to 'piece out' the drama's 'imperfections' in our 'thoughts' (*Henry V*, I. chorus, 23). See pp. 263–4, 313.

The material adduced in my present essay, drawn from my more extended commentary on the various dramatists concerned in *The Golden Labyrinth*, bears indisputable witness to the archetypal status of Shakespeare's drama.

XVII

THE TRAGIC ENIGMA

Introduction, composed in 1964, for Prof. Sadhan Kumar Ghosh's *Tragedy*, Calcutta (Pradeep K. Banerjee), 1965.

WE shall never stop arguing about tragedy, and whenever a devoted scholar engages himself on this inexhaustible question, we are likely to be enthralled. There can be few more devoted students of literature than Professor Ghosh, and it was a good idea of his to set out his views on the tragic drama of our western tradition.[1]

In tragedy the human enigma is expressed, and somehow left as an enigma without inducing in us any final sense of disquiet. If we could rationalize our experience we should come near to resolving the problem of good and evil, together with what Tennyson in his lines on Vergil called 'the doubtful doom of human kind'. A full rationalization will perhaps for ever prove impossible. But every attempt is nevertheless worth-while.

Professor Ghosh turns over the famous phrases of Aristotle, considering the 'tragic flaw', the 'pity and terror' and '*katharsis*'; and also the Greek concept of '*hubris*'. These he applies variously to Greek, Shakespearian and other Renaissance tragedies, showing how far they fit or do not fit our experience. His discussions are characterized by a fine refusal to accept easy solutions, whether in the domain of morals or religion or psychology. The subject is baffling and Professor Ghosh is willing to be, within reason, baffled.

Indeed, in this very sense of perplexity we come near to the heart

1. I would take this opportunity of welcoming also Dr. Amaresh Datta's *Shakespeare's Tragic Vision and Art*, Delhi, 1963, and Dr. Satyaprasad Sengupta's incisive commentary on the various approaches to Shakespeare's tragedies in his *Trends in Shakespearian Criticism*, Calcutta. 1965. [1966]

of the matter. One of Professor Ghosh's most interesting conclusions is his reading of the Shakespearian tragic heroes as men, to use Othello's phrase (v. ii. 345), 'perplexed in the extreme'. This is surely true: it fits Brutus, Hamlet, Othello, Macbeth, Lear, Timon and Antony; though not, it would seem, Coriolanus. Professor Ghosh sees Shakespearian drama as set between, and tugged by, two main conflicting forces, Medieval and Renaissance; and here we have cause enough for mental distraction. The artistic result appeals to us all, whatever our period, for it becomes under Shakespeare's handling a reading of man at any time or place baffled by destiny. Therein lies the universality of Shakespeare.

For my part I enjoy searching in tragedy for definite causes of our paradoxical enjoyment. Professor Ghosh well observes that Lear is the only tragic hero we have who really *repents*.[1] The others attain recognition, including often a recognition of their own inadequacies, but with no psychic act of repentance in anything like the religious meaning of the term. Professor Ghosh lays emphasis on the stature of Shakespeare's heroes and the fight they put up against an implacable destiny. Somehow we do not want to see their pride, or perhaps 'integrity' would be a better word, reduced. Is it possible that, despite appearances, the hero, even a Macbeth, may be *getting somewhere*? I confess that I am myself continually looking for some solution along these lines, finding signs of some hard-to-define advance, what might be called an 'inward victory', in the greater tragic dramas of the west, from Aeschylus to Ibsen.

And yet if we pursue this course too far we may become involved in categories of supernature and human survival beyond death. Professor Ghosh comes near to admitting as much when he writes: 'Part of the pleasure of tragedy is due to men's sense of a sort of victory over death.' His words are deliberately, and wisely, vague. The danger is that too precise a definition of an after-life is liable to dissolve some vital element in the tragic experience which we have grown, rightly, to treasure. If that experience really, as we so often feel, holds the key, the spoiling of it results not merely in a loss of

1. Note however that here, as in *The Winter's Tale*, the repentance is a repentance addressed to the sanctity not of God but of a human being, Cordelia and Hermione.
[1966]

aesthetic pleasure, but in the loss of some great wisdom also. Is too easy a belief in survival, even if survival be—as I for one believe it to be—a fact, in danger of distracting us from some more important and all-containing truth which our minds are not as yet ready to understand, but which we can, at high moments of tragic experience, fleetingly apprehend?

We do not know; and Professor Ghosh is wise to be cautious. He writes with learning, with a great love of literature and a deep concern for man. He knows where dogmatism would be dangerous. But in his central trust he remains firm: 'The spirit of Man, we feel with Abelard, is the candle of the Lord.'

XVIII

SHAKESPEARE AND RELIGION

Six talks for the B.B.C. series *Lift up your Hearts* broadcast during the
Quatercentenary Shakespeare birthday week, 20–5 April 1964.

I. A KING'S PRAYER

WE generally think of religion as belonging to a world
rather different from our ordinary psychology and
everyday affairs. But the 'religion', if there is one, of
Shakespeare's total drama is comprehensive. His
main concerns are human: his plays could be divided into love-plays
and king-plays. The New Testament, concentrating on the highest
good, tends to leave us guessing in the matters of sex and politics, and
so does the religion which descends from it. It is the business of
drama to face, for good or ill, everything.

Many passages witness Shakespeare's religious sensibility. Here is
one:

> My lord of York, it better show'd with you,
> When that your flock, assembled by the bell,
> Encircled you to hear with reverence
> Your exposition on the holy text,
> Than now to see you here an iron man,
> Cheering a rout of rebels with your drum . . .
>
> *(2 Henry IV, IV. ii. 4)*

The thought is of religion as a backwater, apart from the compulsions
of state-affairs, and war.

But what of those who are inevitably involved in this wider,
generally sinful, drama?

A good, if extreme, example is King Claudius, in *Hamlet*. He is
a kindly man and a good king who has nevertheless gained his

227

throne and queen by murder. Now we are all, if we think clearly, in much the same position, since human politics and human sex are saturated in guilt. Claudius pathetically *wants* forgiveness, but is not prepared to alter his whole way of life. Few of us are: and we may even be right not to. Claudius attempts, at a poignant moment, to pray:

> O, my offence is rank, it smells to Heaven!
> It hath the primal eldest curse upon't,
> A brother's murder . . . What if this cursed hand
> Were thicker than itself with brother's blood,
> Is there not rain enough in the sweet heavens
> To wash it white as snow? Whereto serves mercy
> But to confront the visage of offence?
> And what's in prayer but this two-fold force
> To be forestalled ere we come to fall,
> Or pardon'd, being down? Then I'll look up.
> My fault is pass'd. But O, what form of prayer
> Can serve my turn? 'Forgive me my foul murder'?
> That cannot be, since I am still possess'd
> Of those effects for which I did the murder,
> My crown, mine own ambition, and my queen . . .
>   What then? What rests?
> Try what repentance can: what can it not?
> Yet what can it, when one can not repent?
> O wretched state! O bosom black as death!
> O limed soul, that struggling to be free
> Art more engag'd! Help, angels! Make assay.
> Bow, stubborn knees; and heart with strings of steel
> Be soft as sinews of the new-born babe.
> All may be well.
>
>   (III. iii. 36)

He prays, by an act of will. How many of us can do more? And this is the inevitable result:

> My words fly up, my thoughts remain below:
> Words without thoughts never to heaven go.
>   (III. iii. 97)

Try as he may, with his will, religion has not helped him. The world is in that position, today.

Something has been forgotten. We must look deeper.

II. CHRISTIANITY AND MAN

Shakespeare's main task was to establish a relationship between Christianity and the demands of man's sexual and social predicament. In respect to government the ideal was put perfectly by Portia in *The Merchant of Venice*:

> The quality of mercy is not strain'd.
> It droppeth as the gentle rain from heaven
> Upon the place beneath. It is twice bless'd:
> It blesseth him that gives and him that takes.
> 'Tis mightiest in the mightiest: it becomes
> The throned monarch better than his crown.
> His sceptre shows the force of temporal power,
> The attribute to awe and majesty
> Wherein doth sit the dread and fear of kings;
> But mercy is above this sceptred sway,
> It is enthroned in the hearts of kings,
> It is an attribute to God himself;
> And earthly power doth then show likest God's
> When mercy seasons justice.
>
> (IV. i. 184)

That *is* the ideal.

It is less easy to work it out in practice, or even through a whole play. This Shakespeare attempted in *Measure for Measure*, wherein he skilfully combines the two, related, problems of sexual psychology and government.

Duke Vincentio is a studious ruler who has seen so deeply into human nature that the execution of justice becomes impossible. The realm is accordingly in chaos.

So he hands over his office to Angelo, a man of confident rectitude and spotless reputation, to see what happens. Under the test of power Angelo is found to be less virtuous than he thought. He starts by condemning a young man for a sexual lapse, but soon after finds himself overthrown by temptation, and using his place as governor to satisfy his own criminal desires. Like the King in *Hamlet* he tries, ineffectually, to pray.

It is a play about the dangers of hypocrisy, of superficial, mental virtue out of contact with man's true nature. Man really is not as yet fit to judge his fellow men. Isabella is speaking:

> Why, all the souls that were were forfeit once,
> And He that might the vantage best have took
> Found out the remedy. How would you be
> If He, which is the top of judgement, should
> But judge you as you are?
>
> (II. ii. 73)

In any official position man is merely comic:

> O, it is excellent
> To have a giant's strength, but it is tyrannous
> To use it like a giant . . .
> Man, proud man,
> Drest in a little brief authority,
> Most ignorant of what he's most assur'd,
> His glassy essence, like an angry ape,
> Plays such fantastic tricks before high heaven
> As make the angels weep; who, with our spleens,
> Would all themselves laugh mortal.
>
> (II. ii. 107–23)

There is no easy answer. About the same time Shakespeare wrote *Troilus and Cressida* with its famous defence of authority and order:

> Take but degree away, untune that string,
> And hark! what discord follows; each thing meets
> In mere oppugnancy . . .
> Force should be right; or rather, right and wrong—
> Between whose endless jar justice resides—
> Should lose their names, and so should justice too.
> Then every thing includes itself in power,
> Power into will, will into appetite;
> And appetite, a universal wolf,
> So doubly seconded with will and power,

Must make perforce a universal prey,
And last eat up himself.

(I. iii. 109)

Control and order are apparently necessary. And yet, man remains
rebellious. It is this rebellious stuff in him that Shakespeare studies
in the great tragedies.

III. TRAGIC REVELATION

In *Measure for Measure* it was recognized that

best men are moulded out of faults,
And, for the most, become much more the better
For being a little bad.

(v. i. 440)

The thought helps us to understand Shakespeare's greater tragedies.
Their heroes, however wrong, win our admiration. When the
wicked Richard goes to the Battle of Bosworth with

Let us to't pell-mell;
If not to Heaven, then hand in hand to Hell!

(v. iii. 313)

we respond. Somehow, it does us good. Macbeth shows a superb
courage throughout his nightmare course. Lear's refusal to break
down—'No, I'll not weep' (II. iv. 286)—before the cruelty of his
daughters is the pivot of his drama.

Shakespearian tragedy is in one sense a fall, in another a rise.
Under tragedy the weak Richard II takes on true royalty, brands his
accusers, and dies magnificently. Romeo and Hamlet achieve a new
spiritual poise towards the close. So does Othello

It is the cause, it is the cause, my soul;
Let me not name it to you, you chaste stars.
It is the cause . . .

(v. ii. 1)

And Macbeth:

To-morrow, and to-morrow, and to-morrow,
Creeps in this petty pace from day to day,

231

To the last syllable of recorded time;
And all our yesterdays have lighted fools
The way to dusty death. Out, out, brief candle!
Life's but a walking shadow, a poor player
That struts and frets his hour upon the stage,
And then is heard no more—it is a tale
Told by an idiot, full of sound and fury,
Signifying nothing.

(v. v. 19)

The lines do not leave us depressed. On the contrary, we are invigorated. It is as though Macbeth has momentarily risen *above* his own fearful existence.

Lear, reunited after his madness with Cordelia, imagines a life of simple love with her, hearing people talk of 'court news':

and we'll talk with them too,
Who loses and who wins; who's in, who's out;
And take upon's the mystery of things
As if we were God's spies.

(v. iii. 14)

The autocratic old king has won through to a strange serenity *over*-looking state affairs, as from another dimension.

These heroes are all *getting somewhere*. They do not, in the religious sense, repent. They do, however, attain to self-recognition: and that seems to be all that matters. So Wolsey in *Henry VIII*, when his ambitious schemes are revealed and his life in ruins, is suddenly happy:

I know myself now; and I feel within me
A peace above all earthly dignities,
A still and quiet conscience.

(III. ii. 379)

There is no condemnation. Othello in remorse *wishes* to suffer hell-torments, but our own response is nearer the couplet in *Macbeth*

Though his bark cannot be lost,
Yet it shall be tempest-toss'd.

(I. iii. 24)

Today spirit-communicators tell us that after death we are not punished, but that our earthly lives are exposed, to ourselves and others, exactly as they have been. Some of us might prefer to be punished.

Judgement is given by our own, greater selves, which are with us always. That is the meaning of Shakespeare's words

> This above all: to thine own self be true,
> And it must follow, as the night the day,
> Thou canst not then be false to any man.
>
> (*Hamlet*, I. iii. 78)

Towards this truth our tragic heroes advance. The suffering and the evil help. Even Henry V knew that

> There is some soul of goodness in things evil
> Would men observingly distil it out.
>
> (IV. i. 4)

That is as good a text as any for the revelations of Shakespearian tragedy.

IV. BEYOND TRAGEDY

The tragedies are plays of death. But in *Timon of Athens* Timon knew that 'nothing brings me all things' (v. i. 193); and Shakespeare presses beyond tragedy, beyond death. His guiding star is love.

Romeo dreamed of an awaking from death, made an 'emperor' (v. i. 9) by Juliet's love. To Cleopatra, after Antony's death, Antony has become the universe:

> I dream'd there was an emperor Antony . . .
> His face was as the heavens, and therein stuck
> A sun and moon, which kept their course, and lighted
> The little O, the earth . . .
> His legs bestrid the ocean; his rear'd arm
> Crested the world; his voice was propertied
> As all the tuned spheres, and that to friends;
> But when he meant to quail and shake the orb,
> He was as rattling thunder. For his bounty
> There was no winter in't . . .
>
> (v. ii. 76)

She goes to meet him, leaving the 'elements' of 'baser life' for 'fire' and 'air' (v. ii. 291–2).

Two of Shakespeare's last plays might be called 'resurrection' parables. To 'the music of the spheres' (v. i. 231) Pericles finds his daughter Marina, supposed dead, like a symbol of eternity:

> Thou dost look
> Like Patience gazing on kings' graves, and smiling
> Extremity out of act.
>
> (v. i. 139)

His wife, Thaisa, after being buried at sea, is revived, just like the raising of Lazarus, by the saintly Cerimon, and is reunited with Pericles in a temple. In *The Winter's Tale* the penitent Leontes—for these parables have room, as the tragedies did not, for penitence—is shown by Paulina a statue of his supposedly dead queen, Hermione; and he gradually discovers that the statue lives:

> Leontes: What was he that did make it? See, my lord,
> Would you not deem it breath'd, and that those veins
> Did verily bear blood? . . . Still, methinks,
> There is an air comes from her: what fine chisel
> Could ever yet cut breath?
>
> *   *   *   *   *   *
>
> Paulina: Either forbear,
> Quit presently the chapel, or resolve you
> For more amazement. If you can behold it,
> I'll make the statue move indeed, descend,
> And take you by the hand . . .
>
> (v. iii. 63–89)

She demands Leontes' 'faith'. Then:

> Music, awake her: strike!
> 'Tis time; descend; be stone no more . . .
> Leontes: O, she's warm.
> If this be magic, let it be an art
> Lawful as eating.
>
> (v. iii. 95–111)

In both *Pericles* and *The Winter's Tale* correspondences with the New Testament are obvious. But these dramas are not, as is Shakespeare's last play *Henry VIII*, explicitly Christian. Rather, by power of his own dramatic explorations Shakespeare has wrenched from the great enigma, death, a conclusion that corroborates, without copying, the Christian revelation.

Such are the understandings which we must bring to *The Tempest*, and in particular to Prospero's great speech on earthly transience:

> These our actors,
> As I foretold you, were all spirits, and
> Are melted into air, into thin air.
> And like the baseless fabric of this vision,
> The cloud-capp'd towers, the gorgeous palaces,
> The solemn temples, the great globe itself,
> Yea, all which it inherit, shall dissolve,
> And, like this insubstantial pageant faded,
> Leave not a rack behind. We are such stuff
> As dreams are made on, and our little life
> Is rounded with a sleep.
>
> (IV. i. 148)

Though agnostic and non-committal, the words nevertheless expand our perceptions beyond all normal experience. And *The Tempest* has more in it than this: it simultaneously sums Shakespeare's life-work and shows man as wielding powers beyond the human; aureoled, by magic certainly, perhaps by the divine.

V. SHAKESPEARE'S ENGLAND

Shakespeare's thought-adventures, though bold, all work within a framework of respect to the community and to religion. He was a patriot; more, a Christian patriot. In the England of his time he seems to have felt that State and Church had, so far as was humanly possible, come together.

His best known patriot speech is in *Richard II* (II. i. 40–68), 'This royal throne of kings, this sceptred isle'. England is a fortress

'bound in with the triumphant sea' and the English a crusading
people

> Renowned for their deeds as far from home,
> For Christian service and true chivalry,
> As is the sepulchre in stubborn Jewry
> Of the world's ransom, blessed Mary's Son.
>
> (II. i. 53)

Shakespeare sees England, as did Milton later, as a Messiah-nation.

Richard's throne is usurped by Bolingbroke whose reign as
Henry IV is disturbed by civil conflict. It is for his son, as Henry V,
to remove the curse. He is conceived as a strong and good king and a
great leader who, as all secular rulers must, realizes that his position
is tainted with sin. Here is his prayer before the battle of Agincourt:

> O God of battles! steel my soldiers' hearts . . .
>   Not today, O Lord!
> O, not today, think not upon the fault
> My father made in compassing the crown . . .
> Five hundred poor I have in yearly pay
> Who twice a day their wither'd hands hold up
> Toward heaven, to pardon blood; and I have built
> Two chantries, where the sad and solemn priests
> Sing still for Richard's soul.
>
> (IV. i. 309)

I see King Henry here as the type of all secular government, in any
place or time.

Shakespeare's kings must always be understood both as individuals and as representatives of powers beyond themselves. That is
how we must read Cranmer's prophecy at the end of *Henry VIII*,
Shakespeare's last play, composed after *The Tempest*, and serving to
enclose his total work in a national frame. Cranmer is speaking
prophetically of the reigns to follow of Elizabeth I and James I, but
we must read them as symbols of a longer process of which we,
today, form part. Of Elizabeth he says:

> Truth shall nurse her;
> Holy and heavenly thoughts still counsel her;
> She shall be lov'd, and fear'd. Her own shall bless her;

Her foes shake like a field of beaten corn,
And hang their heads with sorrow. Good grows with her.
In her days every man shall eat in safety
Under his own vine what he plants, and sing
The merry songs of peace to all his neighbours.
God shall be truly known . . .

(v. v. 29)

England's royalty is a Phoenix, dying in Elizabeth and reborn in
James I

Who, from the sacred ashes of her honour,
Shall star-like rise, as great in fame as she was,
And so stand, fix'd. Peace, plenty, love, truth, terror,
That were the servants to this chosen infant,
Shall then be his, and like a vine grow to him.
Wherever the bright sun of heaven shall shine,
His honour and the greatness of his name
Shall be, and make new nations; he shall flourish,
And, like a mountain cedar, reach his branches
To all the plains about him. Our children's children
Shall see this, and bless Heaven.

(v. v. 46)

That is Shakespeare's last word—a prophecy of his own country's
creative influence across the globe.

VI. THE SONNETS

Shakespeare saw deep into the abysms of evil in man and society; and
yet his sense of human splendour was preserved.

In his Sonnets he, as Wordsworth says in 'Scorn not the Sonnet . . .', 'unlocked his heart'. More, he explains how he came to see
mankind as glorious.

The Sonnets record his devotion to a beautiful young man:

When in the chronicle of wasted time
I see descriptions of the fairest wights,
And beauty making beautiful old rhyme
In praise of ladies dead and lovely knights,
Then, in the blazon of sweet beauty's best,

Of hand, of foot, of lip, of eye, of brow,
I see their antique pen would have express'd
Even such a beauty as you master now.
So all their praises are but prophecies
Of this our time, all you prefiguring;
And, for they look'd but with divining eyes,
They had not skill enough your worth to sing:
    For we, which now behold these present days,
    Have eyes to wonder, but lack tongues to praise.

(Sonnet 106)

This was the kind of adoration experienced earlier by Socrates, Plato, and Michelangelo, as later by Byron, Tennyson and Wilde. The hero of the Old Testament, King David, experienced it; and the protagonist of the New Testament too, in his relation to the Beloved Disciple, in the Gospel of John (pp. 22, 28–9, 238, 259).

From the external beauty flowers love. Here is another sonnet, where the poet insists that love is, or should be—perhaps he is not quite sure of himself—independent of physical beauty:

Let me not to the marriage of true minds
Admit impediments: love is not love
Which alters when it alteration finds,
Or bends with the remover to remove.
O no! it is an ever-fixed mark
That looks on tempests and is never shaken;
It is the star to every wandering bark,
Whose worth's unknown, although his height be taken.
Love's not Time's fool, though rosy lips and cheeks
Within his bending sickle's compass come:
Love alters not with his brief hours and weeks,
But bears it out even to the edge of doom.
    If this be error and upon me prov'd,
    I never writ, nor no man ever lov'd.

(Sonnet 116)

Is the poet's love failing as the years go by? We cannot be sure.

But of this we can be sure: in the course of it the one beauty has irradiated for him the whole of creation. The loved one, he says, is for him present in all beautiful and in all hideous forms. His own mind is as a great king being flattered by what must, surely, be the eye's deception. Even so, it is an honourable deception:

> Or whether doth my mind, being crown'd with you,
> Drink up the monarch's plague, this flattery?
> Or whether shall I say, mine eye saith true,
> And that your love taught it this alchemy,
> To make of monsters and things indigest
> Such cherubins as your sweet self resemble,
> Creating every bad a perfect best
> As fast as objects to his beams assemble?
> O, 'tis the first; 'tis flattery in my seeing,
> And my great mind most kingly drinks it up:
> Mine eye well knows what with his gust is 'greeing,
> And to his palate doth prepare the cup.
>   If it be poison'd, 'tis the lesser sin
>   That mine eye loves it and doth first begin.
>
>   (Sonnet 114)

'Poison'd' and 'sin' are well-chosen words. There *is* a risk in 'creating every bad a perfect best'; and a glory too, as the actor of Richard III, Iago, or Caliban well knows. Intellectually Shakespeare is himself baffled. But it has happened. The universe has in fact been stamped with God's signature; and that is how the works of Shakespeare were born (pp. 288–9).

XIX

SHAKESPEARE AND THE ENGLISH LANGUAGE

Composed for the Canadian Broadcasting Corporation and broadcast in
Canada on 29 April 1964; subsequently published in *A Garland for Shakespeare* by the Shakespeare Quatercentenary Celebrations Committee,
Jalpaiguri, India in 1964; and now included as a tape-recording published
by Sound Seminars, Cincinnati (p. 13 above, note).

SHAKESPEARE wrote at a time when the English language
was seething with powers and possibilities. On to the central
blend of Anglo-Saxon and Norman French new words
were being grafted from Latin and Greek, from French and
Italian, and from the East. The invention of printing had given
European tongues a new mobility, over-leaping geographic boundaries; education and reading received new impetus. Readers were
greedy for translations. Across Europe Latin, so long the universal
language of western thought, was giving way to native speech; and
the cultures of ancient Greece and Rome were becoming, as they are
again in the translations of our time to a yet wider audience, common
property. Of this grand intermingling and exploitation of cultures
and languages England was, and still is, the main beneficiary. For
some reason words flew towards her, as though magnetized to this
island, and intoxicating even the illiterate with their wonderful
sounds and half-felt meanings. People were in love with words; and
with the words came translations—it was all one process—carrying
new ship-loads of thought and story, myths of ancient Greece and
Rome, romances from Italy, the great Bible itself. Passage after passage in Elizabethan poetry is inspired by exotic dreams of far lands;
and it was just because exploration was only beginning, because the
world was in process of *being opened out*, that men could enjoy, as it

241

were, the *soul* of discovery, could feel earthly existence itself as open-ing out. Geographic discovery was raw material for what Andrew Marvell in *The Garden* called those 'other lands and other seas' of the poetic imagination.

In such a period and in such a land, a poet's mind might well find itself, as did Spenser's, almost over-burdened with riches. A great poet could be, as never before, comprehensive, summing the ages, embracing the earth, prophetic of the future. All that was needed was receptivity balanced by control. Shakespeare had both.

Let us look for a moment at the people's names in what is gener-ally regarded as Shakespeare's most universal play, *Hamlet*. Claudius and Marcellus are Latin; Laertes, from Homer, Greek; Polonius is Greek-Latin; Ophelia Greek-*ish*; Horatio, 'more an antique Roman than a Dane' (v. ii. 355), Latin Italianized; Bernardo, Teutonic-Italian, and Francisco Italian or Spanish; Reynaldo, Italian French. French society is much discussed, and a Frenchman, Lamond or Lamord according to our reading, talked of by Laertes (IV. vii. 92). Fortinbras is a French derivation. Voltimand is Nordic and Cor-nelius Latin-Dutch. Rosencrantz and Guildenstern are German, and Osric, alone, Danish. As for English, Gertrude is Anglo-Saxon and so, though there was the original 'Amleth', is 'Hamlet'. 'Hamlet' is defined in our dictionary as 'a small village, especially one without a church'. Whatever we make of that, we find Hamlet and his Mother English, and about them swirl this universe of cosmo-politan names. The play is a microcosm of Shakespeare's England.

We cannot talk of Shakespeare's 'style' because he has so many. Though his vocabulary was immense and he was a master of metaphor and allusion, the central pith of his writing is native English; and he could when he wished write with an extreme sim-plicity. This he does in *Julius Caesar*, where he relies on simple words, many of one syllable, and a lucid syntax. To the Elizabethan, Caesar was an imperial archetype, and his assassination the very heart of history. In this play, where 'the heavens themselves blaze forth the death of princes' (II. ii. 31), Shakespeare, as Masefield (in *Shakespeare and Spiritual Life*, p. 201 above) puts it, saw life 'start-lingly'; and, as though in reverence before his mighty theme, Shakespeare used a bare style. Here is Cassius urging that Caesar is no more than an ordinary man:

> I cannot tell what you and other men
> Think of this life; but, for my single self,
> I had as lief not be as live to be
> In awe of such a thing as I myself.
> I was born free as Caesar; so were you.
> We both have fed as well, and we can both
> Endure the winter's cold as well as he.
>
> (I. ii. 93)

Even when the thought is grandiose, as in Caesar's comparison of himself to the North Star

> The skies are painted with unnumber'd sparks,
> They are all fire, and every one doth shine,
> But there's but one in all doth hold his place . . .
>
> (III. i. 63)

—even here, the *language* is simple.

But what if all Caesars are cheats? and revolutions too? What if all history is a pointless business? *Troilus and Cressida* is a *mental* drama, probing in thought and critical in purpose. In it Shakespeare sees human engagements as they are when one concentrates on *thinking* about them. 'All thought', said Oscar Wilde, 'is immoral . . . Nothing survives being thought of' (*A Woman of No Importance*, III). It is true; and not very much survives in *Troilus and Cressida*, even though, being Shakespeare, the poet leaves us with too fine a sense of pathos and too electrified a perception for the result to be wholly pessimistic.

When thought becomes divorced from instinct, its language will be abstract; and that means a high proportion of those new Latinized words that were at this time pouring in to supplement the native stock. In *Love's Labour's Lost* Shakespeare makes fine comedy of the new love of Latin derivations. In *Troilus and Cressida*, concentrating on thought alone divorced from that practical faith, or trust, by which we have to live, he indulges in them himself.

Their king Agamemnon is arguing that the failure of the Greeks in the campaign against Troy is no disgrace, since human purposes inevitably go astray. True, even unanswerable, as thought, though scarcely a practical argument for a political leader:

> Princes,
> What grief hath set the jaundice on your cheeks?
> The ample proposition that hope makes
> In all designs begun on earth below
> Fails in the promis'd largeness: checks and disasters
> Grow in the veins of actions highest rear'd,
> As knots, by the conflux of meeting sap,
> Infect the sound pine and divert his grain
> Tortive and errant from his course of growth.
> Nor, princes, is it matter new to us
> That we come short of our suppose so far
> That after seven years' siege yet Troy walls stand;
> Sith every action that hath gone before
> Whereof we have record, trial did draw
> Bias and thwart, not answering the aim
> And that unbodied figure of the thought
> That gave't surmised shape.
>
> (I. iii. I)

It is not only a play made of thought; a great deal of it, as here, is *thought about thought*. Ulysses soon after complains of critics who fail to realize that those who work with their minds are superior to those who perform merely the physical actions:

> They tax our policy, and call it cowardice;
> Count wisdom as no member of the war;
> Forestall prescience, and esteem no act
> But that of hand . . .
>
> (I. iii. 197)

Such critics, he says, quite ignore 'the still and mental parts'.

See what awkward word usages, many of them Latin, these speeches contain: 'conflux', 'tortive', 'bias and thwart', 'surmised', 'forestall', 'prescience'. Shakespeare regularly draws on Latin; indeed, he seems to have coined many of our best known derivations himself. But he seldom *worries* us as he does in *Troilus and Cressida*: generally, as by some uncanny instinct, he only uses or coins words that will have *survival value*. In *Troilus and Cressida* alone do his

244

derivations strike us as awkward and unnatural. They seem to be words that exist only for their paraphrasable meaning, without either sense-perception or magic; and yet men are creatures in a natural and magical setting, and such naked thinking is not quite natural to them, certainly not natural to Shakespeare.

Even in *Troilus and Cressida* we have just found nature asserting its presence, as in that fine metaphor of the 'knots' on a tree made from the 'conflux' of 'sap'. Perhaps what might be called Shakespeare's instinctive style—what the scholarly Milton, himself so prone to Latinized word-coinings that did not survive, called in *L'Allegro* his 'native wood-notes wild'—is one in which nature dominates. Shakespeare's historical plays are redolent of the English countryside; his patriotism is made of it; *Richard II* is a play of what might be called a 'pastoral royalism'. Or France, being near home, may do as well. Here is a French lord, Burgundy, making a plea for peace to return to 'this best garden of the world, our fertile France', now all wild and untrimmed through lack of care:

> Her vine, the merry cheerer of the heart,
> Unpruned dies; her hedges even-pleach'd,
> Like prisoners wildly overgrown with hair,
> Put forth disorder'd twigs; her fallow leas
> The darnel, hemlock and rank fumitory
> Doth root upon, while that the coulter rusts
> That should deracinate such savagery.
> The even mead, that erst brought sweetly forth
> The freckled cowslip, burnet and green clover,
> Wanting the scythe, all uncorrected, rank,
> Conceives by idleness, and nothing teems
> But hateful docks, rough thistles, kecksies, burrs . . .
>
> (v. ii. 41)

England and France are, for Shakespeare, 'home', and his feeling for them is one with his feeling for their especial kind of fertility, their roots in nature; but he can range farther. He can attack more subtle problems involving alien races. Shakespeare's language varies according to the task in hand, and nowhere else is this so clear as in his creation of Shylock in *The Merchant of Venice*.

There were Jews in England, but not many. In his classic study

The Growth and Structure of the English Language Otto Jespersen tells us that, though there was no recognizable Jewish-English dialect for Shakespeare to draw upon, and though one can point to no definitely Jewish trait—apart of course from actual Hebraic references—in Shylock's talk, yet Shakespeare has created for him a number of mannerisms a little off-centre. Such, we may suggest, are 'my tribe', 'my moneys and my usances' and 'flesh of muttons, beefs or goats' (I. iii. 52, 58, 109, 168); together with his way, twice, of explaining, as though an outsider living in his own world, his metaphors: 'land-rats and water-rats, land-thieves and water-thieves—I mean pirates' (I. iii. 23), and 'stop my house's ears, I mean my casements' (II. v. 34). The result does in fact register with us as Jewish. Shakespeare has somehow felt into the *soul* of Jewry, and created from that. This is only one particularly clear example of his usual method.

In *The Merchant of Venice* we meet another interesting alien: the Prince of Morocco. Afterwards Shakespeare built a whole play around a Moor, and called it '*Othello*'.

The Moors were an African race forming part of the great Arabian civilization that stretched from the East to the Atlantic. For centuries it had kept alive Greek thought when Europe was, comparatively, dark, and had been the guardian of scientific knowledge. A number of Arabic words such as 'admiral' and 'algebra' exist in modern English as memorials to its military and scientific ascendancy. The Moors, based victoriously for centuries in southern Spain, penetrated Europe. Through them two great cultural strains, Christian-European and Moslem-Arabian, collided. *Othello* is about this collision.

The hero, Othello, has an aura of warlike adventure such as the Elizabethans loved and admired. But he is very un-English. Shakespeare gives him a language of exotic reference and a music all his own. Francis Berry in *Poetry and the Physical Voice* (1962) has well referred its orotund, full-throated, quality, to African, negroid speech. Othello is of Africa and all its violent sun-bred instincts; but he also bears himself royally as one worthy of a great culture, which is nevertheless not quite ours. A prime agent in the drama is his magical handherchief, from Egypt, woven by a 'sibyl' in a prophetic trance. Heroic action, exploration and magic all contribute to this amazing racial composite, Othello.[1] He is moreover half-Europeanized, and is newly married to a Venetian, and is now himself a Christian, until the tragedy forces him back on his own lonely, mysterious, valuations.

Thinking his wife Desdemona unfaithful, he plans to murder her in her bed as a sacred duty. His speech reflects a remote, almost unearthly, nobility as he addresses the stars:

> It is the cause, it is the cause, my soul;
> Let me not name it to you, you chaste stars.
> It is the cause. Yet I'll not shed her blood,
> Nor scar that whiter skin of hers than snow,
> As smooth as monumental alabaster.
> Yet she must die, else she'll betray more men.
> Put out the light, and then—put out the light.
> If I quench thee, thou flaming minister,
> I can again thy former light restore
> Should I repent me; but once put out thy light,
> Thou cunning'st pattern of excelling nature,
> I know not where is that Promethean heat
> That can thy light relume. When I have pluck'd the rose
> I cannot give it vital growth again.
> It needs must wither. I'll smell it on the tree.
> O balmy breath that doth almost persuade
> Justice to break her sword! One more, one more.
> Be thus when thou art dead, and I will kill thee
> And love thee after. One more, and this the last.
> So sweet was ne'er so fatal. I must weep,
> But they are cruel tears. This sorrow's heavenly,
> It strikes where it doth love. She wakes.
>
> (v. ii. 1)

His thought-processes, his very being, are alien to us, yet noble. This is no speech of a barbarian or a man adrift from ethic. His words 'Promethean', 'alabaster', are marvellous. His global travels (I. iii.

1. For Othello's personality see also *The Wheel of Fire*, 1930, etc.; G. M. Matthews, 'Othello and the Dignity of Man' in *Shakespeare in a Changing World*, essays ed. Arnold Kettle, 1964; Peter Alexander, *Shakespeare*, 1964 (227); Eldred Jones, *Othello's Countrymen*, reviewed *T.L.S.* 15 April 1965; and Miriam Halevy, 'The Racial Problem in Shakespeare—I', *The Jewish Quarterly*, Spring 1966; XIV, 1.

128–70) are being extended to the cosmos, to the stars, or moon:

> It is the very error of the moon,
> She comes more near the earth than she was wont,
> And makes men mad.

(v. ii. 107)

Again, with a splendid Greek derivation:

> Nay, had she been true,
> If Heaven would make me such another world
> Of one entire and perfect chrysolite,
> I'd not have sold her for it.

(v. ii. 141)

No one else in Shakespeare talks quite like that.

Shakespeare's range is such that each speech demands a different speaking; so, for that matter, does every line. Not nearly enough attention is given to the subtleties of Shakespeare's language, its variations in speed and tone and its interplay of homely realism and rhetorical sublimity. Complications are endless. Stage performances too often fail to project vocally the riches that lie before us. They fail to touch the *soul* of Shakespeare's art.

I use the word 'soul' deliberately. Language may seem to correspond simply to 'thought'; yet poetry, when read *aloud*, is—or may be—far more than *thought*; and for what it is we have no easy word. A good speech well spoken is spoken with the speaker's whole, physical and spiritual, personality. Spoken poetry is life distilled.[1]

Shylock and Othello were created, as we say, from 'within', which is the same as saying from their 'souls', and externals found and fitted to the intuition. Shakespeare is always working like this. There is always a something behind, of which his text is the surface.

The coming together of languages and cultures in Shakespeare's England was itself far more than a convergence of geographic and historic externals. England was the meeting place of psychic currents, from all sorts and conditions of mankind, past and present; in England, they became *one*. It was because Shakespeare's England

---

1. I can only point to my own illustrations on the three tapes, especially 'Shakespeare's Rhetoric' and 'Byron's Rhetoric', published by Sound Seminars, Cincinnati (p. 13 above, note).

had made its own so many influences that Shakespeare's poetry could be simultaneously so English, so varied, and so universal, so that even his patriotism has spread its influence across the world. Today it is accepted readily by readers of other nations. In fact, they seem to take it as their *own*. His England is theirs. My brother once called Vergil's Rome a 'spiritual city'; we can say the same of Shakespeare's England.

It is true that Shakespeare's most famous patriotic speech from *Richard II*, 'This royal throne of kings, this sceptred isle', seems at first far from universal. England is felt as an island-fortress guarded by the sea

> Which serves it in the office of a wall,
> Or as a moat defensive to a house,
> Against the envy of less happier lands . . .
>
> (II. i. 47)

But after his speeches of early patriotism—*King John* has another—Shakespeare wrote many dark and probing works, surveying all that was most grim in man's soul and his social, and cosmic, predicament; and then, as though tempered by fire, his human and cosmic trust gives us *Antony and Cleopatra* and the last plays, touched by gleams, or more than gleams, of an insight *beyond tragedy*. After *The Tempest* he returned to a national and near-distance theme in *Henry VIII*. *Henry VIII* concludes with his greatest patriotic speech of all; a speech of spiritualized patriotism, of a subdued yet vast music. In it Shakespeare sees England no longer on the defensive, but as expanding.

Archbishop Cranmer is speaking over the child Elizabeth at her christening, the King, Henry VIII, beside him. He speaks of the reigns to follow of Elizabeth I and James I, but the words take on universality and may be read as a more general, national, prophecy:

> This royal infant—heaven still move about her!—
> Though in her cradle, yet now promises
> Upon this land a thousand thousand blessings,
> Which time shall bring to ripeness: she shall be—
> But few now living can behold that goodness—

A pattern to all princes living with her,
And all that shall succeed. Saba was never
More covetous of wisdom and fair virtue
Than this pure soul shall be: all princely graces,
That mould up such a mighty piece as this is,
With all the virtues that attend the good,
Shall still be doubled on her; truth shall nurse her;
Holy and heavenly thoughts still counsel her;
She shall be lov'd, and fear'd. Her own shall bless her;
Her foes shake like a field of beaten corn,
And hang their heads with sorrow. Good grows with her.
In her days every man shall eat in safety
Under his own vine what he plants, and sing
The merry songs of peace to all his neighbours.
God shall be truly known; and those about her
From her shall read the perfect ways of honour,
And by those claim their greatness, not by blood.
Nor shall this peace sleep with her, but as when
The bird of wonder dies, the maiden phoenix,
Her ashes new-create another heir
As great in admiration as herself,
So shall she leave her blessedness to one—
When Heaven shall call her from this cloud of darkness—
Who, from the sacred ashes of her honour,
Shall star-like rise, as great in fame as she was,
And so stand, fix'd. Peace, plenty, love, truth, terror,
That were the servants to this chosen infant,
Shall then be his, and like a vine grow to him.
Wherever the bright sun of heaven shall shine,
His honour and the greatness of his name
Shall be, and make new nations; he shall flourish,
And, like a mountain cedar, reach his branches
To all the plains about him. Our children's children
Shall see this, and bless Heaven.

(V. v. 18)

England is here a great spreading, and creative, power, destined to make 'new nations'. With this speech Shakespeare's life-work concludes.

Shakespeare had the first American colonies to go upon, and he was probably thinking of those, but his words were truer than he knew. By the very power and nature of his genius he was *likely* to speak truer than he knew, because it is the business of great poets to do just this. Today England is no longer in the old sense an island; the 'moat' is there, but it is no or little defence, and what was recently called her 'empire', and is now known as the 'commonwealth', is rapidly changing. Britain may seem to have little enough of political or military power. Even so, one of the 'new nations' of which Shakespeare wrote has a great deal of power: the United States of America. More—the language spoken in common by Britain and America has not only spread across the globe, but is now *increasing its hold*. Made as is no other language from a multiplicity of tongues, it is now on the way to becoming, as near as any one language can become, a universal medium. One even sometimes feels that some of its best music comes out when spoken by an Oriental, or an African.

While the English language spreads, it takes Shakespeare with it; and yet, since we cannot well assess the power Shakespeare has exerted to make the English language what it is, it may be that it is Shakespeare that is part cause of the language's appeal. Shakespeare has his own undisputed appeal anyway to nations of the West and to nations of the East. Young people all over the world read him and act him at schools and universities. It would not be easy to say which of the two, Shakespeare or the English language, gains most from their joint collaboration, but it *is* easy to see that together they are a power of unpredictable magnitude. Shakespeare once wrote of

> the prophetic soul
> Of the wide world dreaming on things to come.
> (Sonnet 107)

It is not unreasonable to suggest that within the vision of that 'soul' there may lie a world of the future bound together into a spiritual commonwealth speaking—as Wordsworth has it (p. 138 above)— 'the tongue that Shakespeare spake', and finding in that bond their union, and their inspiration.

XX

NEW LIGHT ON THE SONNETS

Broadcast by the B.B.C. on Shakespeare's birthday, 23 April 1964. Published in *The Listener*, as 'New Light on Shakespeare's Sonnets', 30 April 1964; LXXI, 1831. I use below a slightly longer version which had exceeded the time-limit, and had to be cut for broadcasting.

AMONG the many publications of Shakespeare's quatercentenary the Sonnets certainly hold, to use a Shakespearian phrase, 'pride of place'.[1]

The old conflict as to the identity of Shakespeare's friend rages as fiercely as ever. The first edition of the Sonnets in 1609 was dedicated by the publisher Thomas Thorpe to 'Mr. W.H.' (i.e. 'Master W.H.') as 'the only begetter of these ensuing sonnets'. Dr. A. L. Rowse and Mr. Peter Quennell in their recent biographies favour the Earl of Southampton, whose initials were 'H.W.', and follow Mrs. C. C. Stope's biography of Southampton in taking Thorpe's 'W. H.' to apply to Sir William Hervey, the Earl's stepfather, supposing that it was he who gave the manuscript to Thorpe. But the reading of 'only begetter' as 'only producer' has no support in the word-usage of Shakespeare's day, since 'beget' regularly means 'engender' (see below, pp. 329-30, 334-5). W. H. had inspired the poetry: that is obviously what Thorpe meant.

In his new monograph *An Introduction to the Sonnets of Shakespeare*, Prof. Dover Wilson appears at first to be on firmer ground in his support of the Earl of Pembroke, whose initials were W.H. But, as A. C. Bradley noted in his essay 'Shakespeare the Man' in

---

1. My first contributions to this renewal of interest were the letters to *The Times Literary Supplement* printed in my Appendix. The first two were written before I had seen Dr. Hotson's book; of the third I am not sure. I should now add to the names mentioned in my present essay those of W. G. Ingram and Theodore Redpath, whose edition of the Sonnets appeared later in the year. [1966]

Oxford Lectures on Poetry, many of the Sonnets are phrased in a manner, and they are certainly often barbed with a criticism, that we must regard as wildly improbable for a man of Shakespeare's status addressing an earl. In his recent edition of the Sonnets Dr. Rowse himself observes that 'nothing else in our literature' resembles this extraordinary relationship; it is called 'quite unprecedented'. Yes: and when we come up against a supposition without precedent for which there is no evidence, it is as well to be on our guard.

And yet a number of authorities during the last hundred years have supported either Pembroke or Southampton. Why? Partly, I think, from fear of homosexuality. A patron earl sounds so safe.

If Southampton was the Friend the Sonnets would be dated about the middle 1590's; if Pembroke, they could run into the next century.

In 1949 Dr. Leslie Hotson published his challenging essay *Shakespeare's Sonnets Dated*, which followed Samuel Butler in arguing that Sonnet 107

> Not mine own fears, nor the prophetic soul
> Of the wide world dreaming on things to come

referred not to some event of the 1590's or the accession of James I in 1603, but to the defeat of the Armada in 1588. He, like Butler, accordingly dated the Sonnets at the start of Shakespeare's career, and adduced strong corroborative evidence for two other Sonnets which appear to contain contemporary references. Hotson's revolutionary thesis met a varied reception, the most important objections being that the quality of much of the poetry pointed to a later date.

Dr. Hotson at that time produced no candidate for W.H., though he did state in his book (36) that he was 'grooming one'. In my own study of the Sonnets, *The Mutual Flame*, published in 1955, I found Hotson's dating supported by much of my own reading of the Sonnets, which seemed to indicate an early period at least for the events recorded, though I remained, like others, unsatisfied in regard to the poetry. Since I followed Bradley in believing that W.H. was a gentleman but no lord, I threw out the suggestion (9) that should Hotson's candidate eventually 'turn out to be a law student at the Inns of Court, we might suppose him to be in some measure responsible for Shakespeare's love of legal metaphor'.

What was wanted was a young gentleman with whom Shakespeare might have associated on fairly equal terms, whose initials were 'W.H.', whose Christian name, because three of the Sonnets (135, 136, 143) lead us to suppose so, was William, and who was in London at the appropriate time. Did such a man exist?

He did. In his new volume *Mr. W.H.* (i.e. *Master W.H.*) Dr. Hotson tells us how, after some fruitless work on a certain William Heynes, presumably the young man that he was 'grooming' in 1949, he has now discovered a satisfactory candidate. He comes from a distinguished Lincolnshire family, was a younger contemporary of Marlowe at Cambridge, and was admitted to Gray's Inn in the year 1586. His name is William Hatcliffe.[1]

Hotson's candidate meets the demand that though W.H. cannot have been more than a plain gentleman, yet he must also, because the Sonnets say so, have been the centre of some kind of general devotion. Now it turns out that Hatcliffe was in his second year chosen 'Prince of Purpoole' at Gray's Inn. At the Inns of Court there were from time to time Christmas rituals usually led by a Student King, functioning like the Boy Bishop of the medieval Church. These affairs were both sumptuous and serious, involving orations, councils and elaborate ceremonial, all at once less than reality and more than play-acting, though plays too were included, the Inns of Court having been for many years strong centres of dramatic activity. The elected Prince visited the Queen and put on a play for her. Everything was done in high state. The Prince, like the Boy Bishop, had to be good-looking, for the ritual was an adoration of visible perfection, shown best in all the splendour of youth. William Hatcliffe was elected Prince in the winter of 1587.

Hotson rightly observes that the Sonnets address their idol not as a great lord but as a sovereign. In so doing Shakespeare was adjusting himself to what was, at the moment, a social fact; it was more than metaphor.

There is another line of evidence. Hatcliffe's armorial bearings contained three white four-petalled primroses, flowers regarded as

1. My suggestion of an Inns of Court candidate in *The Mutual Flame* leaves me naturally disposed to favour Dr. Hotson's discovery: in this and other respects he seems to have found the man I was expecting. [1966]

emblematic of 'true-love'. These emblems correspond neatly both to the three quatrains of the Shakespearian Sonnets and to their phrases on roses and fidelity. Hotson argues that Hatcliffe's princedom was probably developed according to his private emblems to make him a Prince of True-Love, though here I think that his capitalization of 'Love' for his supporting quotations from the Sonnets where the original has no capitals may be dangerous. Another argument concerns images of 'sun' and 'gold'; and Hotson equates a little heavily certain of Shakespeare's poetic implications with the topaz, a jewel whose emblematic meanings are shown to be apposite for his purpose.

In my own study I listed as dominant in the Sonnets the following impressions: Rose, King, Sun, Gold, Jewels. Hotson's evidence has now shown all these to be exactly suited to the ritual king. What a literary appraisal regards as metaphor he shows to have had a certain actuality. He appears however to have ignored the main jewel references in the poetry which might have strengthened his discussion of the topaz, which as it stands lacks support.

He might also have made use of the reiterated theme of antiquity which is a recurring theme in the Sonnets' metaphysic of time (*The Mutual Flame*, 82–5). He tells us that the aim of the Boy King ritual was to bring back temporarily the Saturnian age of gold in all its truth and loveliness, and leaves it at that. Shakespeare, playing on the words 'antiquity' and 'antique', sees his friend as 'an archetype of all that is best in legend and literature', as one 'who will exist in poetry for ages to come, as he existed in ages past' (*The Mutual Flame*, 85). Here surely we have yet another corroboration.

There is a well-known picture by Nicholas Hilliard showing a young Elizabethan gentleman, hand on heart and leaning against a tree, among roses. Hotson gives reason for supposing it to be a picture of Hatcliffe as True-Love, while also noting that Shakespeare says in Sonnet 16 that his love had been painted by 'this time's pencil', a phrase which, if we accept it—since, though reference to a painter is explicit, the phrase depends for the full effect Hotson gives it on a textual emendation (the removal of a bracket) —might well indicate Hilliard. The hair is of the right colour, auburn, for the 'buds of marjoram' of Sonnet 99, 'The forward violet thus did I chide'. I doubt if Hotson has sufficiently high-lighted the *exact* equivalence of the hair in the picture to T. G. Tucker's conclusion based on this Sonnet (*The Sonnets of Shake-speare*, 1924; Commentary, 173) that W.H.'s 'hair was of a brown auburn and also inclined to curl in *knots*'.

In the printer's lay-out of Thorpe's dedication Hotson is at pains to find the syllables Hat-liv embedded. In the Sonnets themselves he finds a recurring play on the syllable 'hat' (in words such as 'what' and 'that') closely followed by 'live' or 'leave'. Few of us will be at first impressed by this evidence, but when in reference to the Dark Lady, convincingly identified with the Lucy Morgan, court lady, prostitute and finally bawd to whom Prof. G. B. Harrison once drew attention, he finds similar echoes, we begin to wonder. Such echoes might have come unconsciously.

In a matter such as we are discussing proof appears to require: first, absolute faithfulness to whatever evidence exists; second, respect to likelihood; and third, corroborative evidence of various kinds coming from various quarters. Items of corroborative evidence need not be singly impressive, but they should be both varied and exact, and there should be a reasonable amount of it.

Supporters of Southampton have never preserved honesty with themselves in their reading of Thorpe's Dedication; neither they nor the supporters of Pembroke have had regard to likelihood; and no body of varied and exact evidence has been presented for either.

The structure of Hotson's case is this: there was a 'William H' in London belonging to a society, the society so vivid in the memory of Justice Shallow in *2 Henry IV*, with which we have reason to suppose that Shakespeare and his fellow-actors were in close con-tact; he was of the exactly appropriate age for the line 'Thou hast pass'd by the ambush of young days' of Sonnet 70; though a plain gentleman, he was a centre of royalistic adulation; and all this at the precise time to which the Sonnets of historical reference so con-vincingly pointed in Hotson's earlier study. He was living still untitled in 1609, when the Sonnets were dedicated to him as plain 'Master W.H.' The rest of the evidence, and there is quite a lot, is corroborative, and varies in strength. The real test lies ahead. If

Hotson is right, then many more facts, we may be sure, will fly to this new centre like filings to a magnet.[1]

Could such convergences have come about by chance? And there is another, different, convergence. Many of those who have favoured patron peers have been fine scholars; men of literary genius, like Wilde and Masefield, looked for 'W.H.' among Shakespeare's acting associates, intuitively seeing him as some kind of stage personality relating to Shakespeare's art; others again have read the Sonnets as pieces of formal convention. A. C. Bradley's view of him as no more than 'a gentleman of some note' and mine as a young man of 'distinction' but no title (*The Mutual Flame*, 8, 107) were unspectacular conclusions based strictly on the evidence; Bradley ought surely, long ago, to have gained a larger following. And yet none of our theorists has been proved foolish; each was on a strong scent. Who could have supposed that a single historic person could satisfy *all* these conditions? In Prince William Hatcliffe they are all, as near as may be, satisfied.

More: we at last know how Shakespeare became so intimately attuned to nobility, or rather *royalty*, for his nobles speak ordinarily enough and what we really mean is—How did Shakespeare make his kings talk *like* kings? The Prince at Gray's Inn and those around him lived a perfect simulacrum of the Court. Hatcliffe was, it is true, a simple law-student, but all the better as an exemplar of those disparities between man and office that Shakespeare's historical dramas, starting with *Henry VI*, were to study. Of these the young Prince of Gray's Inn was a royal prototype.

While reading Hotson's book we see how the Elizabethans loved to *act* not only on the stage but in their lives too; and it is from this world, so strange to us, of pageantry and emblem that Shakespeare's dramas were born.

It would be a mistake to think that the poetry of the Sonnets is all now explained. Simplified prose versions drawing attention to the main argument of a poem are often valuable and the brief para-

---

1. It occurs ro me that Prof. Peter Alexander's biographical dating of Shakespeare's early life in London is already pointing in this direction: see his *Shakespeare*, 1964, 50–2, 72–3; also his article 'Shakespeare, Marlowe's Tutor', *T.L.S.*, 2 April 1964. See my 'Additional Note', p. 350. [**1966**]

phrases of Dr. Rowse's new edition are likely to give the Sonnets a wider public than they have hitherto enjoyed. But the minute analyses of Dr. Hilton Landry's recent study, *Interpretations of Shakespeare's Sonnets*, are needed too. Hotson's discoveries should serve to enrich but never to limit the poetry's intricate suggestions. They help us to breathe the atmosphere to which the poetry in all its subtlety belongs.

There is another danger. Were we to suppose that these Sonnets, except perhaps for a few of the earlier ones, were in *our* sense wholly artificial or conventional, we should be denying the very impact on which our concern for them depends. They radiate strong personal feeling and all the ups and downs of an intimate relationship. And it is in my phraseology a homosexual relationship: for if a man's impassioned devotion to a younger man, originally prompted and afterwards in part conditioned, for the Sonnets suggest as much, by his beauty, is not to be called 'homosexual', then we must coin some new word. There are, certainly, various levels, and for the more rarefied heights we can consult Plato and the Gospel of the Beloved Disciple, St. John (pp. 22, 28–9, 238). To these visionary insights, which I nowadays call the 'seraphic' intuition, all our Boy Bishops and Student Princes, and the many bisexual disguises throughout Renaissance drama to which I have drawn attention in *The Golden Labyrinth*, are pointing us.

All the same, I think that Mr. Seymour-Smith has, in his recent edition, made a valuable contribution in reading so much of Shakespeare's Sonnets to his Friend as a tussle between physical desire and spiritual adoration. Some of his readings we may dispute; but the often quoted Sonnet 20, 'A woman's face with Nature's own hand painted', explicitly complains that the poet's desire has been *thwarted* by the loved one's sex; and though that may argue physical restraint, it is as certainly a confession of desire. Within and beyond the desire was vision; and it seems natural enough that Shakespeare, born, if ever man was, for drama, should have become so emotionally involved in this high end, and heart, of all drama, this royal and seraphic ideal, as it took life in the ceremony at Gray's Inn.

Hatcliffe had other admirers, among them the Rival Poet, a role easily filled for Hotson, at this earlier date, by Marlowe. At this point the lynx-eyed Hotson is himself gravely at fault. In Sonnet 86, 'Was it the proud full sail of his great verse', he takes the 'affable familiar ghost' who is said to be assisting the Rival to be Robert Greene, then alive. He ignores the context of 'spirits' and 'compeers by night' said to be helping the poet to compose 'above a mortal pitch'. What Shakespeare means is that the Rival has a familiar spirit who directs his writing. Spirit-writing is a well-known practice.

We have not yet answered objections regarding the poetry—Can we believe that all the Sonnets were composed so early? Hotson's answer is that Shakespeare was more of a youthful prodigy than we had supposed. In his support I can point to my own argument in an article published in 1927 and reprinted in *The Sovereign Flower* (App. D) that the second part of *Henry VI* and *Titus Andronicus*[1] show intense writing, different from the operatic fluencies that followed of *Romeo and Juliet* and *Richard II*, such as we do not meet again until the period of *Macbeth* and *King Lear*. Were they not Shakespeare's no one would ever have thought of calling the *Henry VI* trilogy, or even *The Comedy of Errors*, 'prentice work'. It was natural that Shakespeare should have written more intellectual poems such as the Sonnets for a closed circle of cultured readers and should later set himself to the more obviously popular manner, which we perhaps too readily tend to regard as his 'early' manner, of, say, *Richard II*, for the general public. Much the same may be said of *Venus and Adonis* and *The Rape of Lucrece*: in these he may have deliberately aimed at a more sensuous poetry to win favour; and there is perhaps more literary finesse in both those poems than at first appears.

All the same, we must face the impressions received by a number of sensitive scholars, not all of whom had any particular biographical axe to grind, that many of the Sonnets contain fairly late work. And why not? Two of them, Sonnets 138 and 144, had been published by William Jaggard in 1599 and the earlier version of 138 shows variants which T. G. Tucker in his edition regarded as evidence of revision in the later text. Shakespeare may, from time

---

1. For a brilliant interpretation of *Titus Andronicus* see C. Alan Sommers, 'Wilderness of Tigers', *Essays in Criticism*, July 1960; X, 3.

to time, have revised his Sonnets, without disturbing the main narrative. They contain, as we all know, many obscurities, some of which may be due to an imperfect coalescence of versions.[1]

Shakespeare may have used some of them a second time, either for another emotional attachment, or—choosing carefully—for a patron; for Southampton, who had also been a member of Gray's Inn, or Pembroke. In *The Mutual Flame* (134) I found myself wondering what Master W.H. may have thought when he read those warm phrases of devotion expressed to Southampton in the dedication of *The Rape of Lucrece*.

But, and it is the tragedy of such relationships, Hatcliffe's young beauty, as is clear from the later Sonnets, was fading. In Sonnets 113 and 114, 'Since I left you, mine eye is in my mind' and 'Or whether doth my mind, being crown'd with you', Shakespeare tells how the first vision was being in his mind expanded into a spiritualized view of all men; the personal in Platonic wise was being raised to the universal; and that is how Shakespeare's poetic humanism was born. In *The Phoenix and the Turtle* he seems to be recording the swan-song of a romance that died to make poetry live. And which is the better, who can say? Meanwhile he treasured his Sonnets, and from time to time improved them. What they stood for remained the 'star' to the 'wandering bark' of Sonnet 116, 'Let me not to the marriage of true minds, admit impediments'.

I think that Shakespeare himself was behind Thorpe's publication in 1609. I cannot easily accept Hotson's theory that it was arranged by a middle-aged Hatcliffe, wishing to perpetuate his hour of youthful glory. A few textual errors in the main text do not prove

1. In both sonnets Tucker sees possible evidence of revision (xiii). Though the variants of Sonnet 144 are perhaps only those of a 'loose transmission', Sonnet 138 has been deliberately 'rewritten' (223, 218). If one sonnet was rewritten, so may others have been; and perhaps new ones, deliberately, added. In *The Mutual Flame* I tended to regard 'the experience behind the Sonnets' as early and our text as an artistic 're-working' of its significance (137; and see 108-9, 112).

Such a process is natural enough. I myself doctor from time to time my early poems, and those expressing love-visions I have arranged in a single, patterned, sequence. They will appear in a collection entitled *Gold-Dust; with other Poetry*.

The 1609 Sonnets may be as different from their earliest versions as is in all probability the *Hamlet* we know from the lost early *Hamlet* attributed by Peter Alexander (*Shakespeare*, 1964; 69-70) to Shakespeare. [1966]

that Shakespeare did not see the proofs; they are as likely, as every writer knows, to be caused by excessive care, making last-moment alterations leading to new compositorial mistakes. The volume included *A Lover's Complaint*, generally supposed to be about the same young man as the Sonnets.

We must attend carefully to every *nuance* in Thorpe's Dedication,[1] which runs:

> To the only begetter of these ensuing sonnets, Mr. W.H., all happiness, and that eternity promised by our ever-living poet, wisheth the well-wishing adventurer in setting forth.
>
> T. T.

This may be paraphrased as follows:

> To you as the main origin of these following sonnets, Master W.H., I wish every happiness, together with that poetic immortality assured, as he himself in his verses asserts, by the praises of such a poet as William Shakespeare, whose writings will (certainly) live for ever; and this last wish lies behind my boldness in publishing these (so intimate) poems, which is to be regarded as an act of good will towards you (since without their publication the immortality in question could not be yours).

'Setting forth' was a usual word for publishing (p. 330 below). That other influences beside Hatcliffe were contained in the final version may be supposed from the phrase 'only begetter', which I read, following a suggestion of T. G. Tucker, as 'main origin', or 'main inspiration'. The Oxford English Dictionary gives 'preeminent' as a natural meaning for 'only'. Quite apart from such a reading, 'begetter' by itself would probably have served had not others been involved. But it is clear that Hatcliffe still remains central: he is the one that matters. I suggest that Shakespeare himself devised these words.

Shakespeare had attained success and fame. Like Nietzsche he may have become bitterly aware that men welcome the achievements, the visible 'sparks', of genius while remaining blind to the inward psychological workshop and 'the cruelty of its hammer' (*Thus Spake*

1. See also Appendix I, pp. 329–30 below.

Zarathustra, 'Of Famous Wise Men', 30). He had experienced a homosexual idealism of appalling intensity and authority at one extreme and simultaneously, as the Sonnets to the Dark Lady show, a tormenting heterosexual attraction, magnetic and lustful, at the other. These are the two angels, good and bad, of Sonnet 144, 'Two loves I have, of comfort and despair'. The angelic influence was nevertheless mixed with desire and the evil influence shot through with a pathetic love. On the level of event, the seduction of youth by lady neatly symbolizes this deeper truth. Now, in the year 1609, at the top of his fame, Shakespeare was impelled to reveal himself. There was obviously a risk. Why did he do it?

Byron and Wilde both ruthlessly repudiated worldly success by a refusal to preserve a mask. T. E. Lawrence did much the same. The success turns to ashes; it seems all false; it sickens. Social ostracism is dared, almost invited. The reception of the Sonnets seems to have been cold. They were not reissued until 1640. In a recent broadcast conversation (2 January 1964) Mr. Eric Ewens and Mr. Christopher Sykes suggested that the 1609 publication may have had a bearing on the uncanny silence veiling so much of Shakespeare's life.

Shakespeare's challenge had been growing stronger: in *Hamlet*, in *Troilus and Cressida*, in *Macbeth*, in *King Lear*, nihilism is barely controlled. The poet is unleashing the old intensities of *Titus Andronicus* and *Henry VI*, and simultaneously drawing towards the romantics of a later age. In *Timon of Athens* he deliberately enters that more personal and Promethean world: Prof. Allardyce Nicoll has well called it 'Byronic' (*Shakespeare*, 1952; 61).

Timon of Athens reads like an expansion of the sonnets. Timon is a figure of resplendent and universal, almost impersonal, friendship. The old vision is here, but dispersed. That Shakespeare had to do to render the play acceptable, rather as he had done in his own life, expanding vision into writing. Nevertheless drama exerts its own laws and the lack of a personal loved one leaves us aware of a want. Timon's unlimited generosity is never quite convincing: the early acts are as an egg, with the shell and the white but no yolk. But suddenly all is changed: Timon becomes aware of ingratitude. Ingratitude is a recurring Shakespearian obsession corresponding to the general sense in such lonely men as he of no real contact with others, no social reciprocity. Timon throws off his garments, reveals himself naked. There is now no sense of emptiness, the impact of a total personality drives through the poetry and the drama as Timon curses man and communes with the elements, the sea, the heavenly bodies. The only women in the play, apart from the ladies of the Masque who are anyway disguised as Amazons, are two prostitutes, and Timon's curses are loaded with the sexual horror of Sonnet 129, 'The expense of spirit in a waste of shame'. The play as we have it appears to be unrevised. For obvious reasons Shakespeare could not in a drama reveal himself fully. He could show the negative, the social and sexual revulsion, but not the positive; the shadow but not the light that casts it. Perhaps he put the play aside, in disgust, and in this mood decided to publish the Sonnets. The publication was simultaneously an act of self-disclosure and a perpetuation of his vision. Just as Timon was eventually, like Sophocles' Oedipus, wooed by the city that had rejected him, so Shakespeare may have intuitively known that his own personal experience would one day prove a saving power for us all.

It is no use saying that Shakespeare's plays show him to have been sexually normal. Public plays *had* to preserve the accepted code. Who would have expected anything sexually unorthodox behind *An Ideal Husband* or *The Importance of Being Earnest*? In their mixture of affection and disillusion, Wilde's relations with Lord Alfred Douglas insistently recall Shakespeare's relations with his friend; and Shakespeare revealed himself in the Sonnets much as Wilde revealed himself in *De Profundis*.

Shakespeare was not on the evidence of his works a simple one-way 'homosexual' type, but rather both inwardly and in his external affections 'bisexual', or ambisexual. His insight into women probably came from a strong feminine strain in himself and he favoured themes of bisexual disguise. His women speak their best wisdom when so disguised and their love-poetry is always better than the men's, reminding us of Pope's *Eloisa to Abelard* as the Sonnets remind us of Tennyson's phrases in *In Memoriam* (109) on Hallam's 'seraphic intellect' and 'manhood fused with female grace'. We cannot deeply understand men of poetic and religious genius without some understanding too of the bisexual integration to which they are pointing us. Their works we accept—it demands little; whereas the man himself in all the strange agonies of his onward labour may be frightening. Perhaps an honest self-revelation always is, and perhaps genius is merely another name for honesty. However that may be, it was in the Sonnets that Shakespeare, as Wordsworth puts it, 'unlock'd his heart'. And now, with Dr. Hotson's brilliant researches to assist us, we at last have material for a biography in depth.

VENUS AND ADONIS

The Radio Times, 16 April 1964, 38.

In 1593 Shakespeare dedicated *Venus and Adonis* to the Earl of Southampton, calling it 'the first heir of my invention'; meaning, perhaps, his first published work of poetry as opposed to drama. It was an immediate success, especially with the younger generation, including the students of the Inns of Court. Shakespeare's handling may seem almost too English and homely for so classical a theme. But it has an impact denied to more sophisticated works.

Delight in physical creation brings animals vividly to life. Each is described, but each is also known inwardly; physical perception is somehow one with an inward identification. We are made to feel a horse's hot instincts for a mare, a hunted hare's misery, a boar-hound's anguish, the fear in a snail's withdrawn antlers.

We are aware primarily of Adonis' beauty and of Venus' tragic passion, conceived as fire. We see through her fiery, devouring eyes the tormenting charms of the reluctant youth. These are so warmly and intimately before us at every turn that we seem to touch what might be called his 'physical personality'.

The presentation is at once so shameless and so dispassionate that we no more question it than we do the equally sensuous description of the horse. Though we may certainly relate *Venus and Adonis* to Shakespeare's Sonnets, yet it is written as from a more impersonal survey of Nature's tragic miracles, in animal and man. The poem is more of a triumph than it might appear.

XXI

C. B. PURDOM'S SHAKESPEARIAN
THEORY

An unscripted discussion partially smoothed for printing, between the late C. B. Purdom (see p. vii) and G. Wilson Knight on Purdom's book *What Happens in Shakespeare*: broadcast by the B.B.C. on 9 September 1964. C. B. Purdom's views are also to be had on tapes published by Sound Seminars, Cincinnati (see p. 13 above, note).

GWK: Among all these books we've been having lately on Shakespeare—more than ever—there's always been a great number, but now there's been an awful rush—I'm rather interested in yours, because it seems different. I do think that there's some accomplishment in doing a book on Shakespeare that's different from all the others, but I'm not sure that I can agree with it all. Would you like to tell us exactly what is your theory once more?

CBP: Certainly. I don't ask you to agree with me. I ask you to consider what I've said—what I say now. Because unless you see what Shakespeare is doing you can't enter into the meaning of the plays. I think for instance that such literary critics as A. C. Bradley and historians such as A. L. Rowse miss his meaning and misinterpret the plays. I confine myself to one matter only, what I call the fundamental law of drama, which is a definition of dramatic action. I didn't invent this law; I get it from the plays, formulate it from the plays as they were written by Shakespeare. Now let me say briefly what the law is. It is that a dramatic work is performed by actors in words and movements and contains the story in action of a problem confronting a protagonist, which leads to a crisis in which the problem is resolved, the action being presented from the point of view of the protagonist after the crisis. That is to say the action is instantaneous: there's no time or place; it's told by the protagonist not as a story, though it contains a story, but as his vision or experience.

GWK: That 'no time or place' is going to be rather difficult for us, but you may be right. It's not going to be easy to understand 'no time or place', is it? However let's put that by. We'll return to it later.

As regards the theory, I can't see how it fits *A Midsummer Night's Dream*. This has always been one of my favourite Shakespeare plays. You could perhaps find a protagonist in Bottom, or even Theseus, but I don't see how you can say that the play is written from the point of view of one person.

CBP: No, it isn't—it isn't. *A Midsummer Night's Dream* is not a drama, it's an entertainment: it's one of the exceptions in Shakespeare. He wrote other plays which were entertainments as, for instance, *The Merry Wives of Windsor* and *Pericles*. These are not dramas either, for they are not written from the point of view that I've suggested, nor do they observe, or are intended to observe, the fundamental law.

GWK: Well, I don't mind much about *The Merry Wives of Windsor*, but I do mind about *Pericles*. I think that play would suit your theory rather well, as a matter of fact, but let's put that aside. *A Midsummer Night's Dream* does seem to me to be a most admirable work. It acts well, and if we're not going to call this a drama but only entertainment, by which I suppose we mean superficial entertainment, well, where are we?

CBP: Not necessarily superficial. The play is fine entertainment because it's poetic, and a really poetic work is never superficial. No, this play enters into the depths of happiness. It's concerned with marriage, for it was written for a marriage. What starts the play and finishes it is the marriage of Theseus; but Theseus is not a protagonist, because he has no problem at all.

GWK: But he is concerned with the problems of others, and there is magic too, and fairies, and I'm certainly not going to say I don't believe in magic and fairies. And there is Oberon. I don't know, but I think I should vote for Oberon as protagonist if I've got to have your theory. I vote for Oberon, shall we say. May we leave it at that? You won't get me easily to agree, but if I must agree, I should say Oberon.

CBP: I think *A Midsummer Night's Dream* is a perfect example of a play or piece of theatrical work that is not drama.

GWK: Well then, take another play. What about *Hamlet?* It's always been one of my cherished convictions, although I know he had a crime in the background, that King Claudius shows all the marks within the play of being a fine gentleman and even a good, pacifically-minded, king. The kind of king we today should admire. Remember how he makes peace instead of going to war as the old Hamlet would have done. Now, here's this Claudius, who I think is rather pleasant and have said so in my own writings. Hamlet calls him—well, what doesn't he call him? This villain, a kindless villain, which means an inhuman, brutal villain; and at the end 'Here, thou incestuous, murderous, damned Dane' (v. ii. 339). Hamlet sees him as a villain, yet the play shows him as, at least from some points of view, a rather courteous gentleman. Well, how does that fit your theory that the whole play's seen from Hamlet's point of view?

CBP: I think Claudius fits my theory perfectly, because we don't see Claudius as he really is. He may have been the admirable man that you suggest. He may have been the perfect king. But we're not concerned with that. All we're concerned with as far as Claudius is concerned is the place he takes in the dramatic situation that Hamlet presents. What Hamlet is concerned with is his being done out of the throne, his father being killed, and what he's to do about it.

GWK: Then why does Hamlet present him as such a gentlemanly fellow? Why doesn't he present him as a kind of Richard III or Iago or Edmund?

CBP: The reason is that Hamlet presents the whole thing from the point of view of the end. It is when Hamlet has been killed and dies that the story is unfolded. He then tolerates Claudius; he's not concerned with seeing the good in him, he just tolerates him, and therefore he's able to present him.

GWK: He's learnt very quickly, because only a very little time earlier he had said—'Thou incestuous, murderous, damned Dane, drink off this potion'.

CBP: Yes, but in drama there is no time. In drama everything happens at once. Hamlet presents his experience.

GWK: Do you mean . . .

CBP: In this timeless sense.

GWK: Is it the kind of experience we hear of about people who are drowning, who suddenly see their whole life; an experience which we have some evidence for?

CBP: That is a good analogy. Oh yes.

GWK: He sees his whole life . . . and from a more enlightened point of view.

CBP: Yes, but we're not concerned with the whole life, but only with this particular situation. What the actor playing Hamlet has to do is to come before the audience, because the audience is necessary to him, and to say: 'Look, this is my experience, this is my situation. This is what I have to say.' And what he says is spoken not only by himself but by all the other characters. He calls to life all the other characters who took part in this situation.

GWK: But are you suggesting that it would even be better perhaps if something was done in a prologue with the chief character coming on to demonstrate that?

CBP: Not at all, because it's done in the moment in which the action takes place.

GWK: But the audience aren't normally aware of this, are they?

CBP: Well, the actor's business is to make them aware of it. That is the actor's art.

GWK: But Hamlet doesn't come on until the second scene, does he? How can he give the audience the impression that it's all being shown from his point of view?

CBP: Yes, but what happens at the opening of the play, on the battlements, is still Hamlet's vision.

GWK: But do the audience know that? They don't know it, do they?

CBP: They don't need to know it. They don't need to 'think' a vision. All they need to think of is what is happening before them, the dramatic action.

GWK: Yes, I think possibly the theory is stronger if you keep to that, and don't say that the actor is coming forward and presenting it, because in actual fact he doesn't do that. You may say that what the audience experience is, in fact, Hamlet's vision of the whole thing . . .

CBP: Yes.

GWK: But you can't very well say that Hamlet presents it to them.

CBP: Yes, he presents the opening scene of the play . . .

GWK: If it is Hamlet's statement, shouldn't he come on first and say 'Look here . . .'

CBP: I don't think so. Otherwise you would have merely a poem, an epic or a monologue, instead of which you have drama with characters, and the characters are as the protagonist presents them. As he conceives them, as he sees them.

GWK: Mm.

CBP: As they exist in his vision.

GWK: Well, I have raised some objections and my objections are on *A Midsummer Night's Dream* and *Hamlet*: they are chosen ones, and perhaps I could object to others, but let's leave that for a moment. How would you like to tell us what play you would choose to expound from your point of view, giving your point of view every chance you can? What would you take?

CBP: Well, I could take any of the plays except the three that I've mentioned and perhaps the three *Henry VI* plays. But let me take *As You Like It*, which is a comedy where this fundamental law is not so easily perceived perhaps as it is in tragedy; tragedy being simple, comedy being always complex. Now *As You Like It*, written about 1599 or earlier, does present this idea of a protagonist and of a character who asks the audience's participation in an experience, and does so most completely. The leading character of course is Rosalind—no question about that.

GWK: She is the leading character, yes.

CBP: And what we get in the play is how Rosalind sees herself and her situation and the other characters. *As You Like It* is a play of realized happiness. The heart's desire attained. Now, all the other characters are, I say, as Rosalind sees them—and so we get Orlando. Rosalind's comic problem in the play is how to secure Orlando. So, as she presents him, Orlando is a perfect young man, a perfect lover. He does nothing wrong throughout the play, from beginning to end. He is a strong man, handsome, poetic, the heart's delight of the heroine. So we see him, and this makes Orlando very difficult to act, because he's so perfect. In the course of the play Rosalind succeeds, she wins Orlando, and all the other characters also get their heart's desire. All except Jaques, of course. . . . He is a man of common-sense and there's no common-sense in this play. It's poetry, it's about becoming happy—greatest happiness.

GWK: But what about . . .

CBP: And Jaques gives his blessing at the end.

GWK: Oh yes, he gives his blessing, but what about Touchstone and Audrey and so on, are they seen from Rosalind's point of view?

CBP: Yes, exactly, in every word, in everything they do. And they get their happiness, their own particular heart's desire. Certainly.

GWK: When you have a comedy or a romance, the people don't die. It has just occurred to me that isn't there a difficulty there? You can't have any longer any analogy with the drowning man seeing his past life. When is the vision seen? Is it seen on the day of the marriage, looking back in that way? Is it seen then?

CBP: Oh no, you mustn't push this analogy too far. That would be a very feeble description of what happens. Certainly there is consummation in the comedy, you get the problem resolved happily. The comic situation is completed in a way that gives pleasure, undoubted pleasure. That's all you need.

GWK: But you do need, don't you, to make some statement corresponding to the statement you made about tragedy—when you said that it was something like the vision at the moment of death.

CBP: I said at the moment of crisis.

GWK: But what is the moment of crisis in a comedy?

CBP: Well, when they are all reconciled at the end, at the very end of the play, where you get the mask of Hymen—that lovely episode.

GWK: It's a vision of the play as seen by Rosalind at that moment at the end when she has been successful, is that it?

CBP: Oh yes.

GWK: But it's not a vision, you see. There is a slight difficulty because we're dealing with poetic visions rather than natural-ism—a kind of x-ray of life, seeing its spiritual significance, some-thing of that sort. Now when you say it's a man at the brink of death . . .

CBP: Oh no, no, no, no. I said crisis, not death.

GWK: Well, if we *were* to say death, I could say to myself: 'Yes, he is obviously attuned differently, and he can see into it all, but now Rosalind is in life, and it's more difficult for me to see how just because she's happy and going to be married she can be supposed to have this supreme poetic x-ray vision of the whole business'.

CBP: That's because you're thinking of death. I say it's not neces-sary to think of death, think of the crisis, think of the completion. In tragedy, of course, death is the completion. In comedy, it's the very opposite. It's happiness.

GWK: Yes. Well, may we turn to that a little later, because it's still bothering me. We ought to have a tragedy now. Would you take a tragedy and explain your point of view as applied to one of them—one of the big tragedies. Would you like to take *Othello*?

CBP: Yes, the first of the last great plays. This is a tragedy of love, love self-defeated, of the honourable man, Othello, a man of power, and what befalls him; and of his situation with Desde-mona, a high-bred, pure woman whom he loves. Here you get contrasts of race, culture and style of living and a wide gulf bridged by love. Yet the bridge breaks, because of a defect in Othello—and it's that defect that creates the tragedy, because love is an inward comprehension, the knowledge of another. Yet Othello allows himself to be misled, to become jealous, because of the jealousy of his enemy; and the result is disaster. This love which essentially is a pure and perfect love breaks; and this lovely creature Desdemona who is perfect as we see her in the play is destroyed, because of the confusion into which Othello allows himself to get. In the play as he looks at things, the signs of love become proofs of the opposite because his mind is distorted. Therefore the end is death. Death for him and death for Desde-mona. And yet in that death of course, light breaks upon him—it's a marvellous death. That's the tragedy—and that's the drama.

GWK: Othello's different from the others in respect to this 'light' that you say breaks upon him, suddenly, just at the end. What interests me there is, that I'm not sure whether that helps your general theory or opposes it. What I mean is, that something of what you're saying is written into *Othello*. At the end he does have this great illumination about how he has been deceived; and he pushes himself almost into another dimension of being, a kind of hell; not that I'm suggesting myself that he goes to Hell at all, but he does himself imagine that. He calls on the devils to torment him, you remember, at a moment of abandon: 'Whip me, ye devils, from the possession of this heavenly sight' (v. ii. 276). Well, he *is* in rather the mood that you're saying all Shakespeare's tragic heroes are in at this last moment; and so I'm not quite sure what comment to make about it. I could either say that it's evidence that this is how Shakespeare sees his tragedies and therefore it may be so in the others; or I could say, 'Well here it's explicit, and when it's explicit by all means let us follow it. But why doesn't Shakespeare make it then explicit in his other plays?'

CBP: I think he does.

GWK: He doesn't . . . no not like Othello . . .

CBP: Well, you see it's part of the trick of the dramatist to use a certain obscurity—you mustn't be too obvious ever in a play, and therefore you musn't be too obvious even in the ending of the play.

GWK: No-o.

CBP: You mustn't look for too great clarity, too great simplicity.

GWK: Well of course, there again that does help your theory a little because in so many respects *Othello* goes in for clarity where the others are numinous, mysterious. It *would* fit your theory that when we come to *Othello*, where we have clarity, something of this shows through. I'm afraid I've given you a point there! I think you *could* argue like that if you like; that *Othello*, being such a play of precise forms, characters, images, would be likely to be more explicit on this point.

CBP: You see what people do, you see what actors do and what producers do, and what even critics do and even, if I may say so, what you do. You elevate Iago into a second protagonist, as if Iago were a central feature of the play. He is, but only to the extent that he exists in Othello's vision.

GWK: I don't think I ever meant to do that. I may have used bad phraseology which I'm always doing, I'm sure, but surely what I meant to do was to see Iago as the spirit of cynicism, if I recall what I said correctly, and Othello is the one I was interested in. I called the essay, you remember, 'The Othello Music'. It's Othello, that's the one I was interested in, and I called Iago a principle of cynicism and Desdemona the spirit of romance or something like that, with Othello tugged between the two. I never had any doubt that he was central. Of course, what has hampered matters here perhaps a little is that Iago is such a magnificent acting part that many actors either want to play Iago or change over, as Irving and others have done, night by night, Iago one day and Othello the next.

CBP: Yes.

GWK: It's just because Iago's done so well.

CBP: Iago's done so well by Othello, that's what I would say.

GWK: Of course, Othello is a very much harder part to perform.

CBP: Yes, infinitely harder.

GWK: Othello's one of the plays where time is very strange.

CBP: Very strange.

GWK: Very strange, you don't know how long they've been at Cyprus. If you try and work out a time sequence as some critics have attempted, well, you can't succeed.

CBP: You make yourself ridiculous.

GWK: It's the same with many of the plays, and I must say that your book was helpful there, at least if one was following you in the book. When we did come to a question of time, I thought you had as good an answer or perhaps a better answer than many people because from the beginning you were saying that it's a kind of timeless vision, a group of events, an establishing of values and contrasts and actions and qualities, and not a realistic sequence exactly.

CBP: Yes.

GWK: I think you do help there. Also, I think I'd be prepared to say that, as I believe I did say once,[1] that *Julius Caesar* does seem, if you look deeply into it, to be a play viewed more nearly from Brutus' point of view—

CBP: Certainly.

GWK: —than anybody else's. After all, of course, Cassius has a single point of view; the revolution's good and Caesar must be killed. Antony's got a single point of view; the revolution's bad and the conspirators must be downed. They're perfectly simple. But the play's not simple, it's complex, and the whole symbolism of the play is complex and a matter of conflict; and Brutus is, in fact, the man who endures the conflict. And therefore the play as composed is the drama that Brutus experiences.

CBP: Yes, and he sees these other characters so clearly.

GWK: It doesn't mean that you must like him better. I don't like him nearly so much as I like Cassius. I think Cassius is much more attractive. But that's another point.

CBP: That's another point.

GWK: Another point, yes.

CBP: Even another play.

GWK: It is, I think, possible, to say that *Julius Caesar* must be regarded, apart from anything else, as a play seen from Brutus' point of view. I think the same of *Macbeth*, very much the same. And perhaps *Lear*.

CBP: Yes.

GWK: You know, I would rather tend myself to say that I could put it like this. Possibly Shakespeare seems to have matured towards writing plays that fit your point of view. The plays that we regard as the great ones do seem, *Othello, Macbeth, Lear*—I won't have *Hamlet* but certainly *Julius Caesar*—they do seem to fit your point of view fairly well. So you could say that Shakespeare was all the time getting towards that, and that when he has done that, it's the kind of play we regard as terrifically great; but even so, to make a general theory of it—I believe you say it's in all dramas, don't you?

CBP: All plays that are dramas.

GWK: You see, that seems to be going very far.

1. In the essay 'Brutus and Macbeth' in *The Wheel of Fire* (enlarged, 136–8).

CBP: Plays of today as well as plays of Shakespeare.

GWK: Looking at Shakespeare's own work, I feel inclined to say that critics could quite well argue that the two *Henry IV* plays with their wonderful realism and their variety of characters and their mixture of seriousness and humour—there's so much humanity and all so realistically convincing—I can quite believe a literary critic—for myself, I've always gone in for what I call interpretation which I think is different—but if I was a literary critic wanting to be cruel to Shakespeare—all literary critics do tend very often to be very hard on their authors—I could imagine myself saying that *Henry IV* was a more perfect work of art than *Macbeth*. At least, that *Macbeth* was a great enigma, an extraordinary, grotesque, and superb accomplishment, but not exactly from every point of view a satisfactory reading of human affairs, and certainly not the kind of play to put before a would-be dramatist and say 'Try and do something like this'. I suppose that would be fatal, wouldn't it?

CBP: Of course. I agree with you that Shakespeare developed both as a technician and as a genius, that is to say, his genius grew in its application. *Henry IV*, I think, fully expresses what I say. If people were not so much bemused by Falstaff——

GWK: But you must be bemused by Falstaff.

CBP: Yes, but not so much. *Henry IV* is Prince Harry all the time and everyone, even Falstaff himself is as Harry sees him. It shows how great a figure Falstaff was, in Harry's own life and imagination.[1]

GWK: Oh, but in Part Two, that wonderful speech on sherris sack. Prince Hal isn't there at the time.

CBP: No, but that doesn't matter——

GWK: That doesn't matter?

CBP: Whenever the protagonist is not on the stage, we always find that the action is more exaggerated, always.

GWK: Yes, I know you said that in your book.

CBP: It's either more lively or more comic or more ridiculous, but

---

1. It is worth noting that in his speech 'I know you all . . .' (1 *Henry IV*, I. ii. 217–39) Prince Hal does in fact come forward and present, as it were, the drama's action to the audience in the manner which Purdom's phraseology suggested of Hamlet. [1966]

whenever the protagonist is not on the stage, he sees himself in the picture as it were, and the thing has exaggeration. You find that in every play.

GWK: And where the protagonist is there himself, it's more, to put it bluntly and use the usual term, realistic, more normal?

CBP: Well, if you understand realistic in the sense of 'usual', not as 'natural', I'll agree with you.

GWK: Do you mean that Toby and Falstaff are expanded beyond any sort of realism, either the real realism or the 'realism' in inverted commas? They're quite grotesque, you mean?

CBP: They're grotesque. Falstaff's real in Hal's mind.

GWK: Yes.

CBP: And delightful in his mind and—and so he makes them.

GWK: Yes, I'm not quite sure whether that is a clear and convincing statement or whether it's your neat way out to settle all possible differences, because in a way it does cover so many difficulties . . .

CBP: I think you must consider Shakespeare's progress as a dramatist, from *Titus Andronicus* to the last plays. He developed, he wasn't the kind of person at the beginning that he was at the end. His technical accomplishment was not so great, he was not so successful, for instance, in *Romeo and Juliet* as in *Macbeth*. The play is not so good a play; it's a marvellous play, a beautiful play, but it hasn't the profundity, the perfection which, I think, *Macbeth* has.

GWK: I suppose I agree that these great tragedies are the ones which I myself, to be quite honest, think most of; I suppose that is true. And I must say that, among all the theories that are produced about Shakespeare, I find myself very sympathetic with you on one point, one very main point; that is, that you do regard the great tragedies as positive statements, not just miserable readings of people who have unfortunately gone to disaster, leaving the audience there with nothing else. You do bring them to your readers with feeling of something big and important and, on the whole, invigorating. There's a phrase of yours that I liked particularly where you say of Macbeth, saying how he ends—how having faced his end Macbeth in the light of that acceptance is able to accept everything, 'his spirit rising ever higher as his fortunes fall'. That to my mind is worth everything; it's so difficult for people, especially producers and actors, to understand that; and that is the way those last scenes of *Macbeth* read, and ought, I am quite sure, to be performed. I've never wavered in that myself, I've always thought that and believe it deeply. And then again, of *Lear* you say, 'All that matters is the vivid, startling, heartbreaking, yet exhilarating vision.' It's exactly that that we want in all our stage productions. I remember Masefield saying something similar in his very valuable little book on *Macbeth* productions. Although the play's ghastly and grim, nevertheless the production and the effect should be, to use an old-fashioned term, beautiful; and I think that we today need to attend to that.

As for the spiritual quality of your book, there is the sense of the drama seeing things almost from another dimension more deeply, more truly. There again, of course, I naturally agree. My only difficulty is this, that although we must not go outside the play whilst we're discussing it, once we produce a theory, we have already begun to go outside the play, and I should think that if your theory is correct, you have got to suppose either a super-self, a greater self, of the character 'Macbeth', somehow watching himself. You will be involved in one of those doctrines in which there is a greater self; either that or in a view of existence as from another dimension, which would be supposed to happen after death. This, I think, might help some people if they're allowed to think like that. The trouble is, if you say it's a point of time which isn't in time anyway, and it isn't in space, and you don't say what part of the man's experiencing it, only that it's a vision, well, I'm just a little afraid your readers won't have enough to get hold of; but if they were allowed perhaps to say, if it helps them, it's as he sees it after death in another land, or if they're allowed to say it's his greater self because we're all linked on to another self that's watching us—and some doctrines do believe that—if you're allowed to think like that, or even in the extreme to say it's God's vision of the action, it would help a little.

CBP: I don't object to that. What my fundamental law really says is that drama is reconciliation.

GWK: Oh, well, I agree with that.

CBP: Reconciliation of Man, with his environment, with his fellows, and with himself.

GWK: And considering there's so much art and drama today which does just the opposite, we have a right to agree with each other and say that Shakespeare, even though we can't help being what we are in this generation and our best art has to be different, no doubt, yet Shakespeare is still that kind of beacon to us because he does what we can't yet do today. We can't get reconciliation.

CBP: Oh yes, we can get reconciliation. What we have to do is to come to terms with ourselves.

GWK: Yes, but I mean our modern artists don't.

CBP: Our modern artists don't very easily.

GWK: I think we could agree, couldn't we, on this, that though the modern dramatist must be a modern dramatist and can't establish such a reconciliation—he mustn't pretend to—there is no excuse for the producers or the actors who when they produce or act Shakespeare fail to at least try to get this reconciliation. They should do the thing with something of this point of view.

CBP: Yes, in modern art, in all the arts, there's no *conclusion*. In drama there is conclusion and that is what I think makes drama the supreme art.

XXII

SHAKESPEARE AND THE
SUPERNATURAL

An interview with the editor, Dr. V. P. Underwood, published in *Light*,
Autumn 1964; LXXXIV, 3458.

Ed: In this quatercentenary year of Shakespeare, most of us could
think of well-known instances of his using what is generally called
the 'supernatural' not, like most modern writers, as a mere metaphor or device or 'gimmick', without any implied acceptance,
but as a factor essential to the play, and to be taken as seriously as
the play. I am saying 'supernatural' as a concession to popular
habit. Neither you nor I believe that what is not yet, or not often,
within the range of physical science and the five senses is necessarily 'above' or 'beyond' the 'Nature' of our materialist belief-
system. In thinking of 'unscientific' elements in Shakespeare's
plays, most people would recall *Hamlet* and *Macbeth*, but of course
you could give many other instances.

GWK: What we talk of as a 'device' may be intrinsic to the work
concerned. In this sense all great drama, in every age, is likely to
make contact with the spiritualistic or the occult. Shakespeare is
no exception.

The succession of ghosts that speak to Richard and Richmond
before the battle of Bosworth makes a wonderful dramatic climax
in *Richard III*. The portents in *Julius Caesar* include ghosts, and
the ghost of Caesar later appears to Brutus.

Nothing could be more gripping on the stage than the ghost
scenes of *Hamlet* on the battlements of Elsinore. They dominate
the play and reverberate throughout, and that is part of the reason
why *Hamlet* is so fascinating: 'Look, where it comes again. . . . In

the same figure, like the king that's dead. . . . Looks it not like
the king? . . . Most like: it harrows me with fear and wonder'
(I. i. 40–4). What could be more dramatic?

In *Macbeth* we meet the three witches or 'weird sisters'. They
are more than 'witches'. 'Weird' means 'destiny'. They are Shakespeare's creations, based partly on beliefs in witchcraft, partly on
his source, and partly on other traditional lore. In the middle of
this play, in the Cauldron scene, they hold a kind of séance like
the spirit-raising scene much earlier in *Henry VI* (*2 Henry VI*, I.
iv), and apparitions come. Of course Shakespeare works it up for
his own dramatic purposes. An actual séance would scarcely
work out so neatly as our three *Macbeth* apparitions, the 'armed
head', the child covered with blood, and the child crowned, with
a tree in his hand. They constitute in themselves a little drama.
Shakespeare creates symbolic entities that resemble spiritualistic
manifestations. Though he builds them up for his own dramatic
and poetic purposes, he is relying on spiritualistic accounts and
makes, intuitively, a spiritualistic contact. Without such contacts
we are not likely to get a succession of great dramas.

In *All's Well that Ends Well*, which I take to be a fairly late
play, there is a scene of spirit healing. The girl Helena claims to
possess mysterious powers learned from her father. She offers to
heal the king, whom the professional doctors cannot help. The
situation is exactly such as might occur and often does occur
today. The king fears that he will be made to look foolish:

> We thank you, maiden;
> But may not be so credulous of cure,
> When our most learned doctors leave us, and
> The congregated college have concluded
> That labouring art can never ransom nature
> From her inaidable estate—I say we must not
> So stain our judgement, or corrupt our hope,
> To prostitute our past-cure malady
> To empirics, or to dissever so
> Our great self and our credit, to esteem
> A senseless help, when help past sense we deem.
>
> (II. i. 117)

Helena insists, claiming that the power is not hers, but from God. In a brilliantly composed scene she is shown breaking down the king's reluctance. The healing is performed. The play's comment runs:

> They say miracles are past; and we have our philosophical persons to make modern and familiar things supernatural and causeless. Hence is it that we make trifles of terrors, ensconcing ourselves into seeming knowledge, when we should submit ourselves to an unknown fear.
>
> (II. iii. 1)

That suits us, today, admirably.[1]

In Shakespeare's last plays what might be called the dark supernaturalism of the tragedies gives place to a happier mysticism. In *Pericles* and *The Winter's Tale* there are amazing reunions, and those we thought dead turn out to be alive. Pericles finds his long-lost daughter:

> Thou dost look
> Like Patience gazing on kings' graves, and smiling
> Extremity out of act.
>
> (V. i. 139)

The lines suggest an eternity, beyond time, beyond suffering. Pericles hears a mysterious music, which he calls 'the music of the spheres' (v. i. 231).

Even more elaborately dramatized is Leontes' experience in *The Winter's Tale* where, after suffering years of penitence for his sin, he finds that his long-lost wife Hermione, supposed dead through his own fault, is really alive. Paulina, who functions as a kind of dramatic medium, brings him to the supposed new-made statue of Hermione in a chapel. He is staggered by the statue's resemblance to his lost wife: 'What was he that did make it? . . . Would you not deem it breathed and that those veins did

---

1. Helena's powers are discussed in the chapter 'The Third Eye' of *The Sovereign Flower*. Shakespeare's 'triple' (i.e. third) 'eye' (II. i. 111) is 'The Third Eye' of occultism, to be identified it seems with the pineal gland as a 'receiving centre' for spirit power (see Harry Edwards, *The Healing Intelligence*, 1965; 44–5).

verily bear blood? . . . What fine chisel could ever yet cut breath?'
(v. iii. 63–79). Paulina speaks:

> Either forbear,
> Quit presently the chapel, or resolve you
> For more amazement. If you can behold it,
> I'll make the statue move indeed, descend,
> And take you by the hand.
>
> (v. iii. 85)

She fears they will think that she is using 'wicked powers'. But
this she denies. Leontes tells her to go ahead, he accepts it all. She
calls on the statue to come down: 'Music, awake her, strike! 'Tis
time, descend, be stone no more.' There is music, and Hermione
comes down. Leontes says:

> O, she's warm.
> If this be magic, let it be an art
> Lawful as eating.
>
> (v. iii. 109)

The transfixing dramatic force of a seemingly supernatural event
is here present, not in terms of terror and ghosts, but in terms of
blessedness, and it is all simultaneously 'holy'—Paulina uses the
word—and part of nature.

Ed: But do you suggest that the witches in *Macbeth* represent black
magic? They could not be said to do evil, as distinct from making
prophecies.

GWK: In a way they do not even make any prophecy which
Macbeth can claim has prompted him to evil. They say that he is
going to be king, but for all we know he might have been king
—he suggests as much himself—whether he committed the
murder or not: it is *he* who commits the murder. All the same, I
do not think that you can deny that the 'witches' are dramatically
conceived as, in large part anyway, tempters. You cannot call
them good powers. What of the hideous ingredients of their
cauldron? They sow the seeds of temptation in Macbeth's mind,
though what happens is, it is true, his fault. They might be
compared to untactful mediums! They have a message to deliver,
but would have been wiser not to deliver it too exactly. They

could have said: 'Something good is coming for you,' and left it at that. But to say, 'All hail Macbeth, that shalt be king hereafter,' was a very dangerous thing to do at that particular moment.

Here is an important thought: they appear to Macbeth after he has been shedding blood violently in war. He is saturated in death, and this may be what opens his eyes to these strange creatures. I have found an analogy in Byron's *Sardanapalus*. The enlightened emperor is in principle a pacifist but is nevertheless forced to engage in bloodshed. He has a terrible nightmare afterwards; he has lowered himself to the level of those who shed blood, and in his dream feels himself oppressed by the ancestral warlike and imperial powers which he loathes. So, too, Macbeth's eyes have been opened by bloodshed. A seventeenth-century dramatist, Nat Lee, copies in his *Sophonisba* the Cauldron scene of *Macbeth*, but has for dark powers two priestesses to the Goddess of War. Shakespeare's scene is copied, but the relevance is now to open war, not secret murder. Both Lee and Byron see war as murder, and in so doing serve to indicate a possible relationship between Shakespeare's Weird Sisters and the bloodshed that Macbeth has been engaging in.[1]

Prospero in *The Tempest* uses what may be called a 'white magic'. The more intelligent members of Shakespeare's audience would have recognized that. In his *English Literature in the Sixteenth Century* (1954; 8–14) C. S. Lewis discusses beliefs held in Shakespeare's time concerning white magic. He says that there was a strong belief at this period in beneficent spirit agents, with which man could get into direct contact. It is accordingly a mistake to think that there was for them only a choice between the Church on the one side and communication with devils and evil spirits on the other. The possibility of communion with beneficent spirits was, by many, accepted. Though himself a strictly orthodox Christian, Lewis relates *The Tempest* to such beliefs in a kind of 'white magic', and it is interesting to find a scholar of his status

---

1. In discussing the use of blood sacrifices to assist spirit contact in the ancient world my brother writes: 'This general ancient belief, that blood activates spirits, may be true, but we have rightly ceased to practise it' ('Spiritualism among the Ancients', *Light*, Autumn 1965; LXXXV, 3462).

asserting that Shakespeare's *Tempest* derives from this tradition, which may be related to the Platonists of Florence, whose works would have been well known to Shakespeare's contemporaries.

The Tempest is full of mysteries. The academic world should have paid more attention than it has to that strange and fascinating book by Colin Still, *Shakespeare's Mystery Play* (later revised as *The Timeless Theme*), which worked out comparisons between *The Tempest* and the myths and rituals of past ages.

Ed: This leads on to the question of the poet's beliefs. Do you feel that the older Shakespeare believed more firmly in such powers by the time he wrote of Prospero than he had done earlier?

GWK: No, not exactly, because the progress of an artist is very strange. With great authors like Shakespeare, much of what he does in later life may be forecast in words or short speeches in his earlier works. For example, the sublime tragedy *Antony and Cleopatra*, written in his maturity, is a grand-scale drama on love and death, love being felt as victorious. In it Cleopatra gives a full-length description of a wonderful dream of her 'emperor Antony', whom she sees, after his death, as a kind of cosmic force bestriding earth and ocean:

> His face was as the heavens, and therein stuck
> A sun and moon, which kept their course, and lighted
> The little O, the earth . . .
>
> (v. ii. 79)

That dream of a cosmic emperor throws back to the earlier *Romeo and Juliet*. Just before Romeo receives the news of Juliet's death, he refers, briefly, to a dream of life beyond death:

> I dreamt my lady came and found me dead—
> Strange dream, that gives a dead man leave to think—
> And breath'd such life with kisses in my lips,
> That I reviv'd, and was an emperor.
>
> (v. i. 6)

The play is to end tragically; there is no other suggestion of a happy outcome; but we have had a glimpse. Shakespeare has touched the beyond-death intuition. What first appears in this early play in a brief reference he later develops into a whole play.

We can trace the sequence from the tragedies, through *Antony and Cleopatra*, which is both tragedy and revelation, on to the last plays with their 'resurrections', without supposing that every development was quite new to Shakespeare's mind.

As for Prospero's magic, we can observe earlier examples in the Friars of *Romeo and Juliet* and *Much Ado about Nothing*, who control their plays' plots almost like magicians, the first using the powers of herbs, on which he is an expert. Owen Glendower, in *Henry IV* Part I, is a magician with spirit-musicians at his command. In *All's Well that Ends Well*, Helena's father had his mysterious secret of healing. Cerimon, in *Pericles*, is a direct forerunner of Prospero, explicitly claiming god-like powers. All these are summed up in Prospero.

What is important is the way the artistic works unfold. These we can receive each in its own right, without asking at every moment, 'Did Shakespeare as a man think or know this or that?' It is a matter of what he *does* as an inspired artist.

Ed: Of course all this is complicated by first, the question how much the artist could write without believing in what his characters appear to believe; second, how much he was writing for 'box office'.

GWK: Yes. We might find it difficult to say with complete psychological honesty why we are talking here today! A lot of egotism may enter into it. We are all a mass of multiple instincts at every moment. All the same, people can respond to what we are saying on its own merits.

Shakespeare had his ambitions, he wanted to be a gentleman and have a coat of arms. But that does not affect the question as to whether *King Lear* is a great drama. If he could come back from the spirit world and say: 'I wrote *King Lear* for one thing only, money,' it would not make the slightest difference. Perhaps he did, but it is irrelevant. I think the academic world has to be very careful about the way it analyses the motives of authorship. The subtleties are infinite. A masterpiece stands complete in its own right.

Ed: Is a masterpiece more important than the mind, the human experience, that produces it? Does not an artist get satisfaction out

of a work that expresses his deepest beliefs, whether he makes
money out of it or not?

GWK: Shakespeare's deepest beliefs may be *in* his plays; but they
need not be mental concepts. Only one piece of evidence, to my
mind, shows the relation between Shakespeare as a thinking
person and Shakespeare as an artist. That is Sonnet 114.

If there is one thing that especially characterizes Shakespeare's
dramatic artistry, it is his reaction to the wonder and splendour of
human existence. We may deplore the actions of his villains,
Richard III and Iago, morally, but they are dramatically excellent
of their kind, and we are in danger of being more interested in
Iago than in Othello. Shakespeare could see the unity, the harmony, the essential being of men of all sorts, and that is why his
writing is so powerful. To put it theologically, Shakespeare could
accept God's creation of humanity as the marvel which it is. This
may be optimistic, but it is deeply Shakespearian. Now, the
sonnet in question is the one where he describes how his love,
or Platonic vision, born of the beautiful young man, 'W.H.', is
being expanded into his total life-work. Everything, however
ugly, he sees as an expression of the beauty of the young man:

> Or whether doth my mind, being crown'd with you,
> Drink up the monarch's plague, this flattery?
> Or whether shall I say, mine eye saith true,
> And that your love taught it this alchemy,
> To make of monsters and things indigest
> Such cherubins as your sweet self resemble,
> Creating every bad a perfect best
> As fast as objects to his beams assemble?
> O, 'tis the first; 'tis flattery in my seeing,
> And my great mind most kingly drinks it up:
> Mine eye well knows what with his gust is 'greeing,
> And to his palate doth prepare the cup.
>   If it be poison'd, 'tis the lesser sin
>   That mine eye loves it and doth first begin.

Does the eye deceive the mind? he seems to ask. Surely it must be
deception? Is it not morally wrong to enjoy a Macbeth's murders,

an Iago's intrigues? Is the cup then poisoned that brings the mind its delight? At least, he says, it was an authentic vision. It was not a sentimental escape from reality. I did actually *see* this beauty, and to that extent I may be forgiven.

Shakespeare knew that what he was doing was superb. He forestalls criticism by stating firmly the critical viewpoint, but his experience remains intact. I doubt if any great poet has left so crisp and clear a definition of how his poetry was made.

Ed: To come back to *Hamlet*: should we regard the Ghost, clamouring for revenge, as a mere dramatic device, or does it represent acceptance of the idea that the 'other world' may urge us on to violent acts which we would not normally commit? Belief in the 'dark supernatural' was undoubtedly prevalent in Shakespeare's time and later. Thousands of people are said to have attended 'witches' sabbaths' in France.

GWK: There has certainly often been danger in making contact with the supernatural in the past. I have been told that there are black magic societies today. I have had a personal account of a revengeful spirit demanding a murder in India and causing considerable anxiety to the recipient of the message. But my own experiences of Spiritualism have never brought me into contact with anything that one could call dangerous. It has all seemed to come from a plane characterized by what Christians would call Christian love.

In my writings on *Hamlet*, I have from the first regarded the Ghost as being a far from wholly beneficent spirit. I have seen Hamlet himself as a dark figure, made darker, almost demented, after meeting the Ghost. This Ghost is ambiguous. He seems to be in Purgatory; though not in Hell, he is suffering for his sins. On the other side Claudius, the old warrior king's murderer, is a diplomatist, a peacemaker, and in some respects at least appears to constitute an advance on his bellicose predecessor. He is, despite his crime, a king of some dignity and social quality who thinks in terms of this earthly life and all its more common-sense and social valuations. From these Hamlet himself has broken away. He, after conversing with the Ghost, has plunged deep, beyond life, and is distraught and even dangerous. It is because we have such a baffling alignment of values, a criss-cross, a see-saw, that *Hamlet* is such a fascinating play.

How salutary, then, is the Ghost? We cannot be sure. A. C. Bradley saw him as a majestic figure carrying a high degree of authority. From the Christian point of view we are told to let the dead bury the dead and not to think about revenge, and from that angle the Ghost is scarcely an enlightened spirit, and might almost be called evil. Hamlet himself raises the central question: 'The spirit that I have seen may be the Devil' (II. ii. 635). Dramatically we can hardly suppose that it was, but Hamlet's words nevertheless suggest a doubt as to whether it was a wise and good spirit. And the play's total action drives the doubt home.

Hamlet seems to have been written from a consciousness that sees our earthly life being disturbed by alien powers. The Ghost may have some authority from beyond; but how far can we allow it to interfere with the processes of *this* life—even though that life is shown as, in part, corrupt? That is the problem that faces the hero: neither death, in the Ghost, nor life, in Claudius, deserves his allegiance. He himself has intermittent glimpses of a higher state of being than either, and to these we must look for our solution.[1]

Additional Note, 1966

I add an important passage from *1 Henry VI*. Joan of Arc's helpers are 'choice' and 'familiar' spirits subject to a master-devil, 'lordly monarch of the north', and coming from 'the powerful regions under earth' (v. iii. 3–11). The stage direction, which may or may not be Shakespeare's own, calls them 'Fiends', but all this merely designates spiritualism as then generally clouded by ignorance and fear. What is important is Joan's defence:

> First, let me tell you whom you have condemn'd:
> Not me begotten of a shepherd swain,
> But issu'd from the progeny of kings;

1. See a second article 'Shakespeare and the "Supernatural" ', by Beryl Pogson in *Light*, Autumn 1965, LXXXV, 3462; also Cumberland Clark, *Shakespeare and the Supernatural*, 1932.

Virtuous and holy; chosen from above,
By inspiration of celestial grace,
To work exceeding miracles on earth.
I never had to do with wicked spirits.
But you—that are polluted with your lusts,
Stain'd with the guiltless blood of innocents,
Corrupt and tainted with a thousand vices—
Because you want the grace that others have,
You judge it straight a thing impossible
To compass wonders but by help of devils.
No—misconceived! Joan of Arc hath been
A virgin from her tender infancy,
Chaste and immaculate in very thought,
Whose maiden blood, thus rigorously effus'd,
Will cry for vengeance at the gates of Heaven.

(v. iv. 36)

Joan's speech which points on to Byron's *Manfred* (*Byron and Shakespeare*, 298–301), is as powerful a defence of Spiritualism against the Church's traditional condemnation as we shall anywhere find.

XXIII

CHRISTIAN DOCTRINE

Essays in Criticism, entitled 'Shakespeare and Theology', January 1965; XV, I.

LITERARY studies can seldom have produced a more gross misrepresentation than that accorded my Shakespeare commentaries by Mr. R. M. Frye's *Shakespeare and Christian Doctrine* (Princeton, U.P.: London, O.U.P.). Writing in *The Birmingham Post* for 28 April 1964 Sir Ifor Evans states that Mr. Frye is opposing 'G. Wilson Knight's belief "that Shakespeare's plays are essentially and pervasively—even blatantly—Christian"'. Does this reviewer think that those words, quoted from Mr. Frye, were written by me? Perhaps: for he also implies that before Mr. Frye's onslaught such work as mine 'falls flat on its face'. In similar vein Mr. Martin Seymour-Smith in *The Spectator* of 24 April 1964 writes: 'Again and again he shows the outpourings of Professor Wilson Knight to be utter nonsense in the light of the expectations and beliefs of Shakespeare's audience.' These reviews are interesting symptoms of a surreptitious hostility in academic and critical circles of which I am well enough aware. But my opponents will have to find a stronger champion than Mr. Frye.

Referring to work by myself and by others for whom he chooses to hold me responsible, Mr. Frye writes:

> We are repeatedly faced with assertions as to what sixteenth-century Christians would have thought of particular characters, actions, and speeches, but rarely—indeed, almost never—do we find evidence cited from the sixteenth century to buttress the assertions.
>
> (19)

Since one of my central principles has always been to refuse to have anything to do with such pseudo-scholarship, so deeply ingrained in our academic tradition, the charge is fantastic. Have I not inveighed against the tendency 'to label and render nugatory, because docketed, the romantic statement' and insisted on the dangers 'of using Elizabethan scholarship, of one sort or another, to shrivel Shakespearian power to the stature of an academic under-standing' (*The Crown of Life*, 253)? Have I not attacked the recent attempts to confuse the results of my interpretations by such refer-ences to supposedly contemporary thought? Have I not written against all attempts to clothe them 'in a well-cut, twentieth-century, suit of Elizabethan learning', urging that the correct procedure is to 'interpret an age in the light of its great books and men of visionary genius, not the men of genius in the light of their age' (*The Imperial Theme*, 1951 edn., Prefatory Note, xii; and see *The Wheel of Fire*, enlarged, 331, 343; also p. 209 above)? In my 1953 preface to *The Shakespearian Tempest* (vii–viii) I argued that what was most im-portant in my interpretations was discovered 'not by any reading of medieval or Elizabethan philosophies, but by a simple inspection of the poetry'. Again:

> A new layer of symbolic meaning was unearthed by direct interpretation; of this certain elements were abstracted by scholarship and equated with medieval philosophy; and finally the philosophy—not even the Shakespearian elements —is arbitrarily applied to the poetry *from outside* as the one sure canon of judgement and necessary implement of interpretation. The illogicality is patent. Let us inspect the dangers . . .

With reference to a problem of human and dramatic valuation I stated that it would 'not be solved by a whole library of moral text-books, however Elizabethan (or medieval) they may be', since that would be to read genius in the light of mediocrity. Has Mr. Frye not read my books?

He thinks (4) that I regard Shakespeare's plays as 'pervasively' and 'blatantly' Christian, and twists (as shown below) a remark from the 1936 (U.S.A. 1937) edition of *Principles of Shakespearian Production*. That book I opened with the warning that Shakespeare's dramas used various world-views as occasion demanded and that to talk of Shakespeare's religious 'philosophy' was meaningless: 'his massed statement includes many philosophies, but is subject to none' (17). A couple of pages preceding that from which Mr. Frye quotes—did he read only the one page?—I asserted that Shakespeare's last play *Henry VIII* had 'an orthodox' colouring that was 'new', suggesting that in it he 'returned at the last to orthodoxy', finding in Christianity a corroboration 'of what his own exploring poetry had independently discovered'. I added a footnote apologizing for having adventured for once into biography but insisting that though certain earlier plays held Christian suggestions, Shakespeare had never come 'anywhere near' such a 'Christian symbolism' as we find in *Henry VIII* (232). Elsewhere I have shown how Shakespeare's life-work before *Henry VIII* had been philosophically summed up in a work 'without theology'; that is, *The Tempest* (*The Crown of Life*, 251).

Whenever I have compared Shakespeare's dramatic adventures to the New Testament or Christian dogma I have regarded the two powers as independent, though 'whatever our private views'— whether we are orthodox believers or not—'*both are recording the same facts*' (original italics); that is, the same cosmic laws lie behind both. So 'orthodox Christianity and Shakespeare confront each other with a contrast and similarity that challenge our attention' (*Principles etc.*, 231–2). When I pointed a relation to pagan sacrifice and the Christian Mass (233–4) I was concerned primarily, as the whole tenor of my chapter ('Shakespeare and Ritual') makes clear, with the limitations of naturalistic acting and staging rather than with doctrine as such. Again and again I have warned my readers against a misuse of such comparisons. In *The Crown of Life* I emphasized 'the sharp break' between the 'medieval' and the 'Shakespearian' drama; 'the medieval system losing its hold, the way was at once opened for a far more richly varied drama'; the finding of 'medieval thought' in Shakespeare 'in no sense disposes of a sharp distinction'; 'human drama becomes autonomous; the age-old importance of ritual moves from the altar to the playhouse; and this drama of the humanistic imagination is newly wealthy in crowned kings and lovely heroines' (227).

One of Mr. Frye's most insistent complaints is that *my* 'school' adventures rashly beyond the dramatic whole to allot to Shakespeare's protagonists definite places in Heaven or Hell *after death* (Frye, 5, 58, 92). The statement as applied to me is either comic or malicious. I am so far from moralizing that of *Measure for Measure* I wrote that despite its Christian affinities it 'exists more nearly as a challenge to orthodox morality than as an advertisement for it' (*The Sovereign Flower*; 251). Nor have I ever discussed the 'eternal destiny in a future life' (Frye, 5) of Shakespeare's persons, except to oppose with all my strength those who in the process of doing so would have Macbeth damned. I quote from *The Sovereign Flower* (250):

> Though I have compared *Macbeth, King Lear* and *Antony and Cleopatra* to experiences of Hell, Purgatory and Paradise, it makes no sense, within my field of study, to say that Macbeth is damned: the Hell has been experienced during the action. What happens afterwards we are not told, but the whole tendency of Shakespearian humanism counters the doctrine of Hell as a state of lasting torment after death.

I have always in morality's despite viewed Shakespearian tragedy as in some indefinable, Nietzschean, way an advance. In Shakespeare salvation appears, most undoctrinally, to come about 'not through repentance but by recognition and acceptance; and in these there lies a spiritual achievement' (as above, 249). And yet I of all people am supposed to be always finding non-existent references in Shakespeare to 'Christian doctrines of redemption' (Frye, 5)—which, by the way, I have never been able to understand. *Where* do I do this? As for the 'future' life, in reading the last plays as imaginative penetrations beyond tragedy I wrote that they 'do not aim at revealing a temporal survival of death' but 'rather at the thought that death is a delusion' ('Myth and Miracle'; *The Crown of Life*, 22). I have insisted that we must not 'question beyond the framework', saying: 'To argue that Leontes and Hermione must anyhow die after the action is irrelevant: they do not exist after the action' (*Principles etc.*, 44). What *does* Mr. Frye mean?

He quotes from two only of my seven main Shakespearian volumes—one a book on staging where ritualistic comparisons were called for—and these two he has signally failed to comprehend. But this is not all. After suggesting that Shakespeare's dramas show a certain Christian affinity in their un-Marlovian sense of tragic purpose I once called his heroes 'miniature Christs', and wrote:

> In the world of Shakespearian tragedy this unique act of the Christ sacrifice can, if we like, be seen as central. The one general principle is exploited in various human stories, with heroes good, bad and indifferent.
>
> (*Principles etc.*, 1936; U.S.A. 1937; 231, 234)

The terms used are as un-theological and un-doctrinal as the nature of the statement allows and the implied honouring of 'bad' heroes utterly precludes any suggestion of a morality-play. However, this is what it becomes in Mr. Frye's book:

> For Knight, on the other hand, the 'unique act of the Christ sacrifice can . . . be seen as central' to Shakespeare's tragedies.
>
> (5)

Torn from its context and a key reservation omitted, it is so presented as to deceive the reader. He stops his quotation at 'central' and *omits 'if we like' which precludes the rigid doctrinal emphasis which he is imputing.*[1]

Yet worse remains. I once regarded Timon as within the sequence of Shakespeare's plays analogous to Christ according to the Christian scheme within history, since in *Timon of Athens* Shakespeare's tragic emotions are pushed to an extreme and the stage cleared for more visionary dramas. I also wrote:

> When Timon's servants part to wander abroad separated, they are as disciples of the Christ meeting after the crucifixion.
>
> (*The Wheel of Fire*, enlarged; 235)

Such passing comparisons are natural enough, as when I once compared Othello's bearing under arrest to Christ's, and Middleton Murry Antony's farewell to the Last Supper. Considering that the

---

1. I am referring to the 1936 edition used and cited by Mr. Frye. In 1949 and 1964 this rather loose paragraph was condensed, with a change of 'seen' to 'felt' and a note on Shakespeare's humanistic dramaturgy. [**1966**]

Christian drama had almost alone held the imaginations of Western man for fifteen centuries, it was inevitable that such similarities should appear without any forcing of a doctrinal response.

Timon is in fact compared, as was Richard II but no other Shakespearian hero, to Christ by Shakespeare, twice (I. ii. 48–51; III. ii. 73–4). Even so, it would be wrong to regard the reading as more than a partial and passing analogy. Such an extension Mr. Frye nevertheless imputes by omitting my 'as', so that my passage as he quotes it reads: '. . . they are disciples of the Christ . . .' (Frye, 34). That is what his readers, who have been told that I write nonsense, will think that I wrote.

My main contribution has been the relating of Shakespearian drama to dimensions beyond normal awareness through exact attention to Shakespeare's major dramatic symbolisms previously unfocused: such are, the tempests and music, the sea, Othello's handkerchief, the three apparitions in *Macbeth*, the deities in the last plays, the resurrection-themes in *Pericles* and *The Winter's Tale*, Ariel and Prospero's magic. *Now all these are either naturalistic or pagan.* Even the enigmatic ghost in *Hamlet*, so saturated in orthodox suggestion, I myself read as mainly a symbol of Death. How could I ever have been tempted to sully these newly recognized powers by tying on to them doctrinal labels that wrong their autonomy? I rate my discoveries more highly.

Mr. Frye accuses me of an 'essentially medieval analysis' (60). In *The Crown of Life* (35) I wrote:

The step from Aeschylus to Shakespeare is easy: in spite of Shakespeare's obvious Christian sympathies the two dramatists often seem more contemporaneous than either with Dante. They breathe the same air of questioning adventure, sharing the same brooding sense of blood and death as vast antagonists to the soul of man. Shakespeare was, no doubt, an outwardly conforming Christian; more, his plays witness continually a fervent Christianity on the plane of verbal poetry and human delineation; but in that which is equally, perhaps more, important, the infusing of poetic belief into his fable, his dramatic machinery of ghosts and revenge themes, the driving of action to a climax of slaughter, the sense of death as death;

in this Shakespeare is with Aeschylus; at the most with Vergil, not with Dante. Though the thought-forms of Renaissance writers are often medieval, their creative art is not.

When Shakespeare came to the resurrection themes of his final period, I was careful to explain that his guiding star was 'not the Mass', but his own creative genius (35). All this is pretty nearly what Mr. Frye puts forward as his own clever solution, while accusing me of stupidity. It is probable that my own writing—read, forgotten and reproduced—has taught him what he knows. (But I did not teach him to mis-read Shakespeare's 'Men must endure . . .'; Frye, 137-8. 'Endure' = 'await').

In respect to *The Winter's Tale* I wrote (*Crown of Life*, 96-7): 'Though Christianized phraseology recurs, yet the poet is rather to be supposed as using Christian concepts than as dominated by them'; they are 'implemental to his purpose'; but so are 'Apollo' and 'nature'. The play 'remains a creation of the Renaissance, that is, of the questing imagination, firmly planted no doubt in medieval tradition, but not directed by it'. I added: 'There is a distinction here of importance'. After consideration of the resurrection scene the warning was repeated. Orthodox tradition and paganism had been subsidiary influences, 'but the greatest influence was Life itself, that creating and protecting deity whose superhuman presence and powers the drama labours to define' (128).

Mr. Frye cannot in defence say that he is merely writing from a general hostility to the more visionary elements in my interpretations; nor that he is referring not to me but to what he has chosen to call 'my school'. *He makes precise charges and relates them exactly to myself, by name.* Each in turn I have shown to be in glaring contradiction to all my published convictions.

I now ask Mr. Frye to agree that I have never regarded Shakespeare's plays as 'pervasively' and 'blatantly' Christian; that I have not wasted valuable time in trying to guess what some long-forgotten Elizabethan sociologist or theologian or audience might or might not have thought on any point under discussion; that I have not followed the dramatic persons beyond the dramatic action; and that I have treated the plays up to *The Tempest* as autonomous Renaissance products of 'individualistic, Nietzschean assertion', related to the medieval tradition and using it when it suits them, but primarily pointing ahead to the Romantics and Nietzsche and only giving way to a 'Christian mythology' in *Henry VIII* (*The Crown of Life*, 297).

In discussing *Henry VIII* I found all Shakespeare's former heroes—Hamlet, Othello, Lear, Timon, Prospero—guilty of 'wounded pride' (*The Crown of Life*, 277), and continued:

> This is Shakespeare's one explicitly Christian play; but its Christianity is defined not by theological speculation nor any personification of abstract qualities, but rather by the sharp dramatic confronting of the Shakespearian nobility at its best with the yet nobler ideal. Christianity is not treated as an intellectual scheme: it is brought, through drama, to the bar of life. Can the Shakespearian hero live the Christian way, to the end? The presence of Christ himself is thus realized through His absence.

That is a strange paragraph for someone who is charged with finding Christ-heroes everywhere in Shakespeare. Can Mr. Frye not understand that a single passing comparison for a specific purpose may be different from a number of considered *identifications*? And even in *Henry VIII* I found the religious solemnities balanced against an equally emphatic, at times gross, sexuality (306), while 'the King appears as a tower of strength and sanity above intrigue and theological subtlety' (314); 'men, or at least kings', I wrote, 'cannot live by morals alone', for 'all ethical rules and religious doctrines are, in the last resort, provisional' (317). These phrases occur in the most theological of my supposedly 'theologizing analyses' (Frye, 19).

Any Christian tonings which I emphasize in the royalistic history plays are by reason of that very royalism extended beyond dogma into a more comprehensive, part-secular, world-view beyond orthodoxy and more challenging than theology; as is clear from *Henry VIII* which in its balancing of State and Church, though at a particular point in history and not as abstractions, looks ahead to the 'Third Empire' of Ibsen's *Emperor and Galilean* (Ibsen, 1962; 31–46) and Nietzsche's demand in *The Will to Power* (983) for a 'Roman Caesar with the soul of Christ'. Shakespeare has, in fact, left us a new, Renaissance, bible, submitting to no external doctrine and with its own independent authority. He writes the Old Testament of the Elizabethan age, passing from poetic myth and legend to near-distance history and national prophecy; then, plumbing deeper, to the New Testament of personal problem and creative tragedy. In *Antony and Cleopatra* tragedy is, as in the Gospels, reversed, and leads on in the last plays to a consolidation, corresponding to St. Paul's Epistles, of the death-conquest achieved; and lastly the whole is in each completed by a single work, *Revelation* and *Henry VIII*, concerned again, yet more expansively, with nations and prophecy, piercing the future. Official Christianity, concentrating on the Gospels and Epistles, has inevitably narrowed the Bible to the personal and the theological. Shakespeare's royalistic life-work exists for us rather as do their Scriptures for the Jews, including sexual and political substances and Messianic statement; and there is a Rabelaisian and Renaissance humour. Shakespeare is modern and comprehensive.

To see where he has blundered Mr. Frye must learn to distinguish between my making whatever personal comparisons with Greek or Christian mythology or ritual I may find, for my own purposes and to help my readers, convenient, and my supposed 'attempting to prove on the basis of his writings that Shakespeare was a pious believer' (Frye, 46). Have I not in all my formal interpretations most resolutely refused to discuss the dramatist apart from his drama? Mr. Frye should also re-read my chapter 'Some Notable Fallacies' in *The Sovereign Flower*, which has doubtless been of service to him since it develops the main arguments which he so proudly flaunts as his own and attacks what he attacks, saying (250–1):

> Though his drama is no passive reflection of Christian dogma it certainly does very often, in matters both infernal and paradisal, demonstrate, not indeed the truth of the dogma, but the truth of THAT the truth of which the dogma itself exists to establish. The orthodox teaching of damnation may be factually wrong and yet symbolize a great truth. There are similarities both superficial and profound between the conclusion of *The Winter's Tale* and the dogma of the Resurrection, but there is

301

a danger of concentrating on those which are superficial and passing over those which are profound. . . . So we do Christianity itself little service by regarding Shakespeare's plays as no more than pendants to the religious tradition, since in so doing we inevitably end by slighting that human insight and spiritual penetration through which alone the Shakespearian impact exists and what might be called the corroboration of Christian truth in Renaissance terms is accomplished. . . . It would indeed be strange were Shakespeare's poetry so orthodox as is sometimes supposed.

These thoughts of mine were not new. I quote in conclusion the last words of my first independent publication, *Myth and Miracle* (1929; reprinted in *The Crown of Life*) where, after emphasizing the 'mystic truth' active *behind* Shakespeare, Dante and Christian belief, I wrote, in explicit repudiation of all doctrinal limitations:

> We should centre our attention always not on the poetic forms alone, which are things of time and history, but on the spirit which burns through them and is eternal in its rhythm of pain, endurance, and joy.

Can Mr. Frye not see that the comparisons *are only interesting because of the independences*? On certain general un-dogmatic and non-theological truths of life and death and that which negates death Shakespearian drama certainly goes far to corroborate, in purely general terms, the Christian. But there is much else too, and each is less than the one spirit which burns through them. It is that spirit which I assert.

I sometimes wonder whether *Myth and Miracle* has had any deep understanding since Mr. T. S. Eliot, as he recorded when introducing *The Wheel of Fire*, found it (or he may have been referring to its unpublished predecessor, *Thaisa*) helpful. He, if no one else, saw the point of it and subsequently wrote, and sent me, *Marina* (see p. 317 below, note). The inscribed copy is lodged in The Shakespeare Memorial Library of the City Reference Library at Birmingham. But how many others, in all these years, have understood it?

It is a central spirit-force active within all my interpretations, neither constricted by orthodoxy nor inhibited by sense-perception, against which Mr. Frye's misrepresentations have offended.

ADDITIONAL NOTE, 1966

My first protest against Mr. Frye's misrepresentations was registered in a letter to *The New Statesman* on 21 August 1964, and was followed by another in *The Times Literary Supplement* on 7 January 1965. On both occasions I asked for the book's withdrawal. The second letter was answered by Mr. Frye on 28 January, admitting the omission of 'as' by an error in 'proofing'; and the correspondence concluded by my request, on 4 February, that Mr. Frye should tell us whether before dismissing my work wholesale he had or had not read 'Some Notable Fallacies' in *The Sovereign Flower*, wherein I had summed up 'my many earlier warnings against the very errors with which his book now charges me'. My letter concluded: 'I await his reply.'

I am still waiting. Mr. Frye's arguments have been powerfully attacked by Prof. Irving Ribner in 'A Chain of Fallacies', *Tulane Drama Review* (U.S.A.), Summer 1966; X, 4.

An acknowledgment of a debt to Mr. Frye appears in my Preface.

XXIV

SYMBOLISM

A slightly amplified version of an article contributed to *The Reader's Encyclopedia of Shakespeare* edited by Oscar James Campbell and Edward G. Quinn, and published by the Thomas Y. Crowell Company, New York, 1966.

THE word 'symbolism' as used in current literary and dramatic disquisition is not covered by the dictionary definition of it as a *conventional* sign. Rather it tends to mean some effect, person, object or descriptive passage which automatically radiates general significances flowering from that effect's intrinsic nature. The meanings are not imposed by a convention as they may be in 'allegory' but spring *inevitably* from the symbol used. Though in one sense infinite, they are in another strictly limited. For example, the much discussed Falcon in Ibsen's *Brand*, despite the evidence for the reading of it at one point as 'the spirit of compromise', inevitably suggests, as does the falcon throughout Shakespeare, a strong aspiration (see my *Ibsen*, 1962, 21–4). Any external evidence that counters the intrinsic meaning must accordingly be either inaccurate or misunderstood. The laws of symbolism are rigid, and its analysis a disciplined study.[1]

Symbolism exists to give sensory form to values and powers not otherwise easy to express; at the limit, to extra-sensory dimensions of being and spirit realities. Under poetic handling normal events may themselves assume an aura of symbolical suggestion; through imagery and atmosphere they may shade into the numinous. All imaginative writing is to this extent symbolical. But usually, and certainly for our present, Shakespearian, purpose, we do well to limit the term to elements where normal realism is, or appears to be,

1. My extended discussion of the nature and function of 'symbolism' is set out in *The Christian Renaissance*, 1933, 1962; 11.

negated or broken through; to effects which stick out, strangely but meaningfully. In Shakespeare such effects tend to involve the supernatural, though we must not forget that they grow from a soil of semi-symbolic naturalism; they do not impinge from a completely alien world. They have strong dramatic quality.

Shakespeare's major symbolisms were not properly focussed until recently. Imaginative tonings and the occasional dominant image (e.g. fire in *Coriolanus*) were handled by A. C. Bradley; and imagery became a primary study with Caroline Spurgeon and Wolfgang Clemen. But the major symbolisms have proved less inviting. Colin Still's *Shakespeare's Mystery Play* (1921; revised and enlarged as *The Timeless Theme*, 1936) faced them in *The Tempest*, seeing its events in depth and relating them to ancient myth and ritual, but his enquiry was, though brilliant, limited to one obviously symbolic drama. Probably the first real advance into the more general study of Shakespeare's symbolism was made in 1924 by John Masefield in his Oxford Romanes lecture *Shakespeare and Spiritual Life* (see p. 201 above), wherein he took seriously and probed metaphysically the supernatural portents of *Julius Caesar*, *Hamlet* and *Macbeth*. These had too often been treated by commentators as little more than a writer's obedience to his 'sources' or to traditional superstition.[1] The older critics would have called them 'machinery', the term applied in the eighteenth century to Pope's sylphs in *The Rape of the Lock*. The word 'machinery' is not so derogatory as it sounds. It suggests power and action, and that is exactly how such symbolisms function; they are dynamic, and geared to the human action. It is symbolism in this sense to which my own works have been primarily, though not exclusively, devoted.

There were two related discoveries, both of which may be supposed to involve 'symbolism'. One was the recognition of the death-reversals in *Pericles* and *The Winter's Tale* as dramatic equivalents to a truth beyond tragedy; the other—it came, so far as I can recall,

---

1. Mention should here be made of R. G. Moulton's analytic treatment of Shakespeare's dramatic use of such powers in *Shakespeare as a Dramatic Artist*, Chicago, 1885; IX and XX; and of Edward Dowden's remarkable discussion of the Weird Sisters in *Macbeth* in *Shakespeare: his Mind and Art* in 1875. I am aware that there may be others, especially among German commentators, who deserve, as Enobarbus has it, 'a place i' the story'.

second—the recognition within separate plays of imagistic and intellectual coherences as spatial areas of the mind, at high moments crystallizing into direct dramatic symbolisms of supernatural or semi-supernatural quality. Both discoveries derived from the willingness to see within the Shakespearian world, as Keats puts it in *Hyperion*, 'the depth of things' (*The Fall of Hyperion*, 1. 304); that is, to accept every effect in its own right as exerting lines of force according to its intrinsic nature over and above the surface story. These were my main contributions. Imagistic coherences were simultaneously being studied by Caroline Spurgeon (*Leading Motives in the Imagery of Shakespeare's Tragedies*, 1930; *Shakespeare's Iterative Imagery*, 1931). F. C. Kolbe in *Shakespeare's Way* (1930) played on various key-motifs not limited to imagery and handling events, though his results remained, in the main, sketchy. Apart from Masefield's Romanes lecture the major symbolic agencies were not being accorded their due of centrality.

A peculiarly rich discovery of the new method was made in my reading of the three Apparitions in Act IV, Scene i of *Macbeth*: the Armed Head, the Bloody Child, the Crowned and Tree-bearing Child (*The Imperial Theme*, 150–3; *The Shakespearian Tempest*, 192–3; *The Christian Renaissance*, 1962, 45–6). These appear as spiritualistic materializations, recalling the spirit-raising scene of *2 Henry VI* (I. iv); they are also carefully made to constitute an exact symbolism. Though they are related prophetically to the events of the fifth act, they simultaneously exist more metaphysically as a compressed miniature of the total drama, showing: (i) death, destructive and self-destructive; (ii) life-born-out-of-death; and (iii) human life backed by nature and raised by the crown to a yet higher status; so that the second child-figure compactly denotes nature, man and the surpassing of man in royalty. The two child-figures relate to this particular play's pervading use of child-thoughts throughout, and those in turn to the many thoughts of life-forces in nature and human feasting. Nowhere else can we so plainly see how the major symbols may flower from a semi-symbolic soil; and also how they may function ambivalently, since Macbeth is encouraged by their *words* while remaining blind to the *drama* of their visual statement.

Since these three Apparitions together dramatize conflict, they come to thunder. The following procession of kings, suggesting a creative harmony undisturbed by the brief conflict, comes naturally to music. We have here a peculiarly vivid and compact example of Shakespeare's recurring symbolic contrast of thunder-tempests and music. In *The Shakespearian Tempest* it was shown how this recurring balance applies to a large part of Shakespeare's universe, not alone as imagery but as event: in the romantic comedies, the tragedies and the final plays. The tempest-music symbolism, often taking the form of the sea as variously fierce and calm, acts as a principle of unity in Shakespeare's world. Atmosphere, imagery and thought all vary: the unity lies in the symbolism.

In the historical dramas tempests are tragic impressions in the imagery and there are cosmic portents; and music as a backwater of peace countering violence functions in *Richard II* and both parts of *Henry IV* as in the tragedies. But the dominant *symbolism* of the history sequence is the Crown, existing, despite the inadequacies of its various possessors, as a sacred symbol aiming to raise man and his community beyond man and to link the temporal to the eternal. This symbol too applies widely throughout Shakespeare, since nearly all his plays are royalistically centred. There are accordingly two principles of unity in Shakespeare: (i) tempests-and-music, and (ii) the crown. Their mutual relation, which I first expressed in *The Olive and the Sword* (p. 111 above), is found in the Shakespearian will to transmute human conflicts through the agency of the royalistic intuition to a harmony. This harmony is finally stated in Cranmer's prophecy of the Elizabethan and Jacobean ages in *Henry VIII*, where crown and virtue coalesce. The involvement is localized, contemporary and specific, in the manner of Aeschylus, Vergil and Dante, but what was for Shakespeare an actuality becomes symbolic for us, taking its place beside Aeschylus' Athens and Vergil's Rome.

The relation of symbolism to realism, in the popular sense of the word, is well seen in Shakespeare's use of gold and riches in *The Merchant of Venice* and *Timon of Athens*. Max Plowman's 'Money and The Merchant' (1931; p. 97 above, note) analysed in depth the contrast of money-values and life-values ('pound of flesh', 'heart') in the Trial scene of *The Merchant of Venice*; and this reading I grouped not only with the three caskets as symbols of true and false wealth but also with Portia's 'infinite bank-balance' read as a symbol of the true (*Shakespearian Production*, 1964, 127–9; *The Shakespearian Tempest*, 129–31); for by symbolism the material may at any moment assume sacramental properties. In *Timon of Athens* gold has similar two-way pointings: it both stimulates avarice and acts as the expression of a bounteous and warm heart. In the later scenes Timon's new-found gold adds to his prophetic stature; as outcast he is still sought after; in performance the gold *inevitably* helps to build up the dramatic power of his Promethean personality. When Caroline Spurgeon criticized my emphasis on gold in *Timon of Athens*, observing that there were in fact no gold-metaphors, we see the divergence of her approach from mine. The gold in *Timon of Athens* is part of the symbolic action, more important than imagery (*Shakespearian Production*, 1964; 180–4). In *Measure for Measure* the blend of State and Church represented by the Duke's disguise as a Friar, which the reader too easily passes over, should direct our reception of his words; and the visual balance of King Henry and Cranmer at the conclusion of *Henry VIII* interprets all that has preceded. It is with a stage eye that Shakespeare's symbolic effects must be received.

Symbolism often leads us from the ordinary into the imponderables. The Handkerchief in *Othello*, a domestic object in a domestic world, assumes supernal power, to become, as Othello's reiterations drive home, a primary agent. Middleton Murry, who though a pervading influence behind the new Shakespearian movement was not generally at ease with symbolism as such, was nevertheless the first to observe that Desdemona's 'Sure, there's some wonder in this handkerchief' (III. iv. 100) is not merely an acceptance of Othello's account of it but a sudden realization, in view of Othello's extraordinary behavior, of its magic in action (*Shakespeare*, 1936, XIV; he had advanced the reading earlier in an article). In making the handkerchief a semi-supernatural force in relation to conjugal infidelity Shakespeare was, as Byron, according to Thomas Medwin's *Conversations of Lord Byron* (see *Byron and Shakespeare*, 250) noticed, in close accord with Oriental lore: 'The handkerchief is the strongest proof of love, not only among the Moors, but all Eastern nations.'

In *King Lear* the supernatural is not directly dramatized, but

Edgar as pretended madman, naked, fantastic in behaviour and talking of the fiends that torment him, blends with the appalling tempest and wild heath to give us as strong a sense of the supernormal as any apparition. It is Shakespeare's most elaborate and complex raising of realism to symbolism.

Symbols may however be less obviously based in realism. Ghosts have undoubtedly been seen but even so they come as strangers, if not aliens, as from another dimension. We meet them in *Richard III*, *Julius Caesar*, *Hamlet* and *Macbeth*. They are darkly toned and directly related to the drama's deeper issues; they function as authoritative entities, and that in *Hamlet* as a dramatic agent. In *Hamlet* the Ghost is described in terms of folk-lore and religious eschatology, but it has dramatically a more generalized import. Bradley was in part right, at the conclusion of his second lecture on *Hamlet* in *Shakespearian Tragedy*, to relate its 'majestical' qualities to its function as an instrument of supernal judgement; but it is also a spirit suffering in Purgatory. It remains ambiguous. My own reading has been comprehensive, seeing it as a symbol of Death invading Life; just as the Weird Sisters in *Macbeth* are symbols of Evil. Then there are the appearances of divine beings; such are Hymen in *As You Like It*, Hecate in *Macbeth*, Diana in *Pericles*, Apollo in *The Winter's Tale*, Jupiter in *Cymbeline*, the Angels in *Henry VIII*. The academic and stage rejection of Jupiter has at last been reversed, and that it should have taken so long, and been my own unaided battle, shows how blind commentary may be to staging and therefore to symbolism. Jupiter was always potentially a superb stage power and as such he is now recognized.

Academic understanding has been held up by (i) a lack of stage sense and (ii) fear of the supernatural. When a work may be written off as wholly 'fanciful', acceptance comes more easily. The fairies and spirits of *A Midsummer Night's Dream* and *The Tempest* grow from what may be called a highly imaginative soil; within their world they are expected. Nevertheless they, and their soil, are all symbolically loaded and active and require, and have received, analysis in depth (for the one see *The Shakespearian Tempest*, 141–68 and *The Golden Labyrinth*, 70; for the other *The Shakespearian Tempest*, 247–66, and *The Crown of Life*, v).

In *Pericles* and *The Winter's Tale* a human story itself takes on supernatural quality and so becomes to this extent symbolic. The death-reversals come to us dramatically as resurrections. During these reunions and revivals with their sacred tonings and music we experience a reversal of death, just as at the conclusions of *Hamlet* and *King Lear* we experience death; except that the hero himself does not die, it being his experience of his loved one's death that is reversed (*The Christian Renaissance*, 1962; 190), recalling Euripides' *Alcestis*. That Leontes and Hermione must be supposed to die after the drama's action is dramatically irrelevant: they do not exist after the action. Within the structure of a happy-ending romance a death-reversal is felt pressing for statement and recognition. That it may strain the form is arguable, but its presence is dramatically, if not logically, indisputable. We may say that the form is so manipulated and moulded as to 'symbolize' a difficult truth regarding 'immortality'.

Though there is so much else in Shakespeare, we shall only receive his total work as a harmony if we allow his symbolism to be our guide. The study of 'characters' alone leaves us with a wealth of human understanding, rich but chaotic; the study of thought and imagery in isolation will plunge us into a misleading medievalism.[1] Both, the humanistic and the doctrinal, are legitimate constituents, but neither, nor both together, give us the essence. Academically there is always the temptation to concentrate on these more easily definable elements, separately or together, but the dramatic essence will not be found in so comprehensively simple a scheme as (i) the philosophic and imagistic over-lay of (ii) a human story. It lies rather in the *knotting together* of these two elements through symbolism; and this knotting together can only come from intuition of a third reality, or dimension, whereby, or wherefrom, the disparity is dissolved; and so

---

1. Though in one sense the authority in the text is abundant, my tentative suggestion in *Shakespearian Production* (1964; 131, 143–4) of a not 'too definitely ecclesiastical' Madonna and Child for the staging of *Macbeth* might be criticized as a too-bold transference of imagery and thought to the status of dramatic symbolism.

We could say much the same of St. George, invoked as England's protector in the historical plays, though scarcely a dramatic agent. See pp. 106–10 above; also *The Sovereign Flower*, Index C. The importance of St. George in Shakespeare was emphasized by Beryl Pogson, p. 290 above, note.

we have various indications of a supernature, not definable in orthodox terms and yet out-spacing realism, as the resolving agent.

This 'third reality' is necessarily incommensurable with the opposing parties on which it supervenes. Therefore, except for the Crown's religious associations in the English history plays, Edward the Confessor's healing powers in *Macbeth*, the authoritative Duke in *Measure for Measure* disguised as a friar and controlling events 'like power divine' (v. i. 370), and the Angels in *Henry VIII*, Shakespeare never employs a Christian symbolism, the symbolic agencies which we have noted being either naturalistic or pagan. When Glendower's spirit-controlling powers so uncompromisingly falsify Hotspur's scepticism in cutting across Shakespeare's most strongly realistic drama, *Henry IV* (*1 Henry IV*, III. i. 53–62, 226–35), they do so with an occult but not a Christian authority. Cerimon's and Prospero's arts or magic are naturalistic or spiritualistic, not in any orthodox sense doctrinal. It is in part because the study of Shakespeare's symbolism forces us into categories involving occult and spiritualistic categories that the academic mind has proved so reluctant in investigation.

There are many complications. Shakespeare labours to harmonize opposing cultures: Renaissance humanism and medieval doctrine. He uses symbols of disorder, natural and cosmic, to point, it would appear, his moral; so that he might seem to be composing 'morality' plays with 'order' as his deity and fifth-act ritual conclusions in the contemporary manner as symbolic judgements corresponding to the judgement conclusions to the Mystery cycles. And yet matters are not so simple; nor will a great poetic dramatist base his life-work on an abstract concept. Symbols, as I have argued at length in *The Christian Renaissance* (1962; II, especially 24), outspace the concepts which they suggest. The crown, in plays variously Christian or pagan, is irreducible to abstract concepts on the one side or, at least until *Henry VIII*, its human tenants on the other. Richard III before Bosworth knows that the natural portents may apply equally to Richmond and himself; and the Gardeners in *Richard II* (III. iv) appear to adduce their gardening analogy to blame the King both for nurturing weeds and for not cutting off in good time the revolutionary who arises to root them out. In *Julius Caesar* the portents are highly intricate and variously viewed: to Cassius Caesar's assassination is an act of order, to Antony the reverse and to Brutus ambivalent; and every curve is faced and traced by Shakespeare's symbolic artistry (*The Wheel of Fire*, enlarged, 137–8; *The Imperial Theme*, 94–5; *The Shakespearian Tempest*, 1953, xi). 'Order' may apply to the individual, to lovers, to the family, the state, the cosmos; and any one 'order' may, as in *Romeo and Juliet*, conflict with another, or others (*The Imperial Theme*, 9, 16–18; *The Shakespearian Tempest*, 1953, x, 291). In *Troilus and Cressida* Ulysses' 'order' speech is balanced against the tragic mysticism of Agamemnon and Nestor (*The Wheel of Fire*, enlarged, 48–52); the communal necessity is balanced against the personal and the spiritual. The contrast here dramatized is peculiarly important, for it helps us to see why in *Macbeth*, though the disorder-symbols (II. iv) appear clearly to condemn the hero's crime, his tragic soul-strength asserts itself with considerable dramatic authority against them; almost it would seem against destiny itself.

This soul-strength is dramatized in *Timon of Athens*, wherein the hero assumes the powers elsewhere housed in external symbolism. There is necessarily no tempest; what symbols there are, such as the gold and as in *King Lear* animal-references, Timon dominates; he speaks as an equal of the cosmic lights which he finally rejects for the sea, which functions, mainly through sound, for its surf must be heard (*Shakespearian Production*, 1964, 180–5), as what we may call a symbol of 'Nirvana'. There is more here than satire or hatred, nor is Timon a misguided hero. The stage impact counters such negative and partial readings. Following Edgar in *King Lear*, Timon's nakedness marks his approach as man or superman to some beyond-human yet human-rooted dimension, his physical stature and new-found gold together exerting on the stage positive and Promethean radiations. Humanity and symbolism are identified.

The process continues, differently, in *Antony and Cleopatra*, which is throughout so imaginatively fabricated and almost inflated that only once does a direct symbolism need to assert itself in the mysterious music (IV. iii) that is said to denote the leaving of Antony by 'the god Hercules, whom Antony loved'. Here, as with the Apparitions of *Macbeth* and the later scenes of *Timon of Athens*, a realization of stage atmosphere is essential. Though *said* to suggest Antony's fall as a soldier the music, *as music*, in Shakespeare regularly love's language, inevitably supports the countering and victorious theme of love. Its effect is accordingly one of pleasure rather than pain. Here is the incident. Music sounds. Then:

4th Soldier:	Peace! what noise?
1st Soldier:	List, list!
2nd Soldier:	Hark!
1st Soldier:	Music i' the air.
3rd Soldier:	Under the earth.
4th Soldier:	It signs well, does it not?
3rd Soldier:	No.
1st Soldier:	Peace, I say!
	What should this mean?
2nd Soldier:	'Tis the god Hercules, whom Antony lov'd,
	Now leaves him.
1st Soldier:	Walk; let's see if other watchmen
	Do hear what we do.

(*They advance, meeting other Soldiers*)

2nd Soldier:	How now, masters!
Soldiers:	How now!—
	How now!—do you hear this?
1st Soldier:	Ay; is't not strange?
3rd Soldier:	Do you hear, masters? do you hear?
1st Soldier:	Follow the noise so far as we have quarter;
	Let's see how't will give off.
Soldiers:	Content. 'Tis strange.

(IV. iii. 12)

Note that the 2nd Soldier's interpretation significantly contains the word 'lov'd', inevitably reminding us that Antony has replaced love of war with the love, more truly 'love', of Cleopatra. But quite apart from that, how utterly inadequate to the mysterious atmosphere generated is any explicit interpretation in negative terms. Moreover, the music's effect in the theatre will register before any of the spoken words, and will linger on after, dissolving tragedy in harmony. Nowhere can we so plainly see how dangerous it may be for the study of Shakespeare's symbolism to read the text as literature without living the experience as drama.

In *Antony and Cleopatra* humanity is, at high moments, transfigured; and this knitting of the human essence to the symbolic leads on to the beyond-tragedy reversals of the last period. It is as though, having used various symbolisms, including symbolisms of order, as his semi-choric—though on occasion as ambivalent as a Greek oracle—pointers, Shakespeare finds the human essence asserting itself in *Macbeth* against the symbolism and then in *King Lear, Timon of Athens* and *Antony and Cleopatra* drawing level with it and assuming its properties. No precise doctrinal solution is stated. Prospero's island in *The Tempest* itself endures disorder and the revolutionary Caliban may attract actors as the drama's star part, developing as it does the rough nature-contacts of *King Lear* and *Timon of Athens*, as Ariel symbolizes the aspiring poetry that counters them; while Prospero, Shakespeare's achieved, though troubled and testy, superman, has as best he may to control both.

Our final trusts must be placed in (i) the cogent yet non-committal unifiers, the tempest-music opposition and the crown; (ii) the tragic aspirations and later death-reversals, for the *individual*; and (iii) Shakespeare's last play, the semi-ritualistic *Henry VIII*, balancing church and state, theology and humanism—though *not* in the cause of any abstraction such as 'order' or 'nationalism' but exactly located (*The Shakespearian Tempest*, 1953, xxiii) and thence, and only thence, widely symbolic—for the community. To these we may add the-child-as-symbol: in *Macbeth*, in the final myths, and in *Henry VIII*; for in the Child all solutions lie curled.

The researches here recorded have not as yet been widely understood and developed. In respect to symbolism *Macbeth* seems to have received the most attention. Cleanth Brooks in *The Well-Wrought Urn* (1949) has accepted and for his own purpose reviewed certain aspects of the play's child-symbolism explored in *The Imperial Theme*; and Roy Walker in *The Time is Free* (1949) has discussed the Apparitions with a sense of their complexity. Wolfgang Clemen's *The Development of Shakespeare's Imagery* (1951) includes a valuable commentary on Shakespeare's tempest-symbolism; and Kenneth Muir, writing of Pericles in *Shakespeare as Collaborator*

(1960), responds, as did D. G. James in *Scepticism and Poetry* (1937), to its immortality statement; and there are, naturally, others. But the ingrained academic reluctance to face the supernatural has led to a playing down, and often an ignoring, of the major symbolisms, accompanied by an over-emphasis on intellectual and imagistic detail; and also on moral, and sometimes Christian, doctrine. Symbolic interpretation is concerned less with morals than with metaphysics; but there has been, as so often in the past, a tendency to take the easier course of moralizing. Scholarship has too often behaved as does Macbeth in listening to the Apparitions' words while failing to focus their visual quality; it has read and interpreted the text as word-sequences without a sense of the stage totality.

In consequence scholars have responded to what I have designated the plays' 'spatial' qualities as isolated patterns of static thought imposed on the action instead of as an indissoluble part of that dynamic dimension from within which the great symbolic agencies themselves function. Though Shakespeare's thought-world is often medievally toned, his dramatic action is of Renaissance quality. Commentators have been led to take Othello's and Macbeth's words regarding their own damnation at their face value instead of recognizing them as froth on the fierce current which, whatever else it does, cannot without distortion of the dramatic impact be supposed to lead to Hell. They forget that Othello, despite his great cry for damnation, proceeds to die *in pride*; and that Macbeth ends by regarding himself as 'damned' (v. vii. 63) if he does *not* resist to the last! While making Shakespearian drama a series of Christian moralities, with 'order', which can mean anything or nothing, as a deceptive guide, they have remained blind to the action and major symbolic powers, none of which, except for the Duke in *Measure for Measure* and the religious associations of the crown leading up to *Henry VIII*, and the Angels of Katharine's vision, are specifically Christian. Christian tonings accompany romantic love (*The Imperial Theme*, 10–14); but *Shakespeare's main dramatic engagement of Christianity is made through the body politic* (pp. 21–9); it is part of his striving towards a blend of power and love (pp. 180, 229–30), of State and Church.

The best response has come from poets. The movement we are discussing was heralded by John Masefield's Romanes lecture and the first, and it is still the finest, published reaction to my reading of the final plays was T. S. Eliot's *Marina* (1931).[1] In his essay 'Music in Shakespeare' (*Encounter*, December, 1957; included in *Shakespeare Criticism 1935–1960*, ed. Anne Ridler, 1963), W. H. Auden has discussed and developed the exposition of Shakespeare's music symbolism as set out in *The Shakespearian Tempest*. John Heath-Stubbs' *Helen in Egypt* (1958) bears the imprint of Shakespeare's final period. The most striking advance of recent years in the field of Shakespearian interpretation has been made by Francis Berry: in *Poets' Grammar* (1958), handling the metaphysics of Shakespearian time; in *Poetry and the Physical Voice* (1962), exploring Shakespeare's use of vocal sounds; and in *The Shakespeare Inset* (1965), revealing a hitherto neglected element in Shakespeare's imaginative artistry.

From the first the new approach discussed in my present essay demanded what may be called a new 'focal length'; and symbolism could not be high-lighted without a corresponding shadowing of what had come to be known as 'character' study. Nevertheless A. C. Bradley's analyses of Shakespeare's persons remain for the most part unshaken, though on occasion he attempts to render logical Shakespeare's dramatic and poetic compressions by character-enquiries which appear, within the new focus, irrelevant. Though Bradley may ask awkward questions regarding off-stage events where a final interpretation recognizes the necessity of silence, they are nevertheless usually questions which throw into relief problems which a sensitive actor of the role concerned does well, provisionally, to face.

The key-note of symbolic interpretation is the replacing of the moral by the metaphysical; and Bradley's approach, as in especially his first essay on *King Lear*, has at least as much of the one as of the other. I do not deny that my own first attacks on 'character' study inevitably involved certain elements in Bradley's work. I was not however thinking primarily of him, but of a whole century's commentary. That I regarded Bradley as a part-precursor of my own labours is clear from my earliest, 1928, 'manifesto', reprinted in *The Sovereign Flower* (287, 291, notes). Failure to recognize his part in the

1. The relation of *Marina* to *Myth and Miracle* is discussed in my essay 'T. S. Eliot: Some Literary Impressions'. See p. 11, note; also 302.

story of Shakespearian interpretation is a symptom of failure in understanding of the imaginative extensions that have complemented without invalidating his achievement.

In conclusion, the case for the study of Shakespeare's symbolism may be stated as follows: the isolation of plot, character, imagery or philosophy leads, in each instance, to distortion, if not error; but, as I urged in *The Shakespearian Tempest* (13–17), the study of symbolism, even its study in apparent isolation, does not; for it is impossible to discuss these major symbols at all adequately without simultaneously discussing the total drama. Beyond both religion and humanism and corresponding to the 'Third Empire' of Ibsen's *Emperor and Galilean* (p. 24), they contain, and render purposive, the rest.

APPENDIXES

A. LETTERS PUBLISHED IN *THE TIMES LITERARY SUPPLEMENT*

23 December 1926

SHAKESPEARE'S EXPERIENCE

In the correspondence which has appeared recently in your columns I have not noticed what seems to me to be a most cogent argument in deciding the exact significance of the last line of

> . . . and it is great
> To do that thing that ends all other deeds;
> Which shackles accidents, and bolts up change;
> Which sleeps and never palates more the dug;
> The beggar's nurse and Caesar's.
> > (*Antony and Cleopatra*, v. ii. 4)

The root idea of the passage is an attempt to penetrate to the essence of 'that thing' which we call death. If 'nurse' is in apposition to 'dug' (or 'dung')[1] it is expanding in a needless way, and at the most vital moment of the period, what is not even the most important word of the preceding sentence, the whole weight of which, as with the former ones, falls on the verb. Can this be a fitting end for so intensely conceived a passage? Surely we know that the final half-line in this typical Shakespearian (and Websterian) movement is always the ninth wave; it breaks with a crash and is followed by a tidal pause. One calls to mind so many: 'I cried to dream again', 'Is rounded with a sleep' (*The Tempest*, III. ii. 155; IV. i. 158), 'The sun of Rome is set' (*Julius Caesar*, v. iii. 63).

This speech is an attempt to lock the nature of Death's mystery in words. It first emphasizes its grandeur, its aesthetic appeal, and in

---

1. The Folio reads 'dung'. Compare 'dungy earth' at I. i. 35. [**1966**]

expanding this passes on to analyse its reality in material action. The 'thing' 'ends', 'shackles', 'bolts up', and then 'sleeps', 'never palates more'. The first three verbs express momentary action, sudden, violent; the next two action in duration, or rather inaction. The change in aspect from violence to an image (if we read 'dug') of most perfect peace—that of a child sleeping on its mother's breast—is emphasized by contrasting the soft vowels and labials of the line 'which sleeps . . .' with the gutturals and open vowels of the preceding one. (Compare 2 Henry IV, III. i. 67:

> When Richard with his eye brimful of tears,
> Then check'd and rated by Northumberland . . .)

The contrast of the two lines both beginning 'which . . .' is exquisite, and is a strong argument for 'dug'.[1] Now comes the ninth wave. Already suggested by the sweet image of the last line, it expresses not the power and variety of Death's action, nor merely the blessedness of its negative inaction, but what we are waiting for, its attitude or moral relation to men: that of a nurse to a child. Is it likely that Shakespeare would have padded the conclusion of this tremendous speech with an expansion of 'dug' or 'dung', a word which must be relatively weak in a passage whose whole theme is death, and death alone? An interesting parallel to this 'death' speech is to be found in the 'sleep' lines of Macbeth. Surely no one would there read 'chief nourisher in life's feast' as directly in apposition to 'great Nature's second course' (Macbeth, II. ii. 36–41)?

I agree with the author of the article that 'that thing' is never definite. How can it be, since this passage is an attempt to grasp the nature of the mysterious 'thing' by watching it in action and expressing it in metaphor? Therefore I see no difficulty in 'which sleeps . . .' This point is made clearer if we refer to Mr. Middleton Murry's paragraph in the December Adelphi, where he discusses Prospero's 'rounded with a sleep': 'We are the dreams of the great sleeper'. So it is easy to see why in this passage 'the thing' can be said to sleep.

1. Note also the comparison of death-in-association-with love to a baby 'dying with mother's dug between its lips' at 2 Henry VI, III. ii. 393; and see the other references given in The Imperial Theme, 250, note. [1966]

In this note I have used the word 'death' for clarity: but the 'thing' must remain indefinite.

17 January 1929

SHAKESPEARE AND BERGSON

With reference to the recent discussion on 'Questions of Prose', in the difficult matter of literary aesthetic theory we can scarcely do better than appeal to our greatest exponent of its practice. Shakespeare—or his 'poetic genius'—was a master of aesthetic. And his line of thought in metaphysics is essentially Bergsonian: so that the use of the one in the interpretation of the other produces interesting results.

The two modes of literary composition are well demonstrated by your reviewer (*T.L.S.*, 13 September 1928; 638); the intellectual and logical, and the intuitive and metaphorical, ways of thought. At the one extreme we have the geometrical proposition; at the other, such an illogical extract as that from Mme. Blavatsky's *The Voice of the Silence* quoted in William James's *The Varieties of Religious Experience* (1925 edn.; 421). Neither gives us what is usually considered a supreme form of *literature*, though for their purposes, scientific and mystical respectively, they may be perfect. As your reviewer shows, literature takes as its province the territory *between* these limits: there is a mixture of elements. The finest literature appeals to a consciousness neither wholly practical nor wholly mystical, but one in which the spiritual is bodied into 'shapes', or symbols, of actuality, and Wordsworth's 'light that never was, on sea or land' ('I was thy neighbour') illumines the things of earth. Hence

> The poet's eye, in a fine frenzy rolling,
> Doth glance from heaven to earth, from earth to heaven;
> And, as imagination bodies forth
> The forms of things unknown, the poet's pen
> Turns them to shapes, and gives to airy nothing
> A local habitation and a name.
> (*A Midsummer Night's Dream*, v. i. 12)

A precise definition. The poet's pen, at the actual moment of creation,

gives to the unknown 'nothing' of 'imagination's' 'forms' their concrete and verbal literary 'shapes'. The creative act is here definitely
said to be born of a commingling of the divine and the earthly. Also,
'Much is the force of *heaven-bred* poesy', says the Duke in *The Two
Gentlemen of Verona* (III. ii. 72). Human birth is dependent on a
similar creative union (*Romeo and Juliet*, III. iii. 119–20; *Twelfth
Night*, v. i. 246–8).

Now the distinction between intellect and intuition is, in Shakespeare and Bergson, a question of *speed*. Intellect, which can only
analyse the static (B. H. Streeter, *Reality*, 1927 edn.; 94, 104),
necessarily imposes a brake on the swift reality of 'duration', thus
losing touch with the reality. Discontinuous 'time' becomes the
intellectual counterpart to 'duration'. So, too, in Shakespeare the
'unbodied' essences of spirit have to be born into 'shapes' by 'time':
(*Troilus and Cressida*, I. iii. 16, 312–13): this thought, with variations, is recurrent. Thus, the finest values elude the intellect by their
essential swiftness. Now Shakespeare continually refers to the swiftness of abstract thought or 'meditation' (*Hamlet*, I. v. 30)—the
psychic state which Bergson calls a consciousness of pure duration
(*Creative Evolution*, trans. A. Mitchell, 1928 edn.; 210–12); or
the state, perhaps, described by Keats in his letter of 19 March,
1819 (J. Middleton Murry, *Keats and Shakespeare*, 117). This pure
mental activity is compared in point of swiftness with 'thoughts of
love' or love in many passages of Shakespeare: e.g., *Hamlet*, I. v.
29–30; *Love's Labour's Lost*, IV. iii, 330; *Troilus and Cressida*, IV. ii.
13–14; *Romeo and Juliet*, II. v. 4–8; and, in a negative sense pointing
the comparison most clearly, *Othello*, III. iv. 173–8. The swiftness
of thought is referred to in *Henry V.*, Chorus to Act III. 1–3; and
in the Chorus to Act v. at lines 8, 15, 23; in *Antony and Cleopatra*,
IV. vi. 35–6; in *King Lear*, III. ii. 4. The swiftness of love is referred
to in *The Two Gentlemen of Verona*, II. vi. 42; in *Romeo and Juliet*,
II. ii. 119–20; in *A Midsummer Night's Dream*, I. i. 143–9. The
poetic image is 'lightning'. So much for the 'swiftness' of meditation
and love. Now the imaginative connection of love and poetry in
Shakespeare is apparent. The lover, like the poet, is 'of imagination
all compact' (*A Midsummer Nights' Dream*, v. i. 8). Love sees with
the eyes of art (*A Midsummer Night's Dream*, II. ii. 104–5). Creative

literature is born of the erotic impulse—the statement is clear and vivid in *Love's Labour's Lost*, IV. iii. 291–365. Here the speed-imagery is insistent:

> For when would you, my liege, or you, or you,
> In *leaden* contemplation have found out
> Such *fiery* numbers as the prompting eyes
> Of beauty's tutors have enrich'd you with?
> Other *slow* arts entirely keep the brain . . .
>
> (320)

See also [for the comparison of love and art] *Antony and Cleopatra*, v. ii. 96–100. It is clear, then, that love and poetry may be said to induce a consciousness which 'apprehends' a swift reality beyond the lagging attempts of intellect to 'comprehend' (*A Midsummer Night's Dream*, v. i. 5–6; Henri Bergson, *Creative Evolution*, trans. A. Mitchell, 1928 edn.; 134). The difference between the extreme poetic and the extreme prosaic resolves itself into a question of *speed*. And in this connexion it is interesting to note that Mr. Herbert Read states that rhythm 'is the space-time'—i.e., speed—'element in the forms of poetry and prose' (*T.L.S.*, 20 September 1928, 667).

Poetry induces, and appeals to, a consciousness which functions at an abnormal rate: a psychic state in which limitless associations of imagery, metaphor, logic, etc., may be apprehended in a few instants of time. But all poetry is not metaphoric; nor is all prose 'plain prose'; and yet, on the whole, it is probable that the poetic consciousness always tends to move swifter than that of prose. Why? The prose-verse distinction is *entirely one of printing*: and the prose-poetry distinction is one of psychic speed—in the Bergsonian sense. How, then, does the arbitrary splitting-up in lines influence the speed at which the consciousness in the reader functions?

The rhythm of a line of poetry is a compressed rhythm: that of prose a diffused rhythm. Each poetic line is, by reason of its nature, a pure unit confining the rhythm of the words it contains. This compression of rhythm results in a certain explosiveness in the poetic unit which is lacking in prose. Wordsworth's line on the statue of Newton (*The Prelude*, III. 63), 'Voyaging through strange seas of Thought, alone', is great poetry. It reverberates into infinity.

Add one phrase more, say, '. . . into the void of speculation', and the rhythm of the original line is immediately liberated and diffused into a prose rhythm. The results are less explosiveness, fewer and slower psychic vibrations. The very awareness of the nature of a blank verse line, with the expectancy of its limits, creates in the reader's mind a consciousness of force *compressed*: as one reads the charge is, so to speak, exploded, and swift vibrations are sent through the mind: in Bergsonian language, the mind enjoys a consciousness more nearly keeping pace with 'duration'. Now the passage from *Coriolanus* quoted by your reviewer (*T.L.S.*, 13 September 1928, 638), if we print it as prose, has, as your reviewer notes, a positive rhythm: if as poetry, it has the same positive rhythm in addition to the extra rhythmic force derived from the compressed line-rhythms. That Shakespeare uses enjambed and run-on lines does not alter the fact that we are conscious always of the bounding limits of the line, against which the current of emotion hits and rebounds, swirling onwards like a fast mountain torrent. The rigid boundaries of the line-scheme add to the psychic speed of the passion. The torrent metaphor is exact. Hence the Poet in *Timon of Athens* says:

> Our poesy is as a gum, which oozes
> From whence 'tis nourished. The fire i' the flint
> Shows not till it be struck; our gentle flame
> Provokes itself, *and like the current flies*
> *Each bound it chafes.*

(I. i. 21)

No more perfect physical metaphor could be found than this torrential one for the onward rush and whirl of late Shakespearian verse as opposed to the diffused, uncompacted rhythms of prose.

But that is not to say that prose is, as Mr. Read tells us, 'a structure of ready-made words'. The words of prose, just as those of poetry, are 'born or reborn in the act of thinking'. There is no difference in the process, but in the one instance the creating mind is *thinking faster* than in the other. Good prose is a slower but not a less 'creative' medium than poetry, since each equally keeps pace with the writer's consciousness. Prose and poetry are thus written and read from slightly different centres of consciousness: and the difference may be considered, by those who think in terms of Shakespeare's and Bergson's metaphysic, as primarily one of speed.

Additional Note, 1966

The leading article of *The Times Literary Supplement* of 25 February 1965 quotes T. S. Eliot's letter of 27 September 1928, part of the 'Questions of Prose' correspondence to which my own letter was an addendum, wherein he remarks that verse 'whatever else it may or may not be, is itself a system of *punctuation*'.

For my general argument see *The Wheel of Fire*, enlarged, XIII, 'The Shakespearian Metaphysic' and App. B, 339–41; *The Imperial Theme*, 331–3 and note; also the General Index in *The Sovereign Flower*, Index B, VI Miscellaneous, 'Swift Thought'. My many years' concern with this branch of the Shakespearian metaphysic corresponds closely, as my phrase 'psychic vibrations' in the letter here printed had from the first suggested, to the emphases in contemporary Spiritualism on vibratory speed as characterizing higher states of consciousness and reality.

14 July 1950

DR. HOTSON'S ARGUMENTS

Dr. Leslie Hotson's thesis in *Shakespeare's Sonnets Dated* has attracted considerable attention, and some controversy. I am unqualified to enter the arena of historical discussion, but there is at least one point in his argument where a literary and dramatic judgement becomes relevant.

Antony's words

> Alack! our terrene moon
> Is now eclips'd; and it portends alone
> The fall of Antony
>
> (*Antony and Cleopatra*, III. xi. 153)

are taken by Dr. Hotson (10) to refer to the destruction of Antony's navy at Actium. But the context rules out any such reading. The words are spoken at that pivotal moment when he first has evidence

of Cleopatra's apparent duplicity. This it is, and not his master's
folly or failure, that causes Enobarbus' desertion:

> . . . we must leave thee to thy sinking, for
> Thy dearest quit thee.
>
> (III. xi. 64)

Antony's destiny is felt to depend on the validity of his love-relation-
ship; his 'good stars', his 'former guides' have now left their 'orbs'
(III. xi. 145); and his comment on 'our terrene moon' applies clearly
to Cleopatra. Directly before and after it he is concerned with his
personal agony at her betrayal. Can he be supposed, within the full
flood of his passion, to hark back to Actium? The word 'now'
forbids it; the value of 'portends' would disappear; the thought, the
poetry, the drama, all collapse.

The human idealization of *Antony and Cleopatra* tends continually
to identify the protagonists with the cosmic lights, as in Antony's
'Thou day o' the world' (IV. viii. 13) and Cleopatra's dream of him
with sun and moon for eyes (V. ii. 80). Again, at his death:

> O Sun!
> Burn the great sphere thou mov'st in; darkling stand
> The varying star o' the world.[1]
>
> (IV. xiii. 9)

There is now nothing 'remarkable beneath the visiting moon' (IV.
xiii. 67). For a full discussion see my study in *The Imperial Theme*,
240–2.

Finally, the battle of Actium is long past. The lovers are at
Alexandria. A few lines after the disputed passage, Antony, on his
self-recovery and return to practical affairs, specifically remarks, as a
direct *counter* to his former passion, that his forces are certainly doing
well, and his navy 'knit again' and 'threatening most sea-like' (III.
xi. 170–1). Later, it engages in a battle (IV. x).

The sole purpose of this letter is to preserve an important speech
from misunderstanding. It makes no statement concerning Sonnet
107.

1. 'Star' is a dubious emendation, followed by the Oxford text, of the Folio
'shore'. [**1966**]

26 December 1963

SHAKESPEARE'S SONNETS

May I add some suggestions on Shakespeare's Sonnets to those already put forward in *The Mutual Flame*?

The Sonnets, published by Thomas Thorpe in 1609, are in two series characterized respectively by homosexual idealism and heterosexual lust. The first has a rough artistic, though not necessarily an autobiographical, coherence. Thorpe's cryptic yet pregnant dedication goes:

> To the onlie begetter of these insuing sonnets Mr. W.H. all happinesse and that eternitie promised by our ever-living poet wisheth the well-wishing adventurer in setting forth. T.T.

Since the awkward repetition *wisheth*: *well-wishing* obtrudes it may be regarded as our key. Here is my paraphrase:

> To you as the main origin of these following sonnets, Master W.H., I wish every happiness, together with that poetic immortality assured, as he himself in his verses asserts, by the praises of such a poet as William Shakespeare, whose writings will (certainly) live for ever; and this last wish lies behind my boldness in publishing these (so intimate) poems, which is to be regarded as an act of good will towards you (since without their publication the immortality in question could not be yours).

I have bracketed my expansions.

The repetition *wisheth*: *well-wishing* links the two main thoughts: 'I wish you what is best' and 'This wish impels me to risk publishing the poems'. The action might offend: in the reissue by John Benson in 1640 the Youth's sex was suppressed.

For 'onlie' I follow for safety T. G. Tucker, who in his indispensable edition of the Sonnets (1924; xxxix) argued that in contemporary usage it was as likely to mean 'main' as 'sole'. The reading of 'begetter' as 'procurer' is surely inadmissible, since it suits neither 'onlie' nor what follows. Shakespeare regularly used 'beget' in a semi-parental sense, as at *Richard II*, v. v. 6:

> My brain I'll prove the female to my soul,
> My soul the father; and these two beget
> A generation of still-breeding thoughts . . .

In Phoenix-and-Turtle poems the loved one is Phoenix and the poet Turtle-dove, in a kind of male-female relation (*The Mutual Flame*, Part II). The Sonnets are 'born of' the Youth as 'Muse' (Sonnet 78; and see 38). This is Thorpe's meaning.

'Promised' I take to include both 'rendered sure', as in 'Why did'st thou promise such a beauteous day' of Sonnet 34, and also 'asserted'. 'The well-wishing adventurer in setting forth' in contemporary syntax is naturally to be read as 'the adventurer well-wishing (expressing good will) in setting forth'. 'Adventurer' suggests a bold enterprise. 'Setting forth' means both 'starting on my journey' and 'putting before the public', as in 'Romeo, come forth', i.e. 'into the open', in *Romeo and Juliet* (III. iii. 1). In Sonnet 55 we have:

> 'Gainst death and all-oblivious enmity
> Shall you pace forth; your praise shall still find room
> Even in the eyes of all posterity . . .

The editors of the First Folio wished that Shakespeare were alive to 'set forth'—Thorpe's very words—his text personally; and Benson in his 1640 preface (printed by E. K. Chambers, *William Shakespeare*, 1. 557) spoke of bringing the Sonnets 'forth to the perfect view of all men'.

In *The Mutual Flame* (9) I gave reasons for supposing, as did Samuel Butler in *Shakespeare's Sonnets Reconsidered* (VII, VIII) and Bradley in *Oxford Lectures on Poetry* ('Shakespeare the Man'), that 'W.H.' was not of noble birth, perhaps, I suggested, in the Inns of Court. If one of the two patron-candidates were he, the initials indicate Pembroke rather than Southampton. The reading of 'W.H.' as a reversed pseudonym—or even as a composite of the two surnames —appears untenable: as Tucker (xlii) says: 'If two well-known men existed with respective initials W.H. and H.W., it would be a strange contribution to the "eternitie" of the one to give him the initials of the other.' But many of the sonnets, such as those accusing the loved one of being over-fond of praise, comparing him for his vices to the foul smells of rotting plants, and suggesting that he must have been enduring 'hell' through the poet's temporary neglect of him (84, 94, 120), read strangely, whatever the circumstances, as addresses from player to peer. They suit better Francis Meres's phrase on sonnets written 'among his private friends'. Thorpe's dedication is itself nearer intimacy than reverence. Miss Marchette Chute (*Shakespeare of London*; App. I, 300) contrasts it with an obsequious dedication by Thorpe to Pembroke elsewhere. However, if 'onlie'—despite its dominant position—may be read as 'main', it is possible, as Tucker (xlviii) says, that more than one male addressee had been concerned. So the peer-patrons are not completely ruled out; but if Southampton were the *central* theme of the main series, Thorpe's dedication must be read in terms of either camouflage or misprint.

As for the Rival Poet, we hear in Sonnet 86 that his 'spirit' is 'by spirits taught to write above a mortal pitch'; he has 'compeers by night' to give him 'aid'; an 'affable familiar ghost' 'nightly gulls him with intelligence'. The words indicate—for 'affable' my brother suggests 'approachable through direct conversation'—a practice which is today well known and called 'inspirational', or if powerful enough 'automatic', writing. The description suits George Chapman. In his dedication to *The Shadow of Night* Chapman claimed to be assisted by 'Skill' as 'an heavenly familiar' (see J. Middleton Murry, *Shakespeare*, 49–50); and in *The Tears of Peace* he writes (Tucker, Notes, 162) of Homer's spirit as saying 'I invisibly went prompting thee'; though he has doubts regarding the 'unthrifty angel' that 'deludes' his 'fancy'. Chapman's words and Shakespeare's sonnet show the same co-presence of awe and suspicion before a 'familiar' spirit that such occurrences normally arouse. In *The Golden Labyrinth* I have discussed the evidence of occultism in Chapman's dramas. Marlowe was also supposed, by Greene, to have had 'prophetical' spirit-helpers (Peter Alexander, *Shakespeare's Life and Art*, 95).

Chapman's work has a tone approaching the homosexual (the matter is discussed by Havelock Ellis in 'George Chapman', *From Marlowe to Shaw*, essays by Havelock Ellis, editor John Gawsworth,

1950). He and Shakespeare were among the four poets who contributed additional pieces to the collection of esoteric Phoenix poems compiled in honour of Sir John Salusbury and entitled *Love's Martyr* in 1601 (*The Mutual Flame*, Part II). Sir John has already been put forward as the Fair Youth of Shakespeare's Sonnets by Mrs. Frances (Alan) Keen in a Broadside entitled *Phoenix*, printed for the author by the Favil Press, Kensington, October 1957. His age, three years younger than Shakespeare, does not help his candidature for the whole series; nor does his name; but perhaps more attention might be given to his circle.

30 January 1964

SHAKESPEARE'S SONNETS

May I indicate certain tentative conclusions that appear to follow from my paraphrase, which you so courteously printed on 26 December 1963, of Thorpe's dedicatory prefix to his edition of Shakespeare's Sonnets?

This dedication is our only firm evidence regarding the facts behind the 1609 publication; and yet its full meaning seems never before to have been explored; and still less unveiled. From now on the consequences will be manifold and striking. We must henceforth take the passage seriously and as an artistic unit; the initials 'W.H.' can never again be relegated to a procurer of the manuscript; and Southampton, failing new and incontrovertible evidence, must in consequence be dismissed.

What else follows? The writer fears that 'W.H.' may be offended, but his favour is nevertheless sought by pointing to the immortality he will gain. Pembroke was far too powerful to risk offending and too high-placed to be addressed as a mere 'Mr. W.H.' in fear of oblivion. Though his claims are stronger than Southampton's he may, provisionally, be shelved.

Who provided the text? 'W.H.' is now ruled out. The Dark Lady is unlikely to have treasured the whole collection or to have left Sonnet 130 undoctored. If we exclude thieving, we are left with Shakespeare himself.

The dedicatory lines evidence not only a fine technical skill but also a co-presence of diffidence and will to publication thoroughly characteristic of a writer's temperament. There must have been more in Shakespeare than the impersonal artist and litigious man of business; and he must often have felt the compulsion to speak out. At this turn of his life, which would then correspond to the tragic reversals in the lives of Byron and of Wilde, whose relations with Lord Alfred Douglas so closely recall the Sonnets, he was perhaps impelled to a romantic self-revealing by use of what Wordsworth in 'Scorn not the Sonnet' called the 'key' with which he had 'unlocked his heart', exposing the stark opposition he endured of homosexual idealism and heterosexual lust, as defined in Sonnet 144, written into his twin narrative poems, and reflected finally into the sexological pattern of *Timon of Athens*; a drama composed at this period and bearing many marks, driven home by Timon's casting off of his clothes at its pivotal moment, of naked self-disclosure.

So much granted, we may suppose the Dedication, willing as it does the ratification *by the necessary act of publication* of the Sonnets' reiterated promise regarding the literary perpetuation of a great beauty and a great experience, to have been composed by Shakespeare, using Thomas Thorpe, from natural diffidence, as a mask. No one had such good cause as he to desire and defend publication as a necessary fulfilment of his own emphatic predictions; whereas to shirk it would have been treachery to his vision and to 'posterity' (Sonnet 55).

Why has this dedication been neglected while so much labour has been expended on the rival patrons? Shakespeare first became a national concern at a period of strict morality, and the Sonnets raised social and erotic problems that could only be met by treating them as respectable epistles aimed at financial gain and social advancement to be won from lordly patronage; though many do little enough to further such an aim.

Starting with the artistic revolution against Victorian morality at the close of the last century we meet a new and different outcrop of candidates supported by Wilde, Lord Alfred Douglas, Gide, Joyce, Masefield and Samuel Butler, all of whom except Butler, being themselves artists, favoured an actor (*The Mutual Flame*, 7, 105–6). Our academic authorities, concentrating on business and externals, have generally argued for patronage; our literary men, breathing the poetic dimension, concentrate on art. Some, such as 'A.E.', Butler and Wyndham Lewis, admit a 'Greek' element, or more, in Shakespeare's passion (*The Mutual Flame*, 7–8). Where we have a scholar who is also a man of profound human understanding and Shakespearian insight such as A. C. Bradley, we find him a little unhappily but with a characteristic integrity of approach admitting homo-erotic propensities while following Butler in taking 'W.H.', on the evidence of the text, to be a man of quality, but no peer.

We, in a society no longer unduly dominated either by respect to aristocratic privilege and moral taboos or by any too-heady revulsion from them, may surely, now that the word-by-word meaning of the Dedication, which must henceforth constitute the basis of all honest discussion, has at last been unveiled, begin to see Shakespeare's Sonnets steadily and see them whole.

12 March 1964

SHAKESPEARE'S SONNETS

I have in preparation a work on Byron and Shakespeare in which Southampton as Shakespeare's Friend would be a first-rate ingredient were his candidature not countered by our sole available evidence— Thorpe's Dedication (discussed in my recent letters of 26 December and 30 January).

This evidence his supporters avoid by a highly questionable reading of 'beget'. Will any accredited linguistic expert assure us that 'beget' could be naturally used in Shakespeare's day to mean 'procure'? If so, may we have references? None are available in the *O.E.D.*, the Bible or Shakespeare. Reliance on Hamlet's 'acquire and beget a temperance' (III. ii. 8) has been out of date since Samuel Butler's disposal of it in 1899. In *Hamlet* 'beget' obviously means 'engender'. Shakespeare's use is regularly either biological or, as here, metaphoric.

Is there any evidence at all that begetter = procurer was even a *possible* contemporary usage? What we need is a quotation like 'Beget me that stoup of wine from yonder table', or some rebel leader characterized as 'the proud begetter of a troop of horse'. Are there any such? Cannot one of our professors of English language enlighten us, one way or the other, on this central issue? For them this should be simple stuff. I pause for a reply.

1966: There was no reply.

APPENDIX

B. REVIEWS

The Symposium (New York), April 1931; II.

William Shakespeare: A Study of Facts and Problems; by E. K. Chambers.

The twentieth century has proved rich in Shakespearian archaeology. Elizabethan conditions, social, political, dramatic and bibliographical, have been acutely examined, minutely analysed. The extent and detail of these labours have been indeed remarkable: but not unjustifiable. The 'Romantic' critics pursued an imaginative method which came at times dangerously near to the beating of wings in a vacuum. It is not surprising that they stimulated their successors into reaction. Were their romantic hyperboles merely the reflections of their own uncontrolled genius?—did they, after all, add anything of value to the solid scholarship and daylight common-sense of eighteenth century editors? Recent 'realistic' criticism has set itself to answer these questions: to find the cold truth, pleasant or unpleasant. This is, however, merely an aspect of a more general intellectual movement. Criticism of the Bible has run a parallel course. So the inspired word of poetry is analysed, discussed in terms of printer's ink, water marks, multiple authorship, surface contradictions, and so on. The scientific spirit, so ruthless in analysis of all 'values', has necessarily been turning its attention to the origins whence our values flow. Sir Edmund Chambers, writing from the height of a titanic scholarship, now follows his classic studies of the Medieval and Elizabethan stages with a couple of close-packed volumes [my page references apply to the first] which concentrate the matured results of modern Elizabethan investigation on the subject which is ultimately their main mark and justification.

This is a work of exact and careful scholarship: it makes little attempt to entertain, and none to thrill. There are no flashy phrases,

nor any exploitation of favourite passions. Yet it is remarkable for
clarity and general interest. The arduous ascent is eased by recurrent
wit and wisdom. The wit is well aimed, as when we hear of 'un-
metrical ejaculations and connective words, such as actors introduce
to accompany their gestures and demonstrate their indifference to the
blank verse' (157). The wisdom is often profound. In writing of
Elizabethan punctuation Sir Edmund observes that 'the antithesis
between a logical punctuation and a rhetorical punctuation is not
really sound. All punctuation has elements both of logic and of
rhetoric. It has its origin in spoken utterance' (192). This is the
wisdom of common-sense: perhaps of all the hardest kind to achieve
with any consistency. Continually it illuminates vexed questions
long befogged by doubt and insecurity. Heminge and Condell, and
Ben Jonson, have given us brief but incisive portraits of Shakespeare's literary personality: from which we may conclude him to
have been 'the last man . . . in the absence of rigid proof, to tie
himself to the painful following up and meticulous correction of the
thoughts and words of another' (216). That is typical. Where there
are facts, we can be certain they will be duly presented: where there
are no facts, the common-sense conclusion is set down for us.

We thus receive no startling revelations about Shakespeare the
man. What is known is clearly and briefly traced: it amounts to
surprisingly little. But, instead of hypotheses and hazards in the
darkness which envelops the historical Shakespeare, we are given
something far better: we are put in direct sight of what evidence
there is. Our second volume contains 'documents' only: but they are
interesting always, sometimes quite exciting. We have all heard that
there is a legend about Shakespeare's youthful deer-stealing: here we
have an exact copy of the evidence. The report about Shakespeare's
arrival in London, his holding horses outside the theatre—this, with
many vivid details, is printed as described by Robert Shiels in 1753.
No doubt some of it is unreliable. But it is there for us, to make what
we can of it ourselves. Moreover, there are numerous, far more
valuable, 'contemporary allusions', of Francis Meres, John Webster,
Thomas Heywood, and many others. Especially interesting is a poem
'which has not been printed in full before' by Francis Beaumont.
These extracts bring us to an intimacy with the actual Shakespeare

very different from what we gain from the usual biography. The importance of this section to the general as well as the scholarly reader can hardly be exaggerated. Failing any new startling discoveries, we may call it the best possible method. 'Of William Shakespeare's own early days there is but little on record; and it is no part of my object to compete with those gifted writers who have drawn upon their acquaintance with Stratford and with the plays for the material of an imaginative reconstruction' (16). We endorse that attitude, provisionally: provisionally, since 'imaginative reconstruction' is, after all, the essence both of history and biography, since new facts may yet be discovered, and since there is always the possibility of a new and perhaps convincing use of the old landmarks to outline a fresh and living story. At present, Sir Edmund's method which makes biographers of us all, leaving us to draw our own conclusions, seems hard to improve: and it has its own, reserved, excitement.

Chapters on 'The Stage in 1592' and 'Shakespeare and his Company' (the latter partly biographical) give judgements and details which only the archaeologist could properly question or appreciate: the same may be said of 'The Book of the Play', 'The Quartos and the First Folio', and 'Plays in the Printing House'. But all are characterized by so easy a marshalling of facts, and so faultless a style, that even the uninitiated may follow them with pleasure; and, if at times confused, must confess that confusion to be the child of his own ignorance. Probably the most important chapter is that on 'Authenticity'. For it goes to the heart of our subject—at once the centre and circumference of such scientific criticism. Here the result is encouraging: 'the great majority of the plays are Shakespeare's from beginning to end and ... when he had once written them he left them alone' (235). Besides the chapter on 'Authenticity' the problems of each play are presented and discussed in full at the end of the first volume. That so wide and detailed an investigation should have reached so simple a conclusion is not, to those of us who have been similarly convinced on a different route, surprising. But it is very gratifying. Sir Edmund does not accept the canon unreservedly: he is doubtful about *1 Henry VI*, *Titus Andronicus*, *The Taming of the Shrew* and *Henry VIII*—and, necessarily, *Pericles*. For these Shakespeare is considered to have been partly responsible only.

But there are no rash conclusions. 'I do not think that we have adequate *criteria* for distinguishing with any assurance from the style of his contemporaries that of a young writer still under their influence' (287). On the evidence which scholarship has hitherto applied that is true enough. It is, however, likely that such questions will in future revolve on the test of imagery. We are warned, indeed, not to be led astray by 'parallels': 'authors repeat their predecessors; their successors repeat them; they repeat themselves' (222). Now resort to parallels is certainly dangerous unless the listing be more comprehensive than any hitherto attempted. But a careful attention to Shakespeare's work reveals a very clear consistency not only of imagery but of *the use of imagery*. This is partly a matter of intuitive, and subjective, judgement, but it is likely to gain importance. For example, Sir Edmund hands over large quantities of *Henry VIII* to Fletcher, following the usual tradition. But what of

> Alas, poor wenches, where are now your fortunes?
> Shipwrack'd upon a kingdom, where no pity,
> No friends, no hope; no kindred weep for me;
> Almost no grave allow'd me: like the lily,
> That once was mistress of the field and flourish'd,
> I'll hang my head and perish.
>
> (*Henry VIII*, III. i. 147)

Or again, 'He parted frowning from me, as if ruin leap'd from his eyes' (III. ii. 206). Do we not recognize that accent—that effortless use of typical Shakespearian imagery? Moreover, the incidents of Wolsey's fall, his soliloquies and dialogue with Cromwell, are written from a height surely Shakespearian: they can stand beside the best of similar themes in *Timon of Athens*; they show the same surge of emotion, the same throbbing solemnity. Where a purely poetic judgement is concerned, Sir Edmund's authority may be questioned. Our only valid objection to these 'Fletcher' scenes is, after all, the consensus of critical opinion. But this has been based almost entirely on 'metre'; and, as we are elsewhere warned, 'subject-matter has its reaction upon style. . . . Moreover, allowance has to be made for the influence of moods and for deliberate experiment' (253). Exactly: and a poet may well experiment in metre. Shakespeare was always doing it: one might compare Tennyson, Bridges, and many modern poets. But a poet cannot so easily experiment with imagery, cannot, without rendering his work sterile, refuse his characteristic imagery spontaneous and characteristic utterance. Sir Edmund is, indeed, clearly aware of this (he is aware of most things): 'A writer's mind is a well of subliminal memory, into which words and images sink, and to the surface of which they arise again, unbidden, in the act of composition' (224). He knows, too, that 'probably the most striking parallels are the least evidential' (222); and that 'there is a negative value in comprehensive collections of parallels, however slight, to a doubtful play', since, 'if none are found to a given writer, he is not likely to have written it' (222). Probably Prof. Spurgeon's exhaustive study of Shakespeare's imagery (as outlined in *Leading Motives in the Imagery of Shakespeare's Tragedies*) will, when published, put the whole matter in a different light.

The chapter on 'Chronology' results in no revolutionary conclusions. Rightly, no great trust is placed in supposed contemporary references. 'Shakespeare does not seem to have been greatly given to "topical" allusions, and the hunt for them becomes dangerous' (246). Nor is imagery of any great value here, since 'the unconscious memory is a reservoir, giving up from its store things both new and old' (254). Again, 'when an association of ideas exists, it may be due to some other cause than a common date of origin. It may arise from a similarity of situation, or a revival may have recalled old work to Shakespeare's mind' (255). We are also warned against too firm a trust in 'sources'. So the plays emerge in more or less their usual order. But it must be admitted that, firm as is Sir Edmund's impregnability and rock-like assurance where archaeological scholarship is concerned, or in the negative matter of demonstrating the insubstantiality of false methods, he is less safe when hazarding 'a whimsy', as he calls it, of his own: that an 'illness' was responsible for what dissatisfies him in *Timon of Athens*. The tentative suggestion is unconvincing: there may be a truth in it—but the statement is too vague as it stands, and would need an elaborate defence. Perhaps, too, a remark on the Final Plays needs qualification: 'In any case the transition from the tragedies to the romances is not an evolution but a revolution. There has been some mental process such as the psychology of religion would call a conversion' (86). That is well said: but the distinction is not quite so rigid. *Antony and Cleopatra*, hardly a 'tragedy' in the usual sense, may be suggested to bridge the two modes.

There are signs that the tide is turning in Shakespearian criticism. 'Disintegration' has done its worst and the text apparently yet remains 'like a great sea-mark, standing every flaw, and saving those that eye' it. But it would be the extremity of ingratitude and ignorance if those of us who look ahead to new lines of approach and new kinds of Shakespearian 'truth', regarded the older school of 'realistic' criticism as inept, even when its tempests and 'strange screams of death' raged their wildest, and we trembled to hear its exponents 'prophesying with accents terrible of dire combustion and confused events' about the Shakespeare canon. Every intellectual movement has its exaggerations. Out of this nettle, error, we pluck the flower of truth.[1] Sir Edmund's comprehensive work is that flower: albeit rather a solid and weighty posy. Nor does our debt to recent scholarship end there. We shall find more, and still more, meanings in Shakespeare, of profound importance. But we shall never again forget that the plays are cast in a dramatic art form which precludes detailed correspondence with the appearances of life. We shall consider it but a doubtful compliment to the author to raise hypotheses and prosecute arguments as to the childhood of his characters or their actions during the intervals of their dramatic life. We shall see the plays as plays. Realistic criticism has performed a necessary *catharsis*, and henceforward our interpretations will, through their very limitation to the text and the text alone, focus a Shakespearian reality which is inexhaustible.

The Criterion, April 1931, X, 40.

Towards the Stars: being an Appreciation of 'The Phoenix and the Turtle', by 'Ranjee' (Ranjee G. Shahani); printed at Rouen. A copy is lodged in the Brotherton Library, University of Leeds.

The Phoenix and the Turtle has been unjustly neglected. This essay offers both a timely appreciation and a more doubtful argument

---

1. Quotations used in this paragraph come from *Coriolanus*, v. iii. 74; *Macbeth*, II. iii. 62–4; and *I Henry IV*, II. iii. 11–12.

against Shakespeare's authorship; besides an illuminating discussion of the Phoenix legend in general and its Elizabethan vogue in particular.

Ranjee points out that the obscurity of the poem has been over-emphasized. It is 'crystal clear when once the subtle allusions are grasped'. Critical opinion has been somewhat uncertain. Of the authoritative statements quoted, the most interesting is a passage from Emerson: 'I conclude this piece a good example of the rule, that there is a poetry for bards proper, as well as poetry for the world of readers'. Ranjee is perhaps nearer the truth in insisting rather on a certain kind of experience as a necessity to full understanding. Such experience must be, presumably, a purely intuitive one—an intuition of death's excellence such as evoked, in a very different style, Keats's 'Now more than ever seems it rich to die . . .' or the Bright Star Sonnet. In those, death is blended with the Nightingale's music and love, respectively. *The Phoenix and the Turtle* suggests a similar mystic ascension in the fusing of love and death:

> Phoenix and the Turtle fled
> In a mutual flame from hence.

To quote from our essay: 'The divinity of love and constancy has passed beyond our ken for their rightful place far above our futilities of speech and sorrow'. Such intuition of love's immortality can receive no final justice from analysis: it is at once simple and obscure, a matter for poetry and paradox. We are aptly reminded that 'love speaks the language of the gods'.

We have a careful elucidation of phrases derived from scholasticism: 'So the words "property was thus appalled" mean that there was a logical conflict with the very concept of "proprium". Existence in its metaphysical aspect was scandalized at this impossible condition.' 'The language of the alchemists', we are told, explains the use of 'simple' and 'compounded' to suggest two things 'so mingled that distinction of parts was impossible'. The poem touches 'the dialect of Trinitarian doctrine' in point of 'duality transcended into unity'. Such references are valuable. There are, moreover, many fine appreciative phrases justly applied. We have here an 'attitude to love' which 'contains no slightest suggestion of lower levels; it is all pure ether'. Of the stanza 'Truth may seem . . .', the author writes: 'These lines concentrate in one perfect crystal the mellow wisdom of a life-time'. The poem holds something of 'the cosmic tragedy of love'. Again, 'He (Shelley) was not of the celestial fibre of our poet—tenuous as moonbeams yet strong as steel'. The whole analysis is characterized by exact thought and sensitive poetic understanding.

In the wider question of Shakespeare's work and its relation to *The Phoenix and the Turtle* the essay is less convincing. Ranjee tentatively favours Fletcher's authorship. He asserts that 'nowhere in Shakespeare do we find the apotheosis of love that *The Phoenix* embodies'; he suggests that 'to Shakespeare, love was something really secondary', and refers to his 'somewhat tepid patronage of the passion'. Sonnet 147 is quoted in support. All this seems to be clearly contradicted by the plays and poems. Such a phrase as 'an offering of divine honours to the mutual loyalty of married souls' might itself have suggested

> Let me not to the marriage of true minds
> Admit impediments. . . .
>
> > (Sonnet 116)

The 'apotheosis of love' celebrated in *The Phoenix and the Turtle* is the very theme of *Antony and Cleopatra*, and many of Ranjee's general remarks on the one apply with equal exactitude to the other. There is no fundamental experience shadowed by this poem which cannot be thus paralleled. But neither is there anything else in Shakespeare quite like it in expression and form. Thus the clustering reminiscences of scholastic thought are adduced as evidence against Shakespeare's hand: but past commentary surely illustrates the futility of such arguments directed on a poet so richly varied and adventurous in style. Passages quoted from Fletcher prove nothing, presenting a superficial resemblance only, and Sir Sidney Lee with greater justice regarded Fletcher as indebted to Shakespeare. A more interesting parallel might be drawn from Donne's *A Valediction Forbidding Mourning*:

> Dull sublunary lovers' love
> (Whose soul is sense) cannot admit
> Absence, because it doth remove
> Those things which elemented it.

Donne's love poetry is often pitched in a similar thought-sense continuum to *The Phoenix and the Turtle*: it possesses the same allusive quality, the same kind of poetic compression preferring intellectual paradox to emotional colour, the same metaphysic of love's immateriality. Both are happy in use of a medium itself 'like gold to ayery thinnesse beate' (Donne, *A Valediction Forbidding Mourning*). That does not prove anything as to authorship, though it may indicate an unsuspected relation between the two poets.

The weakness of one section only ought not to hinder due recognition of so valuable a contribution to our understanding of an important poem.

Saturday Night (Toronto), 5 December 1931.

Ben Jonson and King James: Biography and Portrait, by Eric Linklater.

Imaginative biographies are the fashion at present. Today, when we suffer so often from a sense of futility and bleakness in our own lives it is natural that we should turn to scrutinizing past heroes in whom we find a power and purpose lacking to ourselves. This is no purely scholarly and academic interest: rather it is creative, originating from that impulse to find sense in things which forces mankind to compose 'literature' even in periods barren of spiritual delight. Mr. Linklater's book is of this sort. It has no footnotes, no detailed references. You can rarely tell exactly whether he is giving you an authenticated fact, making deductions of probability, or filling a gap with fancy. It does not matter in the least, for we can go elsewhere for exactitude and certainties. The book is an attempt to interest a wide circle of readers in a fine and neglected writer and truly heroic man, living in an heroic and amazing period: wherein we find a useful antidote for our own inconsequences.

Elizabethan England, in all its startling paradox, its gutters of reality along with the gold of its romance, is vividly presented. We are shown the grim joys of bear and bull baiting, vulgar tricks with ponies and monkeys, all the blood and beastliness of cruel sport. Then:

The following day some gentlemen who had watched with

the liveliest interest this rude entertainment, heard at court a play called *Endimion*.

From which we may conclude that a purely literary interest in Elizabethan England will ever distort its actuality. The fiery petals of Elizabethan poetry blossomed from a soil only too well manured with dung. Sometimes we may find a contact, as when Mr. Linklater aptly suggests that the frequent plague ravages in London were partly responsible for the death horrors in Shakespeare:

> . . . Then the death rate would mount to four hundred, five hundred a week, and the noise of the bells tolling, the creaking of the death-carts, were in every ear. One summer there were two hundred a day dying, and London was full of fear and a graveyard stench.
>
> (38)

A fit stage for the creation of *Hamlet*. Mr. Linklater shirks no ugly realism. We have a picture of a past age crude, cruel, insanitary; giving birth, however, to great soldiers, adventurers, writers; a time of life asserting itself the more violently for the hideous shadow cast over it all by the omnipresent pall of death. Perhaps this is true of us too. Perhaps we need an insistent memory of death to vitalize our sense of life. Many people were more truly happy on active service in the war than now in peace and security. But, surely, the most exquisite refinements of poetic vision are not likewise conditioned to a curbless luxuriance in cruelty and vice? Because, if so, where are we?

Ben Jonson emerges as the stalwart poet he was. In him art and actuality were perhaps closer than in his contemporaries. Although one of the greatest comic geniuses in our literature, there was no non-sense about him; about his life, or his art. There was never a more manly versifier. We cannot but respect a poet who was first a brick-layer, then a soldier, then a scholar; who was three times—at least—in prison; who was always ready for a duel, and knew how to kill his opponent; who, in the rough and tumble of a turbulent and often heart-breaking struggle for existence, continued to turn out plays and poems in the same assertive and intolerant spirit that made his life often a danger to others and always a danger to itself. With all this, he was a great scholar—scholarly to pedanticism. Yet, again, no dreamer:

> ... his conception of a poet's duties was different from that which would have sweet singers dwell ever apart to contemplate the recondite significances of daffodils, grains of sand, and creaking light.
>
> (67)

Again,

> He wrote with bare fists, as if for the championship of England, and every line was attack, every phrase a measured swing to the ear or sudden straight left to the heart.
>
> (280)

If he could also make some of the most delicate masques and lyrics in our language, as well as classical tragedy and satiric comedy—well, to use Mr. Linklater's phrase, he was 'an Elizabethan'. There was so little they couldn't do. Shakespeare was, after all, really a logical necessity.

This book is a delightful entertainment. Here is a sample of Mr. Linklater's wit: '*A wife* is too dull a poem not to be sincere' (206). And this, of King James: 'His funeral, like his reign, was extravagant and untidy' (278). Or this, of Platonic love:

> Clearly to define it would probably have puzzled most of its protagonists, but it was characterized more by discussion than action. It quickened the imagination, but it did not spoil the figure. It was very important, but poetical rather than pro-creative.
>
> (289)

Which is excellent. Mr. Linklater's study may be whole-heartedly recommended to all who know a little, and yet not too much, about the life and literature with which it deals.

The Criterion, October 1932; XII, 46.

The Essential Shakespeare, by J. Dover Wilson.

This book follows Prof. Dover Wilson's *Six Shakespearian Tragedies* and his lecture *The Elizabethan Shakespeare*: but it is disappointing. Those were valuable: this seems to me to be often dangerously near to fiction.

Many good, and some fine things, are said. The proposed ideal of treating Shakespeare as a poet, comparing him with others, would, if carried out, have been an asset to criticism. This is excellent:

> Falstaff is more than man; he is, like all great mythological figures, the incarnation of a principle of the universe. . . .'
>
> (89)

We hear that 'Shakespeare's plays are drenched in sea-spray and shot with the coloured thread of mariners' tales' (21). The combination of 'social stability with illimitable opportunity for the individual' gave the Elizabethan Age 'its sense of balanced flight, its unique quality of happiness and spontaneity' (19). These are admirable phrases. Remarks on Elizabethan music and dancing, and on the Elizabethan stage in general, are most helpful. But as soon as Prof. Dover Wilson begins to recreate his central figure—and the rest is only introductory—he seems to me to fall from his Pegasus into a morass of hypotheses and contradictions.

Synthetic portraits that would blend a poet's 'life' with his 'work' are fashionable. Their ultimate value is usually slight and they are often dangerous, since to perform the marriage before each is richly mature tends rapidly to impoverish and fog our understanding of either; such a marriage being in the nature of a multiplication rather than an addition. Where biographical facts are scanty, the course is positively perilous. It is only too easy to find oneself first hazarding a biographical fact from the poet's work and next using that fact to condition an artistic response. This has happened often with Shakespeare, and Sir Edmund Chambers' scholarly biography is a model we do well to contemplate.

Prof. Dover Wilson's sketch does not appeal to me. Shakespeare may, certainly, have been a 'keen sportsman'; he may have followed after whenever 'man's business was afoot' (70); he may have possessed the manliness of a Hotspur, the merriment of Mercutio. But I see rather a Shakespeare, from his early years, of mental pain, of sleepless unrest—the young poet who could tune his heart to sympathize with 'poor Wat' in *Venus and Adonis*. And whereas my Shakespeare could well have created in love and longing admiration the more robust poeple in the plays, I cannot see this 'good mixer in companies of all sorts' (70) writing *Lucrece* at the age of thirty. Nor do I find any evidence to justify the dominant thesis of this book. Prof. Dover Wilson argues that *The Merchant of Venice* and *Julius Caesar* were written in part to advise or warn Essex, and complains that Essex was 'unteachable' (102). Does this fit a writer who is 'utterly unlike a schoolmaster or a preacher' (53)? The moral of *Troilus and Cressida* was likewise: 'give up sulking, make terms with your Prince, think of England first' (101). But I do not see how a poet who 'never commits himself deeply to a cause or to a point of view' (76) can with any forcefulness be said to 'offer counsel' in this way to the extent of 'blunt plain speaking' (64). I find too many unresolved discords here. The whole argument about the Shakespeare-Essex relation is shadowy and without evidence. The reference in *Henry V* is too formal and the satire in *Troilus and Cressida* far too insulting for a poet whose tragic period was partly brought about by a personal sense of loss at Essex's fall. And if Hamlet was so clear an Essex portrait, and Polonius a study of Burleigh, surely Gertrude or Claudius must have seemed to correspond to Queen Elizabeth, and would not this have been suicidal? Elsewhere, Prof. Dover Wilson dangerously replaces an authenticated portrait of Shakespeare by a nameless one he likes better, and disbelieves Jonson's avowed description of Shakespeare's way of writing in favour of a passage whose reference is not known. Why should Shakespeare's love for the fair boy of the sonnets be merely 'affection' (59), 'passion' being reserved for the dark lady? And can the statement that 'from beginning to end the comedies and histories were composed for audiences of young men' (91) be reconciled with the epilogues to *2 Henry IV* and *As You Like It*?

I do not say that any one of Prof. Dover Wilson's statements is necessarily false; nor that all may not be true. Life is chaotic and contradictory. But it is the business of biography to impose form on the flux while duly respecting the available evidence. I cannot find that he does this. Where he writes of Elizabethan England in general, Prof. Dover Wilson is excellent; and where he writes of the plays—especially *Romeo and Juliet* and the early comedies—he is always interesting and sometimes original. The disastrous thesis of the Essex-Shakespeare relationship reads as too facile a dramatization of an intense and natural desire to unify these two worlds. It uses valuable space and is, indeed, the outstanding contention of the book. It is a pity, since there is much else we might have been told by so experienced a commentator. That a false aesthetic is ultimately responsible can be seen from the dangerous distinction drawn between the objective and subjective poet. A critic true to the poetic substance will, however, think in terms of poetry, not individual poets. He will assume that all good poetry is equally expressive, or non-expressive. He will not ask whether Shakespeare revealed himself in his work, but in what sense poetry in general can be called self-revelatory. This involves many subtleties: but there are no short cuts to the synthesis Prof. Dover Wilson has, in my opinion, too rashly attempted.

Additional Note, 1966

Conscience has prompted me to refer back to *The Essential Shakespear* before reprinting this review. Though factually still in agreement with its various points, I now doubt whether all my emphases were fair. Prof. Dover Wilson's argument that the details of Portia's mercy speech are not very apt in an address to Shylock (see p. 180 above) whereas they might fit the Earl of Essex at the trial of Dr. Roderigo Lopez carries conviction. My review should be read less as a criticism of *The Essential Shakespeare* than as a statement of my own position in regard to Shakespearian biography.

It occurs to me that Prof. Dover Wilson's third chapter 'Enter William Shakespeare with Divers of Worship' offers some support to the biographical dating of Dr. Hotson's work on the Sonnets.

The Aryan Path, February 1933; IV, 2.

Shakespeare through Eastern Eyes, by Ranjee G. Shahani.

For long the Western World has been content to regard its poetry as a delicate enjoyment, a refining influence, a thing of 'taste' and 'appreciation'. The best contemporary criticism would press further. In Shakespearian commentary, the issue is being fought out with vigour. Much depends on the result. If Shakespeare is a chaos, then poetry has little meaning, but if poetry has any message at all, that message is religious, and the authority of a poet of Shakespeare's stature is overwhelming.

With much of Mr. Shahani's book I cannot agree. To him, and to many other critics, Shakespeare's work is chaotic, not powerfully philosophic, with slight religious content, and no mysticism. Mr. Shahani sees a great poet skilled to depict the actual world, a master of characterization, a myriad-minded but dispassionate observer. Therefore, he tells us, the Indian, to whom actuality is merely a veil obscuring the mystic reality, finds Shakespeare beyond a certain point barren. The 'mystic quality' the Indian desires is 'utterly absent' (142). 'As judged by India,' we are told, 'Shakespeare cannot be called a thinker' (176). And yet Mr. Shahani admits that he is 'a creative thinker' (177): that is, he thinks through the act of 'creating'. Now this is true. Moreover, all good poetry is essentially 'creation'. It is, also, creative: creating life and power and vision in the reader. It awakens, and directs, and whether the poet be American, English, Indian or Chinese, its final purpose and value is not in any particular form of belief or instruction, but in the power of its symbolisms to awaken us to life and recognition. 'The quarrel,' we are told, 'of the Oriental with Shakespeare admits of no compromise or accommodation. It is fundamental' (149). I do not believe it.

For Shakespeare is the great master of symbolic speech. A slight shift of perspective and he is rich in creative meanings. His creative vision necessarily speaks mainly of life and love, and their opposites, death and hate. We watch the drama played out, we see life victorious over death. Is this nothing? The creative process is justified by the poetic creation: so the tempests of *King Lear* and *Macbeth* dissolve in the music of *Pericles* and *The Winter's Tale*. *The Tempest* itself is, I believe, the grandest mystic document in our language. Why is it not so recognized? Simply because the poet has created so well, has so perfectly incarnated his vision in dramatic shapes and action that we fail to see any symbolic significance. Say a thing too well and it becomes poetry, and poetry is not allowed to mean anything. We think crookedly.

But Mr. Shahani's book is valuable. It attacks a vital issue, raises questions on every page of profound importance. His recent essay on *The Phoenix and the Turtle* was one of the finest pieces of Shakespearian commentary I have read. In much of this book he is illuminating. Every page is provocative at the least. He has a gift of phrase, and a wide knowledge, and, what is more important, a natural sympathy with the poetic world. If only he would turn again to prose interpretation, would bring the mystic insight of the East to elucidation, rather than criticism, of the creative visions of the West, he could do work of the very greatest importance in the service of poetry.

Saturday Night (Toronto), 7 December 1935.

Shakespeare's Imagery and What it Tells Us, by Caroline Spurgeon.
What Happens in Hamlet, by J. Dover Wilson.

These are two very important books. Prof. Spurgeon's study of Shakespeare's imagery has already been in part before the public. Here we have a comprehensive volume complete with discussions and conclusions of various sorts, index and charts. The text is divided between a discussion of Shakespeare's imagery as an approach to understanding his mind and a valuable inspection of leit motifs in individual plays. In following the author's analyses we watch the poet in the very act of self-expression, and our knowledge of the image-creating faculty in the poetic mind is considerably enriched. Many valuable sidelights are cast on biographical and other details. Shakespeare and other Elizabethan dramatists are exactly related in point of imagery. Elizabethan life itself becomes strangely tangible and near from this direct study. One warning is, however, necessary. Prof. Spurgeon's system is mainly concerned with metaphors and similes. To that extent it is self-limited. Her positive results are therefore far more impressive than her negative statements. She observes that *Julius Caesar* shows little 'imagery' and deduces lack of excitement in composition. But although this play is peculiarly barren of metaphor it is most vividly alive with things directly rather than obliquely apprehended (especially fire, blood and metals). Negatively, Prof. Spurgeon's system must never be expected to bear too weighty a stress, but her positive results are not merely interesting: they are supremely important.

This book is a definite step towards a richer understanding of the colour and life-blood, as opposed to the plot-skeleton and tissue, of the Shakespearian play. The author's treatment is keenly sensitive and delicate in apprehension, and empowered by a refreshing modesty of assertion strange to recent Shakespearian scholarship. Some of her conclusions will be questioned, but the book's basic content is revelatory rather than argumentative. Prof. Spurgeon's positive results will prove of impregnable and lasting value when most modern commentary is forgotten.

Prof. Dover Wilson is concerned not with colour and impressionistic surface so much as intricacies of plot and situation, the tissue and arteries of the play he is discussing rather than the tint of its complexion and light of its eye. Nor is he at home in its profounder levels of universal meaning, significantly regarding Hamlet's Yorick meditations as 'sentiment'. Similarly, Hamlet's failure to kill the praying King quite eludes his analysis. But passages in his book are nevertheless of striking interest and present surprising discoveries. There is something unique about the personality of Hamlet. He is not only brilliant in himself, but the cause of brilliance in other people. Some of Prof. Dover Wilson's findings are likely to be called 'super-subtle', though I am myself, with a few exceptions, convinced. His reading of the 'nunnery' scene certainly appears strained; for if 'nunnery' means, or contains any suggestion of, 'brothel', what of the otherwise exquisite 'Why would'st thou be a breeder of sinners?' (III. i. 124). But with Hamlet's way of playing up to the different theories of his own behaviour in the Court of Denmark the author is very skilful; and his elucidation of the play scene most original and quite admirable. I am still a little uncertain of his dumb-show theory; I doubt if it could be got across on the stage. But the suggested reference of Lucianus, nephew to the King, to Hamlet rather than Claudius in the eyes of everyone but Claudius himself, is positively brilliant, and adds both power and meaning to the situation that follows.

It is interesting to observe that Prof. Dover Wilson, who has for long been saturating himself in Elizabethan literature and archaeology as an aid to Shakespearian interpretation, seems to arrive here at his most striking results by forgetting all he has learned and returning to a plain and naïve inspection of the text. His book is only another proof that the most profitable interpretative advance will be, like Prof. Spurgeon's work, contemporary rather than historical. True, he offers a lot of Elizabethan reference both as to ghost-lore and melancholia. But, though interesting enough for itself, it retards rather than advances the argument. For what emerges? That the ghost is enigmatic and Hamlet's 'madness' properly a borderline state. And we need no researches come from the records office to tell us either—nor to prove that 'incest' is here a dominating obsession. Prof. Dover Wilson indeed himself admits as much. Strangely, however, he neglects the one point on which something of a deliberately Elizabethan focus is needed. It is all but impossible for us today to realize the true significance and importance of Shakespeare's kings. Dr. G. B. Harrison, in *Shakespeare at Work*, has well emphasized the terror of possible anarchy that oppressed the nation towards the end of Elizabeth's reign. And the whole of *Hamlet* is greatly clarified if we see in Claudius something at least of 'the deputy elected by the Lord' (*Richard II*, III. ii. 57) and a symbol of stability and order which to attack is, in any first instance, black treason; and which demands from the audience a certain instinctive respect irrespective of plot complications. And, of course, I would myself go further than that, having been for long especially fond of this amiable, well-meaning, pious, efficient and essentially avuncular sovereign.

Saturday Night (Toronto), 25 April 1936.

Shakespeare, by J. Middleton Murry.

We have waited long for this book. Certain intermittent Shakespearian brilliances in Mr. Murry's early work promised a more comprehensive, steady and considered illumination shortly to follow. The tale of how that was postponed may be read in Mr. Murry's own *Keats and Shakespeare* and *God*. I have never been quite satisfied with those explanations. They appeared a rationalization of some inward uncertainty and inability to grip the vital issue. Despite its many virtues this new volume confirms me in that opinion.

Mr. Murry's early work on *Antony and Cleopatra* and *Coriolanus* in *Discoveries* and on Shakespearian passages in *The Problem of Style* resulted from a direct and fearless contact with Shakespeare's art. Then something happened. He began to distrust direct analysis and made terms with the falsities of pseudo-realistic interpretation. Hence the occasional notes Mr. Murry has since written from that viewpoint. The present book is a somewhat heroic attempt to bind together incompatible approaches, and certainly has a specious appearance of unity. The direct method of Mr. Murry's *Dostoevsky*, never since quite recaptured, joins with the method of *Keats and Shakespeare*. But that fusion of a well-known and detailed biography with an extant and expansive desultory correspondence which gave us *Keats and Shakespeare*, a book that never aimed at pure poetic interpretation, is not at all analogous to the present attempt to inter-mix an almost non-existent biography with the precise and finished expressions of the Shakespearian art-form. So we watch Mr. Murry describing Shakespearian tragedy as a superimposition of poetic speech on ready-to-hand melodrama; and in the process poetic drama, which undoubtedly contains both but can be understood in terms of neither, nor of both, nearly, if not quite, escapes. The treat-ment given to that stern test of method, *The Merchant of Venice*, is significant.

The result has been unanimous praise from English reviewers. This marks at least an advance. The strong wine of intellectual and poetic appreciation is offered properly diluted for the general public. Mr. Murry's study may thus prove for many readers a most valuable stepping-stone. I hope, and believe, that it will find its way into the hands of undergraduates on both sides of the Atlantic. I would not be thought to deny its great provisional value.

Moreover there are particular discussions of genuine interest. Analysis of the Histories produces some happy results, especially with *Richard III*, *King John*, and *Henry V*. The treatment of Henry V as Shakespeare's perfect king in that his sense of kingship is one with the idea of comradeship so powerful in the Agincourt address—and how delightful to find this magnificent speech honestly praised again—makes a neat blend of Elizabethan royalism with Mr. Murry's own, here severely restrained, communism. I do not follow all Mr. Murry has to say of 'the Shakespeare Man', but the discussion is suggestive: though I can see no profitable continuity between extremes such as Richard II and Falstaff. I suspect 'the Shakespeare Man' is any character in a play who elicits from Mr. Murry (and therefore from most of us) an especially dominating sympathy. As to Mr. Murry's other point, that where the Shakespeare Man occurs the play as a whole is less evenly balanced, I am not sure. But in proportion as it is found to be true, it must be allowed to be acute.

Some good things on the great tragedies are, however, not good enough. The treatment of *Hamlet* I find shaky, though correctly focussing on the concept of death; that of *Macbeth* a mixture of profundity and rather tenuous obscurity; the discussion of the handkerchief in *Othello* somewhat too long drawn out after the fashion of a novelist's description but none the less of great importance; the chapter on *Antony and Cleopatra* a very fine treatment of one strand in a design of which Mr. Murry's earlier work showed nevertheless a more comprehensive grasp; and the critical rejection of *King Lear* a queer admission of failure concerning a play that was once, or so I used to gather, one of Mr. Murry's favourites.[1]

Mr. Murry's treatment of imagery is often sensitive and original: though I am getting a little tired of the 'fawning hounds', which are not very important but seem to have exerted a nightmare fascination on recent criticism. The section on the Final Plays, though genuine profundities are scattered here and there, cannot be said to do much more than flirt with the vast issues involved.

The Modern Language Review, January 1938; XXXIII, 1, 68.

Shakespeare and the Arts of Design (University of Missouri Studies, XII, 1); by Arthur H. R. Fairchild.

This is a valuable account of Renaissance (and particularly English) architecture, sculpture, tapestry and painting referred to a careful selection of relevant Shakespearian passages. Each side of the discussion has its separate interest: the value emerging from their inter-

---

1. Murry's early commentaries on *Antony and Cleopatra* had done much to direct my own insights. As for *King Lear*, Murry had at one time regarded it and *Antony and Cleopatra* as two plays 'apart', forming the 'pinnacle' of Shakespeare's '*expression* in literature' ('The Nature of Poetry', *Discoveries*, 1924; 1930 edn., 37–8; for *Coriolanus*, 85–104). A very strange reversal, countering the more usual process of rejection followed by insight. [1966]

relation varies. Prof. Fairchild's research does something to illuminate the well-known tomb-chair crux in *Coriolanus*, is cleverly applied to the different meanings of 'perspective', and gives us a subtle analysis of the contemporary and philosophic quality in Shakespeare's references to painting. The quotations throughout are extensive with only one surprising omission: the parable of Fortune designed by the poet in *Timon of Athens*. Some attention to the medieval sympathies in Webster's feeling for tombs and ruins would have enriched the general thesis, while serving to modify slightly the stress here laid on Shakespeare's.

Prof. Fairchild's understanding of the Final Plays lags behind recent investigation when he appears unaware of any meaning in Hermione's statue-resurrection beyond what may be attributed to 'sources'. As a rule, however, he is on his guard: as when, after a discussion of possible originals for the horse-description in *Venus and Adonis*, he comes nobly to the conclusion that Shakespeare 'knew horses' 'from personal observation'. Indeed he is, usually, well up-to-date in poetic psychology, and his more archaeological exposition is always both learned and lucid. He is particularly good on the Stratford bust; his final appreciation of Shakespeare's work as a whole has moments of deep insight, especially in his treatment of 'the problem of pity'; and his essay will remain as an original, comprehensive and often striking analysis that should be possessed, and next re-bound, by all serious students. It has affinities with the long-awaited but as yet unpublished life-work of the late Edgar I. Fripp.

The Universities Quarterly, August 1954; VIII, 4.

The Shakespearean Moment, by Patrick Cruttwell.

Literary criticism has for some time tended to regard Shakespeare and Donne as our two supreme masters of poetic style. Theirs was, in Mr. Cruttwell's words, a poetry able to 'build a transcendental meaning out of particular experience', or, conversely, 'concentrate many orders of experience on to a single point' (106–7). His aim is to show that such poetry grew from a society possessing similar qualities and how, the balance lost, poetic drama and the tragic sense became impossible. He compares 'the Shakespearean moment' under James I with Dante's ideal partnership of Emperor and Pope, as a society trying to realize in England 'what had been a dream for Europe' (109). It was a 'moment of convergence' unifying Church and State, city and countryside, under the Anglican settlement and a Stuart monarchy (249). But it was short-lived.

Mr. Cruttwell navigates the attendant complexities with skill; but he must be prepared for certain disagreements. His handling of the Sonnets lacks balance, and in order to preserve the medieval emphasis he ignores the relation of Shakespearian drama through Seneca, who is not mentioned, to the classics. The attack on Milton shows too little recognition of the degree to which his thoughts and poetry were royally centred, but the case against Dryden is better made, and Pope escapes reproof. Mr. Cruttwell's appreciation of the poetry, though he shows less feeling for the action, of Shakespeare's last plays is well pointed, and his treatment of Marvell's *Horatian Ode* as an after-math of the Shakespearian moment excellent. The close reference of Augustan classicism to Puritanism, at first sight startling, at least startles us into thought.

Two general cautions are needed. We too readily assume that poetry can be satisfactorily handled as printed language, forgetting that the greatest poetry comes into being at that point where printed language, however brilliantly handled, ceases to be the main thing. Because certain inclusions and tensions exist in the linguistic thought-play of Shakespeare and Donne, we unwarrantably assume that such riches cannot be found within the total work of poets whose language, in isolation, is less crammed. The error is serious, and its consequences far-reaching.

Another caution—granted that the dramatic manner and great tragedy appear to lie behind us, we must not suppose that they and their attendant contradictions are necessarily the last, though they may be the first, word in human wisdom. The ages of Faith composed no great drama; Shakespeare moved from tragedy to the last plays and *Henry VIII*; and Nietzsche, after yearning for a tragic civilization in *The Birth of Tragedy*, climbed on scorn of it to the heights of *Thus Spake Zarathustra*. There is always the will to transcend tragedy, and of this will we may suppose that the greater Augustans and Romantics were a part.

Nevertheless, Mr. Cruttwell's thesis is important; more, its central emphasis is all-important. We are reminded that Shakespeare could compare Richard II with Christ (189), and that Donne saw Elizabeth I as reigning with Him in Heaven and James I as His vice-gerent on earth (109). But, after the execution of Charles I, 'all those feelings for Church-and-State-as-one which we have found to be dominant in the Shakespearean moment and its society' (188) were first concentrated and then dispelled, to become henceforth the preserve of the half-witted:

> Never again would it be possible for men whose minds were *not* crankish, sentimental, and superstitious, to bring to bear on the head of the secular State that cluster of emotions which centre round saintliness, martyrdom, and, in the last resort, the supreme martyrdom of Christ.
>
> (224)

More than kingship is involved. The problem sinks to the heart of man and his relation to the universe. What was lost was not merely political, nor even religious; not nature, nor supernature; it was both, and neither; and when we respond to Shakespeare's poetry in *Pericles* and *The Winter's Tale*, we get a breath of it. I should call it the sense of the *magical*.

Mr. Cruttwell's service lies in his isolation of this point of time, and just exposition of its nature. His later assessments are more questionable. He is repelled by the heroic idealisms of Milton and the Augustans and says nothing of the great Romantics. But can we not see the successors of the Shakespearian moment as themselves striving, each in his own setting, to recreate the lost contact? Pope did so in one way, Browning in another; Swift was a martyr to the cause; and as for drama, Byron's heroic life and work, taken together, show dramatic tensions and inclusions covering the whole field, and more, of our argument. As the story unfolds, clearer and clearer sounds the need for some new synthesis of Church and State; in Ibsen's *Emperor and Galilean*, in Nietzsche's *The Will to Power* (983, a 'Roman Caesar with the soul of Christ'); with Tennyson, with Bernard Shaw. It would be a pity to rest back on a nostalgic appreciation of the linguistic agilities of Shakespeare and Donne while neglecting this central and still developing tradition. It matters little whether we have any more poetic drama or metaphysical poetry, and those in any age who 'write dull receipts how poems may be made' (Pope, *Essay on Criticism*, 115) grow wearisome. What we have to do is to fix our attention on that *for* which such splendours once existed and whence they drew their magic: else, as Donne has it (in *The Ecstasy*), 'a great Prince in prison lies'.

The Twentieth Century, April 1956; CLIX, 950.

The Man who was Shakespeare, by Calvin Hoffman.

Candidates for the authorship of Shakespeare's plays are numerous, and it may be worth asking why these various enquiries and claims succeed each other with such insistence? Is there, after all, a problem, a mystery? When all the usual answers have been given, it does, I think, remain strange that what we know of Shakespeare the man is at once so scanty, so dull, and so utterly disproportionate to the power radiating from the works. Ought we to remain content? A problem indeed exists, but its solution is more likely to come about from some new understanding of literary genius, its place in society, and the nature of its reception. What we call 'genius' has not yet been placed within our culture—particularly our religious culture—and, while it remains unplaced, these extravagant attempts may be expected to continue.

Mr. Hoffman believes that Christopher Marlowe left England to avoid the consequences of his reckless life and opinions, his tracks being covered by a rigged-up brawl and death which incidentally involved a peculiarly callous murder, since a corpse was necessary to put before the coroner. From then on Marlowe lived abroad writing the works of Shakespeare. The thesis sounds wild enough, but the dates fit and its presentation is not altogether without support. The account (66) of the discovery in 1953 during some repairs at Corpus Christi College, Cambridge, of a portrait, dated 1585 and bearing Marlowe's age, which shows features certainly resembling the Droeshout portrait of Shakespeare is rather remarkable;[1] the word-tests of

1. Mr. Hoffman's account is not quite accurate. On enquiry, I find that the picture may have come from fabric dating not, as he thought, to the period of Marlowe's

Dr. T. C. Mendenhall, which are said (161) some fifty years ago to have revealed identical graphs for Marlowe and Shakespeare, might have been quite intriguing if exact references had been given for those who, like myself, are ignorant of the doctor's labours; and, despite some weak examples, Mr. Hoffman's lists of thought and phrase similarities in the two poets are, for his purpose, at least no less telling than such lists have proved in the past as a favourite technique in the hands of established scholarship; though this is not saying much.

However, I would myself maintain that the works of Marlowe and Shakespeare exist strictly as contraries. True, Mr. Hoffman can quote a number of Shakespearian 'authorities' as saying that this or that work of Shakespeare must in part have been composed by Marlowe; but in so doing he relies on the old 'disintegrating' school discountenanced by recent investigations. Today, surely, we can see that, whatever the at first sight cogent implications of word-graphs and parallel-lists, there is little enough similarity between the sadistic barbarisms, disjointed and cruel humour, purposeless tragedy, and miserable damnation which we find in Marlowe and the deeply purposive and nobly creative reading of tragedy offered, from first to last, by Shakespeare. In comparison, Marlowe's view of human destiny appears, to put it bluntly, whatever his fine passages of verbal poetry, a mess. The two poets exist not even as complements. I see them rather as 'mighty opposites', and can never myself agree that Marlowe's work stands, in any valuable sense, behind Shakespeare; it points rather to Ben Jonson and Milton.

What, then, of Mr. Hoffman's thesis? It just crumbles. Nevertheless, I offer him an answer, to use if he so wishes, in terms of his own story. He appears throughout to be too little conscious of the implications of that ugly crime by which Marlowe allowed Sir Thomas Walsingham to save him from trial and possible execution. Could Mr. Hoffman now argue that the callous murder of the unfortunate seaman over whose death Marlowe scrambled to safety

---

residence, but only to 1820. The *local* evidence is accordingly weakened, and we are thrown back on the portrait itself and its inscriptions. If the subject is Marlowe, the Latin sentence 'Quod me nutrit me destruit' might be taken to refer to the unorthodox nature of his amatory instincts.

might be supposed so to have worked on his conscience that it hence-forth injected into him a nobler humanism, tapping new depths of humility and wisdom? Or did the sailor's soul possess him, and is that why Shakespeare's plays are so rich in sea-poetry? Well ... perhaps. Or perhaps not.

The Twentieth Century, June 1957; CLXI, 964.

Shakespeare's Sources: Comedies and Tragedies; by Kenneth Muir.

Shakespeare's artistry has always been baffling. What makes a work a work of genius cannot be stated; but every attempt to watch the process of creation has its interest, and sometimes the results are important. Prof. Kenneth Muir's volume is of considerable importance.

The sources of Shakespearian drama have been studied by many generations of scholars, and yet this is the first comprehensive account to be published. The reason is, perhaps, that formerly the matter was not regarded as so very complex. It was natural to regard the poet-dramatist as a simple soul 'warbling his native wood-notes wild', with for subject-matter—since it was necessary to have something to warble about—some readily accessible story, or old play, to compen-sate for his lack of inventive ability. All this was not so very satisfying, and recent investigations, concentrating on the close texture and symbolic profundities of the philosophic poetry, have tended to rule out 'sources' altogether as irrelevant.

But now we have a new advance. The sources indeed exist; but they are far more complex than one had supposed. For the Pyramus and Thisbe interlude in *A Midsummer Night's Dream* we are driven to the conclusion that Shakespeare consulted no less than six or seven versions of the story; and we find that Chaucer, Henryson, Homer, Lydgate and Caxton all contributed to the making of *Troilus and Cressida*. We begin to realize that the great poet may be characterized less by his independence of source-material than by the amount of it; by the reading and the memory, the selection, modification and shaping.

We can all be happy at this result. The scholar can enjoy the range and exactitude of Prof. Muir's learning, and remain flattered by the knowledge that Shakespeare was a man of books as well as of the stage; and the more imaginative student can argue that the discovery of so many complexities serves, once and for all, to invalidate the *negative* use of 'sources', since we can never again regard Shakespeare as slavishly dominated by any *one* source at all, the final responsibility being thrown back on the poet's own, ever-active, judgement. So Prof. Muir's work does nothing to clog Shakespearian studies with the 'learned lumber' which Pope (*Essay on Criticism*, 613) so deplored as the temptation of scholarship; rather it serves to let in fresh air, which is exactly the result Prof. Muir himself would welcome, for this is the work of a rarely gifted scholar who knows, and even insists on, the limitations of scholarship.

INDEXES

No distinction is made between references to the main text and those which apply to the footnotes

A. SHAKESPEARIAN WORKS

B. GENERAL